Social Skills Development

Related Titles of Interest

101 Ways to Develop Student Self-Esteem and Responsibility
Jack Canfield and Frank Siccone
ISBN: 0-205-16884-1

Managed Mental Health Care: A Guide for Practitioners, Employers, and Hospital Administrators
Thomas R. Giles
ISBN: 0-205-14838-7

Social Skills Training for Psychiatric Patients
Robert Paul Liberman, William J. DeRisi, and Kim T. Mueser
ISBN: 0-205-14406-3   Paper   0-205-14407-1   Cloth

Handbook of Psychological Skills Training: Clinical Techniques and Applications
William O'Donohue and Leonard Krasner (Editors)
ISBN: 0-205-15261-9

Self-Esteem Enhancement with Children and Adolescents
Alice W. Pope, Susan M. McHale, and W. Edward Craighead
ISBN: 0-205-14455-1

Small Groups: Process and Leadership, Second Edition
Barbara W. Posthuma
ISBN: 0-205-16169-3

Social Skills for Mental Health: A Structured Learning Approach
Robert P. Sprafkin, N. Jane Gershaw, and Arnold P. Goldstein
ISBN: 0-205-14841-7

Social Skills Development

Practical Strategies for Adolescents and Adults with Developmental Disabilities

STEPHEN J. ANTONELLO

Family Psychological Services
St. Paul, Minnesota

Allyn and Bacon
Boston   London   Toronto   Sydney   Tokyo   Singapore

Library of Congress Cataloging-in-Publication Data

Antonello, Stephen J.
    Social skills development : practical strategies for adolescents
and adults with developmental disabilities / Stephen J. Antonello.
        p.   cm.
    Includes bibliographical references and index.
    ISBN 0-205-17411-6
    1. Developmentally disabled—Life skills guides.   2. Life skills-
-Study and teaching.   3. Social skills—Study and teaching.
I. Title.
HV1570.A55   1996
362.1´968—dc20   95-21050

                                                               CIP

Printed in the United States of America
10 9 8 7 6 5 4 3 2   99 98

This book is dedicated to the memory of Bill Antonello, son of immigrant parents, World War II sailor, Brooklyn Dodger, father of seven children, and Alaska pipeline crewman.

Contents

Preface

This book provides a vehicle for various practitioners to facilitate social skills development and reduce vulnerability in persons with developmental disabilities and related conditions. It is a practical therapeutic and educational tool to enhance the day-to-day social-behavioral functioning of individuals with developmental delay. The book offers an integrative approach for special educators, psychotherapists, human service workers, and parents to enhance personal social relationships; resolve emotional and behavioral adjustment disorders; increase adaptive social behaviors; improve educational and vocational performance; and expand recreation, leisure, and community activities for its intended recipients.

The practical importance of developing social skills and reducing vulnerability in persons with developmental disabilities cannot be overstated. What individuals cannot do for themselves, others must do for them. An old Chinese proverb states, "Give a man a fish and he will eat for a day; teach him to fish and he will eat for a lifetime." Individuals with developmental delay experience mental and behavioral disorders up to several times as frequently as their contemporaries in the general population (Matson & Barrett, 1993). These disorders affect the emotional, intellectual, behavioral, social, and physical functioning of persons with developmental challenges. Much of the maladaptive behavior of individuals can be improved with specific social skills training. My underlying assumption is that maladaptive behaviors most frequently occur because of a lack of alternative positive behaviors in the repertoires of individuals.

The approach taken in this book assumes that there is a high degree of similarity between persons with developmental disabilities and their developmentally intact peers. Individuals with and without developmental delay are more alike than they are different. The same social skills may be taught in essentially the same ways to both populations.

All individuals have basic human rights—freedom, dignity, humane treatment, protection from abuse, achievement of maximum potential, expression of feelings and opinions, decision making, and so forth. Each person has a life experience of self and world resulting from the interplay between thought, feeling, behavior, and the environment. Everybody has basic needs, including physiological gratification, safety, love and belonging, self-esteem, and self-actualization (Maslow, 1970). We each experience basic emotions such as fear, anger, frustration, hurt, sadness, and happiness. It may be argued that all individuals progress through similar developmental life stages, beginning life in a state of relative helplessness but gradually developing motor, sensory, speech, language, and cognitive skills that increasingly allow them to adapt to life's challenges. Finally, all persons construct meaning in their lives to the extent to which they are capable, resulting in ethical, spiritual, and mythological beliefs. *Meaning* referents guide behaviors and enable persons to tolerate life situations that they do not understand or cannot control.

Individuals with developmental disabilities differ from their peers in many ways that increase vulnerability, thereby increasing the need for social skills training. They progress more slowly through developmental stages, final level of development in some areas is lower, and certain skill areas (e.g., intellectual, social, physical) may develop unevenly. Global intelligence and specific cognitive abilities typically are more limited. Physical problems (e.g., epilepsy, chronic physical disability), odd or "different" physical appearance, and atypical mannerisms (e.g., stereotyped movements, coordination abnormalities, hypo- or hyperactivity) may be present. Self-control may be limited because of such factors as impulsivity, under- or overactivity, diminished attention, poor concentration, impaired memory, and failure to recognize personal and social boundaries. Personal insight and awareness of others may be diminished. There may be a lower capacity to function either within or without structure because of difficulty connecting past, present, and future; problems monitoring time and activities; and difficulty organizing and integrating activities. Friendships are often limited because of slow development of peer relationships, smaller social networks, a limited repertoire of interpersonal skills, and an inability to differentiate friendship from other types of relationships. Socialization experiences are often restricted by poor memory for previous conversations; frequent caretaker, residence, and day program changes; limited transportation; and less effective skills with which to initiate, plan, schedule, and carry out social liaisons. Communication may involve smaller repertoires of functional communication patterns, more reliance on nonverbal messages, and increased behavioral expressions of feelings and ideas. More rigid behavior patterns, failure to stop unsuccessful behaviors, difficulty utilizing positive and negative feedback, less ability to generalize behavioral successes from one situation to another, and frequent perseverating thoughts and behaviors are common. There is often less ability to elicit sympathy from others because of peculiar physical appearance, inattention, rigidity, egocentrism, distracting mannerisms, and general social deficits. Daily frustrations are likely to be increased by limited anticipation of problems, failure to avoid or solve problems, poor understanding of environmental demands, and less capacity to generate personal and social support. Occupying a minority status, individuals with developmental disabilities may suffer ostracism, experience discrimination, receive fewer opportunities to participate in mainstream cultural activities, and live in lower socioeconomic conditions than their developmentally intact peers. The expectation of dependency may result in a high level of supervision, structure, support, physical caretaking, social-informational assistance, and advocacy by others. Limited mobility is likely to be induced by restricted opportunities for transportation, telephone communication, housing, employment, and general voluntary activity. Emotional expression may be constrained by fewer opportunities to express feelings (e.g., kept from funerals, less frequently asked about feelings), more accumulation of unresolved grief, anger, and other feelings, and more difficulty judging socially acceptable expression of feelings. Finally, persons with developmental disabilities often experience higher levels of family stress because attention and resources are drawn away from other family members' needs, relational imbalances can occur (e.g., one parent overinvolved or overprotective, another parent disengaged, siblings feeling ignored or resentfully overburdened), and family integration may suffer. For all of these reasons, it becomes important to provide specific social skills training to individuals with developmental disabilities.

The development of these materials grew out of my personal experiences treating individuals with developmental disabilities, mental illness, and family relationship problems. As an undergraduate student, I developed an interest in developmental disabilities while working as a teaching assistant in an autism project, the first of its kind in a local school district. After completing my bachelor's degree in psychology in 1977, and a master's degree in clinical psychology in 1979, I began a dual employment position. In one job as a school psychologist, I worked closely with special education teachers in the assessment and treatment of special populations. At the other, as a clinical psychologist and family therapist, I performed psychological testing and individual, group, and family psychotherapy at a community counseling center. During the course of my work in these positions, I was asked to provide psychological assessments, individual psychotherapy, and group psychotherapy to individuals with developmental disabilities at a local sheltered vocational workshop. In 1986, I completed my Ph.D., combining clinical psychology and educational administration, focusing on the assessment of family stress in families of persons with developmental disabilities. In my doctoral dissertation I developed an instrument to compare stress in families with and without children with special needs. At about the same time, I left both employment positions in order to expand a private practice that I had started earlier on a part-time basis. I have continued to work extensively with individuals with developmental disabilities, chronic mental illnesses, and dual diagnoses.

In 1981, when I began my first formal group work with persons with developmental disabilities, I could not find any specific materials related to group psychotherapy and social skills development for this population. I began integrating existing social skills materials, educational techniques, and psychotherapy approaches in order to better serve these individuals.

Eventually, six or seven distinct group curricula were developed and piloted that addressed areas of basic social skills, feelings, self-esteem, problem solving, developmental issues, vulnerability, and personal boundaries. These were revised, reworked, expanded, and field-tested many times. Field testing and curriculum development have taken place largely at a variety of developmental achievement centers, sheltered vocational workshops, and residential facilities. Specific skills have been included and retained because they are directly related to problems occurring in real-life situations for adolescents and adults with developmental disabilities. The result of this process is a set of social skills curricula that are clinically relevant, practically useful, and easily engaged by individuals with developmental disabilities.

Other authors have addressed the issue of social skills development in developmentally intact populations, but very little work has been targeted toward individuals with developmental disabilities. Materials available to teach social skills to persons with developmental disabilities, though helpful, are often narrow in scope and limited to single topics (Benson, 1992; Jackson, Jackson, Bennett, Bynum, & Faryna, 1991). In this book, social skills development is considered a comprehensive endeavor, necessitating that specific skills training be conducted in a wide range of areas that will require individuals to make cognitive, emotional, and behavioral adaptations. A perusal of the eighty topics covered in this book illustrates this point.

Although these materials originally targeted adolescents and adults, most skills can be adapted for younger individuals. The introduction to each topic identifies specific modifications that can be made to accommodate individuals with lower developmental abilities. These may apply to younger persons as well. In defining concepts, reading case vignettes, and asking discussion questions, group facilitators should always modify their language to fit the vernacular and cognitive abilities of participants. An attempt has been made to use age-neutral case vignettes whenever possible, but many of them have been written from the perspective of late adolescents and adults. Instructors and group leaders should feel free to modify both language and scenario to better fit the situations of younger individuals, when appropriate. For example, stories involving work problems may be converted to stories about school problems; cases describing group living counselors may be changed to involve parents. It is also appropriate to change the names of characters, at times, so that participants can more closely identify with the sexual, racial, or ethnic backgrounds of the stories' protagonists.

An effort has been made to make these skills cultural-, ethnic-, racial-, and gender-fair. Throughout the book, the use of sex-identified pronouns has been reduced by referring to mixed groups as often as possible (e.g., *they, their, themselves* instead of *he/she, his/her, himself/herself*). Case vignettes are balanced at approximately 50 percent for each gender. Male and female characters have not been restricted to gender-stereotyped situations and responses but, rather, participate in activities that have traditionally been associated with one gender or the other. The names of characters have been selected to reflect a balance of ethnic and racial groups. When conveying specific information during group sessions, the group facilitator should always try to be cognizant of the backgrounds of individual participants and sensitive to their differing needs. This should be done in a fashion that does not stereotype individuals according to gender, race, ethnicity, or cultural group.

The organization of the book is such that later skills tend to expand on earlier ones. The first chapter begins with the basic social skills on which all other social skills are built. Chapter 2 investigates the recognition and appropriate expression of feelings. Chapter 3 focuses on personal hygiene, self-care, and manners. Chapter 4 takes an experiential approach to self-esteem. Chapter 5 teaches about problem solving and conflict management. Chapter 6 explores friendship and social supports. Chapter 7 examines personal boundaries and sexuality. Chapter 8 deals with developmental issues. Chapter 9 introduces the concept of self-advocacy. Finally, Chapter 10 focuses on decreasing vulnerability in the community.

Each chapter follows the same format: (1) topic, (2) specific skills to be learned, (3) concepts necessary to perform the skills, (4) case vignettes, (5) discussion questions, (6) group activities, and (7) assessment of skills learned.

The reader should use these materials in a flexible fashion. The group leader is encouraged to pick and choose chapters and topics as necessary to develop specific social skills of concern in various populations of interest. Many of these topics work well with widely differing populations, including those with mild and moderate developmental delay, persons with chronic mental illness, and individuals with the dual diagnosis of developmental disability and mental illness.

Group facilitators are encouraged to begin each group session by asking members how they feel and attempting to categorize their feelings on a numerical scale described in topic number one. A few minutes of free time should be allowed at the outset of each session for unstructured socializing and small talk, followed by the numerical rating scale. After members share feelings and engage in small talk, a specific topic should be selected. Before discussing the topic, the group instructor or facilitator should ask if anyone needs time to work on a personal issue or problem. Individuals' specific concerns should be given priority over topical discussions. The intended message is: "Human beings are more important than curriculum materials; you are more important than my need to teach you something." Persons with the lowest numbers should be given the first opportunities to "use" group time (unless certain members abuse this privilege by exaggerating their own problems in relation to those of others). The group leader should allow individuals to discuss problems, express related emotions, and request the support or assistance of other group members. An attempt should be made to reframe problems in terms that can be understood and supported by others. Feedback and support can be actively solicited from fellow participants, either by the person sharing the problem or by the group facilitator. After individuals have addressed relevant personal problems, the group leader should move on to the daily topic.

When the general topic is introduced, participants should be solicited for their personal definitions and current understandings of the topic. The leader may then give a more formal definition and background description of the topic. An ongoing exchange should be held with individual group members while explaining and presenting the topic. After the topic is explained and particular terms defined, the leader may wish to read one or more short case vignettes provided in each section. Next, a full group discussion of the case vignette would be appropriate. If case vignettes are deleted, the group leader may either utilize one or more of the group activities listed in the curriculum, or lead a discussion following the listed discussion questions. It would be good to begin with simple, concrete questions, moving next to feelings and personal experience questions, and finally discussing problem-solving questions.

After the more formal discussion of the topic, discussion questions, case vignettes, and/or group activities, the group may wish to break into pairs (self-selected or chosen by the group leader) to discuss topical materials further in a more personal and informal manner. Afterward, the group should reunite to discuss any unfinished business, make or receive announcements, and orient toward future activities.

The reader will notice that curricula materials are written in a relatively simple fashion but often contain high-level concepts. It is important to reword materials to fit the cognitive ability, frames of reference, and communication styles of group participants. The leader should also remain free to pick and choose portions of chapters or topics that best fit the specific needs and understandings of participants. *All sections will not be appropriate for all persons.* Several concepts are listed that may be necessary to perform specific social skills. The group leader should explain these concepts as concisely as possible utilizing the vernacular of the client rather than a dictionary definition. This may involve different types of explanations for different participants, as described in more detail in the introduction to the first topic.

The assessment of skills learned may utilize both qualitative and quantitative means. Although the curriculum has a substantive and measurable content, the impact of the group process is largely experiential. If the group is presented to participants in too task-oriented a fashion, this may defeat some of the more intangible but important effects of the group process (affective bonding, interpersonal relatedness, belongingness, enhanced self-esteem, and increased social connectedness). Therefore, while the leader may utilize the curricula "assessments of skills learned," it will also be important to assess qualitatively and informally the less tangible influences of the group process.

The issue of "user" qualifications needs to be addressed briefly. This book was written for professionals, paraprofessionals, and parents. The primary user qualification is that one should be thoroughly familiar with the introduction to the book, as well as the introduction to each skill area, before proceeding to facilitate the development of a particular skill in a particular individual. In the ideal circumstance, a social skills trainee would receive help with a particular skill from a number of different facilitators, which may include the special education teacher, psychologist, group therapist, vocational counselor, and parent, each of whom would reinforce the work of the others. Naturally, professional therapists and educators will have more diverse and in-depth backgrounds than most parents or paraprofessionals, and this will enable them to use the materials more effectively at times. In particular, topics related to personal boundaries, sexuality, and developmental issues are probably better understood by those with more advanced training and expertise; but generally, the materials are easy to use at a basic level by persons with very little or no formal psychoeducational training.

The group facilitator should be cautioned that the job of "therapist" or "teacher" of individuals who have developmental disabilities is not to control the person but to enable these individuals to control and direct themselves. The goal is to help empower a disenfranchised segment of society, to enable individuals to express their own preferences successfully, make their own choices, and deal more effectively with the consequences of their own behaviors. Any respect given to other individuals should be extended to those with developmental disabilities, who should neither be patronized nor treated as though they are incompetent. This particular approach emphasizes the individual's competency rather than deficiency. Instead of simply remediating deficits, the group leader builds on existing strengths toward the acquisition of progressively adaptive social and self-management skills.

S.J.A.

References

Benson, B. (1992). *Teaching anger management to persons with mental retardation.* Chicago: International Diagnostics Systems.

Jackson, D. A., Jackson, N. F., Bennett, M. L., Bynum, D. M., & Faryna, E. (1991). *Learning to get along: Social effectiveness training for people with develop-* *mental disabilities.* Champaign, IL: Research Press.

Maslow, A. H. (1970). *Motivation and personality,* 2nd ed. New York: Harper & Row.

Matson, J. L., & Barrett, R. P. (1993). *Psychopathology in the mentally retarded.* Boston: Allyn & Bacon.

Acknowledgments

I want to acknowledge the contributions of the many vocational rehabilitation counselors, instructors, administrative persons, and others who have worked with me and made it possible to provide psychological consultation to individuals with developmental disabilities. I appreciate their valuable input to my social skills groups, psychotherapy sessions, and the development of these materials.

Thanks to Wendy Gilbert-Annis, Karen Edmund, Carol Donahoe, Chris Strong, Anne Tingerthal-Emery, Ann Bumgardner, Alan Martinucci, Rick Johnson, Susan Yahr, Jim Huff, Will Bartsch, Amy Green, Michelle Eischen, Sue Krueger, Vicki Patterson, and others who are or were at one time employed at Midwest Special Services in the capacity of work counselor, instructor, or employment specialist. Thanks to Gene O'Neil, president; Lyth Hartz, vice-president; Tim Finn, director of employment services; Steve Howard and Mary Raduenz, program coordinators; and other employees who have made it easier for me to work as a psychologist and conduct social skills groups at various Midwest Special Services program sites in the St. Paul, Minnesota, and surrounding suburban areas.

Thanks to Lynn Noren, Barb Hesli, Jeff Oakes, Kristin Mulier, Dawn Reagle, Tom Alf, Julie Goergen, and other vocational rehabilitation counselors and specialists who have worked with me during the many years that I have conducted social skills groups and performed psychological consultations at Rise, Inc., in Spring Lake Park, Minnesota. Thanks to John Barrett, president; Don Lavin, program director; and Mary Stransky, human resources manager; for inviting me to work with the staff and clients at Rise, Inc.

I am grateful to Barb Kale, president; Bill Schwartz, vice-president; Dan Reed, marketing director and social skills guru; Debbie Daulton, speech pathologist; Lee Gilcris, seniors coordinator; and the entire program staff who have facilitated my work and helped me to develop my clinical skills at Midway Training Services in St. Paul, Minnesota. I especially have appreciated the opportunity to work with individuals at Midway Training Services who have had multiple disabilities including mental illness, developmental disability, and behavior disorder, and who often have been written off by others as "untreatable."

Thanks to Elizabeth Buchanan, Barb Nelson, Sheila Johnson, and the many administrative and line vocational rehabilitation staff persons with whom I have had the opportunity to work at the Goodwill Industries in St. Paul, Minnesota.

Thanks to Tess Ketelsen, Lori Manthe, and Lisa Dau, program directors; and to Bruce Devenny, Eric Ketelsen, Nancy Bennett-Ott, Joan Decker, Dawn Wright, Darlene Wright, Diane Lovaasen, Teresa Stark, and the many vocational rehabilitation specialists and administrative personnel who have facilitated the provision of my psychological services and social skills groups at Custom Contracts and Services, in St. Paul, Minnesota.

I would like to acknowledge Suzanne Sanscillio, program director; and the many rehabilitation specialists, including Daneen Barnett-Johnston, Deb Hemstad, Joel Hemstad, Doug Kopseng, Brian Larson, and others, for utilizing my group therapy services, acting as cotherapists, and/or facilitating my service delivery at Northeast Contemporary Services in Roseville and Maplewood, Minnesota.

Thanks to Susan Warweg, administrative director; Bonnie Sykora, program director; Toni Quirk, program instructor; and other individuals who have worked with me in the provision of social skills therapy groups at the Phoenix Alternatives Agency in Maplewood, Minnesota.

I would like to acknowledge several other residential facilities that have invited me to provide social skills groups and psychological services to their residents with developmental disabilities and/or chronic mental illnesses. Thanks to Bev Wehe, director of resident services; Colleen Fodness, Tamara Phillips, and Wendy Walker, social workers; and the nursing/administrative staff at Trevilla of Robbinsdale Residence in Robbinsdale, Minnesota. Thanks to Serene Larson, executive program director; Lee Slaghter, program director; Kathy Frost, program counselor and co-therapist; and Carol Marshall, Tina Jewell, Jerry Cole, Lynn Foley, and other residence staff persons at Oakland Home in St. Paul, Minnesota. Thanks to Kent and JoAnne Swenson, program directors; and the entire program counseling staff at Pineview Residence in St. Paul, Minnesota. Thanks to Donetta Johnson, executive director; Barb Hanna, registered nurse; and the program staff at Amy Johnson Residence in St. Paul, Minnesota.

I am grateful to Katie Green, administrative director; Rosalyn Shore, house supervisor; and the many residential program counselors in the Focus Homes Residence Network for utilizing my group and individual psychotherapy services in St. Paul, Minnesota, and surrounding areas. Thanks to the many residence counselors at Boston Healthcare, REM, CCP, Nekton, Inc., and Thomas Allen, Inc., whose clients have utilized my social skills groups and psychotherapy services.

I am indebted to my psychologist interns Rosalyn Bystedt, Elizabeth Burke, Robin Johnson, and Rebecca Whitten, all of whom have acted as co-therapists and whose feedback has helped me to refine my social skills curricula materials ultimately leading to this book.

I am grateful to have had help in my own education from a variety of educators who have provided a basis for critical thinking as well as practical experience in my work with individuals with developmental disabilities. Thanks to Etta and Doug Overland, who helped me get my first job as a teaching assistant in a program for individuals with autism, developmental disabilities, and organic brain disorders. Thanks to Drs. Robert Genthner and Crocker Peoples at Eastern Kentucky University for providing me with my first clinical psychology training. Thanks to my Ph.D. advisor and committee chair, Dr. Neil Nickerson, who taught me about many practical aspects of the educational process, the most important of which was to be aware of the self-esteem of the individual receiving the education. Dr. Nickerson also enabled me to complete my doctoral dissertation on the topic of family stress and disability. Thanks to my other graduate advisors, Drs. Tim Mazzoni, Richard Weatherman, and Hamilton McCubbin, who assisted me in my doctoral training process. I would like to give a very special thanks to Dr. William Charlesworth, who gave me the opportunity to complete my first social science research, was my child psychology and human ethology professor, served on my Ph.D. committee, and has continued to give me encouragement in my career. Dr. Charlesworth has helped me to recognize the importance of human evolution to the understanding of adaptive social behavior.

I am thankful to my wife and fellow psychologist, Judy, for her encouragement, support, and feedback during this project.

I would like to acknowledge the excellent secretarial and office administrative staff who have suffered through my handwriting, typed this document, and completed what have seemed to be endless rewrites. Thanks to Sue Thompson, office manager and secretary; Jo Apman, secretary; and Nanette McCann, secretary. Thanks to Terri Torkko for her assistance in proof-reading this book. Thanks also to the many secretaries and receptionists who have helped me to schedule conference rooms, arrange client schedules, notify transportation, and generally manage logistics at the agencies where I have conducted social skills groups.

I sincerely appreciate the interest which Mylan Jaixen, associate publisher; Susan Hutchinson, editorial assistant; and others at the Allyn and Bacon, Simon and Schuster Education Group have taken in this project. Without their interest, support, critique, and production efforts, the book would not have come to fruition. I also wish to acknowledge the reviewers who read and critiqued the book: Rowland Barrett, Brown University School of Medicine, and Ruth Lynch, University of Wisconsin–Madison.

Thanks to all of the other individuals who have either directly or indirectly had an impact on me and my professional work, and have contributed to my ability to produce this document.

Finally, and most important, thanks to all of my clients with developmental disabilities, the special people who have come into this world at a great disadvantage, yet have taught me at least as much as I have taught them about life, including the virtues of patience, appreciation of the small blessings that life has to offer, courage in the face of overwhelming odds, forgiveness, and living with dignity despite the well-intentioned but often misguided attempts of others to change them.

Social Skills Development

1 *Beginning Social Skills*

1. **Introduction to Group**
2. **Listening Skills**
3. **Introducing Oneself**
4. **Beginning a Conversation**
5. **Asking a Question**
6. **Maintaining a Conversation**
7. **Giving a Compliment**
8. **Saying Thank-you**
9. **Introducing Others**

THIS CHAPTER IDENTIFIES and explores the basic social skills on which most other social skills are built. Individual topics are generally presented in order of increasing complexity such that later topics continue to utilize the skills learned from earlier ones. The nine initial skills are particularly important because they lay the foundation for many other social skills. Although the average person may take them for granted, individuals with developmental disabilities often require concrete, explicit assistance in learning these skills. Listening is the most fundamental skill. Introducing oneself is necessary in order to make initial social contact with others. Beginning a conversation correctly often determines others' response to an individual. Asking questions and sharing personal information are crucial in order to maintain a conversation with others. Giving compliments and saying thank-you are basic to one's ongoing relationships with others. Introducing others is a way of expanding one's social networks and relating to more than one person at a time. Therefore, these skills should receive primary emphasis in the development of general social skills in persons with developmental disabilities.

1. Introduction to Group

The purpose of this topic is to introduce the concept of a *social skills group* to participants. The basic concepts to convey include: privacy/confidentiality, social skill, group rule, group process/format, and group structure. The group leader should hold a loosely structured meeting with new participants to review basic concepts and to solicit members' past experiences and current thoughts and feelings about the group. Participants need to understand that group discussions are confidential. They should be told that they may share the content or topics of groups with others, but should not tell others what particular persons have said in group. It would be helpful for group members to participate in setting specific group rules about peripheral matters such as attendance/commitment, eating snacks or drinking beverages in group, interrupting others' conversation, and so forth. They may be encouraged to support each other and refrain from negative gossip, verbal attacks, other-blame and emotionally destructive behaviors. Introductions need to be made. Individual goals may be discussed if applicable. Members should be instructed that they may ask for group time when they have personal problems to share or when they need emotional support. It would be appropriate to explore the concept of nonjudgmental, nonattacking, nonblaming feedback. Members may be invited to take the risk of sharing feelings. It would be a good idea to encourage them to talk about their current levels of trust and any fears about fellow participants or the group leader. Finally, the group structure and rituals can be discussed and each member encouraged to develop and work on personal goals. They should be informed that toward the beginning of each session the leader will ask how they feel, using a ten-point numerical scale (10 = never felt better in my life; 9 = great, wonderful; 8 = very good, happy; 7 = good; 6 = a little good; 5 = not good or bad; 4 = a little bad; 3 = very bad; 2 = awful; and 1 = suicidal, never felt worse). The group leader may use humor in discussing the numerical scale. For example, he or she may state, "Zero means you're dead, eleven means you're in heaven." The numerical system is fairly easy understood by those with mild developmental disabilities. It may need to be completed by the group leader for lower functioning members. This can be done by simply asking individuals how they feel according to the verbal term applied to each number. Numbers may be assigned by the group leader based on the emotional affect of participants who are reluctant or unable to assign numbers to their own feelings. For verbally lower functioning individuals, the group facilitator may draw five faces with varying degrees of smile or frown and ask which one most reminds them of themselves. Other concepts should be presented in a fashion that most closely matches the language level and vernacular of individual participants. For example, one member may understand that *confidentiality* means "private," but another may need to be told, "What's said in here, stays in here." A third may understand the phrase, "Don't talk about these things with your other friends"; a fourth may relate more to the statement, "Don't blab this to your friends." At the end of the initial group session, free time should be allowed for members to talk to each other, make announcements, ask questions, and orient themselves to the following group.

■ SPECIFIC SKILLS TO BE LEARNED

Understand confidentiality and limits of privacy.
Understand what is a social skill.
Participate in setting group rules:
    Attendance/commitment
    Confidentiality
    Smoking
    Coffee/edibles
    Gossip
    Attacking/judging others
Understand group process and format:
    Introductions and getting acquainted
    Individual goals (Why are you here?)
    Asking for group time to work on personal issues
    Giving and receiving feedback (nonjudgmental/attacking/blaming)
    Interruptions
    Taking risks and sharing feelings
    Trust
    Group structure and rituals:
        Setting/reviewing goals
        1–10 feelings scale (the higher the number, the better you feel)
        How do you feel and what is on your mind today?
        Who needs group time to work on a particular problem?
        Structured activity or exercise
        Volunteers and demonstrations
        Practice (pair and total group exercises)
Share former group experiences.

■ CONCEPTS NECESSARY TO PERFORM SKILLS

Confidentiality: Privacy; keeping private information between friends; not telling secrets to others; not talking about group matters outside of group sessions.

Social skill: Ability to socialize well with others; getting along with others; knowing how to talk to others; ability to listen and talk to others; sociability; good at doing things with others.

Group rule: A thing on which group members agree; order so that everybody can get along together in group; what each person expects or wants from others in a group.

Group format: The kinds of things a group talks about; the order of group activities.

Group process: The way things are worked on in group; the manner in which topics are talked about in group; how things are done in group.

Feedback: Telling others how one things or feels about what was said; sharing how one thinks or feels about others' behaviors; telling a person how one sees his or her appearance; telling somebody how his or her appearance and behavior affect others.

Interrupt: Start to talk before someone else is finished speaking; come into or leave a room when someone is talking; butt in when someone is talking; start talking before somebody else is finished; make noise when someone is talking.

Support: Listen; care about; believe what someone says; tell others they are O.K.; tell a person one is on his or her side; be helpful; treat others kindly; be considerate; tell others one is with them and cares about how they feel.

Attack/blame others: Tell someone, "You're wrong"; say, "You're stupid"; tell people they never do anything right; say, "It's your fault"; tell a person, "I don't like you"; say mean things to someone.

Trust: Feel safe with others; feel you can tell personal things without being attacked by others; feel that others will treat you with respect; know that it is O.K. to tell someone how you feel or what you think; not worry that somebody will try to blame or hurt you; feel good, comfortable, or relaxed with someone.

■ CASE VIGNETTES

—John had several friends. One day he was not feeling well, so he told his friend Jim that he was sad. He said that his mother and father had gotten mad at him because he had stayed outside too late. John felt very good when Jim listened to him. He also felt good because his friend Jim had the same problem and told him about it. Jim never told John's other friends about John's problem because it was his private problem. John wanted only his closest friends to know about it. He felt good because his friend Jim knew how to keep the problem private. He knew that he could trust Jim with his personal feelings.

Why do you think John could trust Jim enough to tell him very personal and private information? Do you think John would share his problems with Jim if he knew that Jim would tell everybody else about the problems?

—Judy had a family problem. She had just started a new group. This was a place to talk to others about problems. It was also a place to learn better social skills. At one of the group sessions Judy talked about her family problem. She cried and was very upset. Later the same day, she overheard two other group members talking about what she had said in group. They told what she said to someone else who was not in group. Judy felt very bad and wanted to cry all over again. She was upset because group members were not supposed to tell what others had said in group. She was very angry and felt let down. Judy was not sure if she ever wanted to talk again in group. She wondered if she could trust the other group members to keep things private.

Why do you think Judy was so upset? Why is it important to keep group information private and confidential?

■ DISCUSSION QUESTIONS

Simple/concrete questions:
  What is confidentiality?
  What is gossip?
  What are the rules for this group?
Personal experience/feelings questions?
  Have you ever been in a group before?
  Have you had good or bad past group experiences?
  How do you feel about being in this group?
Problem-solving questions:
  What should you do if someone breaks the rule about confidentiality and tells other people what you talked about in group?
  How can we make sure our group members do not gossip about each other?
  What is the difference between attacking/blaming other group members and supporting them or being nonjudgmental?
  What does it mean to give feedback to other group members and why is this important?

■ GROUP ACTIVITIES

Share personal background information.
Share past group experiences.
Discuss ways in which group may be helpful to members.
Take turns trying to remember other group members' names.
Take turns stating group rules.

■ ASSESSMENT OF SKILLS LEARNED

Understands concepts of confidentiality and privacy:

ALMOST NEVER	USUALLY NOT	SOMETIMES	USUALLY	ALMOST ALWAYS
1	2	3	4	5

Understands the concept of social skill:

ALMOST NEVER	USUALLY NOT	SOMETIMES	USUALLY	ALMOST ALWAYS
1	2	3	4	5

Gives opinion about group rules:

ALMOST NEVER	USUALLY NOT	SOMETIMES	USUALLY	ALMOST ALWAYS
1	2	3	4	5

Understands and follows group process and format:

ALMOST NEVER	USUALLY NOT	SOMETIMES	USUALLY	ALMOST ALWAYS
1	2	3	4	5

Shares former group experiences:

ALMOST NEVER	USUALLY NOT	SOMETIMES	USUALLY	ALMOST ALWAYS
1	2	3	4	5

2. Listening Skills

Listening is the most basic social skill. Mastering it lays the groundwork for all others. One cannot maintain a conversation or sustain social relationships without listening to others. The group leader should convey the importance of body posture and eye contact. The use of humor is often helpful in order to engage participants in this task. For example, the group leader may converse with a group member while looking at the wall or at some inanimate object, then ask participants if this represents good listening posture. The importance of verbal and nonverbal acknowledgments should be stressed. This can be done with a nod of the head, repeating back what speakers say (paraphrased or verbatim), or asking persons to repeat themselves. To demonstrate a higher level of interest and more involved listening, the speaker can be asked to explain what was said in more detail. This skill is easily understood by individuals with mild and moderate developmental disabilities. It requires more concrete explanation and practice for those with more severe disabilities. Again, it should be emphasized that the language level and vernacular of individual participants should be used whenever possible.

■ SPECIFIC SKILLS TO BE LEARNED

Make eye contact.
Orient toward a speaker.
Lean forward or sit up straight.
Nod head or react to show understanding that one is hearing another person.
Repeat what someone says.
Ask someone to repeat him- or herself.
Ask someone to explain him- or herself.

■ CONCEPTS NECESSARY TO PERFORM SKILLS

Listen: Pay attention what someone says; hear and understand what somebody says; open your ears and close your mouth; let others know that you know what they are saying.

Hear: Open your ears and listen to what somebody says; know what a person is saying because you are listening.

Understand: Know what someone is saying; know what somebody means when he or she tells you something; know what a person is telling you.

Eye contact: Looking someone in the eyes; looking at somebody instead of looking away.

Communication: To send and receive messages; to tell each other things and know what each means; to tell each other news; listen to what somebody says, and the person then listens to what you say; to share information.

Nonverbal and verbal communication: Sometimes our bodies and sometimes our mouths tell things to others; a frowning or smiling face may tell you that someone is sad or happy, but things can also be said with words; say things with either your body or with words.

Active and passive listening: Sometimes people sit back and do not look like they are listening (passive), and at other times they sit up, look at you, and ask about what you are saying (active).

Interrupt: Start to talk before someone else is finished speaking; come into or leave a room when someone is talking; butt in when someone is talking; start talking before somebody else is finished; make noise when someone is talking.

Ignore: Not pay attention; not listen; overlook; disregard; neglect; do something else when a person is trying to talk.

Blocks to communication: Things that get in the way when people are talking; fear of telling one's real thoughts or feelings; anything that makes it hard to listen and share things with others.

■ CASE VIGNETTES

—Marge liked to talk to her friend Gina. One day Gina was trying to talk to Marge, but Marge was not listening very well. Gina would start to tell Marge something, but Marge would interrupt her and start talking about something else. Gina tried to tell Marge about her visit with Aunt Betty. Marge kept changing the subject and talking about what she had done last weekend. Finally, Gina got mad and walked away. She left Marge all alone. Marge was very disappointed because she wanted to tell Gina more about what she had done on the weekend. Marge also felt lonely because she had no one to talk to.

How could Marge have been a better listener? What might happen if you are a poor listener?

—Jim was a nice guy. Everybody liked him. He was a good listener. One day Mike came over to visit him. Mike told Jim all about his visit with Uncle Ed. Uncle Ed had taken him out for pizza. Then they had gone to a movie. Jim looked Mike in the eye. He nodded his head after Mike spoke. Mike knew that Jim was listening well because Jim was sitting up, looking him in the eye, and nodding his head after Mike spoke. Then Jim asked Mike some questions about his weekend. Mike felt very special because Jim listened well. Jim showed that he cared about Mike and about what Mike said.

In what way was Jim a good listener? What did he do that lets you know he listened well? Why do you think good listeners have more friends than bad listeners?

■ DISCUSSION QUESTIONS

Simple/concrete questions:
>   If someone is looking in the other direction, is he or she listening well to you?
>   Can you talk at the same time you listen?
>   Should you look at a person when you are listening to him or her?
>   Do you listen with your mouth or with your ears?
>   Should you let a person know you heard him? How?

Personal experience/feelings questions?
>   Do you know anyone who doesn't listen to you? How do you feel about this?
>   How do you usually feel if someone does not listen to you?
>   How do you feel when people listen well to what you are saying?

Problem-solving questions:
>   If someone does not listen to you, what should you do?
>   How do you feel when people listen well to what you are saying?

Problem-solving questions:
>   If someone does not listen to you, what should you do?
>   What is a good way to get somebody's attention before you talk to them?
>   What prevents somebody from being a good listener? (What blocks communication between people?)
>   What makes somebody a good listener?

■ GROUP ACTIVITIES

Take turns talking about each person's weekend, holiday, and so on, while others practice reflecting back what they have heard.

Each group member selects a partner; partners take turns talking about matters of personal interest and then reflect back what they have heard.

Group leader practices various body postures while asking individuals to listen; asks if it would be helpful to make body posture changes (e.g., look at the wall, hold head down, avert gaze, orient body toward or away from listener); and asks if each body posture reflects good or bad listening posture.

Share various pictures with group members and ask them if the pictures represent good or bad readiness for listening.

■ ASSESSMENT OF SKILLS LEARNED

Makes eye contact:

ALMOST NEVER	USUALLY NOT	SOMETIMES	USUALLY	ALMOST ALWAYS
1	2	3	4	5

Orients toward speaker and has good listening posture:

ALMOST NEVER	USUALLY NOT	SOMETIMES	USUALLY	ALMOST ALWAYS
1	2	3	4	5

Gives reaction to indicate listening:

ALMOST NEVER	USUALLY NOT	SOMETIMES	USUALLY	ALMOST ALWAYS
1	2	3	4	5

Repeats back what someone says:

ALMOST NEVER	USUALLY NOT	SOMETIMES	USUALLY	ALMOST ALWAYS
1	2	3	4	5

Asks others to repeat themselves:

ALMOST NEVER	USUALLY NOT	SOMETIMES	USUALLY	ALMOST ALWAYS
1	2	3	4	5

Asks others to explain themselves:

ALMOST NEVER	USUALLY NOT	SOMETIMES	USUALLY	ALMOST ALWAYS
1	2	3	4	5

3. *Introducing Oneself*

The focus of this topic is to teach participants to make initial social contact with others. It is important to begin relationships properly. Often, the first impression one makes is in a self-introduction. Group members should be encouraged to think about the right times and places for introductions. For example, individuals should introduce themselves when they first meet. This should not be done during work or school time, or if the other person is attending to something else. An initial greeting should be given when an individual is attending sufficiently to the greeter. The greeter should first give his or her own name and then ask for the name of the person greeted. Nonverbal communication is important in the greeting. Eye contact is essential, a smile or pleasant facial expression is welcome, and a handshake is often appropriate. This skill is usually understood by persons with mild and moderate developmental delay. Individuals with more limited social-intellectual development often need more concrete explanations. These elucidations may include pointing to oneself and to the person greeted during the introduction. They may also involve utilizing other nonverbal materials such as picture communication booklets, sign language, and external cues indicating when persons should speak and when they should respond during the greeting. Individuals with shorter attention spans may need to be told very specifically to say, "My name is _____," and, when that is finished, to ask, "What is your name?" A high level of feedback should be given to participants about their verbal and nonverbal behaviors during the introduction.

■ SPECIFIC SKILLS TO BE LEARNED

Decide the right time and place to introduce oneself.
Give a greeting (e.g., "Hi, my name is _____ , what's your name?").
Tell others one's name.
Ask somebody his or her name.
Shake hands.
Look someone in the eyes when introducing oneself.
Smile when introducing oneself.

■ CONCEPTS NECESSARY TO PERFORM SKILLS

Stranger: Somebody a person does not know at all; a person you have never met; a person one sees for the first time; an unfamiliar person.
Acquaintance: Somebody a person has seen before but does not know very well; someone with whom one has gone to school or worked but is not very familiar; a person one knows, but not too well.
Friend: Somebody a person knows well; a familiar person; companion; mate; a person with whom somebody likes to do things; someone to talk to; somebody to whom a person feels close; someone a person can trust.
Greet: Say, "Hi," "Hello," "How are you?" "Nice to see you," "What's happening?" "Nice day," "Good day," etc.; say something to let somebody know that you have noticed the person; say something when first encountering somebody else.
Individual name: What people call themselves; "My name is _____"; a special word for you or me; a word that tells whom one is talking to, whom one is talking about, or who is speaking to an individual.
Nonverbal behavior: What a person's face and body are doing while the person talks; smile, shake hands, nod one's head, wave good-bye, etc.
Verbal behavior: The words people say to each other when they talk; using words to explain things; talking to others and telling them things.

■ CASE VIGNETTES

—*Bob was new in the neighborhood. He had just moved in next door to Bill. Bill saw Bob outside one day but had not yet been introduced to him. He wanted to meet Bob but was afraid to introduce himself. After Bill thought about it, he decided that he would introduce himself. He walked across the street and stuck out his hand to shake Bob's hand. He said, "Hi, my name is Bill." He also asked, "What's your name?" Bob smiled and said, "My name's Bob. I'm new in the neighborhood. I hope we can be friends." Bill said, "That's great, I like to make new friends." They talked some more. Soon they were good friends.*

Do you think it helped Bob and Bill to become friends when Bill introduced himself? Why might it have been helpful for Bill to introduce himself?

—*Sally was new in the neighborhood. She had moved to her new home last week. She used to live with her parents and younger brother. Sally was now moving into a townhouse with three other people who were becoming more independent from their families. As she walked up the steps to her new home, she saw two of her new housemates. She was nervous and did not know what to say. Sally just stood there looking at the two strangers. Finally, one of them blurted out, "Hi, my name is Beth, what's yours?" Beth reached out to shake hands. As they shook hands, Sally felt more comfortable and said, "My name is Sally." Soon they got to know each other and became friends.*

Why do you think Sally was nervous? Do you think she would have felt better if she had known how to introduce herself?

■ DISCUSSION QUESTIONS

Simple/concrete questions:
  What is an introduction?
  How do you ask for somebody's name?
  Do you shake hands when you greet somebody?
Personal experience/feelings questions:
  Have you ever introduced yourself before? How did you do this?
  How do you feel when you introduce yourself to others?
  Is it ever difficult for you to introduce yourself to others?
  Do you introduce yourself differently over the telephone than when you meet somebody
    in person?
Problem-solving questions:
  What should you do if you introduce yourself and someone is rude to you?
  What kinds of problems can happen when you introduce yourself?
  What are some wrong times or places to introduce yourself?
  Are there people to whom you should not introduce yourself?

■ GROUP ACTIVITIES

Each person practice introductions with a partner.
Group leader and volunteer demonstrate introductions.
Fellow group members demonstrate introductions.
Total group gives feedback while pairs of individuals practice introducing themselves in front
  of group.

■ ASSESSMENT OF SKILLS LEARNED

Recognizes appropriate times and places for introduction:

ALMOST NEVER	USUALLY NOT	SOMETIMES	USUALLY	ALMOST ALWAYS
1	2	3	4	5

Gives a greeting:

ALMOST NEVER	USUALLY NOT	SOMETIMES	USUALLY	ALMOST ALWAYS
1	2	3	4	5

Tells name to others:

ALMOST NEVER	USUALLY NOT	SOMETIMES	USUALLY	ALMOST ALWAYS
1	2	3	4	5

Asks others their names:

ALMOST NEVER	USUALLY NOT	SOMETIMES	USUALLY	ALMOST ALWAYS
1	2	3	4	5

Shakes hands:

ALMOST NEVER	USUALLY NOT	SOMETIMES	USUALLY	ALMOST ALWAYS
1	2	3	4	5

Looks others in the eyes when introducing self:

ALMOST NEVER	USUALLY NOT	SOMETIMES	USUALLY	ALMOST ALWAYS
1	2	3	4	5

Smiles when introducing self:

ALMOST NEVER	USUALLY NOT	SOMETIMES	USUALLY	ALMOST ALWAYS
1	2	3	4	5

4. Beginning a Conversation

Knowing how to begin a conversation often determines how others react to an individual. This is one of the most important and fundamental skills to the development of social skills that are more complex. The four basic components of this topic should be presented in a concrete, linear fashion, spending time discussing each element and then practicing an entire, though abbreviated, conversation. Each group participant must be encouraged to choose someone to talk to, as well as something which they would like to talk about. Initially the group participants should practice greeting each other. Next they may engage each other in small talk, utilizing content such as the weather, work, sports, or the news. Third, the group needs to pick a topic of joint interest to discuss in more detail. Finally, members should practice closing a conversation with such phrases as, "Good-bye," "See ya later," "So long," and other colloquialisms familiar to participants. This topic is easily addressed by individuals with mild and moderate developmental disabilities. It can be presented very concretely to lower functioning individuals who may have difficulty initiating and sustaining a conversation, but who are often capable of performing individual conversation elements with the assistance of cues, prompts, and encouragement. The lower the intellectual level, the more necessary it is to use a concrete approach. For nonverbal individuals, sign language, pictures, and symbols, may be used to explain and highlight the essential features of greetings, small talk and closing. For example, group activities may utilize pictures of persons gesturing greetings or waving good-bye, pictures of weather symbols such as sunshine or rain, and other nonverbal materials. This particular topic should be rehearsed rigorously and should be included in occasional social skills reviews.

■ SPECIFIC SKILLS TO BE LEARNED

Choose someone to talk to.
Think of what one would like to talk about.
Greet others (e.g., "Hello," "Hi," "How are you?" "Excuse me," etc.).
Engage in small talk (talk about weather, work, sports, news, etc.).
Pick a topic.
Close a conversation (e.g., say "Bye," "See you later," "Nice talking to you," "Have a nice day").

■ CONCEPTS NECESSARY TO PERFORM SKILLS

Greet: Say, "Hi," "Hello," "How are you?" "Nice to see you," "What's happening?" "Nice day," "Good day," etc.; say something to let somebody know that you have noticed the person; say something when first encountering somebody else.

Small talk: Discussing things that are not too personal; talking about things like news, weather, and sports; conversing about small matters before talking about more important topics; a way to make contact with others without taking the risk of telling them information that is too personal.

Topic: The main thing people are talking about; a particular thing that someone thinks is important; the subject about which people ask questions or tell things; the main point of a discussion.

Closing: Ending a conversation; saying, "See you later," "Good-bye," "Have a nice day," or "Nice talking to you"; a friendly way to stop talking to someone so that you can each do something else.

■ CASE VIGNETTES

—Santino was a friendly person. He liked to talk to people. Even though he was a nice person, he had trouble talking to others. One problem was that he did not know when to start talking and when to listen to somebody. The other day, James and Milford were talking and Santino just broke in talking about something else. James and Milford were talking about a personal matter. Milford's grandfather had died. Santino kept talking about his trip to the zoo. Milford seemed to be quite angry.

Why do you think Milford was angry? What could Santino have done to make sure that Milford was ready to talk to him?

—Cassandra was well liked by her friends. One day she saw Nancy and Rosie talking in the lunchroom. Cassandra wanted to tell them about her trip to the circus; but she noticed that they were very absorbed in their own conversation. She wanted to interrupt to tell them about the trapeze artists, the elephants, and all the fun she had yesterday at the circus. She waited patiently until Rosie noticed her. Rosie looked right at Cassandra so she knew it was O.K. to talk. Even so, she was polite and asked, "Excuse me, Rosie, am I interrupting you and Nancy?" Rosie replied, "Of course not. I heard you went to the circus. Did you have fun?"

Why do you think Rosie and Nancy liked Cassandra? Do you think Cassandra picked a good time to start talking? Why or why not?

■ DISCUSSION QUESTIONS

Simple/concrete questions:
   What are four major parts of a conversation (greeting, small talk, topic, closing)?
   What is an example of a greeting?
   What is an example of small talk?
   What is an example of a topic?
   Give an example of how you would end (close) a conversation?
Personal experience/feelings questions:
   Have you ever had a difficult time starting a conversation with others?
   Are there certain people you have an easy time talking to? Why?
   How do you feel when you are starting a conversation with a friend? Stranger? Acquaintance? Family member? Supervisor?
   Do you ever get nervous or afraid when you start a conversation?
Problem-solving questions:
   When is it a good time to talk to others? Why?
   When is it not a good time to talk to others? Why?
   What should you do if you want to talk to somebody but do not know what to say?
   How do you know when to end a conversation?

■ GROUP ACTIVITIES

Each group member practices giving each other group member a greeting.
Form pairs and practice doing small talk about news, weather, and work matters.
Each participant practices choosing a topic.
Each individual practices giving a closing statement.

■ ASSESSMENT OF SKILLS LEARNED

Chooses someone to talk to:

ALMOST NEVER	USUALLY NOT	SOMETIMES	USUALLY	ALMOST ALWAYS
1	2	3	4	5

Greets others:

ALMOST NEVER	USUALLY NOT	SOMETIMES	USUALLY	ALMOST ALWAYS
1	2	3	4	5

Engages in small talk:

ALMOST NEVER	USUALLY NOT	SOMETIMES	USUALLY	ALMOST ALWAYS
1	2	3	4	5

Chooses a topic of discussion:

ALMOST NEVER	USUALLY NOT	SOMETIMES	USUALLY	ALMOST ALWAYS
1	2	3	4	5

Closes a conversation:

ALMOST NEVER	USUALLY NOT	SOMETIMES	USUALLY	ALMOST ALWAYS
1	2	3	4	5

5. Asking a Question

Knowing how to ask a question is crucial to maintaining a conversation. One reason it is important is that it demonstrates an interest in others. The group leader should begin with a discussion of how a person decides what question to ask and to whom. It may be helpful to point out that the content of most questions involves who, what, when, where, or why. Participants need to know that questions can be prefaced by a greeting, if appropriate, or at least a polite introduction—for example, "Excuse me, can I ask you something?" or "Pardon me, can I interrupt you? I need to ask you something." The importance of smiling and making eye contact should be highlighted. Finally, after the question has been asked, the group participant may be encouraged to acknowledge the answer by saying, "Thank you," nodding, or giving some indication that the answer is appreciated. The concepts of this topic are easily comprehended by those with mild and moderate developmental disabilities. It can be modified for lower functioning individuals, either by giving them simple, rote questions to ask others or by teaching them to make nonverbal requests. These nonverbal requests (questions) may involve pointing to pictures/symbols; making signs; or using other facial expressions, body movements, or agreed-on gestures in a functional manner in order to make specific requests. The lower the intellectual level, the more concrete the language used, and the more likely that nonverbal elements must be used when asking a question.

■ SPECIFIC SKILLS TO BE LEARNED

Decide whom to ask (pick a person).

Decide what to ask (topic of question often involves who, what, where, when, or why).

Give a greeting and ask permission (e.g., "Excuse me," "Pardon me," "May I ask you a question?").

Smile politely.

Make eye contact.

Ask a question.

Thank the person for listening/answering (acknowledge the answer by saying, "Thank you," or showing some indication that one heard the answer).

■ CONCEPTS NECESSARY TO PERFORM SKILLS

Ask: Question somebody; make a request of someone; one can "tell" somebody to do something or can "ask" the person if he or she wants to do it; a person "asks" questions and "tells" statements.

Tell: Say something to someone; give information; explain something; say what one feels, thinks, or wants; make a statement.

Eye contact: Looking someone in the eyes; looking at somebody instead of looking away.

■ CASE VIGNETTES

—*Sue liked to ask questions. The problem was that she did not know the right time to ask them. One day she came into her class meeting late. Everybody was talking about their vacations. Sue did not listen to anyone else. She made a lot of noise when she opened the classroom door. Then she interrupted the whole class and asked the teacher about her class project. A few minutes later, when Sheila was talking, Sue blurted out, "Can I go to the bathroom?" Sheila looked angry when this happened.*

Could Sue have picked a better time to ask her questions? How could she have done a better job asking questions? Why do you suppose some of her classmates were angry with her?

—*Kirby entered the classroom door and noticed that everybody was talking about their vacations. As soon as he saw the others talking, he quietly walked to his seat and listened politely. He wanted to ask the teacher about his class project but waited because he did not want to interrupt his classmates. After a short time, the other students were quiet. Kirby looked at the teacher who looked back at him. He did not raise his hand because he already had the teacher's attention. Mr. Jackson was looking right at him. Kirby politely spoke up, "Excuse me, Mr. Jackson, can I ask you something about my project?" Mr. Jackson responded, "Of course, Kirby. Thanks for waiting patiently. How can I help you?"*

Why do you think Mr. Jackson treated Kirby with such respect? Do you think it was partly because Kirby picked a good time to ask his question? Do you think it had something to do with how Kirby asked his question?

■ DISCUSSION QUESTIONS

Simple/concrete questions:

What is a question?

What are some examples of questions?

What are some things you can ask someone about?

What is the difference between "asking" and "telling" something?

Personal experience/feelings questions:
    How do you feel when you ask someone a question?
    How do you feel if a person ignores your question?
    How do you feel if somebody interrupts your question?
    When do you feel comfortable asking others questions?
    Of whom do you like to ask questions?
Problem-solving questions:
    What should you do if you do not understand the answer to your question?
    What should you do if you do not like the answer you get?
    What problems can happen when you ask questions?
    When and how do you ask a follow-up question?
    When is it O.K. to ask very personal questions? When is it not O.K.?
    What are some times or places which are not appropriate for asking questions of other
        persons? Why?

■ GROUP ACTIVITIES

Group participants take turns asking questions, each person listening to one question and re-
    sponding, then turning to the next individual and asking a new question.
Practice asking questions to the same person about the same topic, trying to solicit more infor-
    mation about the person or topic.
Divide into pairs and ask each other various questions involving personal information (e.g.,
    where each lives, what the person likes to eat, hobbies/interests).
Using humor, ask various questions to group members while looking at the floor, ceiling, door,
    and other inappropriate places; ask individuals if this is a good way to ask questions.

■ ASSESSMENT OF SKILLS LEARNED

Chooses a person to whom to ask a question:

ALMOST NEVER	USUALLY NOT	SOMETIMES	USUALLY	ALMOST ALWAYS
1	2	3	4	5

Selects a topic about which to ask a question:

ALMOST NEVER	USUALLY NOT	SOMETIMES	USUALLY	ALMOST ALWAYS
1	2	3	4	5

Gives a greeting and asks permission to ask a question:

ALMOST NEVER	USUALLY NOT	SOMETIMES	USUALLY	ALMOST ALWAYS
1	2	3	4	5

Smiles when greeting someone:

ALMOST NEVER	USUALLY NOT	SOMETIMES	USUALLY	ALMOST ALWAYS
1	2	3	4	5

Makes eye contact:

ALMOST NEVER	USUALLY NOT	SOMETIMES	USUALLY	ALMOST ALWAYS
1	2	3	4	5

Asks a question:

ALMOST NEVER	USUALLY NOT	SOMETIMES	USUALLY	ALMOST ALWAYS
1	2	3	4	5

Thanks a person for listening or answering a question:

ALMOST NEVER	USUALLY NOT	SOMETIMES	USUALLY	ALMOST ALWAYS
1	2	3	4	5

6. *Maintaining a Conversation*

It is important to know how to maintain a conversation if one is to sustain ongoing social relationships. Many individuals have the skills to initiate a conversation but are unable to sustain it because of their inability to ask follow-up questions or strategically share personal information that is relevant to a particular vein of discourse. In this topic area, the group leader is encouraged to focus on the ability to ask repeated follow-up questions about a topic and to share personal information or experiences related to a topic. First, participants should review the essentials of asking a question. Next, they need to practice sharing personal information about particular topics of interest. Others must be encouraged to ask follow-up questions about the same topics. Participants may be assisted in progressively sharing more personal information as they are asked additional follow-up questions. The questioners can then be urged to share personal information and life experiences intermittently as they continue to ask follow-up questions. This will involve a free sharing of new personal information without being questioned directly. The person being questioned may also be encouraged to share additional information, which may be related to questions but goes further than the particular questions asked. For example, Jim may ask, "Bob, do you watch television at night?" Bob may respond, "Yes, I like to watch sports." The group leader must help individuals recognize the difference between a question and a statement. It is very important for participants to understand that they can show an interest in others by their questions. They can also encourage self-revelation by others if they are willing to reveal personal information. The topic is easily understood by those with mild and moderate developmental disabilities. Of course, those who are intellectually brighter will have an easier time sustaining their questioning and continuing to find new personal information to share with their partners. Lower functioning individuals may need to practice this skill in segments, linking them together later. For example, they may initially practice asking questions, followed by several episodes of sharing personal information about the same topic. Extremely low functioning individuals may participate in a more passive fashion, simply responding to a variety of questions while the group leader and fellow group participants prompt them to respond. This can be good practice for the higher functioning participants., who will learn that a conversation may be sustained by one interested and motivated party who is willing to continue to ask questions and encourage responses from another individual.

■ SPECIFIC SKILLS TO BE LEARNED

Ask a question.
Share personal information (tell about oneself).
Ask follow-up questions about the same topic (also repeat follow-up questions).
Ask follow-up questions in order to move the topic in a new direction (change the topic).
Share more personal information about oneself in response to others' questions.
Share new personal information without being directly questioned.
Recognize the difference between a question and a self-statement (tell a statement; ask a question).
Show an interest in others by asking questions.

■ CONCEPTS NECESSARY TO PERFORM SKILLS

Question: Ask somebody something; ask about something; inquire.
Personal: Private; confidential; intimate; things people usually keep to themselves; things usually told only to friends and family members; something a person does not want everybody to hear about; one's own special thoughts and experiences.

Follow-up: Ask something new after asking the first question; keep talking about the same topic but ask or tell new things about it.

Information: Things that people talk about; ideas individuals share with each other; what people tell each other; messages; knowledge; communication about facts; advice; what people know and report.

Topic: The main thing people are talking about; a particular item that someone thinks is important; the subject about which people ask questions or tell things; the main point of a discussion.

Self-statement: Telling something about yourself; sharing personal information; telling one's thoughts or feelings.

Interest: To show that one cares about what someone else things or feels; to ask about somebody; to have concern for another; to let others know they are important.

■ CASE VIGNETTES

—Mike and Steve were part of the same work group. Their job was to sweep the floor and empty the wastebaskets. They saw each other every day at the job. Mike would say, "Hi, Steve," and Steve would respond, "Hi, Mike." That's as far as the conversation went. Each just did his job. They never asked each other about their weekends. They did not ask about each other's family. They did not even know where each other lived. They simply did their jobs and went home afterward. Steve said, "'Bye, Mike," and Mike said, "So long, Steve." That was it.

Why do you suppose Mike and Steve did not keep a conversation going? Why did they have trouble talking to each other? What could they have done to keep their conversation going?

—Oprah and Sally worked in the lumberyard together, Oprah at the front desk and Sally in the lumber shed. They ate lunch together every day. When the clock struck noon, they met at the pop machine. Oprah would always ask Sally how her job was going. After this, Sally would ask Oprah if she had any news. They asked each other about their families, about their weekends, and about all kinds of things. They were interested in each other. They showed this by asking each other personal questions and by sharing personal information with each other. They were friends. They liked each other. They had a lot of fun talking together.

Why do you think they were such close friends? How did Oprah and Sally show an interest in each other? Did it help to ask each other questions? Did it help to share personal information? Why or why not?

■ DISCUSSION QUESTIONS

Simple/concrete questions:
   What is a question? Give an example.
   What is a statement? Give an example.
   What is a follow-up question?
   What is the difference between telling something and asking something?
Personal experience/feelings questions:
   How do you feel when somebody asks you a question?
   How do you feel when somebody asks you a follow-up question about your answer?
   How do you feel when you ask somebody a question?
   Can you describe a situation in which you enjoyed talking to someone?
   Can you describe a situation in which you had trouble talking to someone?
Problem-solving questions:
   How can you keep a conversation going with someone who does not talk very much?
   When is it a good time to keep a conversation going?

When is it a good time to quit talking to someone?
What are some reasons why people have trouble keeping a conversation going?

■ GROUP ACTIVITIES

Take turns forming pairs and practicing asking questions in front of the group; one person pick a topic and the other person try to keep the conversation going by asking repeated questions and sharing repeated personal information about the topic.

Form small groups and have free discussion about particular topics; encourage question asking.

Take turns standing in front of the group and asking each person a beginning question as well as a follow-up question about the same topic. Ask the follow-up question about the person's answer to the first question.

■ ASSESSMENT OF SKILLS LEARNED

Asks a question:

ALMOST NEVER	USUALLY NOT	SOMETIMES	USUALLY	ALMOST ALWAYS
1	2	3	4	5

Shares personal information without being asked:

ALMOST NEVER	USUALLY NOT	SOMETIMES	USUALLY	ALMOST ALWAYS
1	2	3	4	5

Asks a follow-up question about the topic of discussion:

ALMOST NEVER	USUALLY NOT	SOMETIMES	USUALLY	ALMOST ALWAYS
1	2	3	4	5

Asks a follow-up question to move a topic in a new direction (changes the topic):

ALMOST NEVER	USUALLY NOT	SOMETIMES	USUALLY	ALMOST ALWAYS
1	2	3	4	5

Shares personal information in response to a question:

ALMOST NEVER	USUALLY NOT	SOMETIMES	USUALLY	ALMOST ALWAYS
1	2	3	4	5

Recognizes the difference between a question and a statement (asking versus telling):

ALMOST NEVER	USUALLY NOT	SOMETIMES	USUALLY	ALMOST ALWAYS
1	2	3	4	5

Asks repeated follow-up questions:

ALMOST NEVER	USUALLY NOT	SOMETIMES	USUALLY	ALMOST ALWAYS
1	2	3	4	5

Intermixes questions and self-statements:

ALMOST NEVER	USUALLY NOT	SOMETIMES	USUALLY	ALMOST ALWAYS
1	2	3	4	5

7/8. *Giving a Compliment/Saying Thank-You*

Giving a compliment and saying thank-you are basic to one's relationships with others. Individuals help others feel safe and comfortable by giving them compliments. Being complimentary to others enables them to let down their emotional defenses and to focus on positive aspects of themselves and their relationships with others. Giving a compliment is also a promissory note of sorts, encouraging others to treat one similarly. Saying thank-you is a way of acknowledging the courtesy of others and rewarding them for it. In this section, group members may utilize previously learned social skills involved in choosing someone to compliment and making eye contact. The group facilitator can help participants decide on what to compliment their group mates. The content of compliments may include an individual's personal appearance, behavior, personality or the person in his or her entirety. It is important to select something honest and realistic to compliment about another, lest the compliment not be believed or accepted. It is also important to encourage participants to keep their physical demeanor consistent with their compliments by smiling and appearing friendly when giving them. A compliment should be specific, and the complimentee's name should be used. For example, "Debbie, I like it that you are so helpful today," or "Terry, thanks for sitting quietly and listening to me." Group participants must practice graciously accepting compliments by saying, "Thank you." This particular topic is well received by those with mild and moderate developmental disabilities. It can also be understood by many individuals with more severe disabilities. The material tends to generate enthusiasm among participants. If individuals have difficulty, it is typically in their inability to generate new categories and types of compliments, not in their willingness to use them. The group leader should spend time helping members generate new types of compliments. The facilitator may also help them expand their compliments from superficial (e.g., "I like your shirt,") to more personal foci (e.g., "I like it that you treated me so well today; thanks for helping me with my job.") Less verbal individuals may be able to make complimentary gestures and facial expressions or use picture/symbol booklets to communicate compliments and acknowledgments.

■ SPECIFIC SKILLS TO BE LEARNED

Pick a person to compliment.
Look at the person one is complimenting (make eye contact).
Decide what to compliment:
  Personal appearance (body, face, hair, clothing, etc.)
  Person's behavior ("I like what you are doing," or "I like what you did")
  Person's character or personality (hard-working, friendly, considerate, funny, easygoing, etc.)
  Person in totality ("I like you," "You are great," "You're a nice person," etc.)
Smile and look at others with a friendly face.
Use the person's name before giving a compliment (e.g., "_____ , I like _____ .").
Listen to a compliment.
Recognize a compliment.
Say, "Thank you," after a compliment.
Let the person know for what you are thanking them (e.g., "Thanks for saying that.").

■ CONCEPTS NECESSARY TO PERFORM SKILLS

Compliment: Say something nice to someone; tell others what you like about them; tell someone what you like about his or her behavior; tell somebody what you like about his or her personality; praise someone; congratulate a person; tell others that you like them.
Thank-you: Tell others that you appreciate their compliments; let someone know that you like what he or she said to you; be gracious; accept a compliment.

■ CASE VIGNETTES

—José was a good basketball player. He and Chakiel played in the game together on Saturday. At the end of the game, Chakiel came up to José. He said, "José, nice job. What a great shot you made at the end of the first quarter!" José smiled proudly and replied, "Thanks a lot, Chakiel, we couldn't have won the game without all of your good rebounds."

Do you think José was thankful that Chakiel gave him a compliment? How do you know? Was it a good idea for José to return a compliment to Chakiel? Why might this have been helpful?

—Lavonne and Sue were on the track team together. It was a close race, but Lavonne had crossed the finish line first and helped her team win the race. Sue came up to her after the race and said, "Congratulations, Lavonne, you ran a terrific race." Lavonne replied, "Yes, I ran very fast today. Now I'm going home." Then she walked away. Sue felt badly inside, but was not sure why.

Do you think Sue might have felt badly because Lavonne did not thank her for the compliment? Next time Lavonne wins a race, do you think Sue will give her another compliment? Why or why not?

■ DISCUSSION QUESTIONS

Simple/concrete questions:
  What are some examples of compliments?
  If someone says, "I don't like your shirt," is that a compliment?
  If someone says, "I like you because you are friendly," is that a compliment?
  If someone says, "_____," is that a compliment? (Leader fills in different statements.)
Personal experience/feelings questions:
  How do you feel when you give somebody a compliment?
  How do you feel when you get a compliment?
  How do you feel if someone does not accept your compliment?
  Do you like being with people who never say anything nice to you?
  Do you think other people will want to be around you if you do not say anything nice about them?
Problem-solving questions:
  What should you do if someone does not accept your compliment?
  What should you say to someone who gives you a compliment but you do not agree with the compliment?
  Is it a good idea to give someone a compliment if it is not true? Why or why not?

■ GROUP ACTIVITIES

Group members take turns complimenting the individuals next to themselves. Each person share how he or she feels when getting the compliments.
Take turns having the entire group compliment one person, telling various things which other group members like about the person. Share feedback about how group members feel when giving and receiving compliments.
Form self-selected pairs and take turns complimenting each other.

■ ASSESSMENT OF SKILLS LEARNED

Chooses someone to compliment:

ALMOST NEVER	USUALLY NOT	SOMETIMES	USUALLY	ALMOST ALWAYS
1	2	3	4	5

Makes eye contact when complimenting a person:

ALMOST NEVER	USUALLY NOT	SOMETIMES	USUALLY	ALMOST ALWAYS
1	2	3	4	5

Lists several possible areas to compliment:

ALMOST NEVER	USUALLY NOT	SOMETIMES	USUALLY	ALMOST ALWAYS
1	2	3	4	5

Smiles and is friendly when complimenting:

ALMOST NEVER	USUALLY NOT	SOMETIMES	USUALLY	ALMOST ALWAYS
1	2	3	4	5

Uses the person's name when complimenting:

ALMOST NEVER	USUALLY NOT	SOMETIMES	USUALLY	ALMOST ALWAYS
1	2	3	4	5

Listens to a compliment:

ALMOST NEVER	USUALLY NOT	SOMETIMES	USUALLY	ALMOST ALWAYS
1	2	3	4	5

Recognizes a compliment:

ALMOST NEVER	USUALLY NOT	SOMETIMES	USUALLY	ALMOST ALWAYS
1	2	3	4	5

Says "Thank you" after a compliment:

ALMOST NEVER	USUALLY NOT	SOMETIMES	USUALLY	ALMOST ALWAYS
1	2	3	4	5

Lets the person know why he or she is being thanked:

ALMOST NEVER	USUALLY NOT	SOMETIMES	USUALLY	ALMOST ALWAYS
1	2	3	4	5

9. Introducing Others

Introducing others is an important skill because it enables individuals to share their friends with others, ultimately expanding their own social networks and supports. It enables persons to relate to each other in groups where only some of the individuals know each other at the outset. It is more difficult than introducing oneself because it requires the participant to get outside of him- or herself, to some extent taking on the perspective of another. First, the introducer needs to find out information about the introducee. This requires listening and asking questions. It also demands a certain degree of memory. At the point of introduction, the introducer begins by saying, "This is my friend _____ ; let me tell you about _____" and proceeds to share a short background sketch about the introducee. This should include how one came to know the person and what is their current relationship. The group facilitator must help participants establish a list of categories of interest to use as a reference when introducing their friends. The list should fit the social level and vernacular of the individual group member but is likely to include items such as age, schooling, work, hobbies, interests, family, activity preferences, and so forth. Before practicing introductions in the group, it is helpful to divide into pairs and to spend time questioning partners about categories of interest. It is usually necessary for the group facilitator to ensure that all participants have queried their partners sufficiently to make an introduction. This topic is more difficult than previous ones but is readily accessible to those with mild developmental disabilities. For lower functioning individuals, it is progressively more difficult, necessitating increased structure to be successful. One modification involves the group leader working individually with each pair of participants, helping them to establish a list of categorical information about their partners. This may be followed by the group leader prompting one participant, "Tell us about your friend _____," "How old is _____?" "What does _____ like to do?" "Where does _____ live?" "What does _____ like to eat?" The topic offers a good situation in which to practice other basic social skills, such as listening and asking questions. For nonverbal individuals, pictures, symbols, sign language, gestures, and other types of nonverbal communication can be used to introduce friends more concretely. This may be supplemented by the verbal remarks and descriptions of the group facilitator and other participants.

■ SPECIFIC SKILLS TO BE LEARNED

Find out information about others (collect background information).
Listen and ask questions to others.
Remember what another person says.
Name the person (e.g., "This is my friend, _____").
Tell others about the person one is introducing ("Let me tell you about _____").
Identify categories of interest when introducing someone:

    Age
    Schooling
    Work
    Hobbies/interests/activities
    Best friend(s)
    Family
    Food preferences
    Television and music preferences
    Life story
    Important life events
    Etc.

■ CONCEPTS NECESSARY TO PERFORM SKILLS

Introduce: Present somebody to others; share a new friend with existing friends; help acquaint a person with others; let people know who is one's new friend.

Listen: Pay attention to what someone says; hear and understand what somebody says; open your ears and close your mouth; let others know that you know what they are saying.

Collect background information: Ask somebody about him- or herself; get to know someone; find out what people like to eat, watch on television, do in their spare time, etc.; find out about somebody's present life and history.

Tell: Say something to someone; give information; explain something; say what one feels, thinks or wants; make a statement.

Category of information: A topic somebody wants to know about; something that interests someone; a type of news about someone or something.

Name: What others call someone; a word for somebody so that people know who one is talking about; what a person calls him or herself.

■ CASE VIGNETTES

—*Joseph brought his new friend Peter home for dinner. They walked in the door and sat down at the table. Just then Joseph's mother entered the room. She started putting food on the stove and asked Joseph to please set the table. Peter just sat there quietly. He did not know if he should help Joseph set the table or not. He felt a little bit uncomfortable because he had never met Joseph's mother before. Finally, after several minutes, Joseph's mother looked at Peter and asked, "Joseph, who is your friend?" Joseph replied, "That's my friend Peter, can he stay for dinner?"*

Why do you think Peter felt uncomfortable? Do you think Peter would have felt better if he had been introduced right away? Why or why not?

—*Janet had a job in the school cafeteria. It was her job to wash dishes. One day she met a new friend, Kelly, who cleared dishes off tables and swept the floor. At breaktime she and Kelly sat at a table with some of Janet's other friends. Upon sitting down with Kelly, Janet immediately said, "Everybody, I want you to meet my new friend Kelly.. Some of you know her. She clears tables and sweeps the floor here. She lives on Grove Street by the railroad tracks. Her brother is the cook at a restaurant" After hearing this, Janet's friends asked Kelly some questions and they all got along very well.*

Do you think Janet made Kelly feel comfortable at the table? How did she do this? Did it help to properly introduce Kelly to the others? How did this help?

■ DISCUSSION QUESTIONS

Simple/concrete questions:
    What is an introduction?
    What are some things you can tell others about your friends?
Personal experience/feelings questions:
    Do you have any close friends?
    Have you ever introduced a friend to others?
    How do you feel when you introduce your friends to others?
    How would you feel if your friend brought a new friend to see you but did not introduce
        him or her?
Problem-solving questions:
    What should you do if your friend brings a new person to your activity but does not
        introduce the person?
    Why is it important to introduce new people to others?
    What should you do if you come to school or work and there is a new person that you
        have not met before?

■ GROUP ACTIVITIES

Pick one group member to demonstrate introducing others.
Divide the group into pairs. Each explore background information and categories of interest
    about the other, and then take turns introducing partners.
Repeat the exercise with new partners.

■ ASSESSMENT OF SKILLS LEARNED

Asks someone for personal background information:

ALMOST NEVER	USUALLY NOT	SOMETIMES	USUALLY	ALMOST ALWAYS
1	2	3	4	5

Asks questions and listens to what other people say:

ALMOST NEVER	USUALLY NOT	SOMETIMES	USUALLY	ALMOST ALWAYS
1	2	3	4	5

Remembers what other people say:

ALMOST NEVER	USUALLY NOT	SOMETIMES	USUALLY	ALMOST ALWAYS
1	2	3	4	5

Names a person while introducing him or her:

ALMOST NEVER	USUALLY NOT	SOMETIMES	USUALLY	ALMOST ALWAYS
1	2	3	4	5

Tells background information when introducing a person:

ALMOST NEVER	USUALLY NOT	SOMETIMES	USUALLY	ALMOST ALWAYS
1	2	3	4	5

Identifies and describes categories of interest to introduce someone:

ALMOST NEVER	USUALLY NOT	SOMETIMES	USUALLY	ALMOST ALWAYS
1	2	3	4	5

2 Feelings

THE GENERAL TOPIC of this chapter is *feelings*. These skills are included early in the manual because difficulty in recognizing, accepting, and appropriately expressing feelings is pervasive among persons who have developmental disabilities. The chapter begins with an exploration of different types of feelings, moves on to the areas of recognizing and accepting feelings, and then focuses on the appropriate expression of feelings. Finally, several topics explore how to deal with specific emotions. Individuals with developmental disabilities often experience emotions as unpleasant forces impinging from outside themselves. This chapter assists with the identification of the source of emotions, and helps individuals connect feelings with other thoughts and behaviors in an adaptive fashion.

10. Types of Feelings

The major focus of this topic is to familiarize participants with a wide range of human emotions and to help them differentiate these from thoughts and behaviors. Individuals with developmental delay often have difficulty distinguishing their feelings from their thoughts and behaviors. This frequently results in unnecessary loss of behavior control and confusion about emotions. The concept of a *feeling* or *emotion* should be discussed. This can be followed by a discussion of different types of feelings, differentiating positive and negative emotions from physical feelings (bodily sensations) such as pain, hunger, and tiredness. Next, the difference between emotions, thoughts, and behaviors should be explored. The positive and negative polarities of feelings may be examined, familiarizing individuals with a variety of terms to describe positive and negative emotions. These materials are easily understood by those with mild and moderate developmental delay. This area is also accessible to persons with more severe disabilities. The topic lends itself well to nonverbal communication augmentation. It may be helpful for the group leader to act out particular feelings, asking group participants to guess which feeling the leader is trying to express. It is also beneficial and enjoyable to have group members play a game of charades, acting out feelings while others guess which ones they are communicating. Another modification for nonverbal individuals is to show pictures of persons expressing different emotions, asking participants yes/no questions about the pictures—"Do you think this person is happy?" or "Does this person look angry?" The pictures can be clipped easily from magazines. An additional modification is to draw five faces, two with different degrees of positive expressions, one neutral, and two with different gradations of unhappiness. More severely developmentally delayed and less verbal individuals can be asked to point to the face that reminds them of themselves or of other individuals. The group leader may draw more complex feelings faces or obtain them from other published sources. A final set of modifications for lower functioning individuals is to utilize one or more signs, symbols, gestures, or nonverbal communications to indicate various feelings. For some individuals, the understanding of emotions is very concrete and must be limited to very basic feelings.

■ SPECIFIC SKILLS TO BE LEARNED

Identify what is a feeling (emotion).
Identify different types of feelings:
    Positive emotion:
        Happy
        Relaxed
        Confident
        Interested
        Peaceful
        Excited
        Joyful
        Mellow
        Relieved
        Satisfied
        Etc.
    Negative emotion:
        Sad
        Afraid
        Scared
        Anxious
        Nervous
        Insecure
        Bored
        Depressed
        Helpless
        Hopeless
        Angry
        Frustrated
        Jealous
        Hurt
        Lonely
        Surprised
    Physical feeling:
        Pain
        Hunger
        Tiredness
Identify the difference between a feeling and behavior.
Identify the difference between a feeling and thought.
Identify two major categories of feelings: good and bad.
Identify the difference between emotional feelings and physical feelings of pain, hunger, tiredness, and so on.

■ CONCEPTS NECESSARY TO PERFORM SKILLS

Feeling: Emotion; something somebody feels inside; nervousness, anger, surprise, happiness, sadness, excitement, loneliness, or other emotion; good or bad sensation happening inside someone.

Thought: Something somebody thinks; an idea; a thing that a person believes; activity going on in someone's head.

Behavior: Something somebody does; to act in a certain way; what somebody's body is doing.

■ CASE VIGNETTES

—*Ellen was very happy. She had had a wonderful weekend. It started when she got her paycheck on Friday. Then she went out to eat with her friend Joyce. She ate a hamburger and Joyce had a hot dog. Afterward, they went to a movie. On Saturday, Ellen visited her brother and his wife. She stayed overnight and returned home on Sunday. Now she was eating lunch and feeling very good. She thought that everything in life was perfect and she was enjoying herself.*

Why do you think Ellen was feeling happy?

—*George woke up and rolled out of bed. He felt irritable and grumpy. He had to get ready for work. George was tired and did not feel like going, but he knew he had to work to earn his spending money. At breakfast, he snapped at Dan when Dan asked him to pass the milk. Dan asked, "What's bugging you, George?" but George did not answer. As George got on the bus to go to work, he bumped into Doug but did not say, "Excuse me." Doug got mad but George snapped at him to be quiet. Then Doug sat back and ignored George. At work, one of George's co-workers complained that he was pushing the dishes into the dishwasher too fast. When his supervisor asked him about this, George said it was Ed's fault because Ed worked too slowly.*

How do you think George was feeling? Do you think he was doing a good job handling his feelings? Why or why not?

—*Susan started feeling sick after lunch. She complained that her stomach was upset and she felt dizzy. She was also very tired and her throat was beginning to feel sore. She felt hot and was sweating more than usual. She decided to go home and get some rest. She did not think she could do any more work that day.*

Do you think that Susan was feeling upset because of unhappy emotions, or because her body was getting sick? Why? Is there a difference between having a body that feels sick, and having unhappy emotions?

■ DISCUSSION QUESTIONS

Simple/concrete questions:

Is _____ a feeling? (List various feelings as well as things which are not feelings.)

Personal experience/feelings questions:

Have you ever felt _____ (list feelings)? When and why?

Problem-solving questions:

How do you know what somebody is feeling?

If someone says they are feeling _____ (list feelings), what are some possible ways to react to the person?

If other people are feeling bad, should you try to take care of their feelings? Why or why not?

■ GROUP ACTIVITIES

Ask group members how they are feeling.

Ask each person to list a different feeling.

Divide into pairs and have group members take turns telling each other about all of the feelings they can remember experiencing during the week.

Utilizing a "feelings faces" chart, ask each person to identify a particular feeling based on the picture of a facial expression.

The group leader role-plays various facial expressions and body postures, and asks group members to guess the feelings associated with nonverbal cues. Group members take turns doing the same.

■ ASSESSMENT OF SKILLS LEARNED

Identifies what is a feeling:

ALMOST NEVER	USUALLY NOT	SOMETIMES	USUALLY	ALMOST ALWAYS
1	2	3	4	5

Lists different types of feelings:

ALMOST NEVER	USUALLY NOT	SOMETIMES	USUALLY	ALMOST ALWAYS
1	2	3	4	5

Identifies the difference between a feeling and behavior:

ALMOST NEVER	USUALLY NOT	SOMETIMES	USUALLY	ALMOST ALWAYS
1	2	3	4	5

Identifies the difference between a feeling and a thought:

ALMOST NEVER	USUALLY NOT	SOMETIMES	USUALLY	ALMOST ALWAYS
1	2	3	4	5

Identifies two groups of feelings: good and bad:

ALMOST NEVER	USUALLY NOT	SOMETIMES	USUALLY	ALMOST ALWAYS
1	2	3	4	5

Understands the difference between emotional and physical feelings:

ALMOST NEVER	USUALLY NOT	SOMETIMES	USUALLY	ALMOST ALWAYS
1	2	3	4	5

11. Recognizing and Accepting Feelings

Individuals with developmental disabilities often have great difficulty recognizing and accepting their feelings. Emotional impulses are frequently converted quickly to maladaptive behavioral expressions. The central point of this topic is to help group participants recognize and accept their feelings. The group facilitator should emphasize that while we experience feelings *inside* ourselves, they typically show on the *outside* of ourselves as well. Feelings may be reflected in tone of voice, facial expressions, body posture, and the specific words we speak to others. Participants may be told that it can help them to recognize their feelings if they pay attention to their own bodies and to the feedback they receive from others. For example, the man who has his hand in a fist, feels hot on the neck, is frowning at someone, is speaking loudly, and is hearing other pople ask why he is angry should consider the possibility that he may be feeling angry. The woman who is sitting with her head in her hands crying should consider the possibility that she may be feeling sad. Group members should be informed that it is O.K. to have any type of feeling. They may also be instructed that they must control their behavior even when feeling bad. This topic is easily grasped and enjoyed by persons with mild and moderate developmental disabilities. It is appropriate, useful, and engaging to play a game of feelings charades, as in the previous topic, so that group participants can practice identifying feelings. The modifications used in the previous topic for lower functioning participants also apply to this one. Individuals with more limited intellect will require more concrete explanations and increased use of nonverbal presentations.

■ SPECIFIC SKILLS TO BE LEARNED

Recognize that feelings happen "inside" oneself.
Recognize that feelings show on the "outside" of oneself:
   Voice (e.g., loud, soft, shaky).
   Face (e.g., smile, frown, tearful).
   Body posture (e.g., downcast, toward others, away from others).
   Words spoken (e.g., friendly, angry).
Recognize feelings
   Pay attention to one's body (what one's body tells an individual).
   Pay attention to feedback from others (what other people tell a person).
Accept feelings:
   All feelings are O.K.
   One must control behavior even when feelings are very strong.

■ CONCEPTS NECESSARY TO PERFORM SKILLS

Feeling: Emotion; something somebody feels inside; nervousness, anger, surprise, happiness, sadness, excitement, loneliness, or other emotion; good or bad sensation happening inside of someone.

Inside self: One's thoughts and feelings; the private world of an individual; one's personal experience of the world.

Outside self: How one's voice, face, body, and speech look and sound to others; behaviors and body movements; one's appearance.

Behavior: Something somebody does; to act in a certain way; what somebody's body is doing.

Feedback: Telling others how one thinks or feels about what was said; sharing how one thinks or feels about others' behaviors; telling a person how one sees his or her appearance; telling somebody how his or her appearance and behavior affect others.

■ CASE VIGNETTES

—*Bob was working at his job on the work floor of the assembly shop, putting strips of plastic on boxes. He seemed very frustrated and angry. He threw some boxes and snapped at Earl, "Slow down." Earl did not pay much attention to Bob. He kept putting boxes in front of Bob. Finally, Bob threw a pile of boxes, screamed some bad words at Earl, and stomped off the work floor muttering to himself, "Can't a guy ever have a chance to catch up around here?" He slammed the door. Soon he was leaving the building and walking along a dangerous road. He did not care because he was so upset.*

Do you think Bob was angry? Why? Do you think that Bob was handling his feelings well? What could he have done differently in this situation?

—*Juanita was working at her job on the floor of the assembly shop. It was her job to put ten little boxes inside a big box and to pass this to the next person. She did this all day. She was proud that she could package 500 boxes every day. Brian was giving her new boxes faster than she could finish them. They were piling up. She was becoming frustrated and angry. She noticed that her muscles were feeling tight, her neck was hot, and her voice was very short and impatient. Then her friend Joan asked her if she was angry. She thought about it for a minute and agreed: "Yes, I am feeling mad because Brian is giving me boxes too quickly." Juanita then walked over to Brian and asked him if he would slow down. But he kept pushing boxes in front of her, so Juanita went to the supervisor, Amy, and said, "Amy, can you please talk to Brian? He's giving me too many boxes and I can't keep up." Amy talked to Brian and then he slowed down.*

Why do you think Juanita was feeling angry in this situation? Do you think she handled her feelings well? Why or why not? Was Juanita able to control her behavior even though she was feeling badly?

■ DISCUSSION QUESTIONS

Simple/concrete questions:

How does a person's voice sound when the person is angry? Sad? Happy? Nervous or scared? Down or depressed?

How does someone's face look when he or she is angry? Sad? Happy? Nervous or scared? Down or depressed? Surprised?

Personal experience/feelings questions:

Have you ever felt _____? (happy, sad, angry, down or depressed, etc.) How did you know you felt that way?

Have you ever seen someone who was _____? (angry, sad, happy, nervous or scared, etc.). How did you know they felt that way?

Problem-solving questions:

If you are not sure how you are feeling, what would be a good way to find out? (How can you get in touch with your feelings?)

If you are not sure how somebody else feels, how can you find out?

How can you tell someone that his or her behavior is unacceptable to you?

■ GROUP ACTIVITIES

Form pairs and discuss current feelings of group members.

Ask group participants if they have ever felt angry, sad, happy, nervous, scared, surprised, and so on. Describe the situations.

Take turns imitating persons with various feelings.

Take turns guessing how each person in the group feels while they role-play feelings.

Use a "feelings faces" chart and ask different group members to identify particular feelings.

■ ASSESSMENT OF SKILLS LEARNED

Recognizes that feelings happen inside self:

ALMOST NEVER	USUALLY NOT	SOMETIMES	USUALLY	ALMOST ALWAYS
1	2	3	4	5

Recognizes that feelings show on outside of self:

ALMOST NEVER	USUALLY NOT	SOMETIMES	USUALLY	ALMOST ALWAYS
1	2	3	4	5

Relates feelings to body postures and sensations:

ALMOST NEVER	USUALLY NOT	SOMETIMES	USUALLY	ALMOST ALWAYS
1	2	3	4	5

Recognizes feelings when receiving feedback about them from others:

ALMOST NEVER	USUALLY NOT	SOMETIMES	USUALLY	ALMOST ALWAYS
1	2	3	4	5

Accepts unpleasant feelings while controlling behavior:

ALMOST NEVER	USUALLY NOT	SOMETIMES	USUALLY	ALMOST ALWAYS
1	2	3	4	5

12. Appropriately Expressing Feelings

Human emotions are universal. They become problematic when individuals do not express them appropriately. This may stem from poor recognition of feelings or from lack of feelings-related communication skills. The point of this topic is to enable participants to tell others how they feel in ways that are positive and adaptive. Feelings may be expressed directly or indirectly, assertively or passively. Assertive, direct feelings expression involves telling someone what one feels and why the person feels that way. Passive or indirect expression of feelings includes the performance of ambiguous behaviors that need to be interpreted by the receiver. An example of this type of feelings expression is found when an angry person walks out of a room and slams the door behind himself but fails to say why he is upset. Another example is seen when someone has had her feelings hurt by somebody else but fails to tell the person. Instead, she gives him or her the silent treatment and refuses to talk to the person. The group facilitator should help participants recognize defenses against feelings. The purpose of a defense is to protect oneself from painful feelings; but these defenses also interfere with one's ability to share feelings appropriately with others and, ultimately, this makes it more difficult to let go of bad feelings and move on to other matters. Participants need to be encouraged to take the risks necessary to share their true feelings, and they must be praised for doing so. They should be helped to understand that there is a healthy balance between sharing feelings with others and keeping feelings to themselves. The concepts of assertively or passively expressing feelings are easy to comprehend for those with mild and moderate developmental delay. The concepts involved in feelings "defenses" are more difficult to understand and are most easily understood by persons with mild disability. Like the previous topics, this one lends itself to nonverbal communication augmentation such as playing the game of feelings charades described earlier, utilizing pictures of persons with emotional expressions; drawing feelings faces; and utilizing other signs, symbols, gestures, and nonverbal communication techniques. While many of the concepts involved in the appropriate expression of feelings are difficult to understand, the act of expressing feelings directly is much less complicated and is understood at some level even by individuals with severe disabilities.

■ SPECIFIC SKILLS TO BE LEARNED

Tell others how one feels.
Tell others directly versus indirectly how one feels (e.g., assertive versus passive).
Recognize defenses against feelings:
    Blocking out feelings:
        Forgetting how one feels (repression)

Being unsure how one feels (confusion)

Trying not to think about how one feels (suppression, denial)

Acting the opposite of how one feels:

Acting superior when feeling inferior

Treating someone too nicely even if not liking the person

Pretending one feels happy when feeling bad

Displacement of feelings:

Yelling at one person when feeling angry with another

Acting angry when feeling hurt

Breaking things when mad at someone

Take risks when sharing feelings.

Constructively express feelings.

Achieve a balance between sharing feelings with others and keeping feelings to oneself.

■ CONCEPTS NECESSARY TO PERFORM SKILLS

Direct expression of feelings: Telling others how you feel with words.

Indirect expression of feelings: Letting people guess from your behavior how you feel.

Assertive: Directly telling a person how you feel; saying how you feel and why you feel that way; telling someone what is on your mind.

Passive: Indirectly telling someone how you feel; letting someone guess about how you feel; not say how you feel and why you feel that way; letting people guess from your behavior how you feel.

Aggressive: Trying to hurt someone; acting mean to somebody; attacking someone; swearing or saying nasty things to a person.

Passive-aggressive: Doing mean or hostile things to someone but refusing to say why; giving somebody the silent treatment or refusing to talk to the person but not saying why; doing small things to bother someone but not saying why; walking out of a room and slamming the door behind you.

Defense against feelings: Blocking out your feelings; forgetting how you feel; trying not to think about how you feel; acting the opposite of how you feel; yelling at one person when mad at somebody else; breaking things when angry with somebody; pretending to feel good when feeling bad; acting tough or angry when feeling scared.

■ CASE VIGNETTES

—*Sally was feeling very angry with her boyfriend, Bob. He had invited her to visit him on Saturday at his group home. Bob lived with three other residents. He also had two residence counselors who helped him with cooking and household activities. When Sally called Bob on Friday night, one of the counselors told Sally that Bob had gone to his mother's house for the weekend. He had not even called Sally but just took off, leaving the message with the evening staff person. Sally was very disappointed because she had planned to have a fun day with Bob on Saturday. She was also mad at Bob because he changed their plans without telling her. When Bob returned home on Sunday, he picked up the telephone to hear, "Hi, Bob, this is Sally. I'm very mad at you because you told me to come over on Saturday. Then you changed your mind without telling me. I don't want to be your girlfriend if you're going to keep treating me this way. Why did you change our plans without telling me?" Bob had no good excuse. He apologized to Sally and said it would not happen again.*

Do you think Sally did a good job sharing her feelings with Bob. Why or why not? Was she assertive and direct, or was she passive and indirect in sharing her feelings with Bob?

—Bruce was a quiet guy. He lived in a three-bedroom apartment with two housemates. Bruce felt that his housemates should do more housework, but he was afraid to tell them. One day, his roommate Steve left a big pile of dishes in the kitchen. As Bruce saw Steve come in the door, he walked by the dishes and pushed some of them on the floor. Then he pretended it was an accident. He was afraid to tell Steve to do the dishes, but he gave Steve the silent treatment. He did this by walking past him, not saying, "Hello," and refusing to speak to him all night.

Do you think Bruce did a good job sharing his feelings with Steve? Why or why not? Was he assertive and direct, or was he passive and indirect in sharing his feelings with Steve.

■ DISCUSSION QUESTIONS

Simple/concrete questions:

Is it a good idea to_____ (threaten, scream, yell, shame/blame, keep silent, slam doors, withhold affection, etc.) when angry?

Is it okay to express your feelings directly, to tell someone that you feel_____ (angry, hurt, sad, afraid, etc.)?

Can you give an example of directly expressing anger, hurt, sadness, frustration, etc.?

Can you give examples of indirectly expressing the above feelings?

Personal experience/feelings questions:

Have you ever felt _____ (angry, sad, hurt, fearful, etc.)? How did you express it? How did other people react to you?

Problem-solving questions:

What are some appropriate ways to express anger? Sadness? Hurt? Frustration? Envy/jealousy? Nervousness/anxiety/fear?

What should you do if somebody says he or she is angry with you?

What should you do if someone gets out of control when (e.g., yelling, screaming, hitting, breaking things, throwing things, etc.)? telling you their feelings

■ GROUP ACTIVITIES

Ask participants in turn to give one example of a time when they felt angry, sad, hurt, afraid, surprised, etc. Ask how they expressed their feelings.

Describe various appropriate and inappropriate behavioral reactions to feelings. Ask group members for their opinions about the appropriateness of behaviors and possible better ways to express the feelings.

■ ASSESSMENT OF SKILLS LEARNED

Tells others how one feels:

ALMOST NEVER	USUALLY NOT	SOMETIMES	USUALLY	ALMOST ALWAYS
1	2	3	4	5

Tells feelings *directly:*

ALMOST NEVER	USUALLY NOT	SOMETIMES	USUALLY	ALMOST ALWAYS
1	2	3	4	5

Understands concept of *indirect* expression of feelings:

ALMOST NEVER	USUALLY NOT	SOMETIMES	USUALLY	ALMOST ALWAYS
1	2	3	4	5

Recognizes one or more *defenses* against feelings:

ALMOST NEVER	USUALLY NOT	SOMETIMES	USUALLY	ALMOST ALWAYS
1	2	3	4	5

Expresses feelings in appropriate fashion:

ALMOST NEVER	USUALLY NOT	SOMETIMES	USUALLY	ALMOST ALWAYS
1	2	3	4	5

Recognizes situations in which it is better to keep feelings to oneself:

ALMOST NEVER	USUALLY NOT	SOMETIMES	USUALLY	ALMOST ALWAYS
1	2	3	4	5

13. *Dealing with Fear and Anxiety*

Almost all persons experience the basic emotions of fear and anxiety. Individuals fear realistic threats but also become anxious about potentially dangerous circumstances that may or may not come to pass. Although fear and anxiety each have a somewhat different conceptual focus, the group leader should consider them synonymous for the purpose of this topic. How to recognize when one is feeling fearful or anxious should be examined. Recognition of these feelings may include noticing bodily changes such as chest tightness, stomach butterflies, shakiness, muscle tension, accelerated heartbeat, rapid breathing, sweaty palms, and feelings of weakness. It can also involve the presence of anxious thoughts, including worry about specific matters or general apprehension that something bad might happen. Next, the group can discuss possible ways to deal with fear and anxiety. These may include sharing feelings with somebody, saying positive messages to oneself, meditation, praying, breathing slowly and deeply, distracting oneself with other thoughts, or leaving the anxiety-provoking situation for a short time. The group discussion should examine techniques to prevent anxiety and fearfulness. These may include self-relaxation procedures, listening to relaxation tapes or music, engaging in physical exercise, going for walks, and surrounding oneself with friends. The concept of useless worry and fretting may be addressed to help participants to distinguish those things that they can and cannot change. Group members must be encouraged to take action when they have the power to do so and to use more passive strategies (e.g., relaxation techniques or self-messages) when they have no power to eliminate the feared stimuli. Finally, individuals need to be encouraged to recognize and share their own fears and anxieties. Persons with mild developmental disabilities can understand these concepts well, but lower functioning individuals may experience more difficulty. Nonverbal modifications should be made as was done in the previous topics for individuals with more limited comprehension.

■ SPECIFIC SKILLS TO BE LEARNED

Recognize when feeling fearful/anxious:
    Bodily changes:
        Tight chest
        Butterflies in stomach
        Shakiness
        Muscle tension
        Fast heartbeat
        Rapid breathing
        Sweating palms

Feeling weak
Anxious thoughts:
Worry
Nervousness
Thinking something bad will happen
Decide what to do if anxious/fearful:
Talk to someone about feelings
Talk to self (positive messages)
Meditate/pray
Breathe slowly/deeply
Distract oneself with other thoughts
Leave the situation for a short time
Prevent anxiety and fearfulness:
Self-relaxation procedures
Relaxation tape
Music
Physical exercise
Going for a walk
Surrounding oneself with friends
Recognize useless worry and fretting:
Recognize when dwelling on things that one cannot do anything about
Recognize worries that one has the power to do something about
Recognize what scares an individual.

■ CONCEPTS NECESSARY TO PERFORM SKILLS

Anxiety: Worry; nervousness; feeling threatened; concern; feeling that something bad might happen; afraid something will go wrong; trembling and shaking.

Fear: Worry about a real danger; nervousness because something dangerous is happening; feeling startled by something scary and dangerous; terror; fright; panic.

Relaxed: Calm; peaceful; at ease; restful.

Confident: Brave; sure of oneself; secure; feeling able to deal with things; not worried about what will happen; knowing that one can do something with no problem.

Worry: Nervousness; fretting; uneasiness; fearfulness.

Nervous: Worried; agitated; uptight; edgy; unsettled; tense; fearful; jittery; jumpy.

■ CASE VIGNETTES

—*At the end-of-the-year party, Troy planned to get up in front of all his friends and instructors to make a speech. He would tell them that he had learned a lot from the school program and that he was looking forward to his new job. At first, he was nervous, but Troy soon relaxed because he knew everybody would like his speech. He told himself to relax and have fun, and it worked. He got up in front of everybody and gave his speech. Even though he forgot one of the things he had wanted to say, he kept talking and thought of it later. Everybody clapped when he was done. He felt very good. Troy was proud of his good job speaking in front of the group.*

Why do you think Troy was relaxed and confident? Did he do anything to help himself relax?

—*Laurie was an anxious person. She seemed to worry about everything. Today she was particularly worried about her bus being late. The bus was supposed to be there at three o'clock. It was only lunch time, and she had three hours to wait, but she was already fretting about the bus being late. She worried that the driver would not get her home on time so that she could eat supper and go to her special club that night. Laurie was becoming more nervous, and she could think of nothing else except the bus. After lunch, she had trouble concentrating on her work. She kept going over and over in her mind what might happen if the bus was late. She started thinking that there might be a new bus driver who would not know where her house was. After that she thought, "What if I get lost and nobody finds me?" After she had worried all day, the bus finally came. It got there at five minutes before three o'clock.*

Do you think it helped Laurie to worry all day about the bus? Why or why not? Why do you suppose she worried so much? Could she have done anything to relax so that she would have worried less?

■ DISCUSSION QUESTIONS

Simple/concrete questions:

What are some different things people worry about?

What happens to your body when you are nervous or scared?

Personal experience/feelings questions:

Do you ever feel worried? Nervous? Afraid? What makes you feel this way?

How have you handled your fears and worries in the past?

Do you know anybody who is very relaxed and confident? Why are they able to relax and be comfortable with themselves and their situations?

Do you know anyone who is a worry-wart (someone who worries about anything and everything)?

Problem-solving questions:

How can you prevent yourself from being overly fearful and anxious?

What is a good thing to do if you are really scared?

How can you decide if something is worth worrying about?

■ GROUP ACTIVITIES

Ask each person if he or she has ever felt scared, nervous, or anxious, afraid, and how the individuals handled those feelings.

Take turns role-playing persons who feel nervous, anxious, worried, and afraid. The group leader points out the facial expressions, body posture, and general demeanor of participants.

Ask each person for one suggestion to deal with fear, anxiety, or worry.

■ ASSESSMENT OF SKILLS LEARNED

Recognizes when feeling fearful/anxious:

ALMOST NEVER	USUALLY NOT	SOMETIMES	USUALLY	ALMOST ALWAYS
1	2	3	4	5

Is able to engage in anxiety or fear reducing task(s) when feeling anxious/fearful:

ALMOST NEVER	USUALLY NOT	SOMETIMES	USUALLY	ALMOST ALWAYS
1	2	3	4	5

Recognizes and/or uses anxiety/fear prevention technique(s):

ALMOST NEVER	USUALLY NOT	SOMETIMES	USUALLY	ALMOST ALWAYS
1	2	3	4	5

Recognizes useless worry and fretting:

ALMOST NEVER	USUALLY NOT	SOMETIMES	USUALLY	ALMOST ALWAYS
1	2	3	4	5

Lists things that are anxiety-provoking:

ALMOST NEVER	USUALLY NOT	SOMETIMES	USUALLY	ALMOST ALWAYS
1	2	3	4	5

14. Dealing with Sadness and Depression

Most people feel sad or depressed at one time or another. Individuals may feel sad about many life situations, including the death of a family member or friend, loss of a companion, splitting up with a boyfriend or girlfriend, or losing something important to the person. *Sadness* is the feeling of unhappiness, sorrow, melancholy, and gloominess associated with such a loss. *Depression* is a clinical phenomenon that includes sadness but also a variety of other changes in thinking and behavior. Depressed persons often feel tired, heavy, slowed down, unmotivated, and less concerned about everyday life than they used to be. They may experience sleep difficulties, appetite changes, and increased negative thoughts about themselves, the world, other people, and the future. The group leader should discuss the concepts of sadness and depression, highlighting their associated bodily changes, pessimistic thoughts and negative feelings. There should be a discussion of the possible causes of depression and sadness, emphasizing the role that losses of relationships and other more tangible possessions may play in this process. It can be noted that mistreatment by others may result in sadness and depression. It would be appropriate to review a variety of activities or circumstances that may help reduce the occurrence and impact of these emotions. These include social activities, friendship supports, proper nourishment, interesting tasks, physical exercise, and a regular time schedule for daily activities. Finally, it may be conveyed that sadness and depression are normal responses to loss, signaling that a loss has occurred and reminding individuals what is important to them. These feelings can give persons the opportunity to reorient themselves to deal with problematic situations. The topic is easily understood by those with mild and moderate developmental disabilities, particularly the notion of losses of relationships, which tends to occur at a higher frequency in this population. Relationship losses may be caused by frequent residential caretaker, day program, school, and other life changes. An individual with mild or moderate developmental delay can easily recognize the event of a loss or life change which brings about feelings of sadness and depression. Lower functioning individuals can engage in very concrete communication about losses, perhaps pointing to pictures of family members who have died and making gestures to indicate that they are in heaven. Persons with more limited comprehension will require more concrete, nonverbal assists, such as picture/symbol communication devices, signs, gestures, and abbreviated verbal phrases that are paired with nonverbal messages. This topic tends to elicit significant emotional sharing by participants. Sharing of emotions should be promoted and supported by the group leader and other participants.

■ SPECIFIC SKILLS TO BE LEARNED

Recognize when feeling sad or depressed:
    Bodily changes:
        Heavy
        Slow
        Tired

Crying/tearful
Negative thoughts:
  Self
  World
  People
  Future
Negative feelings:
  Sad or blue
  Unhappy
  Hopeless/helpless
  Worthless/inadequate
Recognize causes of sadness/depression:
  Loss of important person:
    Death
    Divorce/separation
    Split up with relationship partner
    Separation from significant other
  Thinking about losses:
    Loss of job
    Loss of money/possessions
    Lack of social activities/friends
    Something bad happening to someone one cares about
    Ridicule, teasing, ostracism and bad treatment
    Being let down by someone important:
      Someone fails to follow through with commitments.
      Significant other person treats one badly.
  Reduce sadness/depression:
    Social activity (e.g., talking to friends)
    Social support (e.g., friends providing reassurance)
    Proper nourishment (e.g., eating regular, healthy meals)
    Find something to do (e.g., keeping busy with crafts)
    Physical activity/exercise
    Regular time schedule for activities
  Accept sadness and depression as normal responses to loss:
    Signal that one has experienced loss
    Reminder about what is important to a person
    Time to regroup oneself and one's resources

■ CONCEPTS NECESSARY TO PERFORM SKILLS

Sad: Unhappy; gloomy; down in the dumps; blue; heavy-hearted; sorrowful.

Depressed: Down; upset; having a lowered mood; unhappy; tired and gloomy; having the blues; slowed down; feeling badly.

Emotion: Feeling; something somebody feels inside; nervousness, anger, surprise, happiness, sadness, excitement, loneliness, or other feeling; good or bad sensation happening inside someone.

Thought: Something someone thinks; an idea; a thing that a person believes; activity going on in someone's head.

Social support: Someone available who understands a person; friend, family, or relative; somebody to talk to or do things with; the act of listening, believing, caring about, helping, and otherwise considerately treating another person.

Loss: To lose someone or something; not have someone or something anymore; the death of a significant other; the event of a friend or family member moving away; to be cut off from a person, place, or thing.

■ CASE VIGNETTES

—*Marge seemed to be a rather sad and depressed lady. She often cried and looked sad. Marge's mother had died last year. Two years earlier her father had died. All of her grandparents were gone. Her brothers and sisters had died, too. She felt all alone. She had one aunt who saw her on weekends, but Marge lived alone and had little contact with others. One day Marge was crying at work. Her friend Betty came up to her and asked, "Why are you crying?" Marge replied, "Nobody cares about me, I'm all alone in the world." Betty responded, "I like you, Marge, we're friends." Marge continued to talk about all of the things that were wrong in her life. She continued to feel sad and depressed. She did not even seem to notice that Betty wanted to be her friend.*

How do you think Betty felt when Marge continued to talk about all of her problems? Do you think Marge could have been more open to Betty's support? What could she have done to let Betty know that she appreciated her support?

—*One day Muriel came into her group looking very sad. The group was talking about a topic when suddenly Muriel burst into tears. Bruce asked, "What's the matter, Muriel?" And she responded, "My mother died last Saturday." Everyone was silent for a moment. They did not know what to say. Then Sharon came over and put her arm around Muriel, stating, "I'm so sorry to hear that, Muriel. When did she die?" Muriel told the group all about her mother's heart attack. The ambulance had rushed her to the hospital but was too late. The doctor said she died before she got there. It was scary for the group members to hear this and they felt very sorry for Muriel. Muriel felt relieved after she talked. Everyone was very supportive. They told her that they cared about her and asked if there was anything they could do to help her. Sandy said she would pray for Muriel and Dave said the same thing.*

Do you think it helped Muriel to talk about her mother's death in group? Why or why not? Do you think that the group was supportive of Muriel? What did the group members say or do that might have helped?

■ DISCUSSION QUESTIONS

Simple/concrete questions:
    How does a person's body change when feeling sad or depressed?
    What kinds of thoughts do people have when feeling sad or depressed?
    What kinds of feelings do sad and depressed people have?
Personal experience/feelings questions:
    Have you ever felt sad? Depressed? Why?
    How did you know that you were feeling sad or depressed?
    Have you ever had any major losses (e.g., parents, brothers and sisters, friends, relatives, etc.)? How did you feel and how did you react to the loss?
Problem-solving questions:
    What is a good way to deal with sadness and depression?
    When you experience a big loss such as a family member, how long should a "normal" person feel sad or depressed?

■ GROUP ACTIVITIES

Ask each person if he or she has ever felt sad or depressed. Why did the person feel that way?

Take turns giving support to group members who have experienced sadness, depression or loss.

Take turns role playing sad and depressed demeanor (facial expression, body posture, voice tone, etc.)

■ ASSESSMENT OF SKILLS LEARNED

Recognizes when feeling sad or depressed:

ALMOST NEVER	USUALLY NOT	SOMETIMES	USUALLY	ALMOST ALWAYS
1	2	3	4	5

Recognizes causes of sadness/depression:

ALMOST NEVER	USUALLY NOT	SOMETIMES	USUALLY	ALMOST ALWAYS
1	2	3	4	5

Engages in one or more activities to reduce sadness/depression:

ALMOST NEVER	USUALLY NOT	SOMETIMES	USUALLY	ALMOST ALWAYS
1	2	3	4	5

Accepts sadness and depression as normal responses to loss:

ALMOST NEVER	USUALLY NOT	SOMETIMES	USUALLY	ALMOST ALWAYS
1	2	3	4	5

15. *Dealing with Anger and Frustration*

Almost everyone feels angry or frustrated at times. Individuals with developmental disabilities often experience difficulties in expressing these emotions appropriately. This is in part because of more limited repertoires of coping responses, but also because of more limited understandings of the nature of feelings in general. The group leader should first help members understand the difference between angry feelings and angry behaviors. Angry feelings may include anger, frustration and general emotional upset. Angry behaviors are more extensive and include yelling, swearing, screaming, slapping, hitting, pinching, spitting, scratching, throwing things, destroying property, and so forth. It is helpful for the group leader to identify various causes of anger and frustration. Origins may include mistreatment by others, something getting in the way of one's goals, someone preventing person from having what he or she wants, others expecting too much from a person, trying to do something that is too difficult, feeling pressure to do things a person does not want to do, and so forth. It is often productive to focus group energy on identifiying coping skills to deal with anger and frustration. These coping skills include going somewhere to cool off, getting away from anger-provoking situations, talking to others about one's feelings, avoiding situations that cause frustration, asking for help or support from others, engaging in active problem-solving behaviors, venting angry feelings in a harmless fashion (e.g., punching a pillow), and learning to delay gratification by waiting more patiently for things that one wants. It may be helpful to discuss the concept of displaced anger, as in the situation in which Johnny's mother yells at him and Johnny kicks the dog. It is extremely important that group members understand the difference between controlling their behavior and controlling their feelings. One should strive to be in touch with and experience one's feelings while simultaneously keeping behavior under control and within acceptable social limits. Acceptable behavior varies from one context to another. A related matter is to encourage participants to verbalize and express angry and frustrated feelings without violating the rights of others. This topic is easily understood by those with mild and moderate developmental delay, although there may be more difficulty developing anger/frustration coping skills than in identifying anger and recognizing its causes. Lower functioning individuals will again require increased nonverbal assists such as pictures, symbols, gestures, facial expressions, and opportunities for observational learning. The topic lends itself well to humorous examples of angry/frustrated people, which can be acted out by the group leader or individual participants. More severely developmentally delayed persons will require simpler explanations and can be expected to be more concrete and behaviorally oriented in their group participation. Persons with higher levels of conceptual ability will be better able to discuss causes and coping mechanisms related to the topic.

■ SPECIFIC SKILLS TO BE LEARNED

Identify angry feelings/behavior:
    Feelings:
        Angry
        Mad
        Upset
    Behavior:
        Yelling
        Swearing
        Screaming
        Slapping/hitting
        Pinching
        Spitting
        Scratching
        Throwing things
        Destroying property
        Kicking
Identify what causes frustration/anger:
    Others treating one badly
    Someone else preventing one from having what one wants
    Name calling and insults
    Someone taking another's things
    Something getting in the way of an individual achieving a goal
    People expecting too much from a person
    Trying to do something that is too difficult
    Feeling pressure from others to do things one does not want to do
Identify coping skills to deal with anger/frustration:
    Go cool off.
    Get away from the situation that makes one angry.
    Talk to others about one's feelings.
    Avoid situations that are upsetting.
    Ask for help or support from others.
    Talk over problems with someone (problem solving).
    Go for a walk and later talk things over.
    Punch a pillow or punching bag.
    Learn to wait for the things that one wants.

Recognize displacement of anger and frustration (e.g., Johnny's mother yells at him and Johnny kicks the dog; a worker is upset with the boss and yells at a co-worker).
Understand the difference between controlling behavior and controlling feelings.
Verbalize angry and frustrated feelings without violating the rights of others.

■ CONCEPTS NECESSARY TO PERFORM SKILLS

Angry: Mad; upset; rageful; irritated; annoyed; resentful.
Frustration: Irritation; inconvenience; encountering something in one's way; something keeping a person from getting what he or she wants; something or someone in the way of what somebody wants to do; having to wait for things one wants.
Coping skills: Ways to get what a person wants; ways to deal with not having what one wants; behaviors a person can use to handle anger, frustration, and emotional upset; abilities and behaviors that help a person avoid problems.
Displacement: Yelling at one person when mad at somebody else; feeling upset with one person and taking it out on someone else.
Angry feeling: Feeling angry, mad, upset, rageful, irritated, annoyed, or resentful; an unpleasant emotional experience that one feels inside him- or herself.
Angry behavior: Performing angry behaviors such as yelling, screaming, hitting, kicking, and breaking things; doing something mean or nasty when feeling emotionally upset.

■ CASE VIGNETTES

—Richard had a job at the sheltered workshop. He swept floors, emptied trash cans, and also did other odd jobs. Richard was free to roam around from room to room by himself. One day he was talking to himself. He was saying loudly, "That dumb John. I don't like him. He can mind his own business" Then Richard stopped by the secretary's desk and said, "I don't like John anymore, he's stupid." A little while later, he was emptying the trash and someone overheard him saying, "I wish John was dead, I'm gonna get him fired." Richard talked loudly all day. Sometimes he talked to himself and sometimes to other workers. He sounded angry and he looked very frustrated.

Do you think Richard was angry? Why or why not? Do you think Richard handled his feelings well? Why or why not? Was there anything else Richard could have done to cope better with his feelings?

—Raul was a good worker. He worked hard and was very careful as he put together boxes and other parts on the assembly line. One day he was working hard and Brian, his workmate, kept talking loudly and interrupting him. Raul told Brian he was busy and did not want to talk. Brian continued to interrupt him loudly. Raul patiently waited until his break time. He then talked to his job supervisor, who agreed to move him further away from Brian. Raul knew that Brian had problems and did not understand that he was too loud. Raul had solved his problem without hurting Brian's feelings and without engaging in angry behaviors for which he would have felt sorry later. This way he had more peace and quiet at his job while keeping his friendship with Brian.

Do you think Raul did a good job handling his frustration and anger? Why or why not?

■ DISCUSSION QUESTIONS

Simple/concrete questions:
What is the difference between an angry feeling and angry behavior?

Is _____ (hitting, slapping, smiling, swearing, laughing, etc.) an angry feeling or
  behavior?
Personal experience/feelings questions:
  Have you ever felt angry? When?
  What kind of things make you angry? Frustrated?
  Please give an example of a time when you felt angry or frustrated. How did you handle this
    feeling?
Problem-solving questions:
  What is a good thing to do if you are feeling angry? Frustrated?
  Is it O.K. to feel angry or frustrated? Why or why not?
  Is it O.K. to let your behavior get out of control when you are angry? How can you keep
    from losing control when you feel angry?

■ GROUP ACTIVITIES

Facilitate a discussion about group members' experiences in coping with their own and others'
  anger.
Each group member identify one positive way to deal with anger.

■ ASSESSMENT OF SKILLS LEARNED

Recognizes the difference between angry feelings and angry behaviors:

ALMOST NEVER	USUALLY NOT	SOMETIMES	USUALLY	ALMOST ALWAYS
1	2	3	4	5

Identifies causes of frustration and anger:

ALMOST NEVER	USUALLY NOT	SOMETIMES	USUALLY	ALMOST ALWAYS
1	2	3	4	5

Uses one or more coping skills to deal with anger/frustration:

ALMOST NEVER	USUALLY NOT	SOMETIMES	USUALLY	ALMOST ALWAYS
1	2	3	4	5

Recognizes displaced anger:

ALMOST NEVER	USUALLY NOT	SOMETIMES	USUALLY	ALMOST ALWAYS
1	2	3	4	5

Understands the difference between controlling behavior and controlling feelings:

ALMOST NEVER	USUALLY NOT	SOMETIMES	USUALLY	ALMOST ALWAYS
1	2	3	4	5

Verbalizes angry/frustrated feelings without violating the rights of others:

ALMOST NEVER	USUALLY NOT	SOMETIMES	USUALLY	ALMOST ALWAYS
1	2	3	4	5

16. Dealing with Grief and Loss

The final topic in this chapter examines ways to deal with grief and loss. Individuals with
developmental disabilities probably suffer a disproportionately large number of losses com-
pared to their contemporaries, but tend to have fewer supports and coping mechanisms to deal

with these losses. Increased losses may occur because of frequent residential caretaker changes, education/work program changes, and more limited power over everyday activity schedules. In many respects, their lives are regulated according to the convenience of daily caretakers rather than their own individual needs for continuity and social attachment. To complicate this situation further, persons with disabilities are frequently only peripherally involved in major decision making about their own lives, and may be left out entirely from funerals and other rituals to assist family members in dealing with losses. The group facilitator should explain various types of losses that may result in grief. These may include deaths of significant others (e.g., family, friends, relatives), physical/mental illness, and rejection or abandonment by significant others. Next, participants need to be familiarized with various stages or elements of the grief process made famous by Elizabeth Kübler-Ross in her book *On Death and Dying* (1969). The order of these stages is not as important as the fact that each may occur. Stages of grief can include such features as shock/disbelief, anger, bargaining with God, guilt/anxiety, depression/sadness/hurt, and eventual acceptance of the loss, leading to a more stable emotional balance. The discussion should move on to an exploration of coping mechanisms, which include seeking/receiving social/emotional support, giving oneself permission to experience grief, reorienting toward other people, increasing physical/social/recreational activities, and reminiscing about positive memories of the past. Grief can be used as a positive life force. It can help one to redefine priorities, and it can be a learning experience leading to personal growth. Grief and loss are normal parts of life, creating life-boundary situations that no one escapes. Individuals with mild and moderate developmental delay can easily understand the concepts of grief and loss and can readily share their own losses. They may have more limited coping mechanisms and less understanding of the permanence of death. As with non–developmentally delayed persons, this topic should be discussed within the intellectual frameworks of the discussants, focusing on those areas that are meaningful to them. Lower functioning individuals often experience profound loss without having an intellectual understanding of the causality and mechanics of death. It may be helpful and worthwhile for some individuals to point to pictures of deceased parents and utter phrases such as "Mom gone," or "Dad in heaven." Done in the presence and with the support of other group members, this can be a healing experience. Higher functioning individuals may be more articulate about their feelings and the experience of their losses.

■ SPECIFIC SKILLS TO BE LEARNED

Recognize types of losses that can result in grief:
  Death of a significant other person (e.g., family member, friend, relative)
  Physical or mental illness
  Rejection/abuse/abandonment by significant other
Recognize grief reaction process and stages:
  Denial/disbelief/shock
  Anger/bargaining
  Guilt/anxiety
  Depression/sadness/hurt/loss
  Acceptance
  Resolution and getting on with life
Recognize things that are helpful when experiencing grief/loss:
  Receiving emotional support (e.g., people who understand one's feelings)
  Receiving social support (e.g., family, friends, church)
  Allowing oneself to have feelings (e.g., grieving, crying, turning oneself over to one's
    feelings)

Reorienting toward other people (e.g., reaching out to others, helping others, not wallowing in distress)

Increasing social/physical/recreational activities

Talking about memories and reminiscing

Use grief and loss as a positive force in one's life:

A way to define oneself and one's priorities (what is important in life)

A learning experience for personal growth

Accept grief/loss as a normal part of living (life-boundary situation).

■ CONCEPTS NECESSARY TO PERFORM SKILLS

Grief: Sadness; loss; sorrow; distress; negative feelings at the time of a death or another loss.

Loss: Losing someone or something; not having someone or something anymore; the death of a significant other; the event of a friend or family member moving away; being cut off from a person, place, or thing.

Grief stages: Emotional changes that occur after a loss; feelings such as denial, disbelief, shock, anger, guilt, anxiety, depression, sadness, and hurt that take place after a loss; different moods a person may experience after losing somebody or something.

Rejection: To be put aside by others; to be ignored; when family members or friends no longer want to see a person or talk to him or her; when a group of pople do not include another in their activities.

Abandonment: When important people leave and never come back; when someone forgets about another person; when others lose interest and no longer have anything to do with somebody; when people turn their backs on others.

Boundary: Dividing line; space between people or things; rule; way somebody is supposed to act; limit; border; end point; place where one thing leaves off and another begins; something that lets a person know the limits of acceptable behavior.

■ CASE VIGNETTES

—*Joe's mother had died last week. He still felt very sad and hurt. At first he did not believe it was really true. He asked God if he could have his mother back. He promised he would always be good and would clean his room every day if only he could have her back. Then he cried for an hour. Even though it had now been a week since she died, Joe cried every day, but not as much as before. Sometimes he felt guilty because he thought he should have been a better son. He was just beginning to understand that his mother was not coming home. He prayed for her every day. He had gone to the funeral with his family and friends. They were crying, too, so he knew that it was okay to cry. Everybody talked about what a good person she had been, and this made him feel better. Many of his friends told him that they were sorry to hear about his mother and they would give him help if he needed it. Even though he was quite upset, Joe felt supported by his family and friends. He knew that he would be O.K.*

Do you think Joe was dealing well with his mother's death? Why or why not? Were Joe's family and friends helping in any way? How?

—*Donna was in the hospital. She was having trouble breathing and needed to use an oxygen tank. This meant she had to breathe into a mask so that she could get more air in her lungs. She felt very worried and depressed. She had always been healthy, but now she had to lie in a hospital bed. Soon she would move to a nursing home. She could no longer live with her housemates in their apartment. She felt the loss of her independence. This meant that she needed a bunch of doctors and nurses around to give her medicine and oxygen. They needed to watch her to see that she was O.K. At first, this was very hard, but soon Donna realized that she had no choice. She might die without special help. Still, it was hard to be around a bunch of new people. She told herself, "I know I can make it through this, I will pray and I will also call my family and friends so I won't be lonesome." Donna made some new friends at the nursing home and tried very hard to think about happy thoughts. Sometimes she felt sad but found strength in the happy memories of her earlier life.*

Do you think Donna dealt well with her medical problems and losses? Why or why not?

■ DISCUSSION QUESTIONS

Simple/concrete questions:

What is grief? Loss?

List some of the stages of grief.

Name some different types of losses.

Personal experience/feelings questions:

Have you ever lost anybody (family, friend, relative, etc.)? How did you deal with your loss? What did the person mean to you?

How did you feel when you lost an important person in your life?

What are some different types of feelings that you have had when you experienced a loss?

What are some different types of thoughts that you have had when you lost important people?

Have you ever had a bad illness? What are some of the thoughts and feelings you had when you were physically ill?

Problem-solving questions:

What is a normal way to act if you lose somebody?

When you lose somebody, what should you do if you continue to feel very sad and hurt?

What are some things a person can do to work through grief and loss in a positive way?

What can you learn about yourself when you suffer a great loss? How can this help you understand what is important in your life?

■ GROUP ACTIVITIES

Ask each group participant if he or she has ever lost someone close to him- or herself.

Form pairs of group members who have had similar losses. Discuss feelings and reactions to these losses.

Share pictures of important persons whom individuals have lost and reminisce about them.

Take turns receiving social and emotional support related to losses.

■ ASSESSMENT OF SKILLS LEARNED

Recognizes one or more types of loss that can result in grief:

ALMOST NEVER	USUALLY NOT	SOMETIMES	USUALLY	ALMOST ALWAYS
1	2	3	4	5

Recognizes stages of grief:

ALMOST NEVER	USUALLY NOT	SOMETIMES	USUALLY	ALMOST ALWAYS
1	2	3	4	5

Lists one or more helpful activities to deal with grief/loss:

ALMOST NEVER	USUALLY NOT	SOMETIMES	USUALLY	ALMOST ALWAYS
1	2	3	4	5

Understands one positive aspect to grief/loss:

ALMOST NEVER	USUALLY NOT	SOMETIMES	USUALLY	ALMOST ALWAYS
1	2	3	4	5

Recognizes grief/loss as a normal part of living:

ALMOST NEVER	USUALLY NOT	SOMETIMES	USUALLY	ALMOST ALWAYS
1	2	3	4	5

Reference

Kübler-Ross, E. (1969). *On death and dying.* New York: Macmillan.

3 Personal Hygiene, Self-Care, and Manners

17. **Personal Hygiene**
18. **Courtesy, Public Manners, and Socially Offensive Behaviors**
19. **Self-Control**
20. **Dealing with Frustration**
21. **Respect for Others**

THIS CHAPTER EXAMINES personal hygiene, self-care, and manners, areas important to how persons present themselves to other individuals and to the world in general. These topics are important because persons with developmental delay often have quite limited personal insight, and have difficulty reflecting on how they present themselves to others. Specific personal hygiene skills and the rationale for them are discussed. A variety of skills related to courtesy and public manners are presented. Socially offensive behaviors are specifically addressed. The relationship of self-control to public manners is discussed. Specific ways with which to deal with frustration are examined. Finally, a range of ways in which one can show respect for others is explored.

17. Personal Hygiene

Personal appearance and hygiene often create the first impression that one person has of another. Poor hygiene habits may result in immediate negative reactions from others. Self-presentation is particularly problematic for individuals with developmental delay, who often have difficulty noticing subtleties and understanding the impact of their appearance on others. The group leader should systematically identify areas of personal hygiene, including cleanliness, attire, grooming, toileting, and general public considerations. Next, the importance of cleaning personal space can be addressed. This includes one's bedroom, workspace, and shared living spaces. Third, the focus may shift to food-related matters, including the need for clean plates/utensils, hand washing, food refrigeration, and disposal of old foodstuffs. Finally, the leader should emphasize why personal hygiene and cleanliness are important, including the need to kill germs, prevent body odor, and maintain an attractive physical appearance. Because of its concrete nature, this topic is easily understood by individuals with mild and moderate developmental disabilities. Those with more severe disabilities can understand much of the physical mechanics of personal hygiene, although they may not comprehend its underlying rationale. Some of the items such as brushing teeth, combing hair, tucking in shirt, washing hands, and so forth can be made more concrete by utilizing pictures and physical demonstrations.

■ SPECIFIC SKILLS TO BE LEARNED

Identify areas of personal cleanliness/hygiene:
    Cleanliness:
        Shower or bath.
        Brush teeth.
        Wash hair.
        Use soap and deodorant (dirt, body odor, germs).

Shave

Clip fingernails/toenails.

Clean clothes:

Change clothes regularly.

Do laundry (dirt, germs).

Personal appearance/grooming:

Tuck in shirt.

Close buttons and zippers.

Strive for neatness versus messiness/sloppiness.

Comb or brush hair.

Use of the toilet:

Wash hands afterward.

Public consideration:

Cover mouth when coughing.

Excuse oneself if belching/farting.

Keep body clothed.

Recognize areas of personal space that require cleanliness:

Clean room:

Free of old food

Neat versus messy and cluttered

Clothing picked up

Dusted and vacuumed

Work space:

Clean

Uncluttered

Shared living space:

Picked up

Vacuumed and dusted

Recognize food and hygiene skills:

Eat from clean plates and utensils.

Wash hands with soap before eating.

Keep food refrigerated.

Throw out old food.

Understand why personal hygiene/cleanliness is important:

Kills germs and prevents spread of disease.

Prevents body odor.

Personal appearance is more presentable.

■ CONCEPTS NECESSARY TO PERFORM SKILLS

Germ: A very small living thing that can make food spoil; a creature that goes away if you wash your hands, clean your body, and keep your food in the refrigerator; a thing that can give a person a cold, sore throat, or other sickness.

Cleanliness: To keep neat and clean; throw away old food; wash dishes; bathe or shower one's body with soap and water; wash clothes; keep one's room picked up.

Hygiene: Neatness and cleanliness; keeping germs away by washing with soap and water; washing away body odor and using deodorant.

Disease: Sickness; when germs get into food and on a person's body because one is not clean; what can happen if a person eats old and unrefrigerated food; what might occur if a person eats food that has not been cooked long enough.

■ CASE VIGNETTES

—*Sperling was well liked by others. He always dressed nicely with his hair well combed and his shirt tucked in. Sperling took a shower at seven o'clock every morning. He washed his body with soap and water so that he would smell good. Then he used deodorant under his arms so that he did not start to smell bad later in the day, after he had been working. He worked hard, and sometimes he sweated a lot, so it was a good thing that he used his deodorant. People liked to be around him because he looked good, smelled good, and took good care of himself.*

What did Sperling do to take care of his body? Why did he smell good? What is one reason he had many friends?

—*Bill was a nice guy, but he did not take very good care of his body. He did not take a shower every day, and sometimes he smelled bad. Other people were afraid to tell him that he smelled bad, so they just moved away from him and talked to other friends. On hot days, when he was working very hard, Bill started to smell even worse because he did not use deodorant under his arms. Bill's hair was often messy and his shirt came untucked. He looked as though he had been blowing around in the wind, even when it was not windy. He did not shave for two or three days at a time and looked very scruffy sometimes.*

Why do you suppose Bill had no friends? Could he do anything about his personal hygiene to help him get more friends? Why do you suppose people were afraid to tell him that he smelled bad?

—*Sandy was very hungry when she came home one day. She saw that there was some leftover pizza on the kitchen counter. She had forgotten to put it in the refrigerator or throw it away last night after dinner. Sandy sat down and ate three pieces. It tasted kind of funny but she ate it anyway. An hour later, her stomach felt sick and she thought she might vomit. She felt dizzy, was hot, and was sweating on her forehead.*

How do you think Sandy got sick? Do you think it could have been from eating day-old pizza that had not been kept in the refrigerator? What could she do next time to keep from getting sick?

■ DISCUSSION QUESTIONS

Simple/concrete questions:
   What do you do in the morning to make yourself neat and clean?
   What are some things to do to keep your living space clean?
   Why is it important to have good personal hygiene and cleanliness?
Personal experience/feelings questions:
   Have you ever forgotten to take a shower or bath?
   Do you know anyone who wears dirty clothes and does not remember to use soap and
      deodorant? Did they smell good or bad?
   Do you usually look neat or sloppy after you put your clothes on in the morning?
   Would you rather spend time with someone who is neat and clean or someone who is
      sloppy and dirty?
Problem-solving questions:
   What should you do if you work with someone who smells bad and you do not like it?
   How can you improve your own personal hygiene/cleanliness?
   Why is it important to wash your hands before eating meals?
   What should you do if someone coughs in your face and does not cover his or her mouth?

■ GROUP ACTIVITIES

Group members take turns telling about one area of personal cleanliness and hygiene.

Form pairs and discuss personal experiences with other persons who have good or bad personal hygiene.

As a group, list the advantages and disadvantages of having good or bad personal hygiene.

■ ASSESSMENT OF SKILLS LEARNED

Identifies two or more areas of personal cleanliness/hygiene:

ALMOST NEVER	USUALLY NOT	SOMETIMES	USUALLY	ALMOST ALWAYS
1	2	3	4	5

Identifies one or more areas of personal space that require cleanliness:

ALMOST NEVER	USUALLY NOT	SOMETIMES	USUALLY	ALMOST ALWAYS
1	2	3	4	5

Lists one or more food hygiene skills:

ALMOST NEVER	USUALLY NOT	SOMETIMES	USUALLY	ALMOST ALWAYS
1	2	3	4	5

Understands why personal hygiene/cleanliness is important:

ALMOST NEVER	USUALLY NOT	SOMETIMES	USUALLY	ALMOST ALWAYS
1	2	3	4	5

18. *Courtesy, Public Manners, and Socially Offensive Behaviors*

Social etiquette involves a range of obvious and subtle behaviors which often elude persons with developmental disabilities. Others often avoid or mistreat individuals with poor public manners. This is particularly true of persons with developmental disabilities, who may lack compensatory social skills to regain the good graces of others. This topic examines a wide range of courteous behaviors that are incompatible with their socially offensive counterparts. The group leader should highlight the respectful and courteous nature of each behavior, exploring the negative consequences of rude or discourteous behaviors. Some of these behaviors include saying "please," graciously thanking others, listening without interrupting, waiting for others to go first, complimenting, avoiding sarcasm, avoiding abrupt conversations, avoiding overtly rude behaviors, smiling, showing an interest in others, speaking in a friendly tone of voice, taking turns, excusing oneself before interrupting, doing helpful things, sharing possessions, acting in a kind and gentle way, holding doors, and so forth. Participants may be encouraged to bring up their own ideas about courtesy. Most individuals with mild and moderate developmental disabilities understand this topic well enough to participate actively in its discussion. Those with more severe disabilities can often understand nonverbal components of courtesy, including smiling, waving, stepping aside to let someone else take a turn, holding doors, and so forth. The nonverbal elements of courtesy offer a good entry point for work on this issue with less verbal and more intellectually limited individuals.

■ SPECIFIC SKILLS TO BE LEARNED

Say, "Please."

Say, "Thank-you."

Listen without interrupting.

Let others go first (wait).
Compliment others.
Avoid sarcasm and put-downs.
Avoid abrupt conversation.
Avoid rude behaviors (belching/farting, talking with food in mouth, etc.).
Smile at others.
Show an interest in others.
Speak without raising one's voice.
Take turns (doorway, talking, waiting lines, etc.).
Say, "Excuse me" before interrupting (or after rude behaviors).
Be helpful to others.
Share things (e.g., food, possessions).
Be kind/gentle.
Hold doors.
Speak without screaming.
Speak without coughing in someone's face.
Follow simple directions.

■ CONCEPTS NECESSARY TO PERFORM SKILLS

Please: People say "Please" to get something; "Please" means you are asking for something.

Thank you: Tell others that you appreciate their compliments; let someone know that you like what he or she said to you; be gracious; accept a compliment.

Listen: Pay attention to what someone says; hear and understand what somebody says; open your ears and close your mouth; let others know that you know what they are saying.

Interrupt: Start to talk before someone else is finished speaking; come into or leave a room when someone is talking; butt in when someone is talking; start talking before somebody else is finished; make noise when someone is talking.

Wait: When a person cannot have what he or she wants right now but can get it later; to let somebody else go first; to take your turn after someone else.

Compliment: Say something nice to someone; tell others what you like about them; tell someone what you like about his or her behavior; tell somebody what you like about his or her personality; praise someone; congratulate a person; tell others that you like them.

Sarcasm: Saying something mean and funny; embarrassing someone with a snappy remark; humiliating a person; making fun of somebody with an angry joke.

Rude: Mean; discourteous; offensive; doing something that bothers another person; insensitive; not paying attention to how other people feel; not caring how others feel; disregarding; vulgar; neglectful.

Show interest: Listen to others; pay attention; care how others feel and let them know it.

Courtesy: Saying "Please" and "Thank-you"; waiting your turn; letting others know you care about how they feel; helping others in small ways such as holding doors for them or letting them go first; kindness and consideration.

Polite: Courteous; caring; kind; considerate of others; letting others know that you care about how they feel; to show respect for others.

Share: Take turns using things; give some of your treat to somebody else; take turns doing something.

Help: Do something for somebody; share the work; work with somebody so that the person can get the job done faster; do things for others that they cannot do for themselves; assist someone.

Kind: Considerate; helpful; showing someone that you care about how he or she feels; avoiding doing things to hurt or upset others; being mindful of the needs of others.

Respect: Esteem; consideration; showing others that you care about them; letting people know that you care about how they think and feel; listening and paying attention to someone; treating others well.

■ CASE VIGNETTES

—*Earl was a very rude man. He talked very loudly even when others could hear him just fine. Earl did not say "Please" when he wanted a cookie; he just took one out of Joe's lunch box. He spoke loudly, even with food in his mouth. Sometimes part of his sandwich came flying out of his mouth when he was talking at the lunch table. Earl interrupted people, even when they were talking to others. He burped loudly at the lunch table but did not say, "Excuse me." He did not seem to be at all interested in how other people felt, as long as he got what he wanted. Earl often asked for other people's snacks, but he never shared his own snacks with them.*

Do you think Earl's behaviors were rude? Which behaviors? How could he have been more polite and courteous? If he had more courtesy, do you think he would have had more friends?

—*Eileen was a very polite woman. She seemed to care a great deal about others. She always said "Please" if she wanted something and thanked others for giving her things. Eileen was generous with her own things, often sharing her cookies with lunchmates and letting friends play with her video games. She was gentle with others, never yelling, raising her voice, or saying mean things to them. Eileen listened when other people talked, and she waited her turn in lines. Sometimes she held doors for others. When someone held a door for her, she thanked the person. Everybody seemed to like Eileen.*

Why do you think others liked Eileen? Was she polite and courteous, or rude and offensive?

■ DISCUSSION QUESTIONS

Simple/concrete questions:

Is it rude or inconsiderate to burp? Interrupt others? Smile? Cough in someone's face? Talk in a friendly voice? Interrupt someone who is talking?

Give some examples of courtesy and good public manners.

Personal experience/feelings questions:

Has someone ever been rude to you? When? How?

Have you ever given something to somebody and the person did not thank you? How did you feel?

How do you feel when someone is rude to you?

Has anyone ever treated you with respect or kindness? How did you feel?

Problem-solving questions:

What should you do if you have a co-worker or acquaintance who acts rude or offensive to you? How should you tell the person that he or she is being rude?

What are some different ways you can tell others they are being rude or offensive?

What are some ways in which you can show courtesy and respect to other people?

How do you know if other's think you are being rude or offensive?

■ GROUP ACTIVITIES

Take turns practicing polite phrases.

Take turns sharing experiences about other people being rude in public.

Each person give one example of a time in which they were treated very well by others.

Each person pick a partner and talk in detail about an important experience which involved either rude or courteous behavior of another person.

■ ASSESSMENT OF SKILLS LEARNED

Says, "Please," "Thank you," and "Excuse me," at appropriate times:

ALMOST NEVER	USUALLY NOT	SOMETIMES	USUALLY	ALMOST ALWAYS
1	2	3	4	5

Listens without interrupting:

ALMOST NEVER	USUALLY NOT	SOMETIMES	USUALLY	ALMOST ALWAYS
1	2	3	4	5

Speaks politely without sarcasm, abruptness, and rudeness:

ALMOST NEVER	USUALLY NOT	SOMETIMES	USUALLY	ALMOST ALWAYS
1	2	3	4	5

Smiles, compliments, and shows an interest in others:

ALMOST NEVER	USUALLY NOT	SOMETIMES	USUALLY	ALMOST ALWAYS
1	2	3	4	5

Speaks in a normal tone of voice:

ALMOST NEVER	USUALLY NOT	SOMETIMES	USUALLY	ALMOST ALWAYS
1	2	3	4	5

Waits for others, holds doors, takes turns, and shares things with others:

ALMOST NEVER	USUALLY NOT	SOMETIMES	USUALLY	ALMOST ALWAYS
1	2	3	4	5

Helps others at appropriate times:

ALMOST NEVER	USUALLY NOT	SOMETIMES	USUALLY	ALMOST ALWAYS
1	2	3	4	5

Follows simple directions:

ALMOST NEVER	USUALLY NOT	SOMETIMES	USUALLY	ALMOST ALWAYS
1	2	3	4	5

19. Self-Control

A large part of social etiquette and manners is knowing how to control one's behavior. The skill of self-control includes moderating one's behavior after becoming upset. It also involves projecting ahead to the possibility of losing one's temper, and engaging in behaviors that lessen this possibility. Individuals with developmental delay often experience major difficulties in this area. The group discussion should begin with a description of out-of-control behavior, followed by an examination of how to think ahead to avoid losing control. This topic is easily accessible to persons with mild developmental disabilities, but it becomes progressively more difficult for lower functioning individuals. Again, the game of charades, acting out well-controlled and poorly controlled behaviors, might be a more engaging exercise than verbal discussion for many individuals. Another way to bring in nonverbal assists would be to make videotapes, perhaps with group members, of persons who are either well-controlled or poorly controlled in their behaviors. It also might be helpful for individuals with less verbal ability to practice pointing to feelings faces or pictures of real people with various emotional expressions, later connecting these with role-plays of group members acting out good and bad behavior control.

■ SPECIFIC SKILLS TO BE LEARNED

Control behavior when angry or upset.
Think ahead and avoid losing control before getting upset.

■ CONCEPTS NECESSARY TO PERFORM SKILLS

Bad feelings: Bad feelings happen on the inside of a person; someone can have bad feelings of anger, hurt and upset, but not demonstrate any bad behaviors; to feel emotionally upset.

Bad behaviors: Bad behaviors happen on the outside; yelling, swearing, hitting, and other misbehaviors; what people do when they get out of control.

Temper: Mood; disposition; anger; emotional outburst; tantrum.

Impulsive: Acting before thinking; not controlling your behavior; doing or saying things right away instead of thinking about them.

Personal responsibility: Deciding to control one's own behavior; taking control of one's life and behavior; not blaming others when losing one's temper; deciding to keep self-control; making a choice to do or not to do something; not blaming others for one's problems; deciding to do something and doing it; being held accountable for your behavior; taking charge of one's own life; being dependable and reliable; doing what one says one is going to do.

Child behavior: To act like a child; lose control; have a temper tantrum; act like a youngster.

Adult behavior: To act like an adult; behave like a grown-up; control one's behavior; not tantrum and lose control; think before acting.

■ CASE VIGNETTES

—Loren was quite impulsive. He often did things before thinking about them. One day he wanted a cookie, but his sister would not give him one. She knew he had diabetes. Diabetes is a medical problem in which a person cannot eat too many sweets. Before he even thought about it, Loren jumped up, demanded that she give him a cookie, and began screaming. When she still would not give him one, he threw himself on the floor and kicked a chair. Then he banged his head very hard on the floor. It took him a long time to settle down.

Do you think Loren had good behavior control? Why or why not? What could he have done differently?

—Sherry was a friendly and sociable person. She came into her social group one day and said "Hi" to everybody. As she talked to her friends, John looked at her and said, "Sherry, be quiet, why do you always have to talk so loud?" Sherry was not really talking too loudly and felt hurt by John's criticism. She thought he was rude and she started to feel angry. Then she told herself, "No big deal. Relax, Sherry. John didn't mean it the way it sounded." Instead of losing control and starting a fight with John, she said, "John, I don't think I'm too loud, and I'd appreciate it if you would be more polite to me." John thought about what she had said and he apologized: "I'm sorry Sherry, I guess I'm not feeling too well, and I took it out on you."

Do you think Sherry did a good job controlling her behavior? Why or why not? How did she stop herself from having a fight with John?

■ DISCUSSION QUESTIONS

Simple/concrete questions:

What are some examples of out-of-control behaviors?

Do these behaviors reflect good or bad self-control? Screaming? Yelling? Swearing? Throwing things? Hitting oneself? Kicking? Scratching? Stealing? Damaging property? Breaking things? Why or why not?

Personal experience/feelings questions:

Have you ever felt out of control?

Have you ever lost control of your behavior?

How do you feel when you are out of control?

How do you feel when another person is out of control?

Has anybody ever (screamed, sworn, hit, kicked, scratched, etc.) you? How did you feel?

Problem-solving questions:

What is the difference between emotional upset and out-of-control behavior?

What are some things you can do when feeling emotionally upset?

What should someone do after losing control? Should the person apologize for the behavior? Should he or she talk it over with the other person?

■ GROUP ACTIVITIES

Each group member relate one personal experience with out-of-control behavior.

Group members each relate one experience in which they controlled their behavior even when emotionally upset.

■ ASSESSMENT OF SKILLS LEARNED

Controls behavior when angry or upset:

ALMOST NEVER	USUALLY NOT	SOMETIMES	USUALLY	ALMOST ALWAYS
1	2	3	4	5

Thinks ahead to avoid losing control when upset:

ALMOST NEVER	USUALLY NOT	SOMETIMES	USUALLY	ALMOST ALWAYS
1	2	3	4	5

20. Dealing with Frustration

This topic is an extension of the previous one, focusing more specifically on how to deal with various frustrations. Once again, this issue is problematic for many individuals with developmental disabilities. The discussion should begin with the notion that sometimes everyone must wait for people or things. It can then shift to how one handles disappointment and anger. It must be emphasized that individuals need to react calmly when having to wait for things and that losing control will not necessarily help the situation. Concepts of stopping and thinking about what to do while keeping anger, irritability, and negative emotions in check may be addressed. It would be good for participants to brainstorm possible courses of action when they cannot immediately have the things that they want. The difference between active and passive coping skills should be described, and participants encouraged to relate situations that require each type of coping. For example, if someone does not have enough money to buy a snack at the end of the week, the person can actively cope by saving more of his or her spending money. If somebody's grandmother dies, the person can passively cope by praying or learning to let go emotionally of a situation over which they have no control. This topic can be grasped by individuals with mild developmental disabilities and to some extent by those with more severe limitations. Lower functioning individuals may have difficulty comprehending some of the concepts but can be taught, using concrete situations, to cope with many frustrations. Coping may include learning a few key words such as "wait," "not now," and "later," which the individual gradually associates with various activities or tangible objects that are reinforcing. The use of videotape role-plays of individuals dealing well or poorly with frustration would be an entertaining and helpful learning aid, complementing verbal discussions in this skill area.

■ SPECIFIC SKILLS TO BE LEARNED

Wait for people and things.
Handle disappointment, letdown, and anger.
React calmly when having to wait for things.
Stop and think about what to do (react calmly to a bad situation).
Keep anger, irritability, and negative emotions in check while trying to solve a problem.
Decide what to do if unable to have something one wants right now.
Recognize the difference between "active" and "passive" coping skills:
    Active (doing something to change the situation)
    Passive (changing one's own thoughts and attitudes when the situation cannot be changed)

■ CONCEPTS NECESSARY TO PERFORM SKILLS

Frustration: Irritation; inconvenience; something is in somebody's way; something is keeping a person from getting what he or she wants; something or someone is in the way of what somebody wants to do; when people have to wait for things they want.
Negative frustration reaction: Lose control when frustrated; tantrum; act like a spoiled child; anger, emotional upset, and out-of-control behavior.
Frustration tolerance: Ability to deal with frustrating situations; patience to wait for things; ability to control one's behavior while upset; ability to manage tough problems without getting too upset; ability to solve problems without losing control.
Coping skills: Ways to get what a person wants; ways to deal with not having what someone wants; behaviors a person can use to handle anger, frustration, and emotional upset; abilities and behaviors that help a person avoid problems.

■ CASE VIGNETTES

—Diana loved to work; but she hated noisy co-workers. It reminded her of when she was younger and have to live in a state hospital. When her co-worker Warren talked too loudly, she felt herself becoming angry inside. The more Warren talked, the angrier she got. Diana was afraid to speak up and tell Warren to quiet down. Inside, she felt like a pot of boiling water, ready to spill over on the stove. Finally she screamed at him, "Yick, yack, yick, yack, why don't you shut up and be quiet? I'm going to tell the boss to tape your mouth shut." Then she banged her work things down on the table and stomped off.

Do you think Diana was frustrated? Why or why not? Could she have done a better job handling her feelings and coping with stress? How?

—Jody was a friendly person who lived in her own apartment with one housemate. They had some counselors who came to their house to help them cook and do housework. Jody liked her housemate Jean but got frustrated with her, too. Jean was very nosy and got into Jody's business too much. One day Jody caught Jean snooping around her bedroom. Then Jean asked Jody why she had a letter from her mother on her bedroom desk. Jody's bedroom was her own private space, and she was upset that Jean did not respect her privacy. Jody felt that Jean was out of line, prying into her personal and private matters. Just as she was about to yell at Jean, Jody thought to herself, "Oh, well, I bet Jean doesn't understand that she's supposed to keep

out of my bedroom." She told herself, I'll be getting a new housemate soon, maybe I'll just wait for Jean to move out next week." Jody was proud of herself because she had thought ahead and avoided a fight with Jean. Jody was very patient, and the next week Jean moved away.
Do you think Jody did a good job dealing with her frustration? Why or why not?

■ DISCUSSION QUESTIONS

Simple/concrete questions:
    What is the difference between a frustrating feeling and a frustrated behavior?
    What are some things that can cause people to feel frustrated?
Personal experience/feelings questions:
    Have you ever felt frustrated? Why?
    Have you ever had to wait for somebody who did not show up on time? How did you feel?
    Have you ever been told by someone that you could not have what you wanted? How did you feel?
    When you become frustrated and angry, how do you handle these feelings?
Problem-solving questions:
    What should you do if you put money in a pop machine and the machine does not give you any pop?
    What should you do if you want something that someone else has, such as a new shirt or jacket, but you do not have enough money to buy one?
    When you become frustrated, is it ever okay to lose control of your behavior (e.g., start to scream, have a tantrum)?

■ GROUP ACTIVITIES

Waits patiently for people and things:

ALMOST NEVER	USUALLY NOT	SOMETIMES	USUALLY	ALMOST ALWAYS
1	2	3	4	5

Handles disappointment, letdown, and anger without negative behaviors:

ALMOST NEVER	USUALLY NOT	SOMETIMES	USUALLY	ALMOST ALWAYS
1	2	3	4	5

Reacts calmly when having to wait for things:

ALMOST NEVER	USUALLY NOT	SOMETIMES	USUALLY	ALMOST ALWAYS
1	2	3	4	5

Thinks calmly about possible solutions to problems without a display of anger, irritability, and negative emotions:

ALMOST NEVER	USUALLY NOT	SOMETIMES	USUALLY	ALMOST ALWAYS
1	2	3	4	5

Tells oneself an appropriate positive message if cannot have something immediately:

ALMOST NEVER	USUALLY NOT	SOMETIMES	USUALLY	ALMOST ALWAYS
1	2	3	4	5

Recognizes one active and one passive coping skill:

ALMOST NEVER	USUALLY NOT	SOMETIMES	USUALLY	ALMOST ALWAYS
1	2	3	4	5

21. *Respect for Others*

Having respect for others is a unifying theme, underlying all the topics in this chapter. It is important to one's ability to sustain social relationships over time. The group leader should begin with a discussion of the Golden Rule, pointing out the importance of treating others the way one wants to be treated. Politeness and courtesy can be reviewed, followed by the notion that it is good to act generously toward others. This includes sharing things with others as well as forgiving their faults and inadequacies. Attention should be given to how one gets to know others better. Avoidance of rude behaviors and "talking down" to others may be discussed. This topic is understood and fairly easily discussed by individuals with mild and moderate developmental disabilities. Persons with more severe developmental delay can often grasp specific respectful behaviors but have more difficulty with underlying concepts related to the topic. One modification for lower functioning individuals is to use active role-play of respectful and disrespectful behaviors, which may be presented on videotape or in live demonstration by the group leader or other group members.

■ SPECIFIC SKILLS TO BE LEARNED

Understand the Golden Rule: "Treat others how one wants to be treated."
Understand how to speak and act politely to others:
  Listen.
  Smile.
  Hold doors.
  Let others go first.
Recognize how to act generously:
  Share.
  Ignore faults of others.
  Give gifts/tokens of affection.
Understand how to get to know a person:
  Ask about thoughts.
  Ask about feelings.
  Ask about interests.
  Ask about preferences.
Avoid rude behaviors:
  Swearing
  Screaming
  Turning one's back on someone
  Coughing in someone's face
  Shaming/blaming
  Hitting/slapping
  Yelling
Know how to treat others as though they are competent (not talk down to others):
  Not treat others as if they are little children.
  Not act as though one is better than others.

■ CONCEPTS NECESSARY TO PERFORM SKILLS

Golden Rule: Treat others the way you want to be treated.
Polite: Courteous; caring; kind; considerate of others; letting others know that you care about how they feel; showing respect for others.

Generous: Sharing one's things with others; ignoring others' faults and shortcomings; giving things to people in need; sharing one's time with others; doing things for others; kind; not blaming or criticizing; being helpful, considerate and giving.

Rude: Mean; discourteous; offensive; doing something that bothers another person; insensitive; not paying attention to how other people feel; not caring how others feel; disregarding; vulgar; neglectful.

Competent: Knowing how to do a job; able to do things; can do things for oneself; able to understand things; able to make choices and decisions; not helpless and dependent; good at things.

■ CASE VIGNETTES

—Don is a respectful man. He is blind. Although he cannot see others, he hears them. As he passes people in the hallway, Don calls out, "Hi, how are you? Nice day, isn't it?" He smiles when he says this. One day Gail was crying, and Don said, "What's the matter, Gail, are you all right?" Don listens to others and tries to be helpful. When he has an extra treat, he shares it with a friend. He likes to ask his friends what they think and how they feel. He also talks to them about his life. Don does not swear or yell at others. He is very patient and ignores it if someone is rude. Everybody likes Don.

Why do you think everyone likes Don? Is he respectful to others? In what ways?

—Bjorn is a grumpy man. He frequently shakes his fist at others and pretends he is going to hit them. When someone asks him a question, he says, "It's none of your business." Bjorn brags about his good work. He does not listen to other people talk about theirs. Bjorn thinks of himself first and does not seem to care much about others. Sometimes he turns his back on others when they are talking. He does not share his things with friends, not even if he has extra treats and they have none.

Do you think Bjorn has respect for others? Why or why not? How could he show more respect to others?

■ DISCUSSION QUESTIONS

Simple/concrete questions:
  Is it respectful to _____ (cough in somebody's face, yell at somebody, help somebody with something, turn your back on somebody, burp in somebody's face, listen carefully to someone, hold the door for someone, etc.)?
  What are some things that show respect for other people?
  What are some things that show disrespect and rudeness to others?
Personal experience/feelings questions:
  Has anybody ever been rude to you? How? How did you feel?
  Have you ever been rude to anyone else? What did you do?
  How do you feel when others treat you with respect? Can you think of an example when you were treated with courtesy and kindness?
Problem-solving questions:
  How can you deal with somebody who acts disrespectfully to you?
  When other people act rudely to you, should you act the same way to them?

■ GROUP ACTIVITIES

Ask each person if particular behaviors are respectful or disrespectful.
Participants select partners and share personal experiences in which they were either treated well or badly by others. Return to the larger group and each person share an experience that was learned from his or her partner.

■ ASSESSMENT OF SKILLS LEARNED

Recites Golden Rule:

ALMOST NEVER	USUALLY NOT	SOMETIMES	USUALLY	ALMOST ALWAYS
1	2	3	4	5

Recognizes polite behaviors:

ALMOST NEVER	USUALLY NOT	SOMETIMES	USUALLY	ALMOST ALWAYS
1	2	3	4	5

Recognizes generous behaviors:

ALMOST NEVER	USUALLY NOT	SOMETIMES	USUALLY	ALMOST ALWAYS
1	2	3	4	5

Understands how to ask questions to get to know someone better:

ALMOST NEVER	USUALLY NOT	SOMETIMES	USUALLY	ALMOST ALWAYS
1	2	3	4	5

Avoids rude behaviors:

ALMOST NEVER	USUALLY NOT	SOMETIMES	USUALLY	ALMOST ALWAYS
1	2	3	4	5

Avoids condescending to others:

ALMOST NEVER	USUALLY NOT	SOMETIMES	USUALLY	ALMOST ALWAYS
1	2	3	4	5

4 Self-Esteem

THE GENERAL TOPIC of this chapter is self-esteem. These exercises are qualitatively different from the earlier ones for social skills. The topics included here provide a framework within which the group facilitator may take an experiential approach to the development of self-esteem. The chapter begins with an introduction and cohesion-building exercise. Some of this may be skipped if the group is not new but has already been through an introductory session. Basic individual needs and areas of personal growth are explored. Next comes a discussion of self-worth and self-acceptance, identifying positive and negative aspects of each individual's self-esteem. The ensuing exercise takes a more in-depth approach to specific areas related to self-esteem. The topic of self-identity, which in many respects provides a basis for individual self-esteem, comes next. The areas of personal history and family constellation are then explored. It may be a good idea to spend more than one session on each of these topics because of the large amount of information they are likely to elicit from group members. The areas of socialization and nurturance are subsequently examined. They are followed by the topic of guilt and shame, which helps group members understand many painful emotions related to self-esteem. A segment on positive self-affirmations is included to give each participant a concrete tool for increasing self-esteem. The chapter ends with discussions of wellness and physical/mental energy. These topics highlight the importance of a range of wellness activities that are more indirectly related to self-esteem than are previous ones.

22. *Introduction and Cohesion Building*

Feeling good about oneself is invariably tied to the feedback one receives from others. A sense of cohesion with one's friends and peers tends to lead to increased personal sharing, mutual support, and positive feedback. This topic begins with an introduction to the group format, process, and rules. For those who have participated in the first topics of the book, or if the group has been meeting prior to this section, these preliminaries may be abbreviated. The leader should ensure that participants have been introduced, understand the general topics to be addressed, and have personal goals related to self-esteem. The format of sharing feelings, asking for group time, working on specific skills, partner exercises, and group mechanics should be discussed. Group rules should be established, with specific emphasis on confidentiality and the importance of giving positive feedback to fellow group members who take the risks to share personal information. Finally, the "meat and potatoes" of group should consist of a group cohesion exercise and personal sharing. Several possible cohesion exercises are offered. In each case, the group leader can move around the room asking each person, "If you could be any kind of animal (famous person, movie star) what (or who) would you be? Why?" After each has had an opportunity to share his or her identification, others should be encouraged to guess why he or she picked that particular animal or person, and what it might say about the individual's personality. For example, the person who identifies with a tiger may feel weak and want to be stronger. The person who identifies with a bird may have a desire for more freedom. Someone who identifies with a puppy may want more affection from others. The cohesion-building exercises tend to open people up, which is an ideal lead-in to additional personal sharing exercises in which individuals share where they live, what they like/dislike, life goals, beliefs, values, and other personal data. The topic is appropriate for those with mild and moderate developmental delay, who generally enjoy the exercises and are capable of understanding necessary concepts. Lower functioning persons are capable of indicating preferences by pointing to pictures of various animals or famous persons, and communicating preferences through facial expressions and gestures. Often group participants enjoy adding physical demonstrations to show their animal or person identifications. This may involve flexing their muscles to indicate toughness, flapping their arms to represent wings, or other such mannerisms. A further modification for individuals with more severe disabilities is for the group leader to take a more active role, questioning them about preferences and personal information in a context that allows for "yes" or "no" responses.

■ SPECIFIC SKILLS TO BE LEARNED

Recognize and understand general group topics and format:
    Introductions
    Overview of topics
    Individual goals
    Sharing feelings (1–10 scale)
    Asking for group time
    Skill-building
    Partner exercises
Understand group rules:
    Confidentiality
    Positive and negative feedback to others
    Smoking/refreshments
    Attendance/punctuality
Participate in building group cohesion:
    Cohesion-building exercise (to foster trust, security, community and group belongingness):
        Animal identification metaphor (If you could be any kind of animal, what would you choose?)
        Famous person identification
        Movie star identification

Personal sharing exercise:
    Name, age, residence
    Likes/dislikes
    Life goals
    Beliefs/values

■ CONCEPTS NECESSARY TO PERFORM SKILLS

Group cohesion: Togetherness; when people find it easy to talk to each other; individuals enjoying being together; when persons are feeling emotionally close to each other.

Group belongingness: People feeling they are accepted in their group; a person feeling that he or she has a place in a group; feeling that one is like others in a group; feeling cared about by fellow group members.

Personal sharing or self-revelation: Telling things about yourself; letting others know personal information about oneself; telling your real feelings; telling people what you think; telling others about your life.

Trust: Feeling safe with others; feeling you can tell personal things without being attacked by others; feeling that others will treat you with respect; knowing that it is O.K. to tell someone how you feel or what you think; not worrying that somebody will try to blame or hurt you; feeling good, comfortable or relaxed with someone.

Security: Feeling safe to tell others about yourself; feeling accepted as you are; feeling comfortable with others; trusting others with one's feelings.

■ CASE VIGNETTES

—*John, Steve, Bill, and Mike often liked to play basketball with each other. Steve was never sure what John was going to say. Sometimes, for no reason, John would snap, "Steve, that's a terrible shot, can't you ever hit the basket?" Steve would then wait for John to make a bad shot and sarcastically say, "Boy, that was a good one, where did you learn to play ball, at a nursing home?" Bill would look at both of them and say, "You guys play ball like babies." Each of them tried to shoot better than the others, often bumping into each other just as one was making a good shot. They added up the points as each made a basket. Mike always lied about his score, giving himself more points than he really had. Nobody ever talked about personal feelings or private information because they were afraid the others would make fun of them.*

Do you think John, Steve, Bill, and Mike had much group cohesion or togetherness? Why or why not? Do you think they trusted each other? Did they feel safe and secure with each other? Why or why not?

—*Rita had a small group of friends. They got together for lunch on Saturdays. As they sat down for dinner, they would tell each other about their weeks. They were very excited to tell each other everything. They listened with interest as the others talked. They paid attention to each other because they liked and cared about one another. Today Jessie was very sad because her uncle died. Rita listened and then put her arm around Jessie's shoulder, stating, "I'm so sorry to hear that. When is the funeral?" Jessie talked some more and felt very good because everyone was concerned for her. She felt safe telling them all of her feelings because she knew they cared about her. This was a very cohesive group. They had a feeling of togetherness and caring about each other.*

Why do you think this group was so cohesive and had such togetherness? Did it have anything to do with how they listened and shared things with each other? Why do you think they trusted each other when they talked about very personal information?

■ DISCUSSION QUESTIONS

Simple/concrete questions:
 What is group cohesion?
 What is confidentiality?
 What is positive/negative feedback?
Personal experience/feelings questions:
 Do you like who you are? Why or why not?
 Tell us something about who you are?
 Tell us about who you would like to be?
 What makes you feel comfortable with other people?
 Have you ever felt scared about sharing your feelings with others? Why or why not?
Problem-solving questions:
 What should you do if you do not trust the other people you are with?
 Can you learn to trust others better? How?

■ GROUP ACTIVITIES

Ask each person to list one animal which they would like to be, or that they are like in some way. Discuss each person's selection.

Each participant take a turn sharing personal information starting with name, age, and residence, and following up with more personal information such as likes, dislikes, or life goals.

Group members form pairs to discuss information from the first two exercises.

■ ASSESSMENT OF SKILLS LEARNED

Recognizes/understands group topics and format:

ALMOST NEVER	USUALLY NOT	SOMETIMES	USUALLY	ALMOST ALWAYS
1	2	3	4	5

Understands group rules:

ALMOST NEVER	USUALLY NOT	SOMETIMES	USUALLY	ALMOST ALWAYS
1	2	3	4	5

Shares personal information and bonds with others:

ALMOST NEVER	USUALLY NOT	SOMETIMES	USUALLY	ALMOST ALWAYS
1	2	3	4	5

23. *Basic Needs and Personal Growth Opportunities*

Self-esteem is related to one's ability to meet basic needs and to undergo personal growth experiences. It is one on a continuum of basic needs. Individuals who do not sufficiently satisfy a range of basic needs tend to have difficulty feeling good about themselves. Persons with developmental disabilities frequently experience frustrations in attaining basic needs and wants, resulting in more than the typical difficulty establishing solid, positive self-identities. The group facilitator should begin with a discussion of survival needs such as safety, food, clothing, shelter, medical care, and the like. Next, needs for belongingness, social affiliation, competence, other-respect, and self-respect may be discussed. It can be pointed out that self-esteem often involves positive feelings about one's group identification, individual competencies, and positive feedback (respect) from others. Next, more complex aspects of self-esteem can be considered. These may include intimacy with others, personal identity (continuity of a sense of self over time), and self-actualization, which involves achieving one's potentials, continuing to undergo personal growth, and doing the best one can given his or her own special life circumstances. This discussion should be followed by an examination of various personal growth opportunities. These include socialization with others, new life experiences, recreational pursuits, work or productive activity, and continuing education. Finally, the difference between a need and want should be discussed, noting that there may be differences of opinion about what fits into each of these categories. Individuals with mild and moderate developmental disabilities can easily understand very basic needs, but as the needs become more abstract and socially related, they may have more difficulty comprehending them. Pictures, symbols, and gestures can be used with lower functioning persons to communicate about basic physical needs and particular personal growth activities.

■ SPECIFIC SKILLS TO BE LEARNED

Identify basic needs for survival and happiness:
   Safety from threats (personal security)
   Physical needs (food, clothing, shelter, toilet needs, medical care, etc.)
   Belongingness and social affiliation (being with others, being part of a group or family)
   Competence (having skills, knowing how to do things)
   Respect from others (other esteem)
   Respect from self (self-esteem)
   Intimacy (loving and being loved by others, caring)
   Identity (continuity of life experience, ability to relate past, present, and future, being someone
      special; individuality)
   Self-actualization (achievement of self-potential, continuing personal growth, doing the
      best with who one is and one's position in life)
Identify personal growth opportunities:
   Socialization (e.g., sharing thoughts and feelings with others, interacting with others, shar-
      ing social feedback with others)
   New life experiences (e.g., doing new things, meeting new people)
   Recreation (e.g., art, music, physical activity, etc.)
   Work (opportunity for productivity)
   Education (learning new things)
Distinguish between a need and a want:
   A need is more important; one "must" meet a need.
   A want is not really necessary but is desirable.

■ CONCEPTS NECESSARY TO PERFORM SKILLS

Need: Something a person must have; sometng an individual cannot live without; something
   very important and necessary to someone; things that are necessary to stay alive and healthy;
   individuals demand that their needs be met.
Want: Something a person would very much like; a thing that somebody can live without;
   something very important but not necessary for survival; people want certain things to
   make them happy; individuals hope that their wants are satisfied.
Safe: Secure; not worrying that bad things will happen; comfortable with others; not afraid to
   tell others how one feels and thinks.
Secure: Trusting others with one's feelings; confident; safe; comfortable with oneself and
   feeling accepted by others.

Socialize: Talk to others; get together with friends; tell people about one's life and ask about theirs; take an interest in people; do things with others; relate to people.

Belongingness: Feeling that one belongs somewhere; feeling as though one fits into a group; feeling like a part of the gang; feeling that one has a place with others.

Competent: Knowing how to do a job; able to do things; able to do things for oneself; able to understand things; able to make choices and decisions; not helpless and dependent; good at things.

Other respect: Having respect of others; being important to others; being valued by people; others think that one is worthwhile.

Self-respect: Respect for oneself; feeling that one is important; valuing oneself; feeling worthwhile; seeing yourself as a good person.

Intimate: Feeling close to someone; loving closeness; two people feeling care and affection for each other; emotional closeness between people; sharing very personal thoughts and feelings with someone.

Personal growth: Making changes for the better; improving oneself; maturing; growing up; learning new things; developing a better understanding of life, people, and oneself.

Potential: Something that a person might do; something one may achieve; a person has not yet done something but may do it; a thing that has not yet been done but could be if one worked at it; a dream that may or may not come true.

Self-actualization: To reach one's potential; what happens when somebody works hard to achieve something; to continue to get better at things; to become more mature; to do the best one can with his or her abilities; to make things happen; to act and make choices.

■ CASE VIGNETTES

—*Dave was a talented fellow. He could run fast and was good at sports. He was smart enough to do many things. Dave had a job working as a janitor, and he lived in his own apartment with the help of his independent living counselor; but Dave could be lazy. He did not deal well with frustration. For example, Dave often got mad at his co-workers because they worked too slowly. When he got mad, he would swear at them and then would work very slowly to get back at them. Dave got fired from a job once because of these problems. He often blamed his problems on others. For example, he drank too much beer once and was too tired to get up and go to work the next day. He blamed his girlfriend for his drinking because she was too crabby. Another time he blamed the bus driver when he overslept, telling his boss, "The darn bus was late, I couldn't help it." Dave was kicked out of his apartment one time because he did not pay his rent. He blamed this on his boss because he felt he should be paid more money at work. What really happened was that Dave had spent too much money on other things and did not have enough left for his rent.*

Do you think Dave was living up to his potential? Could he have done a better job and taken more responsibility for his own behavior? Why do you think he blamed everyone else for his problems?

—*Faith was a slow learner, but she worked very hard and graduated from her special school program. Then she went to another school to learn how to do a job. She became a bus person at a restaurant. She cleared dishes off tables and wheeled them to the dishwasher. Even though Faith had a hard time keeping her mind on the job, she worked hard to do her job well. She did not blame other people when she had work problems. She simply went to the boss and asked for help if she needed it. Because she worked hard and took responsibility for her work, Faith was able to earn extra money. She used the extra money to pay for movies, dinner out, and other fun things. She also paid her own telephone bill and bought groceries for herself. Faith's social worker helped her with her checkbook, but she watched closely to make her money last until the end of the month. Faith continued to go to cooking classes at night. Even though she was grown up, she continued to learn many things.*

Do you think Faith was living up to her potential? How did she take responsibility for her own behavior? Did she blame other people for her problems? Why do you think Faith had the respect of herself and other people?

■ DISCUSSION QUESTIONS

Simple/concrete questions:
  What are some things that every person needs? Why?
  What are some things most people want but do not necessarily need?
Personal experience/feelings questions:
  Have you ever felt that your needs were not getting met? Which ones?
  Do you ever feel that others do not care about your needs? How do you feel about this? How
    do you handle this?
Problem-solving questions:
  If your needs are not getting met, what should you do?
  What can you do to get others to respect your wants and needs?
  What is the difference between *needing* something and *wanting* it?

■ GROUP ACTIVITIES

Take turns identifying basic needs.
Discuss the difference between needs and wants.
Form pairs and each person tell a partner about met and unmet needs or wants.
Entire group brainstorm different ways to help individual members meet personal needs.

■ ASSESSMENT OF SKILLS LEARNED

Identifies basic needs:

ALMOST NEVER	USUALLY NOT	SOMETIMES	USUALLY	ALMOST ALWAYS
1	2	3	4	5

Identifies personal growth opportunities:

ALMOST NEVER	USUALLY NOT	SOMETIMES	USUALLY	ALMOST ALWAYS
1	2	3	4	5

Distinguishes between a *need* and *want*:

ALMOST NEVER	USUALLY NOT	SOMETIMES	USUALLY	ALMOST ALWAYS
1	2	3	4	5

24. *Self-Worth and Self-Acceptance*

Accepting and feeling that one is worth something are integral aspects of one's self-esteem. Persons with developmental disabilities often experience repeated failures and rejections, which lead to feelings of low self-worth and poor self-acceptance. This topic is primarily an experiential one. It begins with participants identifying several positive aspects of themselves (strengths) and several things they would like to change about themselves (weaknesses or areas needing improvement). If group members have difficulty listing positive items, and they usually do, the group facilitator and cohorts may help them. Next, the leader should emphasize that personal limits do not mean personal inadequacies. All people have faults, shortcomings, and limitations with respect to their abilities, but this does not automatically mean they are no good. The discussion may continue with individuals identifying potential areas of self-fulfillment, areas in which they would like to develop further and improve their lives. An attempt must be made to convey the importance of accepting oneself, even when desiring changes. Finally, the importance of reaching for things beyond one's grasp and trying things that are difficult can be stressed. This topic is readily comprehensible to individuals with mild and moderate developmental delay. It can be modified for lower functioning individuals by adding external structure. For example, the facilitator and group members can help list strengths and areas for improvement for the lower functioning individuals, who may communicate using yes/no responses or various methods of nonverbal communication.

■ SPECIFIC SKILLS TO BE LEARNED

Identify five positive things about oneself (strengths).
Identify five negative things about oneself (weaknesses or things to change).
Understand that personal limits do not mean personal inadequacies.
Identify areas of potential self-fulfillment.
Understand the concept of accepting oneself even if wanting to make changes.
Understand the importance of reaching for things beyond one's grasp (trying and working on oneself).

■ CONCEPTS NECESSARY TO PERFORM SKILLS

Personal strength: Something somebody does well; something good about a person; a skill; knowing how to do something; a thing someone likes about him or herself; something others like about a person.

Personal weakness or limitation: Something a person wants to do better; a thing about oneself that is not yet as good as one would like; something an individual wishes he or she could do better, but even when trying hard it continues to be difficult; what a person does not like about him or herself; a characteristic that somebody does not like about a person.

Self-acceptance: To like yourself for who you are; to know that one is a good person even if needing to change some things; to feel good as you are.

Self-worth: What individuals think they are worth; how important a person feels; how good or bad someone feels about him- or herself; what people think they deserve from others and from their lives.

Valuing self: To feel that one is important; to have positive self-worth; to think that one deserves something good from life; to feel that one deserves good treatment from others.

Positive: Good; has desirable qualities; agreeable; pleasant; helpful; worthwhile.

Negative: Bad; has undesirable qualities; disagreeable; unpleasant; not helpful; not worthwhile.

■ CASE VIGNETTES

—Sally was a very special woman. She was slower to learn some things than her schoolmates, but she worked hard and finally graduated from high school. She felt good about herself because she was a hard worker, a friendly person, and a good runner. She rode her exercise bicycle every night and tried not to eat too much junk food. Lately she was having some problems because she wanted to live more independently but was not quite ready for this. Sally had

not learned how to cook, do laundry, and take care of her own apartment. Even though she was not yet ready to live by herself, Sally liked herself and had positive feelings of self-worth. She knew that she was an O.K. person even if she was not perfect. It was partly because Sally knew she was worthwhile that she kept learning new things and improving her skills. She knew that someday she would live in her own apartment.

Do you think Sally had good self-worth and self-acceptance? Why or why not? How do you think she was able to have good thoughts and feelings about herself, even when she was having problems?

—Jack did not like himself very much. He did not accept himself for who he was. Jack often talked about other people not liking him. He felt that they unfairly left him out of fun activities. One day Linda overheard Jack saying he was no good because he was too fat. Another time Jack said he was too dumb, because he did not know how to read the directions on a microwave dinner. Jack felt that because he had some problems, he was no good. Often he would not try new things because he was afraid he would fail. When some of his friends decided to take a cooking class, Jack stayed home because he was afraid he would make too many mistakes.

Why do you think Jack had trouble accepting himself? Do you think he paid too much attention to his problems and not enough attention to his strengths? What could Jack do to learn how to like himself more?

■ DISCUSSION QUESTIONS

Simple/concrete questions:
  What is self-worth?
  What is self-acceptance?
Personal experience/feelings questions:
  What do you like about yourself? Why?
  What do you dislike about yourself? Why?
  What would you like to change about yourself? What would you like to keep the same?
  Do you feel like a worthwhile person? Why or why not?
  What makes you feel worthwhile?
  What makes you feel inadequate or not good enough?
Problem-solving questions:
  How can you improve your positive feelings about yourself and acceptance of yourself?
  What can be done to help a person who does not like him- or herself?

■ GROUP ACTIVITIES

Ask each person what they like and do not like about themselves. Find out what each person would like to change.
Ask individual group members to demonstrate body postures and demeanor of people who like or do not like themselves.
Choose partners and talk about personal goals for change.

■ ASSESSMENT OF SKILLS LEARNED

Lists several personal strengths:

ALMOST NEVER	USUALLY NOT	SOMETIMES	USUALLY	ALMOST ALWAYS
1	2	3	4	5

Identifies several personal weaknesses or things to change:

ALMOST NEVER	USUALLY NOT	SOMETIMES	USUALLY	ALMOST ALWAYS
1	2	3	4	5

Differentiates personal *limits* and *inadequacies:*

ALMOST NEVER	USUALLY NOT	SOMETIMES	USUALLY	ALMOST ALWAYS
1	2	3	4	5

Identifies an area of potential self-fulfillment:

ALMOST NEVER	USUALLY NOT	SOMETIMES	USUALLY	ALMOST ALWAYS
1	2	3	4	5

Accepts oneself even if wanting to make changes:

ALMOST NEVER	USUALLY NOT	SOMETIMES	USUALLY	ALMOST ALWAYS
1	2	3	4	5

Understands the importance of self-improvement:

ALMOST NEVER	USUALLY NOT	SOMETIMES	USUALLY	ALMOST ALWAYS
1	2	3	4	5

25. Self-Esteem

Self-esteem is how individuals feel about themselves. It is influenced to a great extent by their self-concepts, what they think about themselves. Persons with developmental delay are vulnerable to the development of poor self-esteem. They tend to receive high levels of negative feedback from others because of their many limitations. This is sometimes internalized as negative thoughts and emotions. They also may overgeneralize or selectively abstract negative views of themselves from meager evidence. For example, one may say, "I'm no good because I'm in a special class," or, "I can't do this; therefore, I can't do anything." This session continues to be highly experiential, unlike more didactic topics, and begins with each member receiving encouragement to verbalize several positive self-statements. Positive self-talk may include a spectrum of self-related categories including body, appearance, behavior, talent, skill, total person characteristics, and other self-attributes. Group members should be taught to differentiate positive and negative feelings related to self-esteem. Some negative esteem components include guilt, shame, inadequacy, isolation, and loneliness. Positive esteem components include confidence, security, competence, belongingness, and adequacy. This topic continues to be readily accessible to individuals with mild and moderate developmental disabilities. Lower functioning persons are able to comprehend and practice the more concrete elements of the session. Again, they may require modifications such as the use of pictures/symbols and more active questioning on the part of the group leader. Framing questions in a yes/no format may be helpful—for example: "Do you like your hair?" "Do you do a good job?" "Do you like yourself?" These questions can then be narrowed—for example: "What do you like about your good job? Is it that you are a fast worker?" Or "What do you like about yourself? Is it that you are a friendly person?"

■ SPECIFIC SKILLS TO BE LEARNED

Verbalize several positive self statements:
    Body/appearance
    Behavior

Talent/skill
Total person
Other attributes
Differentiate positive and negative feelings related to self-esteem:
Guilt, shame, inadequacy, isolation, loneliness, etc.
Confidence, security, competence, belongingness, adequacy, etc.

■ CONCEPTS NECESSARY TO PERFORM SKILLS

Positive statement: Say something good; tell a good thing about yourself; say something nice; tell a good thing about a person.

Negative statement: Say something bad; tell a bad thing about yourself; say something that is not nice about yourself or someone else; tell a bad thing about a person.

Self-talk: What a person says about him- or herself; say good or bad things about oneself; talk about yourself.

Thought: Something somebody thinks; an idea; a thing that a person believes; activity going on in someone's head.

Statement: Something that someone says; tell something; say something about yourself or someone else.

Feeling: Emotion; something somebody feels inside; nervousness, anger, surprise, happiness, sadness, excitement, loneliness, etc.; good or bad sensation happening inside of someone.

Behavior: Something somebody does; to act in a certain way; what somebody's body is doing.

Personal experience: A thing that happens to someone; something a person thinks or feels; what happens in a person's life; how a person sees him- or herself and other people.

■ CASE VIGNETTES

—Alan felt good about himself because he had finally learned how to control his behavior. He used to scream and throw things but had worked very hard to learn how to relax and calm down. He liked himself more now because he had learned how to control himself. One day, his friend Tony asked him, "Alan, how did you learn to control your behavior?" Alan replied, "Talent, I got talent." Then he said, "I try harder, I think about good things." Alan now paid attention when he was just starting to get angry and told himself, "Calm down, Alan, you can do it."

Why do you think Alan felt good about himself? How did he learn to control his behavior? Did Alan say any positive statements to himself?

—Judy did not like herself very much. One of her problems was that she could not stop herself from making noises and body movements. She did this because of a medical problem that the doctor told her parents about. She took medicine to help her control the noises, twitches, and body movements, but she continued to have trouble controlling these behaviors. Sometimes she would call out when everyone else was quiet. At other times she swore at people. Judy told herself: "I can't help it. I hate myself because I'm different from everybody else." She also said to herself, "I'm no good because I can't control my behavior."

Why do you think Judy said bad things about herself? Do you think she could learn how to like herself more? How could she start feeling better about herself?

■ DISCUSSION QUESTIONS

Simple/concrete questions:
Do people who say mean things to others feel good about themselves?

Do people who say nice things to others feel good about themselves?

What are some areas of a person's life in which they can have good thoughts about themselves?

Personal experience/feelings questions:

Do you like yourself?

Do you like your body?

Are you a smart person?

Do you feel like a worthwhile person?

Do you ever feel guilty, shameful, or inadequate (not good enough)?

How do you feel when saying nice things about yourself?

How do you feel when saying nice things about other people?

Problem-solving questions:

What can a person do to feel better about him- or herself?

How can somebody practice positive self-esteem (practice feeling good about him or herself)?

■ GROUP ACTIVITIES

Participants take turns saying positive things about themselves (body, appearance, behavior, talent, skills, personality, entire self, etc.).

Group members take turns saying positive things about others.

Form self-selected pairs and talk about how each person feels about him or herself.

■ ASSESSMENT OF SKILLS LEARNED

Verbalizes several positive self-statements:

ALMOST NEVER	USUALLY NOT	SOMETIMES	USUALLY	ALMOST ALWAYS
1	2	3	4	5

Recognizes positive and negative feelings related to self-esteem:

ALMOST NEVER	USUALLY NOT	SOMETIMES	USUALLY	ALMOST ALWAYS
1	2	3	4	5

26. *Self-Identity*

A clear self-identity contributes to one's ability to experience positive self-esteem. If one is unable to develop a coherent identity or to formulate a lasting sense of self, then one's self-esteem is entirely dependent on external factors, changing with each situation. Having personal identities means that people see themselves as the same persons they were yesterday, last month, and last year, even though they have undergone a variety of changes. Personal identity tends to be based on various group identifications, reflecting how the person is similar to others, and on personal differences, how one stands out in contrast to others. Because of their more limited intellectual development, persons with developmental disabilities often experience more difficulty than their peers establishing and maintaining positive self-identities. At the outset of the session, the leader may help participants identify a range of similarities and differences. This can be done in a question/answer format, each asking him- or herself such questions as: "What do I enjoy?" "What do I do well?" "What is important to me?" "Whom do I admire? "What things describe my personality?" "How am I the same as or different from others?"The conversation should ultimately result in a discussion that helps the participants recognize and accept their differences while also enjoying their commonalties. The topic is straightforward for those with mild and moderate developmental disabilities. It may be modified for lower functioning individuals by increasing external feedback about individual characteristics, asking very specific questions that facilitate self-descriptions, and using nonverbal communications to elicit information. Examples of more simple and specific yes/no questions include: "What color is your shirt? Is it the same as or different than_____'s shirt?" "Do you like to play softball? Do you know anyone else who likes to play softball?" "Are you a fast worker?" "Is your work faster or slower than others'?" The lower the intellectual level, the more concrete, specific, and closed-ended the questions need to be.

■ SPECIFIC SKILLS TO BE LEARNED

Identify similarities and differences between oneself and others:
What do I enjoy?
What do I do well?
What do I value? Why?
What am I proud of? Why?
Who do I admire? Why?
What are my favorite places?
What things describe my personality?
Things I know I am?
Things I know I am not?
What are my hobbies? Interests?
What are my goals? Ideals? Hopes?
Recognize and accept differences between people.

■ CONCEPTS NECESSARY TO PERFORM SKILLS

Similarity: How people or things are the same; how people or things are alike.
Difference: What is not alike between people; what is not the same about things; something that sets two people apart; something that is special about a person or thing.
Personal history: What happens to a person over time; a person's past, present, and future life; how somebody lives and changes over time; someone's life story.
Past: What has already happened; five minutes ago, an hour ago, yesterday, last week, last month, last year, and a long time ago
Present: what is happening right now; this moment; what we are doing, seeing, hearing and talking about now; here and now.
Future: What will happen later; five minutes from now; an hour from now, tomorrow, next week, next month, next year, and a long time from now; what is yet to come; what will happen.
Identity: Who you are; who I am; who each person is; what is special about a person; how one is like or unlike others; to be a separate person; to be an individual; to have one's own thoughts, feelings, and behaviors; to know who you are and how you are the same as or different from others; individuality; distinctiveness.

■ CASE VIGNETTES

—Richard was a very distinctive person. He was special and had a personality all of his own. Richard was about six feet tall and had brown hair combed straight back, with a little bit of gray. This made the edges of his hair look like salt and pepper. He ate quite well and his belly was starting to hang over his beltline. He wore glasses with plastic gray frames. He also had a

black wristwatch that flashed the time, day, and date. Richard spoke rapidly and did not leave much room for others to talk. He was friendly and became easily excited. Richard often talked over and over about things that bothered him. He frequently repeated what others said and then smiled, trying to be as friendly as possible. One of Richard's problems was that he took things too personally. He became upset about small things others said. Sometimes he made a mountain out of a molehill; but he tried hard to be friendly. Richard was special. He had his own personality. There was no mistaking Richard for somebody else.

Can you tell me something about Richard's identity? What did he look like? What kind of personality did he have?

—Whitney was a pretty woman. She was about five feet, five inches tall, and weighed about one hundred and ten pounds. She had dark, chocolate brown skin and dark brown eyes. Her hair was black and she wore it in braided curls, nicely held together with beads. Whitney was proud of her appearance and was always well dressed. She often wore colorful outfits. Whitney had a lot of energy and liked to joke around with her friends. She was a good reader, and enjoyed doing crossword puzzles. She enjoyed eating pizza and going out to restaurants. She had a goal to get married someday and have two children. First she wanted to get a job and learn how to live by herself. Right now she was continuing to go to school so she could get a good job later. Whitney was a special person who had her own personality and way of dressing. One reason others liked her was because she knew who she was, and she liked herself.

What sort of person was Whitney? How did she like to dress? Did she have any goals? Why do you think she liked herself?

■ DISCUSSION QUESTIONS

Simple/concrete questions:
   What are some areas in which people are different?
Personal experience/feelings questions:
   What do you like to eat?
   What are your hobbies and interests?
   What do you like to do on weekends?
   What kinds of things do you do well?
   What are your favorite places?
   What do you value (what do you think is important)? Why?
   In what way(s) are you proud of yourself? Why?
   Who do you admire? Why?
   What kind of a personality do you have?
   What are your goals in life?
   How do you feel about yourself? Do you like your identity?
Problem-solving questions:
   How can you change who you are?
   Is it a good idea to change who you are?

■ GROUP ACTIVITIES

Describe a particular group member, but do not give his or her name; other group members guess whom you are describing.
Take turns describing a mystery person (another group member), and have others guess who is being described.

Individuals share personal information about their own identities and indicate things that they would like to keep the same or change.

■ ASSESSMENT OF SKILLS LEARNED

Identifies similarities between self and others:

ALMOST NEVER	USUALLY NOT	SOMETIMES	USUALLY	ALMOST ALWAYS
1	2	3	4	5

Identifies differences between self and others:

ALMOST NEVER	USUALLY NOT	SOMETIMES	USUALLY	ALMOST ALWAYS
1	2	3	4	5

27. Personal History

To a large extent, a person's identity is related to his or her personal history. Therefore, personal history plays a major role in the development of one's self-esteem. Individuals with developmental disabilities often have chaotic personal histories because of frequent school, work and residential changes. They also may have a limited understanding of their histories because of more limited ability in memory retention, association, and integration of life experiences. The group facilitator should begin with a recognition of the importance of each individual's personal history to his or her identity and self-concept. An attempt must be made to convey the importance of the continuity and relatedness of various aspects of one's life. This should be followed by a detailed discussion of the personal histories of specific group members. It may involve intensive questioning and in-depth sharing by each participant, or by comparing individuals across various categories of history information. Categories may include earliest memories/feelings, school, family relationships, friendships, family activities, sexuality development, hobbies/interests, changes in family patterns/roles, major attachments, discipline, successes/failures, achievements, work, physical health, aging, and others. The topic is appropriate for individuals with mild and moderate developmental delay. As the participants' intellectual levels decrease, there is a need for more active questioning and structure by the group leader. For extremely low functioning persons, this may involve concrete yes/no questions. For these individuals in particular, but also for brighter persons, sharing family pictures can be enjoyable and appropriate.

■ SPECIFIC SKILLS TO BE LEARNED

Recognize the importance of a personal history (continuity of life experiences).
Share personal history information with others:
  Earliest memories and feelings
  Preschool, grade school, junior and senior high school, etc.
  Relationships with parents and siblings (family closeness)
  Relationships with extended family members (e.g., grandparents, aunts, uncles, cousins, other relatives)
  Family activities (good and bad times with family)
  Sexuality awareness and development
  Friendships (home, school, other)
  Major hobbies and interests over time

Changes in family patterns/roles over time (feelings about family roles and place in family)
Major attachments to family, friends, relatives
History of discipline (methods, feelings about discipline)
Major life successes/failures
History of achievements and achievement expectations
Changes in feelings about self/family
Work history
Major life events (e.g., developmental milestones, losses)
History of physical health
The aging process and associated changes

■ CONCEPTS NECESSARY TO PERFORM SKILLS

Autobiography: One's personal story; an individual's life story.
Life timeline: The order of experiences that have happened in someone's life; the order of important events in a person's life.
History: Somebody's life story; a story; all the things that happen to a person in his or her life; all of the things that someone experiences during his or her life.
Past: What has already happened; five minutes ago, an hour ago, yesterday, last week, last month, last year, and a long time ago.
Present: What is happening right now; this moment; what we are doing, seeing, hearing, and talking about now; here and now.
Future: What will happen later; five minutes from now, an hour from now, tomorrow, next week, next month, next year, and a long time from now; what is yet to come; what will happen.

■ CASE VIGNETTES

—Tom was a friendly young man who greeted others with kind words and a smile. One day he told his friends part of his own life story. He was born into a family with five children. Because he had special medical problems, his mother did not think she could take care of him properly. She was raising five children alone because Tom's father had died. Tom had a different father than his brothers and sisters. His mother gave him up for adoption when he was three weeks old. He had wonderful adoptive parents who loved him very much. They had no children of their own and were very happy to have Tom. As he was growing up, Tom had regular visits with his birth mother and his brothers and sisters. Tom went to many good schools, sometimes changing schools because one had a better special education program than another. Tom participated in sports and was a good baseball player. As he became older, he saw less of his brothers and sisters but continued to have regular visits with his mother. Last year, one of his sisters died in a car accident. He felt very sad and went to the funeral. As Tom has grown up, he has learned to be a good worker. Soon he will move into a new house with three other people similar to himself. He is excited to become more independent but is somewhat afraid to leave home. He cannot help but think that his life has changed a lot over the years.

What do you remember about Tom's history? Can you recall anything about his past, present, and future life? What are some things that have happened during Tom's life?

—Rita is an older woman. She has had many problems in her life, and has moved from one home to another. She has worked in a few different places but has not been employed for the last ten years. She has trouble paying attention at a job. Rita's memory is getting worse as she gets older. She knows that she lived with her mother and father until age three and then went

into an institution. That was a place people went if they had very bad problems and their families could not take care of them anymore. She stayed there until she was about ten or twelve years old. After that, she moved into a foster home. Then she was placed in so many different group homes that she cannot remember them all. Sometimes the people treated her nicely, but at other times they were not so friendly. Rita cannot remember much about her childhood. She thinks that she went into the hospital when she was a teenager but cannot remember why or for how long. Now she is living in a group home, but she may have to move into a nursing home if her medical problems become worse. Rita becomes confused about her life story. She has not seen any relatives or family members for a long time. She is not even sure if they are still living.

What do you remember about Rita's history? Can you remember any important things about her past, present, and future life? Do you think Rita has a clear idea about what has happened in her life? How do you think you would feel if you could not remember your own life story?

■ DISCUSSION QUESTIONS

Simple/concrete questions:

What are some important things to ask about when taking someone's personal history?

Personal experience/feelings questions:

What are your earliest family memories?

Tell us about your school history? Did you enjoy school? Why or why not?

What kind of relationships did you have with your parents? Brothers and sisters?

Do you feel very close to your relatives?

How have your interests or hobbies changed over time?

Do you relate to your family any differently now than when you were younger?

How were you disciplined as a child? How do you feel about that now?

What are your biggest life successes? Failures?

What sort of work history have you had?

Has your physical health changed over time?

Problem-solving questions:

If someone does not like his or her own personal history, what should he or she do about it?

Does what happened to people in the past make them behave in certain ways right now?

If a person has had terrible past experiences, can the person do anything to feel better later in his or her life?

■ GROUP ACTIVITIES

Ask each group member to share a short autobiography.

Participants form pairs and discuss personal histories in detail.

Facilitate a discussion about the importance of a personal history as this relates to self-identity and continuity of life experiences.

■ ASSESSMENT OF SKILLS LEARNED

Recognizes the importance of a personal history:

ALMOST NEVER	USUALLY NOT	SOMETIMES	USUALLY	ALMOST ALWAYS
1	2	3	4	5

Shares personal history with others:

ALMOST NEVER	USUALLY NOT	SOMETIMES	USUALLY	ALMOST ALWAYS
1	2	3	4	5

Lists several important areas of personal history:

ALMOST NEVER	USUALLY NOT	SOMETIMES	USUALLY	ALMOST ALWAYS
1	2	3	4	5

28. *Family Constellation*

A person's family constellation consists of his or her parents, brothers, sisters, aunts, uncles, cousins, grandparents, and other relatives. The family constellation is often referred to as a family tree. To have a solid sense of one's own identity, it is helpful to be aware of one's family background. Family relationships are frequently pivotal in the development of self-esteem. Individuals with developmental delay often experience difficulty in understanding family relationships and the impact of these relationships on their feelings and behaviors. This topic is more complex than most previous ones. It tends to generate much discussion and can be stretched easily into two or more group sessions. The group facilitator should decide whether to do an in-depth or more superficial exploration of family relationships, depending on particular group member needs. It is sometimes useful to help participants draw three-generational family trees, including grandparents, parents, and siblings. They should be asked to share information about their families-of-origin (the families they were born into) and current nuclear families (families in which they currently reside). It may be helpful to discuss such elements as coalitions or alliances between family members, rigidity or flexibility of family boundaries (family's ability to change in order to meet new situations such as father losing job), hierarchical relationships (who falls where in the pecking order), family power structure (who controls authority and by what means), and family cohesion (closeness or distance). It may be helpful to discuss family communication patterns, roles, rules, values, mythology (special family beliefs), secrets (things family members are prohibited from talking about), stresses and strains acting from inside or outside the family, special roles (e.g., helper, black sheep), how members were taught to deal with emotions, relationships with other family/friends, major family member losses (e.g., death, divorce), ongoing chronic family stressors (e.g., illness, chemical dependency, abuse), and/or family socioeconomic conditions. Because of the range of concepts included in this topic, the group facilitator will need to be selective in focus. Persons with mild and moderate developmental delay usually enjoy and easily share information related to this topic. Lower functioning individuals require more concrete tasks and are more limited in their information sharing. One modification is to ask group members to draw pictures of their families and tell stories about the pictures. Another modification is to ask specific yes/no questions about various aspects of family life, beginning with simple questions such as, "Do you have any brothers and sisters?" or "Do you live with your mom and dad?" Lower functioning individuals may use pictures, symbols, gestures, pointing responses, and other types of nonverbal communication to share family information. This is a good topic in which to share family pictures.

■ SPECIFIC SKILLS TO BE LEARNED

Identify a three-generational family tree.
Describe family of origin and current nuclear family.
Identify family boundaries:
    Dyads, triads, coalitions, and alliances
    Rigidity/flexibility of family boundaries (adaptability)
    Hierarchical relationships
    Family power structure

Family cohesion (closeness/distance)
Recognize family communication patterns.
Identify family values/roles/rules/mythology.
Recognize family secrets.
Identify stresses and strains affecting family.
Describe special roles in family (angel, helper, black sheep, etc.).
Identify family emotional tone.
Describe family relationships with other families.
Identify major family member losses (e.g., death, divorce, separation, changes of residence).
Identify negative or stressful family situations (e.g., mental illness, chemical dependency, physical/sexual/emotional abuse).
Identify family socioeconomic status and physical surroundings.

■ CONCEPTS NECESSARY TO PERFORM SKILLS

Family tree: Everybody in a family; all of a person's relatives; parents, children, aunts, uncles, cousins, grandparents, and all other relatives.

Generation: A group of people about the same age; you and your friends are one generation, and your parents are another generation; a whole group of people who were born at about the same time.

Family boundaries: Family rules; space between family members; how close family members feel; how close family members are to each other; how much privacy family members have; how much sharing family members do with each other,

Communication: To send and receive messages; to tell each other things and know what each means; to tell each other news; to listen to what somebody says, and the person listens to what you say; to share information.

Value: What is important to a person; a belief; guideline for behavior; what somebody thinks is right or true.

Role: What job somebody performs; a person's position in a family or group.

Rule: Guideline; boundary; limit; expectations; what each person agrees to do or not do.

Mythology: Things family members believe; things that people believe that may or may not be true; ways that families see things and think people should act.

Family loss: Someone dying or leaving the family; a family member going away to school; theft of family property; illness or disability of a family member; a family member getting separated or divorced.

Dyad/triad: Two family members or three family members; how any two or three family members get along together; family teams; who is on whose side in family disagreements; who gets along with whom in a family.

Coalition: When two family members team up together against someone else in the family; two or more family members who disagree with others in the family.

Flexible: Able to change behavior in new situations; able to make changes to deal with new problems; able to do things differently than before when a person or family has a new problem; ability of individuals or family members to trade jobs.

Rigid: Not willing to change; unable to change; doing the same thing even if it is not working anymore; not flexible or adaptable.

Adaptable: Able to make changes; can change behavior in new and different situations; flexible; willing to try new things.

Hierarchy: A group or family pecking order; who is the boss over whom; who makes group or family decisions and who follows them; who gets to decide what happens in a group or family.

Power structure: Who controls the power in a group or family; who can make what decisions; who does what jobs; who has the authority to decide things in a group or family.

Cohesion: Togetherness; when people find it easy to talk to each other; individuals enjoying being together; when persons are feeling emotionally close to each other.

■ CASE VIGNETTES

—*Joel came from a very unhappy family. The social worker called it "dysfunctional." That meant that family members did not work very well together and everyone was unhappy. Dad was always trying to boss everyone around, saying that he worked hard and nobody appreciated him. No one listened very well to Dad, and sometimes he got mad and hit Joel. He also hit Joel's mother after he had been drinking. Joel's sister, Courtney, was very shy and quiet. She did not say much. When Dad was angry, she hid in her bedroom, sometimes under the bed. Mom tried hard to talk to Dad and to get the children to behave, but she did not know what to do when Dad got mad. It seemed that in this family, whenever one person was upset, everybody became upset. Nobody had much privacy. Mom walked into the bathroom one day when Joel was in the bathtub. He was very embarrassed and felt angry. Last week, Dad lost his job. He started drinking more beer than usual and seemed to be angry with everyone. Dad did not want Mom to get a job, even though she used to be a secretary before they got married and knew how to work. Dad told her, "I don't want any wife of mine working. We need you here to cook and clean." The family did not have much money, but it was not able to change after Dad lost his job. One time the social worker came to the house to talk to Mom and Dad. Dad did not listen to her because she was a female social worker. No woman was going to tell him what to do.*

Why do you think this was an unhappy family? What could they have done differently to be happier? Do you think the power and authority were used fairly by Dad? Why or why not? What should a person do if he or she is living in this kind of family?

—*David came from a large family. They did not have much money, but Mom and Dad loved all of the children and did their best to buy what each child needed. Each person was treated specially. When it was David's birthday, Mom and Dad took him out for pizza because that was his favorite food. Each child had his or her own job. This was fair because each person was asked to do something he or she was able to do. David took out the garbage and washed dishes. His sister, Roxanne, helped with dishes and also did yardwork. She especially liked to help weed the garden. Mom and Dad made the rules but they were different, depending on the age of each child. Older children were allowed to stay up later at night. Once in a while family members got mad at each other, but they usually apologized later if they hurt others' feelings. There was a family rule that everybody should talk about things that bothered them. That way, problems were solved quickly. Mom and Dad shared the power in the family, and they let David and the other children make some of the smaller family decisions. For example, if the family was going to a restaurant, sometimes the children were able to decide where they would go. Sometimes David's family had relatives over to visit. They also spent time by themselves, doing things with their friends or as a family.*

Why do you suppose David had a happy family? Do you think the parents were fair in his family? Could people say what they thought and felt in David's family?

■ DISCUSSION QUESTIONS

Simple/concrete questions:

Can you describe some things that are important to know about a person's family?

Can you describe your own family? List brothers and sisters, parents, and relatives.

Personal experience/feelings questions:

Do you like your family? Why or why not?

How often do you see your family?

To whom do you feel closest in your family? Who is most important to you in your family? Why?

What was your role in the family in which you grew up? How were you expected to act?

What were some of the things that your family members believed? What did your family think was important in life?

Have you suffered from any major family losses? Who? How do you feel about this?

If you could change your family in some way, what would you change?

Problem-solving questions:

What is a good way to deal with family problems?

If you are unhappy about something in your family, what should you do?

What are some different ways to deal with situations that you think are unfair in your family?

■ GROUP ACTIVITIES

Ask group members to give short descriptions of their families-of-origin.

Facilitate a discussion about various family stressors and ways that families deal with these.

Facilitate a discussion about different family boundaries, communication patterns, and uses of authority. Try to elicit group members' feelings about how these processes took place in their own families.

Form pairs in order to discuss personal family information.

■ ASSESSMENT OF SKILLS LEARNED

Describes personal family tree:

ALMOST NEVER	USUALLY NOT	SOMETIMES	USUALLY	ALMOST ALWAYS
1	2	3	4	5

Differentiates family of origin and current family situation if different:

ALMOST NEVER	USUALLY NOT	SOMETIMES	USUALLY	ALMOST ALWAYS
1	2	3	4	5

Understands concept of family boundaries:

ALMOST NEVER	USUALLY NOT	SOMETIMES	USUALLY	ALMOST ALWAYS
1	2	3	4	5

Recognizes family communication patterns:

ALMOST NEVER	USUALLY NOT	SOMETIMES	USUALLY	ALMOST ALWAYS
1	2	3	4	5

Identifies family values, roles, rules, and mythology:

ALMOST NEVER	USUALLY NOT	SOMETIMES	USUALLY	ALMOST ALWAYS
1	2	3	4	5

Recognizes family secrets:

ALMOST NEVER	USUALLY NOT	SOMETIMES	USUALLY	ALMOST ALWAYS
1	2	3	4	5

Identifies stresses and strains acting on family:

ALMOST NEVER	USUALLY NOT	SOMETIMES	USUALLY	ALMOST ALWAYS
1	2	3	4	5

Describes family member roles:

ALMOST NEVER	USUALLY NOT	SOMETIMES	USUALLY	ALMOST ALWAYS
1	2	3	4	55

Identifies family emotional tone:

ALMOST NEVER	USUALLY NOT	SOMETIMES	USUALLY	ALMOST ALWAYS
1	2	3	4	5

Describes family relationships with outsiders:

ALMOST NEVER	USUALLY NOT	SOMETIMES	USUALLY	ALMOST ALWAYS
1	2	3	4	5

Identifies major family member losses:

ALMOST NEVER	USUALLY NOT	SOMETIMES	USUALLY	ALMOST ALWAYS
1	2	3	4	5

29. Socialization

Socialization is crucial to self-esteem. Individuals only have identities to the extent to which they are either part of groups or can differentiate themselves from others. Group belongingness and individual self-differentiation occur in the context of social relationships. Persons with developmental disabilities often have more limited social networks than their peers. Consequently, the persons with whom they socialize take on a greater significance in their lives. This topic begins with the identification of the concept of a social experience. The facilitator should foster a discussion of different social areas, including family history, friendship patterns, relationships with neighbors, relationships with teachers/schoolmates, and other relationships such as babysitters/caretakers, boyfriends/girlfriends, relationship partners, workmates, acquaintances, and strangers. Group participants should be assisted in understanding why socialization is important. Advantages of socialization may be discussed, including safety/security, learning skill development, communication of important information, achieving a sense of belongingness/attachment to others, decreasing isolation/loneliness, enjoyment, sharing positive/negative life experiences, sharing burdens, giving help, releasing emotions, and sharing feelings. Individuals with mild and moderate developmental delay usually have no difficulty engaging in significant discussion about their socialization. Lower functioning persons may require modifications of more concrete yes/no questioning, use of pictures/symbols, and increased nonverbal communication strategies. They will not understand many of the concepts involved in this topic but can often identify important events connected with family, friends, and significant others.

■ SPECIFIC SKILLS TO BE LEARNED

Identify what is a social experience:
    Family history (parents, siblings, relatives, etc.)
    History of friendships
    Relationships with neighbors
    Relationships with teachers and schoolmates
    Caretakers and baby-sitters
    Boyfriends, girlfriends and relationship partners
    Work relationships
    Professional helpers (counselors, social workers, medical providers, etc.)
    Acquaintances and strangers

Identify why socialization is important:
>   Safety/security
>   Learning, education, development of skills, communication of important information
>   Sense of belonging/attachment to others, decreased loneliness/isolation
>   Enjoyment, sharing positive/negative experiences with others
>   Sharing burdens, support and help
>   Emotional release, sharing feelings

■ CONCEPTS NECESSARY TO PERFORM SKILLS

Socialize: Talk to others; get together with friends; tell people about one's life and ask about theirs; take an interest in people; do things with others; relate to people.

Social: Related to people; to do with relationships; talking to people; taking an interest in others; doing things with people; getting together with friends; rules about how to get along with others.

Relationship: Connection with somebody; when people know each other; to relate or do things with others; togetherness; family, friend, or acquaintance.

■ CASE VIGNETTES

—Patricia was a social isolate. She had no close friends. She usually sat by herself at the lunch table and worked quietly by herself at her job. Sometimes she wanted to make friends, but she did not know what to say. Patricia was afraid that others might not like her, so she kept to herself. She had been this way for many years. She had spent so much time by herself that she had no idea what other people liked to talk about. Sometimes she saw others happily talking to each other and wished she had more friends. Patricia would have liked to tell them about her work, about where she lived, and about her family. Last year her father had died of a heart attack. Now she lived with her mother, who was also quiet and shy. Neither Patricia nor her mother left the house very often. Her mother often told Patricia that she was afraid when Patricia did not come home right away after work.

Did Patricia have many social relationships? Did she socialize with people at work? Do you think she ever felt lonely? What could Patricia have done to improve her social relationships and make friends with others?

—Sol has many friends. He sees people at home, at work, and in the community. Everybody knows Sol. He came from a very talkative and friendly family. Now that he lives in his own apartment with two housemates, Sol carries on the family tradition. He and his housemates usually talk after work and when they eat supper together. They also do things together like going to the circus or out to eat. Sol goes to work fifteen minutes early so that he can talk to his friends in the cafeteria. He usually works with his friend Dave. Sol has a girlfriend whom he dates on weekends. Sometimes they go to movies. At other times they just stay home and watch videos. On Thursday night, Sol goes to a club, where he joins in different activities with his social group.

Does Sol have many social relationships? Do you think Sol is lonely? Why or why not? Why do you think other people like Sol?

■ DISCUSSION QUESTIONS

Simple/concrete questions:
>   What is a social experience?

Can you list some different types of social experiences?

Personal experience/feelings questions:

Do you have a family? Friends? Workmates? Schoolmates? Teachers? Supervisors? Counselors? Boyfriends? Girlfriends?

Describe your friends. What do you like to do with other people?

Do other people ever bother you? Why?

Do you like talking with others? Doing things with them? Why or why not?

Can you describe your own social history (history of different kinds of relationships with people)?

Problem-solving questions:

Why is it important to have social relationships?

If you have no friends or close social relationships, how can you develop them?

How can you meet other people?

What are some things that make it easier to socialize with others?

■ GROUP ACTIVITIES

Facilitate a discussion and sharing about individual social histories.

Divide into pairs to talk about specific aspects of each person's social history.

■ ASSESSMENT OF SKILLS LEARNED

Identifies one or more social experiences:

ALMOST NEVER	USUALLY NOT	SOMETIMES	USUALLY	ALMOST ALWAYS
1	2	3	4	5

Recognizes why socialization is important:

ALMOST NEVER	USUALLY NOT	SOMETIMES	USUALLY	ALMOST ALWAYS
1	2	3	4	5

30. *Nurturance*

It is impossible to develop a sense of self-esteem without nurturance. Nurturance is the love, concern, physical comfort, and emotional sustenance given to individuals by themselves and others. The group should begin with a discussion of the different components of nurturance, which include care from others, care for self, attention, affection, love, positive treatment, respect, and physical comfort. Next, the conversation may turn to each participant's personal sources of nurturance, which may include parents, siblings, relatives, friends, teachers, counselors, therapists, and other concerned persons. Finally, the focus can be on understanding how to influence others to provide nurturance. This may involve saying positive things to others, asking outright for attention/love/affection, avoiding criticism of oneself or others, and maintaining positive attitudes. It may also involve actions such as treating others with kindness, treating oneself well, and refraining from pushing others further away when attempting to gain their affection and attention. Individuals with mild and moderate developmental disabilities typically have no problem discussing these matters. Lower functioning individuals may require the increased specificity, concreteness, and nonverbal modifications utilized in earlier topics.

■ SPECIFIC SKILLS TO BE LEARNED

Identify the concept of nurturance:
    Being cared for by others
    Caring for oneself
    Attention
    Affection
    Love
    Being treated well
    Respect
    Physical comfort
Identify personal sources of nurturance:
    Parents, siblings, family
    Grandparents, relatives, extended family
    Friends
    Teachers, counselors, supervisors, therapists
    Other
Understand how to influence others to provide nurturance:
    Things one says:
        Saying positive things to others
        Asking for attention/love/affection
        Avoiding criticism of oneself/others
        Having a positive attitude
    Things one does:
        Treating others well (kindness)
        Treating oneself well
Not pushing others away in attempts to gain affection/attention

■ CONCEPTS NECESSARY TO PERFORM SKILLS

Nurturance: Love; affection; attention; care; kindness; comfort.
Attention: Look at somebody; talk to someone; be mindful of others; notice others; see some-one; listen; watch; look, listen and notice; take notice and remember what one is doing; notice what someone is saying; keep alert; be involved in something.
Affection: Kindness; consideration; to treat somebody well; feel for someone; love; feel good about someone and show it.
Love: Kindness; attention; affection; admiration; care for someone; nurturance.
Respect: Esteem; consideration; show others that you care about them; let people know that you care about how they think and feel; listen and pay attention to someone; treat others well.

■ CASE VIGNETTES

—Sandy feels that no one gives her any respect. She says that her father yells at her for no reason and her mother does not listen to her. When she is watching television, her little brother turns the channel without asking her. Sandy's father is gone at work all day. He comes home late at night, tired and crabby. He just wants to eat and watch television while he has his beer. If Sandy makes too much noise, he yells at her to be quiet. Sandy feels as though she is in the way at home. She likes to talk to her mother while she cleans the house, but her mother is too busy and tells Sandy to watch television or do something in her bedroom. Sometimes Sandy wonders if her parents love her. She tries hard to do what they say so that they will like her more. It never seems to be enough.

Do you think Sandy receives enough nurturance? Does she get enough love and affection? Is there anything she can do to get more attention from her parents? How do you think Sandy feels when she gets no respect from her family?

—Jack receives a lot of attention from others because he is very friendly and talkative. He says, "Hello," and greets everybody he sees. He was at work yesterday and finished forty-five boxes on the assembly line. That was a lot of boxes and Jack was very proud of his good job. When nobody noticed his work he went up to his supervisor and asked, "Did I do a good job today?" The supervisor answered, "Yes, Jack, you are a hard worker." Then Jack told the secretary about his good job. She also told him he was a good worker. Jack never said mean things to others, but often gave them compliments or said nice things to them.
—Do you think Jack gets enough nurturance? Does he get enough love and affection? Why or why not? Does Jack do anything that makes other people want to give him attention and nurturance?

■ DISCUSSION QUESTIONS

Simple/concrete questions:
>   What are some ways to show others that you care about them?
>   What is nurturance?
>   What are some different ways to get love, affection, and attention?

Personal experience/feelings questions:
>   Do you feel cared for? By whom?
>   From whom do you receive attention and affection?
>   To whom do you give love, attention, and affection?
>   How do (did) your parents take care of you?
>   How do you feel about how your family takes (took) care of you?

Problem-solving questions:
>   If others are not giving you enough love, attention, and affection, what can you do to get more of it?

■ GROUP ACTIVITIES

Facilitate a discussion about various sources of nurturance.
Hold a discussion about personal nurturing experiences.
Form pairs in order to share personal background related to nurturance.

■ ASSESSMENT OF SKILLS LEARNED

Understands the concept of nurturance:

ALMOST NEVER	USUALLY NOT	SOMETIMES	USUALLY	ALMOST ALWAYS
1	2	3	4	5

Identifies personal sources of nurturance:

ALMOST NEVER	USUALLY NOT	SOMETIMES	USUALLY	ALMOST ALWAYS
1	2	3	4	5

Lists one or more ways to influence others to provide nurturance:

ALMOST NEVER	USUALLY NOT	SOMETIMES	USUALLY	ALMOST ALWAYS
1	2	3	4	5

31. Guilt and Shame

The emotions of guilt and shame are at the opposite pole from positive self-esteem. These feelings often occur in individuals who do not feel good about themselves. Persons with developmental disabilities may experience transient feelings of guilt or may develop more deeply entrenched shame-based identities. They often have very little insight into these feelings.

This topic begins with a discussion of the nature of guilt and shame, identifying each emotion and how it develops. Guilt is usually associated with specific behavioral acts for which individuals feel guilty, whereas shame is a more generalized negative sentiment about oneself in which the person labels his or her entire self as "bad" or "unworthy." Guilt is a useful emotion, which lets us know that we must change certain behaviors; shame is a maladaptive emotion involving pervasive negative self-labeling that does not serve any useful purpose. Shame may develop when one receives chronic negative treatment from primary caretakers and family members. It may stem from physical or sexual abuse, yelling, swearing, excessive blame, and receiving messages of one sort or another that one is a "bad" person. Other precipitators are neglect, failure to meet basic needs, caretakers who do not listen or let individuals know they are important, being told that one is stupid or dumb, or being told to keep one's feelings to oneself. One or a few episodes of negative treatment are not usually consequential, but repeated shaming experiences may result in negative, shame-based identities, in which individuals feel inadequate and "no good."

Group members should learn about feelings that often accompany guilt and shame. These may include anger, fear, loneliness, isolation, and anxiety. Finally, a discussion can be held about how to overcome feelings of guilt and shame. These may include rehearsing positive self-affirmations, surrounding oneself with positive and supportive people, becoming more competent and successful at things, learning that one is a special person even if bad things happen to one, and learning not to blame oneself for the bad behaviors of other people. Conceptually, this is a very complex and difficult topic, but most individuals with mild and moderate developmental delay can understand the experiences of guilt and shame and can carry on adequate conversations about things that make them feel guilty or badly. Some individuals will share a great deal of personal pain when discussing this topic; others are much more restricted in their understanding and sharing. The topic is much more difficult for individuals with severe disabilities, who may or may not be able to participate with adaptations previously described in this chapter.

■ SPECIFIC SKILLS TO BE LEARNED

Understand emotions of guilt and shame:
    Guilt (feeling bad about doing something wrong)
    Shame (feeling like a totally "bad" person, inadequate, worthless, not good enough)
Understand how shame develops:
When others treat one badly (especially parents, caretakers, relatives):
    Physical or sexual abuse (touching without permission, hitting, slapping, threatening to hurt, etc.)
    Yelling or swearing
    Blaming for things which the person is not responsible
    Calling someone a bad person
    Neglecting and not taking care of a person's needs
    Not listening to somebody
    Not letting someone know he or she is important
    Calling someone "stupid," "dumb," "silly," etc.

Telling a person to keep his or her feelings to him- or herself
Understand feelings that accompany guilt/shame:
    Anger
    Fear
    Loneliness
    Isolation
    Anxiety
Learn ways to deal with guilt and shame:
    Positive self-affirmations (saying nice things to oneself)
    Surrounding oneself with positive and supportive people
    Learning to be more competent and successful at things
    Learning that one is a special person even if bad things happen
    Learning not to blame oneself for bad behavior of other people

■ CONCEPTS NECESSARY TO PERFORM SKILLS

Guilt: Feeling bad because one has done something wrong; a bad feeling that lets a person know that a behavior should be changed; a bad feeling resulting from a bad behavior.

Shame: Feeling like a "no-good" person; feeling as though one is "totally bad"; feeling inadequate; feeling "not good enough"; feeling like a disgrace.

■ CASE VIGNETTES

—*Juanita came from a large family. She always felt like she was the family scapegoat. That meant that she got blamed for everything. She was yelled at more than her brothers and sisters. When something went wrong in the family, she was the first one questioned. For example, last week Juanita's brother ate the beef stew mother wanted to make for the family dinner. Their mother yelled at Juanita and told her that if she had watched her brother more closely, he would not have eaten the stew. The mother said, "It's your fault, Juanita. You should pay attention to what your brother is doing." Another time, Juanita's father could not find his shoes. He swore at Juanita and called her a name because he thought she might have had something to do with his shoes getting lost. After many years of getting shamed and blamed by her parents, Juanita began to feel that she was a no-good person. She felt so low and awful that sometimes she wished she were dead.*

    Do you think Juanita felt guilty or shameful? Why or why not? How did she get to feel that way? Is there anything she could have done to feel better about herself?

—*Nikki came from a big, happy family. She was the oldest of five children. Ever since she was a baby, she knew that she was loved and cared for. Her mother and father told her how pretty she was. They let her know that she did a good job at school and tried hard to listen to her when she talked to them. Nikki felt safe, secure, and confident because she knew that even if she made a mistake, her parents would still love and care about her. She was a special person, even if she was not perfect.*

    Do you think Nikki felt guilty or shameful? Why or why not? What do you think Nikki's parents did to help her feel good about herself?

■ DISCUSSION QUESTIONS

Simple/concrete questions:
    What are some things about which a person might feel guilty?
    Should a person feel guilty if he or she lies? Cheats? Steals?

What is the difference between guilt and shame?

Personal experience/feelings questions:

Have you ever felt guilty (felt bad about something you did)?

Have you ever felt shameful (felt like a totally bad person)?

Has anybody ever yelled at you? How did you feel?

Has anybody ever hit you? How did you feel?

Has anybody ever sworn at you? How did you feel?

Has anybody ever touched you in ways that you did not want to be touched? How did you feel?

Problem-solving questions:

If you are feeling guilty about something, what would be a good way to feel better?

If you are feeling shameful and inadequate, what should you do in order to feel better about yourself?

■ GROUP ACTIVITIES

Facilitate a discussion about personal experiences with guilt and shame.

Hold a discussion about the distinction between guilt and shame.

Brainstorm and problem-solve different ways to deal with guilt and shame.

■ ASSESSMENT OF SKILLS LEARNED

Understands emotions of guilt and shame:

ALMOST NEVER	USUALLY NOT	SOMETIMES	USUALLY	ALMOST ALWAYS
1	2	3	4	5

Recognizes events that lead to the development of shame:

ALMOST NEVER	USUALLY NOT	SOMETIMES	USUALLY	ALMOST ALWAYS
1	2	3	4	5

Recognizes feelings that accompany guilt and shame:

ALMOST NEVER	USUALLY NOT	SOMETIMES	USUALLY	ALMOST ALWAYS
1	2	3	4	5

Lists one or more ways to deal with guilt and shame:

ALMOST NEVER	USUALLY NOT	SOMETIMES	USUALLY	ALMOST ALWAYS
1	2	3	4	5

32. Positive Self-Affirmations

Positive self-affirmations are phrases that individuals can say to themselves to practice thinking positive thoughts about themselves. These represent the opposite extreme from the emotions of guilt and shame. Positive self-statements affirm the good qualities of a person. Rehearsing positive self-statements out loud leads to increased spontaneous thinking of positive self-thoughts. This in turn gives rise to enhanced self-esteem. In this case, positive behaviors lead to positive thoughts, which lead to positive feelings. Individuals with developmental disabilities often have rather vague self-thoughts, many of them more negative than positive. At the outset of this topic, the concept of a self-affirmation is explained and participants are encouraged to generate several positive self-statements. The group leader and individual members should help others develop their lists of positive self-statements. Next, members are encouraged to rehearse their lists in front of the others. Fellow participants are encouraged to add to each individual's list by giving them compliments, which they may convert into additional positive self-affirmations. Finally, participants are told that they can learn through practice to think positive thoughts and to direct their minds away from negative thoughts. This section is understood by those with mild and moderate developmental disabilities. It can be modified for lower functioning persons by focusing on more concrete self-affirmations and utilizing a yes/no questioning process—for example: "Do you like your pretty hair? You have very pretty hair." "Do you like to help others? You are very helpful." Later, these questions and statements can be paired with pictures or symbols, such as one person helping another, or someone with distinctive hair. For more intellectually limited individuals, positive self-statements will often need to be abbreviated—for example: "Me good," "My hair nice," "Me good worker," "I happy," "Me come school on time." Combining positive self-statements with external compliments reinforces the affirming value of each statement.

■ SPECIFIC SKILLS TO BE LEARNED

Identify: What are positive self-affirmations?

> I am smart.
> I am a good cook.
> I am an on-time person.
> I am a good worker.
> I am a friendly person.
> I am a kind person.
> I have a good sense of humor.
> I get along well with others.
> I am good at helping myself.
> I am an independent person.
> I am a considerate person.
> I am a helpful person.
> I am a good talker.
> I am a nice person.
> I am a patient person.
> I am a good person.
> I am a healthy person.
> I am a happy person.
> I am an important person.

Utilize positive self-affirmations.

Learn to think positive thoughts and direct one's mind away from negative thoughts.

■ CONCEPTS NECESSARY TO PERFORM SKILLS

Self-affirmation: Say something nice about oneself; think a positive thought about oneself; say something that is good about yourself; talk about a happy thought or feeling.

Positive: Good; having desirable qualities; agreeable; pleasant; helpful; worthwhile.

Negative: Bad; having undesirable qualities; disagreeable; unpleasant; not helpful; not worthwhile.

■ CASE VIGNETTES

—*Dick was a very negative thinker. He often thought about all of the bad things that might happen to him. He was in a wheelchair and often apologized for getting in someone's way, even when he was not. He frequently apologized about his behavior, saying, "I'm sorry if I'm not talking loud enough," or "I'm sorry if I'm not doing this right." Dick worried about everything. If it started to thunder, he thought he would get hit by lightning. If it got cold outside, he thought he would freeze. Dick worried that he was not smart enough. He thought he would be late to his program even when he was on time. He felt he was not funny enough for others. Dick thought most people did not like him. He was afraid to do things by himself because he thought he would do a bad job. Dick did not like himself very much and thought he just was not a good enough person.*

Was Dick a positive or negative thinker? How could he have used positive self-affirmations to learn how to feel better about himself?

—Yvonne was a positive thinker. She worked hard and felt good about her work. She knew she was smart because she could do the things she needed to do. When she made a mistake, she did not blame herself too much. She just said, "I'm sorry, I'll try to do better next time." Then she forgot about it. She believed she had a good personality because she got along well with others. Yvonne liked her pretty brown hair and the clothes she wore. She was friendly and considerate of others, and she knew it. She liked herself and thought that she was an O.K. person.

Why do you think Yvonne liked herself? Do you think she used positive self-affirmations? Why or why not?

■ DISCUSSION QUESTIONS

Simple/concrete questions:
>   What are some positive things that people can say to themselves?
>   What are some negative things that persons often say to themselves?

Personal experience/feelings questions:
>   What do you like about yourself? Why?
>   How do you feel about yourself? Why?
>   How do you feel when you say nice things about yourself?
>   How do you feel when you say bad things about yourself?

Problem-solving questions:
>   How can you learn to feel better about yourself?
>   Does it help you to sit and think about all the bad things which are happening in your life?

■ GROUP ACTIVITIES

Take turns verbalizing positive self-affirmations in front of the group.
Encourage group members to help their peers make lists of positive self-statements.
Form pairs and recite positive self-affirmations.

■ ASSESSMENT OF SKILLS LEARNED

Understands the concept of a positive self-affirmation:

ALMOST NEVER	USUALLY NOT	SOMETIMES	USUALLY	ALMOST ALWAYS
1	2	3	4	5

States several positive self-affirmations:

ALMOST NEVER	USUALLY NOT	SOMETIMES	USUALLY	ALMOST ALWAYS
1	2	3	4	5

Demonstrates the ability to direct mind away from negative thoughts:

ALMOST NEVER	USUALLY NOT	SOMETIMES	USUALLY	ALMOST ALWAYS
1	2	3	4	5

33. Wellness

Wellness is a term used to describe the positive functioning of individuals with respect to personal, social, and environmental contexts. Wellness is indirectly related to self-esteem in that it creates the underlying conditions from which self-esteem may develop. Areas of wellness are important to individuals with developmental delay just as they are consequential to others. Physical wellness includes sleep, nutrition, and exercise. Intellectual wellness involves positive thinking about oneself, others, the world, and one's future. Emotional wellness includes self- and other-esteem. Familial wellness involves supportive relationships with parents, siblings, and extended family members. Social wellness stems from positive relationships with friends, acquaintances, and other persons in general. Occupational wellness develops from productive life activities including hobbies, interests, self-improvement endeavors, schooling, and employment. Spiritual wellness comes from a belief in something greater than oneself, whether this is a religious belief or general values/beliefs about the world and one's place in it. Persons with mild and moderate developmental disabilities find this topic engaging and not overly difficult. Individuals with more severe developmental disabilities may understand the concept of physical wellness or sickness, but have more difficulty with the other, more abstract categories of wellness. The use of pictures/symbols, yes/no questions, and gestural/nonverbal communication may be useful for lower functioning individuals. These modifications can work well in the more concrete areas of wellness. For example, when talking about the need for sleep, the facilitator may point to a picture of a sleeping person. Or when talking about work, one may point to the picture or symbol of someone working.

■ SPECIFIC SKILLS TO BE LEARNED

Identify seven areas of wellness:
  Physical (body):
    Sleep
    Nutrition (healthful eating habits)
    Exercise
  Intellectual (thoughts):
    Positive thoughts about oneself
    Positive thoughts about others
    Positive thoughts about the world
    Positive thoughts about the future
  Emotional (feelings):
    Positive feelings about oneself (self-esteem)
    Positive feelings toward others (other-esteem)
  Familial (family relationships):
    Supportive relationships with parents and siblings
    Supportive relationships with relatives and extended family
  Social (relationships with people in general):
    Positive relationships with friends, acquaintances, co-workers, etc. (affective involvement)

Sense of belongingness and connectedness with others
Occupational (work):
Productive life activity:
Hobbies/interests
Self-improvement
Schooling
Employment
Belief in something greater than oneself:
Positive beliefs about the world and one's place in it
Security through recognizing a power greater than oneself

■ CONCEPTS NECESSARY TO PERFORM SKILLS

Physical: To do with a person's body; something one can see, touch or feel; concrete; something that has substance; rules about whom, when, and how to touch.

Intellectual: To do with thoughts; a person's thinking; rules about a person's thoughts and how to express them.

Emotional: To do with feelings; a person's emotions; rules about who has what feelings and how to express them.

Familial: A family relationship; to do with family; something about one's family; oneself, parents, brothers, sisters, grandparents, and one's entire family.

Social: Related to people; to do with relationships; talking to people; taking an interest in others; doing things with people; getting together with friends; rules about how to get along with others.

Occupational: Related to work; things related to jobs, hobbies, schoolwork, and productive activities; things done to improve oneself.

Spiritual: Related to beliefs and values; what one thinks is important in life; a belief in something greater than oneself; something having to do with the meaning of life; what is important to a person.

■ CASE VIGNETTES

—Margaret was in rough shape. She was not a well person. Her body was often sick. For example, last week she had a cold and this week her diabetes was acting up. She had many bad thoughts about herself and the future. She also had many awful feelings. She was afraid that she would need to go to the hospital again, and she was scared about doing her job well. Sometimes her hands, arms, and mouth would quiver and shake. This was partly because of her medicine but partly because she was so nervous. Margaret had very little contact with her family. They only saw her on Christmas and Easter. Even then, she might see only her mother and sister. Sometimes Margaret felt very lonely because others did not seem to care about her. She had no close friends. The only people she saw regularly were her psychiatrist and her social worker. Margaret used to have a job, but she no longer worked full time. She worked only a few hours per week when she was able. She usually sat around the house watching television. Sometimes she was afraid to go out. Margaret used to go to church but no longer went there because she was afraid she would fall on the sidewalk and hurt herself.

In what ways was Margaret not a very well person? What could she have done to increase her wellness?

—José is quite a well young man. His body feels good because he eats the right food, exercises, and gets enough sleep. He thinks good thoughts about himself and others, usually looking on the bright side of bad situations. For example, when he lost his wallet, he said, "I'm sure

someone will find it and turn it in" José has many happy feelings about his family, work, and friends. He sees different family members once every two weeks, and does things with his friends almost every day. He has finished his job training program and now works fifteen hours per week at a restaurant washing dishes. José believes that he was put on this earth for a purpose, and he feels that he has a special place in the world.

In what ways is José a well person? Why do you suppose he is such a well person?

■ DISCUSSION QUESTIONS

Simple/concrete questions:

What are some areas of wellness?

What does it mean to have a healthy body? Thoughts? Feelings? Family relationships? Relationships with others? Work life? Spirituality?

Personal experience/feelings questions:

Do you have a healthy life in the area of (physical, intellectual, emotional, familial, social, occupational, spiritual) needs?

Problem-solving questions:

How can a person improve his or her wellness in _____ (the above seven areas?)

■ GROUP ACTIVITIES

Group members share self-perceptions of wellness in the seven areas.

Form pairs to discuss specific areas of wellness.

Facilitate a discussion about wellness and illness as this relates to different areas of group members' lives.

■ ASSESSMENT OF SKILLS LEARNED

Identifies several areas of wellness:

ALMOST NEVER	USUALLY NOT	SOMETIMES	USUALLY	ALMOST ALWAYS
1	2	3	4	5

States several ways to increase wellness:

ALMOST NEVER	USUALLY NOT	SOMETIMES	USUALLY	ALMOST ALWAYS
1	2	3	4	5

34. *Physical and Mental Energy*

It is difficult to feel good about oneself without having sufficient physical and mental energy. This topic explores the reasons for physical and mental tiredness versus energy. The topic applies equally well to those with and without developmental disabilities. The group leader should begin by examining physical and mental sources of energy. A detailed discussion identifying reasons for physical/mental tiredness should follow. Physical causes of tiredness may include insufficient sleep, overwork, inadequate diet, lack of exercise, health problems, medications and weather conditions. Mental causes may include stress (life demands), anxiety, worry, sadness, grief, losses, depression, unhappiness, loneliness, boredom, thinking negative thoughts, and harboring negative feelings about oneself. Equal attention should then be given to the identification of methods to combat tiredness. These may include getting enough sleep, working in moderation, eating healthy foods in reasonable amounts, exercise, engaging in fun/

interesting activities, reducing life changes, socializing, letting go of worries and bad feelings, redirecting negative thoughts, actively focusing on positive thinking, working on specific goal achievements, and sharing natural positive feelings with others. Most of these concepts can be understood by individuals with mild and moderate developmental delay. Lower functioning persons may grasp the more concrete concepts if accompanied by pictures, symbols, gestures, and yes/no clarifying questions.

■ SPECIFIC SKILLS TO BE LEARNED

Identify physical and mental sources of energy.
Identify reasons for physical and mental tiredness:
    Physical:
        Lack of sleep
        Overwork
        Poor diet (unhealthful foods, over/undereating, lack of nutrients/vitamins, etc.)
        Lack of exercise
        Health problems
        Medications
        Weather conditions (hot, humid, dreary, etc.)
    Mental:
        Stress (environmental changes and demands)
        Anxiety, worry and nervousness
        Sadness, grief, and loss
        Depression, despondency, despair, unhappiness
        Helplessness and hopelessness
        Loneliness and boredom
        Thinking negative thoughts
        Negative feelings about oneself
Identify methods to combat tiredness:
    Get enough sleep.
    Work in moderation.
    Eat healthful foods in reasonable amounts.
    Exercise (at least thirty minutes, three to four times per week).
    Do what one would like to do (fun and interesting activities).
    Manage one's life to reduce total life changes (avoid stress overload).
    Socialize with others.
    Let go of worries, anxieties, and bad feelings.
    Redirect negative thoughts.
    Actively focus on positive thinking.
    Set goals and work toward their achievement.
    Let one's natural positive feelings come out (share positive feelings with others).

■ CONCEPTS NECESSARY TO PERFORM SKILLS

Physical: To do with a person's body; something one can see, touch or feel; concrete; something that has substance; rules about who, when and how to touch.
Mental: To do with one's mind; thinking; what happens in somebody's head.
Energy: Enthusiasm; what makes a person feel excited; vigor; life; vitality; high spirits; get-up-and-go; pep, vim and vigor.

■ CASE VIGNETTES

—Bill was a tired person. When he sat at the table, he slumped in his chair. His head hung down and his eyes closed. No one was sure if he was asleep or awake. René nudged him to find out if he was awake. Bill lifted his head for a moment and then put it back down, almost like a turtle. Bill did not get much sleep at night, yet he worked eight hours every day. By the end of the day, his feet were dragging. Bill had a problem with his kidneys and needed to be hooked up to a special machine at night. He was a worrier, and this made him more tired. He did not think very good thoughts about himself and was always on the lookout for something bad to happen. Outside of work, Bill got no exercise. He did not socialize much with others and did not do many activities. He just sat in his favorite chair and watched television.

Was Bill an energetic person? Did he have much energy? What could Bill have done to get more energy?

—Madeline has a lot of energy. She can be heard all the way down the hallway because of her high-pitched, energetic voice. She eats healthful meals, gets eight hours of sleep each night, and works hard all day. After work, she plays softball and goes to crafts class. She likes to be active and do things with her friends. They often go out to movies and restaurants. Madeline is excited to do new things and is always looking forward to some new experience.

Is Madeline an energetic person? Does she have much energy? Why or why not?

■ DISCUSSION QUESTIONS

Simple/concrete questions:
> What are some physical and mental sources of tiredness?
> What are some possible sources of energy and enthusiasm?

Personal experience/feelings questions:
> Have you ever felt tired? What makes you feel tired?
> Have you ever felt physically or mentally down but then felt more energetic (gotten your second wind)?
> Do you like to spend time with other people who feel very tired?
> How do you think other people feel about spending time with you when you are very tired?

Problem-solving questions:
> How can a person develop more energy?

■ GROUP ACTIVITIES

Share individual experiences of physical and mental tiredness.
Share experiences of high energy and enthusiasm.
Facilitate a discussion about different sources of physical/mental tiredness and energy.

■ ASSESSMENT OF SKILLS LEARNED

Identifies physical and mental sources of energy:

ALMOST NEVER	USUALLY NOT	SOMETIMES	USUALLY	ALMOST ALWAYS
1	2	3	4	5

Identifies several reasons for physical/mental tiredness:

ALMOST NEVER	USUALLY NOT	SOMETIMES	USUALLY	ALMOST ALWAYS
1	2	3	4	5

States several methods to combat tiredness:

ALMOST NEVER	USUALLY NOT	SOMETIMES	USUALLY	ALMOST ALWAYS
1	2	3	4	5

5 *Problem Solving and Conflict Management*

THIS CHAPTER ADDRESSES areas of problem solving and conflict management. The specific topics discussed represent some of the most common categories of difficulty for which individuals with developmental disabilities are referred for psychotherapy and behavioral treatment. The chapter begins with general discussions related to problem solving and decision making. These are followed by a variety of specific skill areas, including asking for help, getting help for personal problems, following directions, keeping on task, and giving and receiving constructive criticism. Next, conflicts with housemates, family, and friends are examined. The two succeeding topics are particularly important to reducing conflicts in the workplace. These include dealing with negative gossip, teasing and false accusations, and staying out of others' problems. The final topic of how to deal with mistreatment from others explores some of the more adaptive ways with which to deal with genuine negative treatment from others.

35. *Problem Solving*

Problem-solving limitations are of central concern to those with developmental disabilities. Faced with a wider than usual array of problems, persons with developmental delay are intellectually, and otherwise, less well equipped to deal with these problems. The group facilitator should begin with definitions of different types of problems, including disagreements between people, insufficient money for specific purchases, inaccessible help for particular tasks, unavailability of others with whom to engage in activities, lack of transportation for activities, and so forth. Next, specific elements of conflict can be shared. These may include two individuals competing for something in limited supply, someone taking offense at the behavior or words of another, two individuals having different ideas or feelings about how something should be done, one person feeling that another is blocking his or her goal achievement, and so on. Participants should be encouraged to identify their feelings about problems and to explore possible alternatives to solve them. This process may include listing several ways to solve a problem, asking others to generate solutions, and brainstorming a number of possible solutions, even if they are not one's first choice. Finally, the leader should encourage group members to decide on, and choose, good solutions from those available in any given situation. This topic is appropriate for persons with mild and sometimes moderate developmental disabilities. Lower functioning individuals will require simplified language, visual assists, and a format that lends itself to yes/no questioning.

■ SPECIFIC SKILLS TO BE LEARNED

Define different types of problems:
    Having disagreements with people
    Having too little money to buy something
    Needing help with a task
    Wanting to do something with someone who is unavailable
    Wanting to go somewhere but not having transportation
Identify the concept of a conflict:
    Two people want something that is in limited supply.
    Someone takes offense at something somebody says or does.
    Two people have different ideas or feelings about how something should be done.
    A person feels that someone else is in the way of goal achievement.
Identify feelings about a problem:
Think of possible alternatives to solve a problem:
    List several ways to deal with a problem.
    Ask others to help think of possible solutions to a problem.
    List possible solutions even if they are not one's first choice.
    Decide on a good solution to a problem.

■ CONCEPTS NECESSARY TO PERFORM SKILLS

Problem: Conflict; puzzle; disagreement with somebody; when a person needs help; an argument with somebody; when someone or something gets in one's way.

Conflict: Problem; disagreement; argument; when a person sees something differently than someone else does and becomes upset about it.

Solution: The answer to a problem; when a person gets rid of a problem; when a person's problem goes away.

Alternative: One possible choice; something a person may pick or choose; one of the different choices someone can make; one way to do things; one way to solve a problem; one of several things that will make a problem go away; solution; answer.

Disagreement: When two people fight; when two individuals have different ideas about what to do; when people each have different answers to a problem; when someone argues or yells at somebody else.

■ CASE VIGNETTES

—*Tom was a poor problem solver. One day he needed more money to buy music tapes. When Tom's residence counselor told him he did not have enough money in his checkbook, Tom threw his Walkman across the room. After that, he needed even more money to buy a new Walkman as well as to purchase some new tapes. If Tom had thought about it more carefully, he would have known that payday was the next day and he would then have had enough money to buy his tapes. Tom often acted before he thought about situations, and then his problems became worse.*

    What could Tom have done differently to solve his problem? Do you think it was a good idea for him to throw his Walkman across the room? Why or why not?

—Georgette was a good problem solver. One day she did not have a ride to her evening crafts class. Instead of becoming angry or upset, she asked her group home counselor for a ride. Her counselor could not give her a ride because there was only one staff person on duty and she had to stay with the other residents. Next, Georgette called her sister, but she was busy doing something else. Finally, Georgette decided to take the bus, but first she had to call the bus company to find out about the bus schedule. She asked her residence counselor for help, and the counselor helped her to make the call. Georgette got to the crafts class on time and had a lot of fun.

Was Georgette a good problem solver? Did she think of more than one way to solve her problem? Do you think it helped her to stay calm and keep trying to find a ride? Why or why not?

■ DISCUSSION QUESTIONS

Simple/concrete questions:
>   What are some different kinds of problems?
>   Is there ever more than one way to solve a problem? Give an example?
>   What is a conflict?
>   Can a person have a conflict without another person with whom to disagree?

Personal experience/feelings questions:
>   Have you ever had a problem? Describe your problem?
>   Have you ever had a conflict with another person? What happened?
>   Do you have any problems right now? Describe them?
>   How do you feel when you have problems or conflicts?

Problem-solving questions:
>   What should you do if you have trouble solving a problem?
>   How can you prevent problems and conflicts from happening? Give an example?

■ GROUP ACTIVITIES

Facilitate a discussion about current problems of individual group members, and brainstorm possible solutions.

Each person share one major life problem and current/past attempts to deal with the problem.

Facilitate a discussion about different types of problems and conflicts which require different types of solutions.

■ ASSESSMENT OF SKILLS LEARNED

Lists different types of problems:

ALMOST NEVER	USUALLY NOT	SOMETIMES	USUALLY	ALMOST ALWAYS
1	2	3	4	5

Identifies what is a conflict:

ALMOST NEVER	USUALLY NOT	SOMETIMES	USUALLY	ALMOST ALWAYS
1	2	3	4	5

States personal feelings about a problem:

ALMOST NEVER	USUALLY NOT	SOMETIMES	USUALLY	ALMOST ALWAYS
1	2	3	4	5

States more than one possible alternative to solve a problem:

ALMOST NEVER	USUALLY NOT	SOMETIMES	USUALLY	ALMOST ALWAYS
1	2	3	4	5

Picks one of several possible solutions to a problem:

ALMOST NEVER	USUALLY NOT	SOMETIMES	USUALLY	ALMOST ALWAYS
1	2	3	4	5

36. Making Decisions

Making a decision is often the end point to problem-solving activity. This topic explores the elements involved in making decisions. Individuals with developmental disabilities tend to be relatively more limited in their personal choices and decisions because of their more protected status and intellectual limitations. For them, making decisions is often very confusing. The group leader should assist participants in understanding the concept of a decision and what it means to decide something. It can be highlighted that a decision requires a choice, often forcing an individual to pick between two or more alternatives. Group participants may be taught to list possible alternatives and to rule out choices that do not make as much sense as others. They should be encouraged to practice making choices that they feel represent the best alternatives in given situations. A discussion can be conducted about various stressors associated with decisions. These may include missing the opportunity to make other good or acceptable choices, choosing the least bad of two alternatives (e.g., washing the dishes or sweeping the floor), losing out on one option by choosing another (e.g., drinking soda pop or fruit juice), experiencing anxiety associated with a good alternative (e.g., desire to go to the movies but fear of getting lost on the bus), and not always being free to make the choice one would most like because of monetary and other resource limitations. Finally, the importance of making commitments (choices) and following through on decisions should be emphasized. This topic is conceptually more difficult than many others and is most appropriate for individuals with mild developmental disabilities. Lower functioning persons can certainly learn to make simple decisions and choices but will need more concrete options, higher levels of external structure, more detailed explanations about options, and possibly nonverbal channels of communication with more simple yes/no response options.

■ SPECIFIC SKILLS TO BE LEARNED

Understand what is a decision (what it means to decide something).
Recognize what it means to make a choice (pick between different alternatives).
List alternatives in a decision-making process (some possible choices).
Be able to rule out less good alternatives (rule out choices that do not make as much sense as other choices)
Make a selection of the best alternative in a specific situation (arrive at the best choice).
Identify different types of decisions.
Recognize various stressors associated with decisions:
  When all choices are very desirable (e.g., choosing cookies, cake, or ice cream)
  When no choices seem pleasant (e.g., do your work or lose your job)
  Choosing between bad alternatives (e.g., either washing the dishes or sweeping the floor)
  Losing out on one option by choosing another (e.g., either going to a movie or going out for pizza)
  Fear/anxiety associated with difficult decisions (e.g., desire to go to the movies but fear of getting lost on the bus)
  Not always being free to make the choice one would really like (various constraints related to other people and resources)

Recognize the importance of following through on decisions/choices, and making the best of a situation (commitment).

■ CONCEPTS NECESSARY TO PERFORM SKILLS

Decision: Deciding something; making a choice; picking one thing or another; doing one thing or another; doing this or that; picking this or that; making up one's mind.

Choice: Choosing something; picking something; deciding something; picking one thing or another; doing one thing or another; selecting something; making up one's mind.

Alternative: One possible choice; something a person may pick or choose; one of the different choices someone can make; one way to do things; one way to solve a problem; one of several things that will make a problem go away; solution; answer.

Option: An alternative; a choice someone can make; one way to decide something; one possible pick.

Commitment: Making a decision to do something and then doing it; making a choice and staying with it; keeping on doing something that one has chosen to do; not giving up; not changing one's mind; staying with what you decide.

■ CASE VIGNETTES

—Carlis could not decide if she should go to the picnic or stay home. She wanted to go partly because there would be a lot of fun, games, and good food at the picnic, but she was afraid because she did not like riding the bus alone, and she had no one to give her a ride. The more she thought about it, the more she thought she would like to go, but she was not sure she wanted to pay the five dollar cost for the food. One reason she thought she might like to go was that her friend Melanie would be there; but she was nervous because Bill would be there too, and he was sometimes mean to her. As she continued to think about it, she became more confused. She spent several days thinking about the picnic. When she finally decided to go, Carlis found out that it was too late. The sign-up sheet had been collected the day before, and she had missed her chance to go to the picnic.

Was Carlis a good decision maker? Why or why not? What could she have done differently to be a better decision maker?

—Farshad was a good decision maker. He seemed to know what he wanted. When he went to a restaurant with his friend Jacob, the waiter asked, "How can I help you?" Farshad knew there were many good things to eat on the menu, but he replied, "Give me a cheeseburger, french fries, and a large chocolate milkshake." Jacob did not know what he wanted and took a long time deciding. Later, the two were watching television. Jacob was not sure what to watch, but Farshad said, "I like to watch football," so that's what they watched. Sometimes his choices were more difficult—for example, the time his mother told him he could either carry out the garbage or sweep the floor. He did not like to do either, but he picked the garbage because it was quicker.

Why do you think Farshad was a good decision maker? Did he make decisions and choices even when they were difficult? Did he waste much time when he was deciding things? Did he know how to choose between different alternatives?

■ DISCUSSION QUESTIONS

Simple/concrete questions:

List some different kinds of decisions.

What are some things that are stressful about making decisions and choices?

Personal experience/feelings questions:

What are some easy decisions for you? Difficult decisions?

Describe a difficult choice that.you have had to make during your lifetime? Why?

How do you feel when you make a difficult choice?

Have you ever felt bad about a decision or choice you have made?

Have you ever changed your mind about an important decision? Why?

Have you ever had trouble making a choice because you were afraid of what would happen?

Problem-solving questions:

What would help a person to make good choices?

If someone is having trouble making a decision, how can he or she get help to make a good decision?

When a person has a hard decision to make, is it a good idea to leave the decision to someone else? Why or why not?

■ GROUP ACTIVITIES

Ask each person about typical life decisions and choices that must be made on a daily basis. Include such decisions as what to eat, wear, do, and the like.

Ask each participant to share one difficult life decision or choice.

Present individual group members with particular decisions and ask them how they would go about making those decisions.

Entire group give positive and negative feedback to individual members about particular decisions.

■ ASSESSMENT OF SKILLS LEARNED

Understands what is a decision:

ALMOST NEVER	USUALLY NOT	SOMETIMES	USUALLY	ALMOST ALWAYS
1	2	3	4	5

Recognizes that making a choice involves picking between alternatives:

ALMOST NEVER	USUALLY NOT	SOMETIMES	USUALLY	ALMOST ALWAYS
1	2	3	4	5

Lists possible alternative choices in a decision-making process:

ALMOST NEVER	USUALLY NOT	SOMETIMES	USUALLY	ALMOST ALWAYS
1	2	3	4	5

Rules out less desirable alternatives in a decision-making process:

ALMOST NEVER	USUALLY NOT	SOMETIMES	USUALLY	ALMOST ALWAYS
1	2	3	4	5

Identifies different types of decisions:

ALMOST NEVER	USUALLY NOT	SOMETIMES	USUALLY	ALMOST ALWAYS
1	2	3	4	5

Recognizes one or more stressors associated with decisions:

ALMOST NEVER	USUALLY NOT	SOMETIMES	USUALLY	ALMOST ALWAYS
1	2	3	4	5

Follows through on decisions/choices:

ALMOST NEVER	USUALLY NOT	SOMETIMES	USUALLY	ALMOST ALWAYS
1	2	3	4	5

37. Asking for Help

Asking for help is often a crucial element in solving problems because individuals cannot always solve or eliminate their own problems. This is particularly true of individuals with developmental disabilities because they generally have fewer intellectual, monetary, and other resources at their disposal. Persons who are good at soliciting assistance are able to solve a wider range of problems with less effort than individuals with less skill in this area. The group leader should begin with a short discussion of the importance of asking for help. The remaining focus should be on ways to solicit help in different situations. Some situations calling for help include wanting directions, dealing with threats from others, desiring assistance at a job, requiring school help, trying to remember things, getting hurt, being in a fire emergency, having household emergencies, losing a pet, and needing transportation to events. Because these areas are rather concrete, the topic can be easily presented to those with mild and moderate developmental disabilities. It can also be modified using more simple choices, pictorial diagrams, gestures, sign communication, and increased external structure, for individuals with more severe disabilities.

■ SPECIFIC SKILLS TO BE LEARNED

Recognize how to get directions:
    Whom to ask (e.g., parent, family member, friend, police, stranger)
    When to ask
Understand how to get help if lost:
    Call home.
    Ask the bus driver.
    Call the police.
    Ask a restaurant manager or shopkeeper.
    Carry identification, address, and telephone number.
Understand possible alternatives if threatened:
    Walking/running away
    Screaming
    Calling police
    Contacting social worker, counselor, or friend
Recognize possible means of help in a job situation:
    Co-worker
    Supervisor
Understand possible sources of help when trying new things:
    Teacher/instructor
    Peer
    Watching someone else
Recognize ways to help remember things:
    Ask for reminder.
    Write it down.
Recognize possible sources of help if hurt:
    Anyone at the scene
    Emergency telephone numbers
    Nurse/doctor
Recognize sources of help in case of a fire:
    Emergency telephone numbers
    Fire department

People at the scene
Understand what to do if a burglar comes into one's home:
    Call the police.
    Call for help.
    Get out.
Recognize what to do in case of the loss of a pet:
    Ask neighbors.
    Call the humane society.
    Have friends help you look.
Recognize what to do if needing a ride:
    Ask caretaker, parent, or counselor.
    Take a city bus.
    Take special transportation.
Recognize an alternative to lifting something that is very heavy:
    Ask for help.

■ CONCEPTS NECESSARY TO PERFORM SKILLS

Help: Do something for somebody; share the work; work with somebody so that the person can get the job done faster; do things for others that they cannot do for themselves; assist someone.

Threaten: Say one will hurt another; try to hurt someone; do something to scare somebody; intimidate.

Directions: Telling somebody which way to go; telling someone how to get somewhere; telling a person what to do; giving instructions; letting a person know how to do something.

■ CASE VIGNETTES

—*Whoopie often liked to take the city bus to visit her friend. She was usually good at reading the bus schedule but sometimes became confused. One day she took the 4A bus when she was supposed to take the 4B. Soon she noticed that the bus had turned the wrong way and she did not recognize the neighborhood anymore. Whoopie did not panic. She walked to the front of the bus and asked the driver for help. He said, "No problem, just stay on the bus and we'll soon be back in your neighborhood. Then you can take another bus."*

Do you think Whoopie did a good job asking for help? Should she have gotten off the bus when she noticed that she was in the wrong neighborhood? Why or why not?

—*Greg was good at asking for help. When he got out of bed on Saturday he asked his room-mate, Bob, how to get to the new drugstore. Bob explained that it was only one block away from the old one that had burned down four months ago. After he walked to the drugstore, he stopped to mail a letter at the post office. Greg asked the clerk in which box to drop the letter so that it would get there most quickly. On his way home, a stranger asked him for some money. When he said, "No, it's my money," the man asked him again. So Greg walked to the nearest corner, where he saw a police officer and asked for help. The police officer sent the other man away and told him not to come back. Greg knew that if he would not have seen the police officer, he could have called 911 for help. That was one reason he always kept some extra money in his pocket. Later that day, Greg was raking the yard but his rake broke. He told his residence counselor about it, and he said that he would help Greg get a new one next week. In the meantime, he borrowed one from a neighbor.*

Do you think Greg was good at asking for help? Why or why not? For what kinds of help did he ask?

—Laurie was a nervous person. She often took the bus by herself to the YMCA. One day she got on the bus, but it was the wrong one. She did not know what to do when she recognized that she was in a strange neighborhood. So she just sat there, mile after mile. She kept hoping to see a familiar place, but she did not recognize anything. She did not ask the bus driver for help because she was afraid. She thought that he might be upset if she bothered him. She also did not ask any of the other passengers because she did not know them. Finally, afterLaurie had ridden the bus for several hours and seen most of the other people get off, the bus driver noticed her. He asked her where she was going and she told him. He said, "We're a long way from there. I think you got on the wrong bus." Laurie agreed that it was the wrong bus and said she did not know what to do. He stopped and called her foster home, because she had the telephone number in her purse. Then he took her back to the bus station, where her foster provider picked her up. By then, it was very late.

Was Laurie good at asking for help? What could she have done differently to get help sooner?

■ DISCUSSION QUESTIONS

Simple/concrete questions:
>What are some different kinds of help for which a person may ask?

Personal experience/feelings questions:
>Have you ever needed help? What kind?
>Have you ever asked someone for help? Did they help you?
>How do you feel when you ask someone for help?

Problem-solving questions:
>What is a good way to ask someone for help?
>What should you do if someone does not want to help you?

■ GROUP ACTIVITIES

Facilitate a discussion about different kinds of help that people need. Ask each person about different types of help that they receive at the present time.

Each group member shares a personal experience about asking someone for help.

Participants talk about particular feelings that they experience when needing help from others.

Form pairs and discuss different ways that people can help each other with everyday problems.

■ ASSESSMENT OF SKILLS LEARNED

Recognizes various sources of "help":

ALMOST NEVER	USUALLY NOT	SOMETIMES	USUALLY	ALMOST ALWAYS
1	2	3	4	5

Recognizes several situations which may necessitate help:

ALMOST NEVER	USUALLY NOT	SOMETIMES	USUALLY	ALMOST ALWAYS
1	2	3	4	5

Understands how and when to ask for help:

ALMOST NEVER	USUALLY NOT	SOMETIMES	USUALLY	ALMOST ALWAYS
1	2	3	4	5

38. *Getting Help for Personal Problems*

This section more fully addresses problems of a personal nature. Individuals with developmental disabilities often have difficulty discriminating between personal problems and general everyday ones. The group leader may initially help participants identify different types of personal problems. These may comprise feelings of emotional upset (sad, angry, worried, unhappy, etc.), family conflicts, abuse from others, school or work difficulties, conflicts with friends, medical illness, unpleasant life changes, and so forth. Next, the group should review a range of persons with whom to talk about personal problems—family members, friends, counselors, teachers, social workers, therapists, and others. Finally, the discussion can focus on identifying ways to work through personal problems. These may include talking to somebody about the problem, engaging in a problem-solving process (see previous topic), and developing coping skills. Specific coping skills may range from developing positive attitudes, to engaging in solution-oriented behaviors, to seeking social-emotional support. Though somewhat more abstract than many previous topics, this one is accessible to individuals with mild and moderate developmental disabilities. It can be modified easily for lower functioning persons. One modification is to take pictures of a variety of helping persons and to communicate via signs, gestures, pointing, and nonverbal mannerisms about different types of help provided by each person. Another modification is to make pictures or symbols to represent different types of hardships, and use nonverbal communication to match these with different helpers, either pictorial or live persons who are available for the exercise.

■ SPECIFIC SKILLS TO BE LEARNED

Identify what is a personal problem:
  Feeling emotionally upset (sad, :angry, depressed, worried, etc.) about something
  Family problem
  Abuse by others
  School/work problem
  Conflict with friends, family, boyfriend/girlfriend, relative, etc.
  Medical illness
  Unpleasant life change (moving to a new residence, new job, new relationships, etc.)
Identify with whom to talk about personal problems:
  Family member
  Friend
  Counselor
  Teacher
  Social worker
  Professional therapist
  Other
Identify ways to work through personal problems:
  Talk to somebody about the problem.
  Go through a problem-solving process (see previous topic).
  Develop coping skills:
    Positive attitudes
    Solution-oriented behaviors
    Seeking social/emotional support

■ CONCEPTS NECESSARY TO PERFORM SKILLS

Personal: Private; confidential; intimate; things people usually keep to themselves; things usually told only to friends and family members; something a person does not want everybody to hear about; one's own special thoughts and experiences.

Problem: Conflict; puzzle; disagreement with somebody; when a person needs help; an argument with somebody; when someone or something gets in one's way.

Coping skills: Ways to get what a person wants; ways to deal with not having what someone wants; behaviors a person can use to handle anger, frustration and emotional upset; abilities and behaviors that help a person avoid problems.

■ CASE VIGNETTES

—One day Donna was having a terrible time at work. Warren kept talking loudly and standing very close to her. She did not like all the noise he made. Warren just did not know when to stop talking. He did not seem to notice that it bothered Donna when he stood right next to her. He did not notice that she was upset either. In fact, he tried joking with her and putting his hand on her arm. Donna did not want to be touched and she was fed up with his talking. She was ready to explode with anger but controlled her anger as she walked to her supervisor's office. She explained that Warren was a "loudmouth," and that he was coming into her private work space. She stated, "He even touched me when I didn't tell him to do it." Donna's supervisor had a talk with Warren. Warren was moved to a new job, farther away from Donna.

Was Donna able to get help for her personal problem? Did she ask the right person for help? Was there anything else she could have done to make sure the problem did not happen again?

—Geraldine had been having a problem with her boyfriend. She had dated Peter for several years. At first he was very nice to her. But one day, he was visiting at her house and became very angry. Instead of just talking to her, he slapped her. Afterward, he said that he felt awful and promised he would not do it again. The next week, they had a disagreement about whether or not to go to a movie, and he hit her again. This time he hit her twice, and harder than the first time. Geraldine really loved and cared about Peter, but she was very angry about what he had done to her. She was afraid that if she told her residence counselor about what Peter did to her, they would not let her see him anymore. Peter kept promising that he would change his behavior and quit hitting her, but when he became angry, he continued to lose control.

Do you think Geraldine did a good job getting help for her personal problem? Why or why not? What else could she have done to get help? Who could she have talked to about the problem?

■ DISCUSSION QUESTIONS

Simple/concrete questions:

What are some different types of personal problems?

Is _____ a personal problem? (group leader uses various examples)

Personal experience/feelings questions:

Have you ever had a personal problem?

Did you ever receive support or help for a problem? From whom?

How do you feel when you ask for help?

Problem-solving questions:

What is a good way to get help for a personal problem?

How can you decide if you can solve your problems yourself, or if you need help from others?

■ GROUP ACTIVITIES

Each group member share one personal problem, past or present. Talk about any help received for the problem.

Individuals form pairs to work on personal problems. Each partner provide social and emotional support as well as helpful information to the other partner.

Entire group focus upon one person with a significant problem. Share various ideas and solutions.

■ ASSESSMENT OF SKILLS LEARNED

Identifies one or more personal problems:

ALMOST NEVER	USUALLY NOT	SOMETIMES	USUALLY	ALMOST ALWAYS
1	2	3	4	5

Recognizes one or more persons who might help with a personal problem:

ALMOST NEVER	USUALLY NOT	SOMETIMES	USUALLY	ALMOST ALWAYS
1	2	3	4	5

Identifies one or more ways to work through personal problems:

ALMOST NEVER	USUALLY NOT	SOMETIMES	USUALLY	ALMOST ALWAYS
1	2	3	4	5

39. *Following Directions*

Following directions is often a way to avoid problems. It may be difficult for the individual with a developmental disability because of limitations in attention, memory, and general intellectual functioning. The topic should begin with a review of listening skills. The importance of looking at others while receiving directions should be stressed. Equally important is the act of attending well to instructions. This can be explained as "keeping your mind on what the person says" and "not talking while listening to directions." The act of following through and doing what someone tells an individual should be stressed. Finally, participants need to understand when it is necessary to follow directions. Appropriate circumstances may include times when one is going someplace new, cooking, dealing with an emergency, seeking help, learning something new, or working at a new job. The topic is appropriate for individuals with mild and moderate developmental disabilities, and may be modified for individuals with more limited functioning. Those with more severe disabilities will require more concrete explanations. The topic lends itself well to behavioral demonstrations. For example, the group leader may give instructions to one of the intellectually brighter participants to do a particular task. This individual can help the group leader demonstrate features of listening, eye contact, and attention, performing the task followed by the same request of an individual functioning at a lower level. While some persons may not be able to understand and differentiate situations calling for direction-following behaviors, they can often grasp specific instructions of a concrete nature when given sufficient cues, prompts, and encouragement.

■ SPECIFIC SKILLS TO BE LEARNED

Listen to a person giving instructions (listening).
Look at a person talking (eye contact).
Pay attention to what a person says (attending):
    Keep one's mind on what the person says.

Do not talk.
Do what a person tells one (follow through with behavior).
Recognize when it is necessary to follow directions:
    At work or school
    In an emergency
    When transporting or going places
    When cooking
    When going to appointments

■ CONCEPTS NECESSARY TO PERFORM SKILLS

Listen: Pay attention to what someone says; hear and understand what somebody says; open your ears and close your mouth; let others know that you know what they are saying.

Eye contact: Look someone in the eyes; look at somebody instead of looking away.

Pay attention: Listen; remember what somebody says; do what you are told; hear what someone says; keep one's mind on something; not talk while listening to somebody.

Instruction: Direction; tell someone what to do; an order; a command.

■ CASE VIGNETTES

—*Tony was a stubborn man. He had just gotten a new job. He was happy about the job but he did not like anybody telling him what to do. His new boss tried to tell him how to package different objects into boxes; but Tony did not listen. He said, "That's stupid, why not just put them in there like this?" His boss tried to explain why it was important to put the pieces in a certain order. Tony grumbled and said, "O.K.;" but when the boss was not looking, he did it his own way. Later, the supervisor reviewed Tony's work and said he had to do half of it over again because Tony had not listened. Tony was upset because he did not make much money that day. He was paid by how many boxes he completed. Because he had not followed directions, he earned less money. Tony was not able to go out for pizza on Friday because he did not follow directions.*

Was Tony a good listener? Was he good at following directions? What happened to Tony when he did not follow directions?

—*Judy liked to cook her own lunch on Saturday. One day while she was cooking, she cut herself badly with a knife. She tried to slice the potatoes, but accidentally sliced her own finger. No one was home, so she called 911. The lady on the other end of the telephone told her to hold a towel on her finger and press very hard. She told her not to let go and someone would be there soon. A little while later, Judy heard a siren and the ambulance came. They took her to the emergency room of the hospital and put seven stitches in her finger. Judy was scared, but she had done what the lady told her to do. Soon her finger healed and Judy was all right.*

Did Judy do a good job following directions? What might have happened if she had not listened to the emergency worker?

■ DISCUSSION QUESTIONS

Simple/concrete questions:
    What are some kinds of instructions that people need to follow?
    What are some times and places in which people need to follow directions?
Personal experience/feelings questions:
    Do you ever have trouble paying attention?

When must you follow directions? Is this ever difficult?

How do you feel when someone asks you to follow directions?

Problem-solving questions:

What should you do if you have trouble following directions?

How can someone get better at following directions?

■ GROUP ACTIVITIES

Ask each person for particular times at which the person needs to follow directions. Share any problems in following directions.

Discuss the importance of following directions in certain situations (work, medical needs, emergencies, etc.).

■ ASSESSMENT OF SKILLS LEARNED

Listens to a person giving instructions:

ALMOST NEVER	USUALLY NOT	SOMETIMES	USUALLY	ALMOST ALWAYS
1	2	3	4	5

Makes eye contact:

ALMOST NEVER	USUALLY NOT	SOMETIMES	USUALLY	ALMOST ALWAYS
1	2	3	4	5

Pays attention to what others say:

ALMOST NEVER	USUALLY NOT	SOMETIMES	USUALLY	ALMOST ALWAYS
1	2	3	4	5

Complies with simple requests:

ALMOST NEVER	USUALLY NOT	SOMETIMES	USUALLY	ALMOST ALWAYS
1	2	3	4	5

Recognizes when it is necessary to follow directions:

ALMOST NEVER	USUALLY NOT	SOMETIMES	USUALLY	ALMOST ALWAYS
1	2	3	4	5

40. *Keeping on Task*

Staying with tasks until completion is extremely important to one's school and work success. Individuals with developmental disabilities often experience extreme difficulties in this area. In addition to limiting school and work performance, poor task-oriented behaviors can limit social relationships as well. This section begins with a discussion of how to focus one's attention, which involves keeping a person's mind on one thing, and maintaining visual, auditory, and behavioral contact with a particular task. Next, the discussion may focus on maintaining a train of thought by staying with one topic, not allowing distractions to interfere with one's thinking, and not changing the subject of conversation. Attention should be given to how to ignore distractions and keep one's mind focused. Next, the group can examine how to continue an activity without interruption, placing an emphasis on staying with one activity and continuing to do the same thing without stopping for interruptions. Finally, the discussion may shift to recognizing how to self-monitor. This can include looking at the clock periodically, asking oneself if enough work is getting done, and noticing if one is working fast enough to get the job done. The topic is easily conducted with individuals with mild developmental disabilities, but lower functioning persons are likely to experience difficulty understanding and discussing these concepts. One way to adapt the topic for individuals with more limited intellectual functioning is to make up games requiring sustained attention. For example, see how many blocks someone can put in a box in thirty seconds while others make distracting sounds and movements. Or have two group members talk to each other about their weekends, while others engage in distractions. Another adaptation would be to set a sixty-second egg timer, which one individual resets while performing a speed task such as that involved in packaging or assembly jobs. An additional modification may be to teach a person how to make positive self-statements about staying on task. For example, "Good job, Rich, keep working," or "Work fast, John, don't pay attention to those sounds."

■ SPECIFIC SKILLS TO BE LEARNED

Understand how to focus attention:
  Keep one's mind on one thing.
  Look, listen, and be involved.
Understand how to continue with a train of thought:
  Continue to stay with one topic.
  Do not let distractions interfere with one's thoughts about an important matter.
  Do not change the subject of conversation.
Know how to ignore distractions:
  Ignore sights and sounds which are unimportant.
  Keep one's mind on the person or topic at hand.
Know how to continue an activity without interruptions:
  Stay with a job or activity.
  Continue to do the same thing without interrupting the task.
Recognize how to do self-monitoring:
  Look at the clock periodically.
  Ask oneself if one is doing one's work.
  Ask oneself if one is doing the job fast enough and getting enough done.

■ CONCEPTS NECESSARY TO PERFORM SKILLS

Attention: Look at somebody; talk to someone; be mindful of others; notice others; see someone; listen; watch; look, listen, and notice; take notice and remember what one is doing; notice what someone is saying; keep alert; be involved in something.

Train of thought: Keep one's mind on one thing; follow along during the conversation; stay with one topic; not let distractions interrupt a person; not get off task because of noises and movements of others.

Distraction: Something that interrupts a person; an event that makes somebody lose concentration; something that gets somebody's attention while the person is trying to do something else.

Self-monitor: Pay attention to what one is doing; notice what you are doing and how you are doing it; notice how fast or slow one is doing something.

On-task: Stay with one thing until it is done; keep at what one is supposed to be doing; keep doing what you are doing; do not stop something until you finish it; do not become distracted.

■ CASE VIGNETTES

—Debbie had great difficulty paying attention. She often attended a social group and enjoyed talking about her problems. Sometimes, right in the middle of somebody else's conversation, she interrupted and started talking about her problems. The group leader told her she had to wait her turn and she tried to wait; but soon her mind wandered and she paid no attention to what others were saying. Once again she was interrupting somebody else. She seemed to have the most difficult time listening, and this resulted in others getting mad at her a lot. Sometimes she felt very bad and did not understand why others were angry with her. That was because she had not listened well, and she did not know that her friends were talking about very personal things.

Why do you think Debbie interrupted others so often? What could she have done to keep on task in group? Would it have helped for her to listen better?

—Jack goes to his social group once every two weeks. He enjoys talking with his friends and helping them solve problems. Jack is a good listener. When someone else is talking, he is very quiet and keeps looking right at the person. If he hears noises or sees somebody else moving around, he ignores the distraction and keeps his attention on the speaker. He does this because he knows it is rude to interrupt others, especially when they are talking about personal matters. Jack does not change the subject until the group is done talking about whatever they are discussing. Once in a while, he looks at the clock to see how much time there is left before the group is over. He wants to make sure he gets a chance to talk but does not want to interrupt anyone else.

Why is Jack good at staying on task? What does he do or not do that helps him stay on task? Do you think others like him more because he does not interrupt them?

■ DISCUSSION QUESTIONS

Simple/concrete questions:
   What does it mean to keep on task?
   What are some tasks or activities in which people need to ignore distractions?
   What must a person do to keep on task?
Personal experience/feelings questions:
   Have you ever had problems keeping on task? Please describe?
   What are some important activities and times in which you must keep on task?
   Have you ever been distracted or interrupted when you were trying to do something? How
      did this feel?
   Do you ever interrupt others who are trying to do a job?
Problem-solving questions:
   What are some ways you can help yourself stay on task?
   If you have trouble keeping on task, is there any sort of help that will make this easier?

■ GROUP ACTIVITIES

Ask each person about particular activities and times for which it is important to keep on task.
Group members share any difficulties that they experience keeping on task.
Group volunteers demonstrate how to keep on task in situations where other persons interrupt.
Facilitate a discussion about why it is important to keep on task in certain situations.

■ ASSESSMENT OF SKILLS LEARNED

Focuses attention on a task:

ALMOST NEVER	USUALLY NOT	SOMETIMES	USUALLY	ALMOST ALWAYS
1	2	3	4	5

Stays on topic of conversation:

ALMOST NEVER	USUALLY NOT	SOMETIMES	USUALLY	ALMOST ALWAYS
1	2	3	4	5

Ignores distractions during activities:

ALMOST NEVER	USUALLY NOT	SOMETIMES	USUALLY	ALMOST ALWAYS
1	2	3	4	5

Performs a task without interruptions:

ALMOST NEVER	USUALLY NOT	SOMETIMES	USUALLY	ALMOST ALWAYS
1	2	3	4	5

Self-monitors activities for specified time periods:

ALMOST NEVER	USUALLY NOT	SOMETIMES	USUALLY	ALMOST ALWAYS
1	2	3	4	5

41. *Giving and Receiving Constructive Criticism*

To become more proficient at tasks, deal better with conflicts, and become better problem solvers, individuals need to be able to give and receive feedback. Giving and receiving constructive criticism is one such type of feedback. Often individuals with developmental disabilities have difficulty recognizing, giving, and receiving healthy criticism. The first task of this group is to identify and understand the concept of criticism. Next, the group facilitator should help members identify the difference between *constructive* and *destructive* criticism, highlighting that constructive (good) criticism is meant to help someone, and destructive (bad) criticism is an attempt to hurt someone. Third, the group leader must focus on how to use constructive criticism successfully. Important elements to consider include the notion that constructive criticism tells someone that he or she needs to change something (it gives information), it needs to be prefaced with a compliment (so that it is more easily accepted), it should focus on the person's behavior (bad behavior, not a bad person), it should give ample information about what behavior needs improvement, and it should be emphasized that just because one receives criticism, the individual is not a bad person. Next, the group may discuss the features of destructive criticism. Its essential elements include an attempt to hurt somebody and a lack of sufficient information given to the person about how to change. For example, if a person is working too slowly, a constructive criticism would be to ask, "Can you please work faster?" and a destructive criticism would be to ask, "Why can't you ever do anything right?" Finally, it would be helpful to discuss various ways to deal with destructive criticism. Some of these include asking the person specifically what he or she does not like about one's behavior, ignoring hurtful remarks, acknowledging appropriate and constructive criticism (e.g., "Yes, I'll try harder"), standing up for one's rights, telling the inappropriate criticizer how one feels and asking him or her to avoid the destructive criticism, and asking the person to explain more fully what is meant by the inappropriate criticism. This topic is accessible to individuals with mild developmental delay and to some lower functioning persons. It is more difficult for those with moderate and severe disabilities. One modification is to simplify the conversation and focus on very concrete behavioral criticisms. The group leader can add behavior demonstrations to complement various criticisms. For example, the leader may say, "Can you please work faster?" and then demonstrate both slow and fast work. Another example would be to say, "Please keep your voice down," and then demonstrate loud and soft voices. A further modification would be to use pictures/symbols that are functionally connected to various criticisms. For example, there may be different symbols for loud, soft, fast, slow, and so forth.

■ SPECIFIC SKILLS TO BE LEARNED

Identify what criticism is?

Identify the difference between constructive (good) and destructive (bad) criticism:

    Constructive or good criticism is meant to help someone.

    Destructive or bad criticism is meant to hurt someone.

Effectively use constructive (good) criticism:

    Constructive criticism tells one that something needs to be changed (it gives important information).

    Give a compliment before criticizing.

    Remember that one is criticizing a person's behavior, not the person (there are no bad people, only bad behaviors).

Constructive criticism is used in order to help someone improve his or her behavior (it gives information about how to improve behavior):

    Can you please work faster?

    Can you please do it this way?

    Can you please keep your voice down?

    Can you please listen to me?

Remember that one is not a bad person because one is being criticized (you may have bad behavior).

    Recognize and avoid destructive (bad) criticisms.

    Destructive criticism tries to hurt somebody.

Destructive criticism does not give enough information about how the person should change:

    You are stupid.

    I don't like you.

    Shut-up.

    Why can't you do anything right?

    You never do it right.

    Why can't you ever listen?

    You are a lousy worker.

Respond appropriately to destructive criticism:

    Ask the person specifically what he or she does not like about your behavior; focus upon behavior).

    Ignore inappropriate criticism.

    Acknowledge appropriate (constructive) criticism and let the person know you will try to do better.

    Stick up for your rights if you are unfairly criticized.

    Tell the person how you feel and ask him or her not to use bad criticism.

    Ask the person to explain more about what they mean.

■ CONCEPTS NECESSARY TO PERFORM SKILLS

Criticism: Give someone feedback about his or her behavior; tell others what you think about their behavior; help someone make changes by telling the person what you think about what he or she is doing; say what you think is good or bad about a person's behavior; judge someone's behavior; tell a person how you feel about his or her behavior.

Constructive: Good; positive; helpful; give information to help somebody change his or her behavior.

Destructive: Bad; negative; hurtful; not helpful; wasteful; put someone down; shame or blame a person; trample on someone's feelings.

■ CASE VIGNETTES

—*Olé was not very well liked by others. He was grumpy, irritable, and cranky. One day Miles told him that he had gotten a new bicycle. Olé snapped, "So what, I don't care." Later that day, Olé came to dinner with his three housemates. He looked at his residence counselor, who had cooked dinner, and said, "Boy, this food stinks." As he ate some more food, he said loudly, "I don't like anybody here, I hate this house." John tried to say something and Olé snapped, "You're stupid, John, you're stupid."*

Do you think Olé was good at using constructive (good) criticism? Was his criticism destructive? Why or why not? How could Olé have criticized others in a more constructive or positive way?

—*Jean was a good, constructive criticizer. She never tried to shame or blame people, but would tell them if she thought they needed to change their behavior. For example, Wanda came into group crying one day and Jean put her arm around her, saying, "Wanda, I hope you are O.K. Can you please stop crying and let's talk about what is bothering you?" Wanda told her what was wrong and then she felt better. Another time, Ines was yelling at MaryJo, and Jean told her she did not think it was right for her to yell so loudly. She said that MaryJo also needed a chance to talk. Jean was friendly as she talked to both Ines and MaryJo.*

Do you think Jean used constructive (good) criticism? Did she use destructive (bad) criticism? Why or why not? Why do you think other people listened to Jean's criticisms?

■ DISCUSSION QUESTIONS

Simple/concrete questions:

What is the difference between constructive (good) and destructive (bad) criticism?

When might criticism happen?

What are some different types of good and bad criticism?

Personal experience/feelings questions:

Have you ever been criticized? Was it good or bad criticism?

Have you ever criticized others? Was it good or bad criticism?

How do you feel when someone criticizes you?

What makes it easier for you to listen to criticism? Does it help if a person gives you a compliment first? Does it help if it is a person that you like?

Problem-solving questions:

How can you deal with a person who is a destructive (bad) criticizer?

How can you make sure that when you criticize others, it is good criticism?

■ GROUP ACTIVITIES

Group members practice giving good and bad criticism to others. Entire group critique whether or not the person is using good or bad criticism.

Individuals share times in which they were criticized in bad or negative ways by others. Give support as appropriate.

Practice making constructive and destructive critical remarks, asking individual group members whether they reflect good or bad criticism.

■ ASSESSMENT OF SKILLS LEARNED

Understands the difference between constructive and destructive criticism:

ALMOST NEVER	USUALLY NOT	SOMETIMES	USUALLY	ALMOST ALWAYS
1	2	3	4	5

Effectively uses constructive criticism:

ALMOST NEVER	USUALLY NOT	SOMETIMES	USUALLY	ALMOST ALWAYS
1	2	3	4	5

Responds appropriately to constructive criticism:

ALMOST NEVER	USUALLY NOT	SOMETIMES	USUALLY	ALMOST ALWAYS
1	2	3	4	5

Responds appropriately to destructive criticism:

ALMOST NEVER	USUALLY NOT	SOMETIMES	USUALLY	ALMOST ALWAYS
1	2	3	4	5

42. Conflicts with Housemates, Family, and Friends

This section examines specific conflicts with other people. Most of the disagreements experienced by the general population occur with housemates, family and friends. Individuals with developmental disabilities are no exception. The group leader should begin by helping participants understand the nature of conflict, focusing on arguments, disagreements, fights, or squabbles between persons who know each other well. The attention should then shift to the types of problems that result in interpersonal conflict. These may include an individual using, borrowing, or stealing the possessions of another, saying nasty or untoward things to someone; yelling at a person; swearing at someone; being too loud (e.g., at bedtime, when someone is trying to concentrate on something else), attempting to use a part of the house at the same time as another (e.g., bathroom, telephone, television); taking somebody's food, verbally or physically threatening a person; and bossing others around. The group facilitator should identify specific ways to deal with conflict. These may include speaking up and asserting oneself, asking somebody for help, asking or telling others to respect one's property, talking things over calmly, ignoring negative behavior of others, compromising or making agreements about sharing physical space or possessions, leaving or taking oneself out of a situation, writing down and/or thinking about problems, ventilating frustration (e.g., punching a pillow), and engaging in relaxation procedures (e.g., music, deep breathing, or massage). Finally, time can be spent identifying negative reactions to conflicts that group members should avoid. These may include hitting, yelling, screaming, crying, pouting, refusing to talk (silent treatment), destroying property, biting, and so forth. While conceptually more abstract, these concepts are intuitively understood by individuals with mild and moderate developmental disabilities because of the ubiquitous nature of the problems. For lower functioning persons, it is easy to construct pictures and symbols to identify specific types of conflicts. These may include pictures of characters attempting to use a telephone or television, persons raising their fists to others, and similar schematics. Other diagrams can show individuals talking things over, holding hands, sharing physical possessions, relaxing, and so forth. Yes/no questions can be asked about either the conflict or conflict resolution pictures. Lower ability individuals can be trained to use these pictures in a functional way in order to signal the presence of conflicts or desired solutions.

■ SPECIFIC SKILLS TO BE LEARNED

Understand what conflict is:
   Argument
   Disagreement
   Fight, squabble
Recognize what sorts of problems result in conflict:
   Person taking (using, borrowing, stealing, etc.) one's things
   Saying something nasty to someone
   Yelling at someone
   Swearing at someone
   Being too loud (especially at bedtime)
   Two people trying to use the same part of the house at the same time (e.g., bathroom, telephone, television)
   Asking for someone's food
   Verbally or physically threatening somebody
   Bossing someone
Identify ways to deal with conflict:
   Speak up for oneself, be assertive (tell how you feel, what you think, and what you want).
   Tell somebody that one needs help (e.g., ask staff person for help).
   Tell others to respect one's property.
   Talk things over calmly.
   Ignore negative behaviors of others.
   Make agreements about sharing physical space or possessions (compromise).
   Take oneself out of the situation (leave).
   Write down problems and think about them.
   Punch a pillow to relieve frustration.
   Use relaxation procedures (music, deep breathing, etc.).
Identify and avoid negative reactions to conflict:
   Hitting others
   Yelling/screaming
   Crying/pouting
   Silent treatment (refusing to talk)
   Destroying others' property
   Hitting or biting oneself

■ CONCEPTS NECESSARY TO PERFORM SKILLS

Conflict: Problem; disagreement; argument; when a person sees something differently than someone else does and becomes upset about it.

Disagreement: When two people fight; when two individuals have different ideas about what to do; when people each have different answers to a problem; when someone argues or yells at somebody else.

Argument: Disagreement; conflict; a problem between two people; dispute; spat; squabble; to yell or swear at somebody.

Assertive: Directly telling a person how you feel; saying how you feel and why you feel that way; telling someone what is on your mind.

■ CASE VIGNETTES:

—*Judy and Sandy were both in the same group. As Sandy came in the door, Judy asked, "Why are you late today?" Sandy replied, "It's none of your damn business." Judy immediately felt hurt, but she did not quite know how to express this to Sandy. Instead, she told Sandy, "You don't have to be so mean, I was just asking you a question." Sandy replied, "Mind your own business, I can come in here when I want to." Judy started to cry, and then she apologized to Sandy for asking her the question. Sandy swore at Judy one more time and then stomped out of the room.*

Do you think Sandy and Judy did a good job dealing with their conflict? Why or why not? What else could either of them have done to handle this situation better?

—*John liked to play his music tapes. He liked all different kinds of music and sometimes played his tapes very loudly. One day he was sitting in the lunchroom playing his tapes when Bruce came over and told him he was making too much noise. John retorted, "Well, anybody who knows anything at all should know that this is good music. Why should I have to turn it down?" Bruce was upset and told John that he was a big baby. John quickly got even angrier and told Bruce to shove off. Bruce went to the other side of the lunch room and ate his lunch with different workmates. Later John came up to him and apologized. He said he would try to play his music more softly next time. Bruce and John decided that they would remain friends. They were glad that they talked about their problem.*

How did John and Bruce resolve their conflict? Why do you think it is important to deal with conflicts? Are there any behaviors that you should not do when you are having a problem with someone?

■ DISCUSSION QUESTIONS

Simple/concrete questions:

What are some different types of conflicts?

Personal experience/feelings questions:

Have you ever had a conflict with someone? Describe it.

How do you feel when you argue and fight with others?

How do you usually handle conflicts with others? Does this work well for you?

Problem-solving questions:

What are some ways in which a person can avoid having conflicts with family members, housemates, and friends?

If two people are having a big argument, what can one person do to help the situation before it becomes an even bigger problem?

■ GROUP ACTIVITIES

Individuals share specific conflicts that they have experienced with family, housemates and friends.

Facilitate a discussion about how to avoid conflicts with others.

Lead a discussion about how to end conflicts once they have begun.

Group members form pairs in order to talk about personal conflicts.

■ ASSESSMENT OF SKILLS LEARNED

Understands what is a conflict:

ALMOST NEVER	USUALLY NOT	SOMETIMES	USUALLY	ALMOST ALWAYS
1	2	3	4	5

Recognizes one or more problems that may result in conflict:

ALMOST NEVER	USUALLY NOT	SOMETIMES	USUALLY	ALMOST ALWAYS
1	2	3	4	5

Identifies one or more positive ways to deal with conflict:

ALMOST NEVER	USUALLY NOT	SOMETIMES	USUALLY	ALMOST ALWAYS
1	2	3	4	5

Avoids negative reactions to conflict:

ALMOST NEVER	USUALLY NOT	SOMETIMES	USUALLY	ALMOST ALWAYS
1	2	3	4	5

43. Dealing with Negative Gossip, Teasing, and False Accusations

Negative gossip, teasing, and false accusations represent three areas of conflict commonly experienced by persons with developmental disabilities. The group leader should explain these terms to group participants, indicating that negative gossip is talking hurtfully behind somebody's back, teasing is saying hurtful things to a person's face, and a false accusation is saying untruthfully that somebody did something that the person did not really do. It should be explained that gossip can harm others by starting rumors, spreading damaging information that may or may not be true, giving a person no opportunity to respond and address the issue, and making somebody ultimately feel embarrassed and uncomfortable. It can be noted that false accusations can harm individuals by getting them into trouble, damaging their reputations, making them suspect for things for which they are not responsible, and ruining their trust in others. It may also wound others by embarrassing them or degrading them. Finally, a discussion about how to respond to negative gossip, false accusations, and teasing might include confronting persons, ignoring them, and/or correcting them with true information. This topic is appropriate for individuals with mild and moderate developmental delay. Individuals of more limited intellect will have difficulty grasping the concepts but may be able to respond to very concrete, yes/no questions about specific examples of these items.

■ SPECIFIC SKILLS TO BE LEARNED

Recognize negative gossip, teasing and false accusations:
    Talking behind someone's back
    Saying that persons did things that they did not do
    Hurtfully teasing or making fun of others
Understand how gossip can hurt others:
    It starts rumors.
    Rumors are not always truthful.
    There is no opportunity for the person to respnd and address the issue.
    It perpetuates problems for the person.
    It makes a person feel embarrassed and uncomfortable.
Understand how false accusations can hurt others:
    They can get someone into trouble.
    They can damage someone's reputation.
    They make someone a suspect even if he or she did not do something.
    They ruin trust of others.
Understand how teasing can hurt others:
    It can embarrass someone.

It can hurt someone emotionally.

It can humiliate or degrade someone.

Understand how to respond to negative gossip, false accusations, and teasing:

Confront persons (ask how they knew things, where they got the information, why they are gossiping/accusing, etc.).

Ignore gossip, accusations, and teasing.

Correct the gossiper or accuser with true information.

■ CONCEPTS NECESSARY TO PERFORM SKILLS

Gossip: Say things about someone that may or may not be true; say something behind somebody's back without telling the person; spread rumors; whisper about somebody.

Accuse: Say that somebody did something; blame somebody for something; slur; condemn; complain about someone's behavior.

Tease: Make fun of; ridicule; laugh at; poke fun of; embarrass; harass; mock; tantalize.

Rumor: Something that may or may not be true; hearsay; gossip; reporting something without knowing all of the facts.

■ CASE VIGNETTES

—*One day Myrtle was feeling very angry with Rosa because Rosa was flirting with Myrtle's boyfriend, Tom. Myrtle saw Rosa sitting very close to him in the lunchroom, batting her eyes at him and listening to everything he said. Instead of confronting Rosa or Tom, Myrtle told some of her other friends that Rosa was pregnant and would have to quit work to have her baby. This was not true, but Rosa had no chance to say so because Myrtle was secretly telling this to people behind her back. By the next day, all of Rosa's friends and workmates had heard the gossip that she was pregnant and had to quit work. Her job supervisor even asked her about it. Rosa was very upset.*

Do you think that Myrtle was fair to Rosa when she secretly spread this rumor? Why or why not? Would you want somebody to spread a rumor or gossip about you? Why or why not? What should Rosa do now that a false rumor has been spread about her?

—*Ron was eating lunch one day when he overheard Richard say something he knew was not true. Richard told Bill that Ann, the work supervisor, had gotten fired. Ron knew this was not true because he had just left a meeting with Ann, who had told him she would continue to be his job coach next year. Ron spoke up and said, "Excuse me, Richard, but I think you are giving people the wrong information. I talked to Ann and she plans to keep her job for this next year." He then asked, "Where did you get your information, Richard? Who told you that Ann was leaving?" Richard paused for a moment and said he might have heard it from somebody else. He thanked Ron for setting the record straight. Ron then suggested that in the future, Richard should talk to Ann first before he started telling people she was leaving her job.*

How did Ron prevent negative gossip from spreading? Do you think he did the right thing by speaking up? Why or why not?

■ DISCUSSION QUESTIONS

Simple/concrete questions:

What are some different kinds of gossip?

What is a false accusation?

What are some different kinds of teasing?

Personal experience/feelings questions:

Have you ever been teased before? How did it feel?

Have you ever teased someone else? How do you think they felt?

Has anybody ever told a lie about you before? How did it feel?

Problem-solving questions:

What should you do if someone teases you?

What should you do if someone gossips or makes false accusations about you?

■ GROUP ACTIVITIES

Facilitate a discussion about the negative effects of gossip, false accusations, and teasing. Form pairs in order to discuss personal experiences with gossip, false accusations, and teasing.

■ ASSESSMENT OF SKILLS LEARNED

Recognizes negative gossip, teasing and false accusations:

ALMOST NEVER	USUALLY NOT	SOMETIMES	USUALLY	ALMOST ALWAYS
1	2	3	4	5

Lists one or more ways in which gossip can hurt others:

ALMOST NEVER	USUALLY NOT	SOMETIMES	USUALLY	ALMOST ALWAYS
1	2	3	4	5

Lists one or more ways in which false accusations can hurt others:

ALMOST NEVER	USUALLY NOT	SOMETIMES	USUALLY	ALMOST ALWAYS
1	2	3	4	5

Lists one or more ways in which teasing can hurt others:

ALMOST NEVER	USUALLY NOT	SOMETIMES	USUALLY	ALMOST ALWAYS
1	2	3	4	5

Identifies one or more positive ways to respond to gossip, false accusations, and teasing:

ALMOST NEVER	USUALLY NOT	SOMETIMES	USUALLY	ALMOST ALWAYS
1	2	3	4	5

44. Staying Out of Others' Problems

Individuals with developmental disabilities, while not intentionally creating many problems, are often more easily triangled into others' problems than are their peers. The group facilitator should begin this section by helping the discussants recognize when, and when not, to help others. Help may be warranted if someone is in trouble, if a person is hurt, if one has a close relationship with the person in question, or if someone requests another's help. It may not be a good idea to get involved if people are not in serious trouble or pain, if they do not ask for help, and if they are not particularly close relations. Various ways of avoiding involvement in others' problems should be discussed. These include ignoring, walking away, not initiating conversation, minding one's own business, helping only when asked, and refraining from butting into someone else's business. The topic is appropriate for persons with mild and moderate developmental disabilities. Lower functioning individuals can be taught to associate simple pictures or signs with specific types of help, but may not be able to comprehend the higher level concepts. They may not have the judgment required to discriminate appropriate and inappropriate times to get involved in others' troubles. One simple modification along these lines is to help the person recognize an emergency telephone number, and to recognize one or more specific signs for "help" that the individual may communicate to teachers, supervisors and others.

■ SPECIFIC SKILLS TO BE LEARNED

Recognize the difference between one's own and others' problems.
Recognize when to help others (and when not to help others):
    If someone is in trouble
    If someone is hurt
    If one has a close relationship with the person (family/friend)
    If someone asks for help
Understand how to avoid getting involved in others' problems:
    Ignoring
    Walking away
    Not talking to someone
    Minding one's own business
    Helping only when asked
    Not butting into someone else's business

■ CONCEPTS NECESSARY TO PERFORM SKILLS

Problem: Conflict; puzzle; disagreement with somebody; when a person needs help; an argument with somebody; when someone or something gets in one's way.

Ignore: Not pay attention; not listen; overlook; disregard; neglect; do something else when a person is trying to talk.

Help: Do something for somebody; share the work; work with somebody so that the person can get the job done faster; do things for others that they cannot do for themselves; assist someone.

Interfere: Get in the way; butt in; meddle; hinder; try to help when others do not want help.

■ CASE VIGNETTES

—One day Tom was walking down the hallway and saw Jesse screaming at Min Lee. Jesse was swearing very loudly and Min Lee was arguing right back. Before he knew what was happening, Tom told Jesse to be quiet and leave Min Lee alone. Jesse turned to Tom and began swearing at him, screaming that he had better keep his nose out of her affairs and mind his own business. Before he could say anything more, Jesse walked over and slapped him across the face. Then Min Lee started yelling at Jesse again.

*   Do you think it was a good idea for Tom to get in the middle of the argument between Jesse and Min Lee? Why or why not? Is there anything else Tom could have done instead of getting involved? Is it ever a good idea to offer help when two people are arguing? When and why?*

—Abda had just arrived at his evening crafts class. As he walked into the room, he noticed that Michele and Gina were arguing. Michele told Gina that she was a baby, and Gina retorted back that Michele was selfish and did not care about anyone else. Soon Abda figured out that Gina was probably mad because Michele had forgotten to bring her the pictures that she had promised to bring that night. She told Gina she would bring them next Thursday. Gina thought Michele did not care about her, and that is when the fireworks started. Abda had to make a decision. Should he help, or should he mind his own business? He thought about it for a minute. No one was in real trouble. No one was hurt. No one had asked him for his advice or

help. He realized it would be better for him to keep his mouth shut and let Michele and Gina work out their own problem. They soon calmed down and worked on their crafts.

Did Abda make a good or bad choice not to get involved in this problem? Why or why not? What might have happened if Abda interrupted the argument between Michele and Gina?

■ DISCUSSION QUESTIONS

Simple/concrete questions:
>   What are some different types of problems that happen to people? Should you interfere in these problems?
>   What are some ways to keep out of other people's problems?

Personal experience/feelings questions:
>   Have you ever had someone interfere with one of your problems when you did not want help? How did you feel?
>   Have you ever tried to help someone who did not want your help? How did they react?

Problem-solving questions:
>   How should you decide whether or not to offer someone help for their problem?
>   If you offer someone help with a problem, and they do not want your help, what should you do?

■ GROUP ACTIVITIES

Facilitate a discussion about the advisability of helping other people with various types of problems.

Members share personal problems and indicate if they are the types of problems for which they would like others to offer help. Discuss various respectful ways to be of help.

■ ASSESSMENT OF SKILLS LEARNED

Recognizes the difference between one's own and others' problems:

ALMOST NEVER	USUALLY NOT	SOMETIMES	USUALLY	ALMOST ALWAYS
1	2	3	4	5

Understands one or more ways to avoid getting involved in others' problems:

ALMOST NEVER	USUALLY NOT	SOMETIMES	USUALLY	ALMOST ALWAYS
1	2	3	4	5

45. *Dealing with Mistreatment from Others*

There are times when one needs to deal with genuine mistreatment. Individuals with developmental disabilities do not always understand and discriminate the subtle differences between real and perceived mistreatment. This topic is an attempt to provide further clarification in this area. Initially, the group facilitator may help individuals recognize different types of mistreatment. More obvious forms of maltreatment may include swearing, name calling, bullying, yelling, degrading, threatening, hitting, and so forth. More subtle but nevertheless annoying mistreatments include rude remarks, cutting in front of others in line, interruptions while on the telephone, interference with activities, and minor embarrassments and annoyances. Even more elusive maltreatment includes individuals borrowing money without paying it back, taking things without permission, and taking advantage when individuals do not completely understand how they are being taken in. The session should focus on understanding different ways to deal with mistreatment, including making assertive demands, repeating requests, refusing to take "no" for an answer, going to outsiders for help, ignoring, and refusing to be mistreated by leaving the situation or protecting oneself. This topic is most appropriate for individuals with mild developmental disabilities. More intellectually limited individuals may respond to simple closed-ended questions about types of mistreatment and ways to deal with it, but they may have great difficulty making finer judgments concerning mistreatment. Previous adaptations using nonverbal communication may apply here as well.

■ SPECIFIC SKILLS TO BE LEARNED

Recognize mistreatment:
    Swearing
    Calling names
    Pushing around
    Yelling
    Degrading (e.g., calling "stupid")
    Bossing
    Threatening
    Hitting
    Rudeness
    Cutting in front in line
    Borrowing money and not paying back
    Taking things without permission
    Embarrassing
    Racial/ethnic slurs
    Interrupting someone on the telephone
    Interfering with someone's activity
Understand ways to deal with mistreatment:
    Assertiveness:
        Tell how you feel.
        Tell what you think.
        Ask for what you want.
    Standing up for your rights:
        Repeatedly tell what you want.
        Refuse to take, "no" for an answer.
        Be persistent.
    Getting help:
        Family/friend
        Counselor/teacher
        Other
    Ignoring (e.g., ignore name calling)
    Refusing to be mistreated:
        Walking away
        Protecting oneself

■ CONCEPTS NECESSARY TO PERFORM SKILLS

Mistreat: Treat badly; act with disrespect; abuse; do bad things to someone; say bad things to a person.

Assertive: Directly tell a person how you feel; say how you feel and why you feel that way; tell someone what is on your mind.

■ CASE VIGNETTES

—*Jack was an African-American man and he was proud of it. He liked his dark brown skin, black curly hair, and the rest of his body. Sometimes he had problems with other people. Jack lived in a neighborhood and went to school in an area where most people were very light-skinned. Sometimes others would make sarcastic or insensitive remarks about Jack's skin color, and this made him feel different from his friends. Jack knew the color of his skin had nothing to do with the kind of person he was, and he felt hurt that somebody would make those kinds of remarks. It also made him feel that other people thought the same things but just did not say them. Jack had a problem. He could either ignore the hurtful remarks by a few people, or he could say something. He felt if he said something back, it might just call more attention to himself and he would feel even more different from the others. He also wanted to avoid having a fight with somebody, and thought if he argued back, this might result in a bigger conflict.*

How was Jack mistreated in this story? Why was it difficult for him to decide how to react to mistreatment from others? What would you do if you were Jack? Is there anything else Jack could have done to deal with this mistreatment from others?

—*Linda sat down to eat her lunch. She had a delicious ham and cheese sandwich, an apple, and two cookies. She had enough money to buy a can of pop, so she went to the pop machine and got one. It was nice and cold. As Linda was eating her sandwich, Regina snuck up behind her and grabbed the soda. Regina drank half of her soda before Linda could grab it back. Linda was very upset about Regina's rude behavior. She told Regina that she would have to pay Linda back fifty cents for stealing her drink. When Regina refused, Linda marched into the supervisor's office, told her the entire story, and asked for help. Regina's supervisor made her buy Linda a new can of pop and said it better not happen again or Regina would be in big trouble.*

Did Linda act assertively when she was mistreated? What was assertive about her behavior? What else might have happened had Linda reacted differently?

■ DISCUSSION QUESTIONS

Simple/concrete questions:
    What are some different types of mistreatment?
    What are some different ways to deal with mistreatment?
Personal experience/feelings questions:
    Has anyone ever treated you badly? What did they do? How did you feel?
    Have you ever treated anyone else badly? Why? How did they react?
Problem-solving questions:
    What should you do if you think someone is mistreating you or taking advantage of you?
    What should you do if you if you feel that someone is being inconsiderate or rude to you?
    What are some ways in which a person can prevent others from mistreating them?

■ GROUP ACTIVITIES

Each group member share personal experiences of mistreatment. Engage in problem-solving behaviors with each person.
Form pairs and discuss personal experiences with mistreatment.
Encourage group support for individuals who are currently being mistreated in some way.

■ ASSESSMENT OF SKILLS LEARNED

Recognizes various types of mistreatment:

ALMOST NEVER	USUALLY NOT	SOMETIMES	USUALLY	ALMOST ALWAYS
1	2	3	4	5

Recognizes one or more ways to deal with mistreatment:

ALMOST NEVER	USUALLY NOT	SOMETIMES	USUALLY	ALMOST ALWAYS
1	2	3	4	5

6 *Friendship and Social Support*

THIS CHAPTER IS A SHORT but important one that deals with the areas of friendship and social support. Persons with developmental disabilities frequently have difficulty making friends, maintaining friendships, and generating adequate social supports in their lives. These topics are directed toward the possibility of increasing friendships and expanding social networks, thereby reducing excessive dependency on a small number of overly important persons in the social networks of individuals with developmental disabilities. The section on making a friend examines specific skills involved in the initiation of friendships. The section on keeping a friend examines specific skills involved in being a good friend. The areas of giving and receiving support are addressed because they are important in achieving a depth of friendship with others. Finally, the theme of trust is examined because persons with developmental delay oftentimes have difficulty assessing the trustworthiness of others and responding accordingly.

46. *Making a Friend*

Individuals without friends lead isolated, lonely lives. Those with few friends rely heavily on each of their relationships for camaraderie, support, and social connectedness. Individuals with developmental disabilities typically have more difficulty than their peers in initiating and maintaining friendships. This topic addresses skills involved in initiating a friendship, understanding how to be a friend to someone, and recognizing how friendship fits into the wider spectrum of social relationships. First, the leader should help individuals recognize how to initiate friendships by introducing themselves, engaging in small talk, discussing common interests (similarities between persons), and sharing unique aspects of themselves (differences among individuals). Next, participants may review behaviors associated with being a friend to others. These include listening, asking questions, sharing personal information, treating someone with consideration, doing things together, inviting a friend to go places, and generally engaging in pleasantries. Finally, the role of friendship can be examined in the context of other relationships, including spouse/mate, immediate/extended family, girlfriend/boyfriend, workmate/schoolmate, acquaintance, and stranger. Most of these skills are borrowed from earlier topics and, when used in combination, result in friendship skills. The topic is easily discussed by individuals with mild and moderate intellectual limitations. Persons with more limited understandings and fewer verbal abilities may respond more effectively with the help of nonverbal communication assists, live demonstrations, and concrete activities. For example, two individuals may communicate using pictures and symbols about a joint task such as putting puzzles together, which is demonstrated by the group leader who provides verbal and nonverbal cues for task completion.

■ SPECIFIC SKILLS TO BE LEARNED

Recognize how to initiate a friendship (how to make friends):
    Introducing oneself

Making small talk
Talking about common interests (how individuals are the same)
Talking about unique aspects of oneself (how a person is different from another)
Understand how to be a friend to others:
Listening
Asking questions
Sharing personal information
Treating a friend nicely
Doing things together
Inviting a friend to do things
Being pleasant and respectful
Recognize where friendship fits into the range of relationships:
Spouse/mate
Immediate family member
Extended family member
Girlfriend/boyfriend
Friend
Workmate/schoolmate
Acquaintance
Stranger

■ CONCEPTS NECESSARY TO PERFORM SKILLS

Initiate: Start; begin; introduce; begin to talk to somebody; ask to do something with somebody.

Friendship: Companionship; togetherness; neighborliness; comradeship; fellowship; brotherhood; closeness with others; to share thoughts, feelings, and activities with others; what a person has with friends and companions.

Relationship: Connection with somebody; when people know each other; to relate or do things with others; togetherness; family, friend, or acquaintance.

Acquaintance: Somebody a person has seen before but does not know very well; someone with whom one has gone to school or worked but is not very familiar; a person one knows, but not too well.

Stranger: Somebody a person does not know at all; a person you have never met; a person one sees for the first time; an unfamiliar person.

■ CASE VIGNETTES

—Mike was good at initiating friendships. That meant he knew how to begin a friendship with somebody. Last week he was entering the front door of his workplace and recognized another man who was on his way out the door. Mike stopped and greeted him: "Hello, aren't you David Bernstein? I heard you play the piano last month at the concert hall." David said, "Yes, I am, thanks for remembering me." The two of them talked for a few minutes because they both liked music. Before David left, Mike had asked him when his next concert was and said that he planned to see him there. Mike went to the concert and later became better friends with David. They asked each other questions and had a great time talking together. Every once in a while they got together for lunch.

Do you think that Mike was good at initiating friendships? Did he know how to get a conversation going with David? What did Mike and David do to keep their friendship going?

—Susan had no close friends. She felt uncomfortable around people and was afraid to introduce herself or say "Hello." Because of this she usually walked by herself, ate lunch by her-

self, and spent her evenings alone. Often when she talked to people she quickly withdrew into herself and did not say much. She did not ask many questions of others and did not tell others much about herself. She was a lonely woman. Others seemed to be having fun together, but she had no one to talk to.

Do you think Susan was good at making friends? Why or why not? What could she have done differently to make some friends? Why do you suppose she was afraid to talk to others?

■ DISCUSSION QUESTIONS

Simple/concrete questions:

What does it mean to be a good friend?

What is the difference between a friend and a family member? Spouse? Girlfriend/boyfriend? Acquaintance? Stranger?

Personal experience/feelings questions:

Do you have any friends?

How did you meet your friends?

Have you ever talked to a stranger? How was this different than talking to a friend?

Problem-solving questions:

What are some things you can do to make more friends?

What problems can happen between friends, and how do you deal with these problems?

■ GROUP ACTIVITIES

Facilitate a discussion about who has which friends and how they met each other.

Take turns telling what makes someone a good friend.

Share personal experiences with successful and unsuccessful friendships.

■ ASSESSMENT OF SKILLS LEARNED

Recognizes how to initiate a friendship:

ALMOST NEVER	USUALLY NOT	SOMETIMES	USUALLY	ALMOST ALWAYS
1	2	3	4	5

Lists several ways to be a friend to others:

ALMOST NEVER	USUALLY NOT	SOMETIMES	USUALLY	ALMOST ALWAYS
1	2	3	4	5

Recognizes where friendship fits into the range of relationships:

ALMOST NEVER	USUALLY NOT	SOMETIMES	USUALLY	ALMOST ALWAYS
1	2	3	4	5

47. *Keeping a Friend*

Once a friendship has been established, individuals must engage in friendship maintenance behaviors, or their relationships fall by the wayside. Persons with developmental disabilities often have difficulty recognizing and performing these maintenance behaviors because of a failure to understand what friendship requires, difficulty in taking on the perspective of others, and limited repertoire of friendship maintenance skills. The group facilitator should begin by helping participants recognize the difference between friendship and other types of relationships. Some contrasting relationships include spouse/mate, family member, acquaintance, and stranger. The conversation may proceed with a detailed discussion of friendship maintenance behaviors, which include listening, remembering what a friend says, showing an interest in the friend, sharing information about oneself, doing things together with friends, talking about topics of mutual interest, being open to doing new things, compromising, sharing thoughts and feelings, supporting, helping, trusting, believing, being respectful, and showing everyday kindness and understanding. This is a higher level topic than most, more appropriate for individuals with mild than with moderate or severe developmental disabilities. A modification for lower functioning persons is to ask specific yes/no questions about each skill area—for example: "Do you feel closer to a friend or to a stranger?" "Would you expect more from a spouse or from a friend?" "Is it important to listen to what a friend says?" "Would you be more likely to do things with an acquaintance or with a friend?"

■ SPECIFIC SKILLS TO BE LEARNED

Recognize the difference between a friend and other types of relationships:
    Spouse/mate
    Family member
    Friend
    Acquaintance
    Stranger
Identify what it takes to be a good friend (and keep friendship going):
    Listening to a friend
    Remembering what a friend says
    Showing an interest in a friend (asking questions)
    Sharing information about oneself
    Doing things together
    Talking about topics which interest both oneself and one's friend
    Doing new things with a friend
    Compromising (sometimes doing what you want, and sometimes doing what others want)
    Sharing thoughts and feelings together
    Supporting and helping a friend
    Trusting and believing a friend
    Being respectful, kind, and considerate

■ CONCEPTS NECESSARY TO PERFORM SKILLS

Friend: Somebody a person knows well; a familiar person; companion; mate; a person with whom somebody likes to do things; someone to talk to; somebody to whom a person feels close; someone a person can trust.

Compromise: Do both what you want to do and what a friend wants to do; give a little and take a little; settle for part of what you want so that others can have some of what they want; one person can choose this time and the other may pick next time.

Support: Listen; care about; believe what someone says; tell others they are O.K.; tell a person one is on his or her side; be helpful; treat others kindly; be considerate; tell others one is with them and cares about how they feel.

Acquaintance: Somebody a person has seen before but does not know very well; someone with whom one has gone to school or worked but is not very familiar; a person one knows, but not too well.

Family member: Brother, sister, or parent; someone in a person's family; somebody with whom a person lives.

Stranger: Somebody a person does not know at all; a person you have never met; a person one sees for the first time; an unfamiliar person.

■ CASE VIGNETTES

—*Lauren was good at making friends but had trouble keeping them. At first, when she met someone, she was always friendly. She introduced herself and was good at small talk; but after a while she became rather bossy and told her friends what to do. She did not listen well. For example, her friend Joan tried to talk about her trip to the zoo, but Lauren ignored her and talked about something else. Lauren had trouble remembering what her friends told her, and this made some of them feel angry. When they did things together, Lauren often tried to decide what activities to do. She did not compromise but had to have her own way or she would not do things with others. She was not very kind or considerate. Soon, all her friends left her and found new friends. Lauren was all alone and had to do things by herself.*

Why did Lauren have trouble keeping friends? Do you think she was too bossy? Why did her friends get mad at her? Why did they find new friends? Do you think Lauren liked being all alone? Why or why not?

—*Geno had many friends. Once he became friends with someone, they usually stayed friends. That was because Geno listened well to his friends, remembered what they told him, and asked about it later so they knew he cared about them. He often asked them questions and told about how his life was going. Yesterday he asked Tony how he liked camp the week before last. He also told Tony that he would be going to camp next week. Geno knew how to find things to talk about that interested others. He often asked friends to come and play ball, go to movies, and do other things. When a friend wanted to do something different than Geno, he compromised. One day they might do what Geno wanted to do, and another day they might do what the friend chose. He liked to do new and different things, so he did not mind compromising. Geno was very supportive of his friends. He helped them with problems if he could. He was a respectful and considerate man.*

Why do you think Geno had so many friends? What did he do to make others want to be his friend?

■ DISCUSSION QUESTIONS

Simple/concrete questions:
    What are some characteristics of a good friend?
    What are some different kinds of relationships besides friendships?
Personal experience/feelings questions:
    Do you have any friends?
    How do you feel when you are with your friends?
    How do you feel if you cannot find any friends to do something with?
    Have you ever had difficulty making friends?
Problem-solving questions:
    What are some ways a person can keep a friendship going?
    If you have an argument or disagreement with a friend, what should you do?
    If someone does not want to be friends with you, what should you do?

■ GROUP ACTIVITIES

Ask each person to describe the characteristics of a good friend.
Ask each person what can be done in order to keep a friendship going.

Form pairs with others with whom individuals would like to be friends. Talk about common interests as well as differences.

■ ASSESSMENT OF SKILLS LEARNED

Recognizes the difference between a friend and other types of relationships:

ALMOST NEVER	USUALLY NOT	SOMETIMES	USUALLY	ALMOST ALWAYS
1	2	3	4	5

Identifies several ways to keep a friendship going:

ALMOST NEVER	USUALLY NOT	SOMETIMES	USUALLY	ALMOST ALWAYS
1	2	3	4	5

48. *Giving and Receiving Support*

Giving and receiving support are significant parts of friendship. To be a good friend to another, one must be prepared to offer support when needed. One also needs to be open to receiving it when offered. Persons with developmental disabilities may experience difficulties in this area. The group leader should begin with a focus on recognizing different types of support. These include social, emotional, physical, esteem, and informational. Social support means being available to participate in friendships. Emotional support involves understanding and acknowledging the feelings of others. Physical support includes any sort of physical assistance or comfort, ranging from putting one's arm around another person to helping someone perform a task. Esteem support means giving one's positive regard to another. Informational support is any communication of information that helps other individuals deal with their life situations. This may range from telling someone when the bus will come to providing detailed instructions on how to perform an activity. The group leader should direct the focus of the group to various ways individuals can provide and receive support. One can ask another to listen, and the other can be open to what the first says. An individual can ask for advice, and this can be given in a nonjudgmental way. A person can request to talk, and another can provide a safe place for the person to share thoughts and feelings. One may ask if another has ever had a similar feeling, and the other can relate a common experience. An individual can ask to be believed and accepted, and another may accept and believe the person. One person can ask another to take his or her side, and the other may be an ally. Help can be sought and it can be offered. Acceptance can be requested, and it be given. An individual can ask for comfort and another can give the person a hug or pat on the back. Of all the topics which generate enthusiasm and interaction, this one, when handled properly, is one of the most enjoyed by individuals with mild and moderate developmental disabilities. Lower functioning participants tend to be better at receiving than requesting support, but can learn to give support in very concrete ways using picture/symbol, gestural, and other nonverbal communications.

■ SPECIFIC SKILLS TO BE LEARNED

Recognize types of support:
Social
Emotional
Physical
Esteem
Informational

Recognize ways to give support:

Being open to other persons (e.g., smiling, speaking in a friendly voice, asking how a person feels, asking what the person wants)

Giving reassurance (e.g., "You are O.K.," "It will be O.K.," "Things will turn out all right")

Providing a safe place for someone to talk (e.g., "I will listen to you," "I care about you")

Giving acknowledgment (e.g., "I understand how you feel," "I've felt that way before," "I know how much it hurts")

Giving acceptance (e.g., "You are O.K.," "I believe you," "I accept you")

Being an ally (e.g., "I'm on your side," "We're with you")

Giving physical comfort (e.g., holding a person's hand, patting someone on the back, giving a hug)

Recognize ways to request (receive) support:

"I want you to listen to me" (listen).

"I want your advice" (advice).

"I just want to talk" (talk).

"I want to know if you've ever felt this way" (common experience).

"I want you to believe/accept me" (believe/accept).

"I want you to let me know you understand me" (understand).

"I want you to be on my side" (take sides).

"I want you to give me some help" (help).

"I want to know that you like me" (like).

■ CONCEPTS NECESSARY TO PERFORM SKILLS

Social: Related to people; to do with relationships; talking to people; taking an interest in others; doing things with people; getting together with friends; rules about how to get along with others.

Emotional: To do with feelings; a person's emotions; rules about who has what feelings and how to express them.

Physical: To do with a person's body; something one can see, touch, or feel; concrete; something that has substance; rules about whom, when, and how to touch.

Esteem: How individuals feel about themselves; how much people like themselves.

Information: Things that people talk about; ideas individuals share with each other; what people tell each other; messages; knowledge; communication about facts; advice; what people know and report.

Reassure: Tell somebody that everything is O.K.; let someone know you will help; tell someone that things will turn out all right; promise help or support.

Acknowledge: Listen; let individuals know that you hear them; repeat back what one hears; show that a person understands what someone has said.

Accept: Take; receive; like yourself for who you are; know that one is a good person even if needing to change some things; feel good as you are.

Ally: On somebody's side; friend; companion; someone who supports another; willing to fight for someone; helper.

Listen: Pay attention to what someone says; hear and understand what somebody says; open your ears and close your mouth; let others know that you know what they are saying.

Understand: Know what someone is saying; know what somebody means when they tell you something; know what a person is telling you.

■ CASE VIGNETTES

—*Raul was a supportive person. One day Bill came into the group and said that he was upset because his mother was dying. Raul listened closely and then said, "Bill, I'm very sorry to hear about your mother." Bill cried and told Raul that his mother had been sick for a year and finally died at the nursing home. Raul told him, "I know just how you feel, Bill. My dad died three years ago from a heart attack." Then he asked, "Is there anything I can do to help?" Bill said there was not, but he appreciated Raul listening and sharing his own story. Then Bill thought again about Raul's offer. He asked, "Raul, can we have lunch today so I can tell you more about my mom?" Raul said, "Of course, Bill, how about I meet you at twelve-thirty in the lunchroom?" Bill agreed. He felt that Raul understood him and supported him.*

How did Raul give Bill support? Do you think this made them closer friends? Why or why not?

—Delores had difficulty giving others support. She was quick to give advice but did not listen very well to others. One day Beverly announced that her mother had died of cancer. Delores did not listen, and Beverly again stated, "I'm feeling awful because my mom died of cancer two days ago." Beverly started to cry. Delores snapped, "Don't cry over spilled milk. She was old and now she's in heaven anyway." Beverly felt badly hurt. What she wanted was some support, someone to understand how she was feeling. Delores did not seem to understand Beverly's feelings, and she did not give any real support. Beverly felt rejected and walked into the next room, where she saw Joyce. She told Joyce about her mother, and Joyce put her arm around Beverly and said, "I'm very sorry to hear that, Beverly. Why don't you tell me all about it? You must feel awful." Beverly received support from Joyce and felt much better.

In what ways did Joyce give support to Beverly? What do you think Beverly wanted from Delores that she did not get from her? Do you think Beverly felt closer to Delores or to Joyce after talking about her mother that day? Why?

■ DISCUSSION QUESTIONS

Simple/concrete questions:

What are some ways to give/receive support?

Personal experience/feelings questions:

Have you ever needed support? What kind of support?

Have you ever asked someone for support? Did they give it to you?

How would you feel if you asked someone for support and they did not give it? How would you feel if they gave you support?

Problem-solving questions:

What are some ways that people can ask for support if they feel they are not getting enough?

If someone does not want to give you support, what should you do?

■ GROUP ACTIVITIES

Participants share times when they needed support, and whether or not this support was forth-coming.

Demonstrate verbal and nonverbal support. Hold a group discussion about whether or not different types of support are helpful.

Take turns supporting each other on issues for which individuals request support. Talk about how each person feels after receiving support.

■ ASSESSMENT OF SKILLS LEARNED

Recognizes several types of support:

ALMOST NEVER	USUALLY NOT	SOMETIMES	USUALLY	ALMOST ALWAYS
1	2	3	4	5

Recognizes one or more ways to give support:

ALMOST NEVER	USUALLY NOT	SOMETIMES	USUALLY	ALMOST ALWAYS
1	2	3	4	5

Requests one or more types of support:

ALMOST NEVER	USUALLY NOT	SOMETIMES	USUALLY	ALMOST ALWAYS
1	2	3	4	5

49. Trusting Others

Trust is basic to friendship. Individuals need to know that they can trust others with their thoughts and feelings. They need to know that they can count on each other for support when needed. Persons with developmental disabilities often have difficulty recognizing whether or not others are trustworthy. This section should begin with a discussion about how to recognize the trustworthiness of others. Some of the essential features of trustworthiness include following through and doing what one says one will do, telling the truth, not exaggerating what one can or will do, admitting mistakes, apologizing for failure to live up to commitments, making amends or making restitution for one's failures, not making excuses for mistakes, refraining from taking other's things without permission, and not violating confidences with others. Participants can be helped to distinguish the difference between intentional and unintentional unreliability or breeches of trust. This skill area is most appropriate for persons with mild developmental disabilities. Individuals with more severe disabilities often have difficulty understanding differences between intentional and unintentional behaviors. For example, they may not know the difference between a lie and a mistake, or between stealing and borrowing. They do not always have the level of comprehension necessary to make fine discriminations in the area of trust. It may be easier for them to identify obviously good or bad treatment, and how this treatment makes them feel. One modification here might be to ask a number of yes/no questions to help individuals learn to discriminate different elements of trust—for examples: "Ed took a cookie from his friend Tom without asking. Did he borrow it or steal it?" "Joyce said she would come back in a few minutes, but she did not return for a half hour because she forgot what time it was. Did she tell a lie or make a mistake?" "Ed asked Jeff if he could use his baseball glove. He used it and gave it back. Did he borrow it or steal it?"

■ SPECIFIC SKILLS TO BE LEARNED

Recognize trustworthiness of others:
    Telling the truth
    Doing what you say you are going to do
    Not exaggerating what you can or will do
    Apologizing for failing to live up to a commitment, and doing something to make it right
    Admitting mistakes
    Not making excuses for mistakes
    Not stealing or borrowing things without permission
    Violating a confidence
Recognize the difference between intentional and unintentional unreliability of others (e.g., a lie versus a mistake):

■ CONCEPTS NECESSARY TO PERFORM SKILLS

Truthful: Telling the truth; honest; telling the real facts; saying what is true; telling what really happened.

Honest: Truthful; telling the truth; saying what really happened; saying what is true.

Falsehood: Lie; not the truth; fable; made-up story; saying something that is not true.

Fable: Lie; untruth; falsehood; a made-up story; fiction.

Fiction: Falsehood; fable; untruth; made-up story; lie.

Lie: Saying something that is false; telling an untruth; making up a story that is not true; deceiving.

Trustworthy: Deserving the trust of others; truthful; not lying; honest; direct; doing what you say you will do; telling the truth; keeping one's word; not stealing, lying or cheating.

Good faith: Give your word and try to keep it; mean what you say; not lie; try not to deceive someone.

Steal: Take something without permission; borrow with no intention of giving something back; secretly take something from somebody; take something and not plan to give it back; rip something off.

Borrow: Ask permission to use something and give it back when done; use something that belongs to someone else but give it back; take something with permission; take with the intention of returning.

Private: Personal; something to be shared with only one or a few people; confidential; something told to a friend that is not to be shared with anybody else; personal and confidential talk between friends; intimate.

Violate a confidence: Tell private things to somebody without permission; when one friend tells another to keep something private but the person tells it to somebody else anyway; break a trust.

■ CASE VIGNETTES

—Richard had a new residence counselor, Laura. One day she advised him that he should open up and tell her about his problems. She said to him, "If you tell me what's bothering you, and why you broke the window yesterday, I'll keep it private, just between you and me." Richard told her all about what made him angry. He said that his mother agreed to take him for the weekend, but she had not come to get him. He had also had a bad day at work. He had been so frustrated and angry that he had thrown his softball through a window. Richard felt better when he talked to Laura about it. The next day his mother called him. She told him that she was disappointed in him because he had broken a window. She also said that Richard's new counselor, Laura, had told her that Richard was mad at her. Richard's heart sank. Laura had promised to keep their conversation private and confidential. He became angry all over again and felt that he could not trust his new counselor, Laura.

Why do you think Richard was feeling angry and let down? Do you think his counselor, Laura, was honest with him? Did she tell him a lie? Did she violate a confidence? Do you think that she might have made a mistake telling Richard's mother about the private conversation she had with Richard? Was Laura a trustworthy person?

—Jamal borrowed his friend Michael's softball glove on Saturday. He promised he would give it back on Sunday. When Sunday came, he walked over to Mike's house and returned the glove. Mike said, "Thanks, Jamal, I know I can always count on you to return something you borrow." Jamal then asked, "Would you like to go to the circus later today, Mike? My dad says he

has an extra ticket." Mike said, "Yes," and returned home. At their agreed on departure time, Jamal and his father picked up Mike and went to the circus.

Did Jamal follow through on his word? Can you give an example of how he did what he said he would do? Was he a trustworthy person?

■ DISCUSSION QUESTIONS

Simple/concrete questions:

What is the difference between the truth and a lie?

If a person says, "I'll pay you back," and does not pay you back, is the person trustworthy? If the person pays you back, is he or she trustworthy?

What is stealing? Borrowing?

Personal experience/feelings questions:

How do you feel if someone opens your mail and reads it without your permission?

Has anyone ever lied to you before? Can you give an example?

How do you feel when somebody lies to you?

Have you ever given somebody money and they did not pay you back? How did you feel?

How do you feel if somebody borrows something from you and does not give it back?

Problem-solving questions:

What should you do if somebody lies to you?

What should you do if someone borrows your money and does not pay it back? What should you do if a person borrows your things and does not give them back?

If somebody says he or she will do something with you on a certain day, at a certain time and place, and the person fails to show up, what should you do?

■ GROUP ACTIVITIES

Divide into pairs and talk about experiences of being lied to by others.

Ask each person to share one example of a situation in which somebody lied to him or her.

Each group member give one example of a time when someone made a promise and did not follow through.

Facilitate a discussion about how a person can feel let down if someone lies to them or does not follow through on their word.

■ ASSESSMENT OF SKILLS LEARNED

Recognizes the level of trustworthiness of others:

ALMOST NEVER	USUALLY NOT	SOMETIMES	USUALLY	ALMOST ALWAYS
1	2	3	4	5

Recognizes the difference between intentional and unintentional unreliability of others:

ALMOST NEVER	USUALLY NOT	SOMETIMES	USUALLY	ALMOST ALWAYS
1	2	3	4	5

7 *Personal Boundaries and Sexuality*

THIS CHAPTER EXPLORES the areas of personal boundaries and sexuality. Problems in these areas represent some of the most frequent reasons that persons with developmental disabilities are referred for psychotherapy and behavioral treatments. The chapter begins with the area of personal boundaries, followed by a more detailed discussion of physical and sexual boundaries. After this, the area of social boundaries is examined. The subsequent topic deals explicitly with various ways to set personal boundaries. It helps each individual clarify diverse areas related to personal boundaries. Next, a discussion of different kinds of relationships continues to examine personal boundaries in relationships. The topic of public, private, and secret behaviors is included to help individuals develop an appropriate awareness of personal privacy. The topic of borrowing and stealing, is added because it touches on an important area of personal boundaries. The final topic focuses on communication and personal boundaries, assisting individuals to communicate in appropriate ways, at appropriate times, and in appropriate places, about personal matters.

50. *Personal Boundaries*

Personal boundaries are the rules and lines of demarcation that define the physical, social, intellectual, and emotional space between individuals. The violation of rules related to interpersonal space is perhaps the single biggest factor for which individuals with developmental disabilities are referred for psychological-behavioral treatments. This section may begin with a definition of the concept of boundaries. The discussion should focus on rules about how close or distant to be with others; general rules of social interaction; sharing physical space; who, when, and how to touch or not to touch; and which types of behaviors are permitted in which contexts. By its nature, this can be a very abstract conversation. It may be simplified, and concrete examples can be given of the different types of boundaries discussed. This should be done through a question-and-answer process that addresses each category of boundaries separately. Some examples of boundary questions are: "Whom do you allow to touch you?" "In what ways do you like to be touched?" "Is this different for family members than strangers?" "When should you look a person in the eyes?" "Are there some people with whom it is not a good idea to talk about personal matters?" In this way, group participants can begin to understand the concept of boundaries in a concrete way and can relate to real-life applications of this concept. The topic is one of the most difficult. It is appropriate for those with mild and for some individuals with moderate developmental disabilities, but lower functioning persons have progressively more difficulty understanding and relating to the topic. The major modification for individuals with more limited ability is to use a question-and-answer format and to restrict questions to concrete, yes/no inquiries. A further modification is to focus more on physical or tangible boundaries. This can be done by taking a person's arm and asking whose it is, then listing a sequence of other body parts and asking to whom they belong. Next, the questions may be repeated, asking the same individual to whom another person's body parts belong, in this way teaching the concept of physical boundaries. Another way to examine social-physical boundaries concretely is to have one individual walk toward another person until the person feels he or she is at a "most comfortable" talking distance. This can be repeated by other individuals to highlight that each person feels most comfortable with a different level of physical-social distance.

■ SPECIFIC SKILLS TO BE LEARNED

Understand the concept of boundaries:
>   Sets of rules for how to act (limits you put on yourself and limits others set for you):
>   >   How close or distant to be with others
>   >   How to interact with others
>   >   How to share physical space
>   >   Whether or not to touch others
>   >   Whom, how, and when to touch
>   >   Which behaviors are permitted in which situations (context)

Differentiate (identify) different types of boundaries:
>   Physical and sexual:
>   >   Who can touch you and whom can you touch?
>   >   When do you let people touch you?
>   >   How do you let people touch you?
>   >   How close do you sit to people?
>   >   When do you make eye contact?
>   >   How close do you get to others in an elevator?
>   >   How do you share your living space (television, telephone, sleeping space, living room, dining room, etc.)?
>   >   Whom do you let touch you in a "sexual" way?
>   >   Who can see you with your clothes off (how do you decide whom to let see your body)?
>   >   What permission do you need to touch others?
>   Social:
>   >   To whom do you talk?
>   >   When do you talk to others?
>   >   With whom do you do things?
>   >   How loudly do you speak?
>   >   Do you talk with food in your mouth?
>   >   When do you "socialize" with others?
>   >   How do you socialize?
>   Intellectual and emotional:
>   >   Whose thoughts and feelings do you have?
>   >   Who controls your thoughts and feelings?
>   >   Do you have a right to talk about your thoughts and feelings?

■ CONCEPTS NECESSARY TO PERFORM SKILLS

Social: Related to people; to do with relationships; talking to people; taking an interest in others; doing things with people; getting together with friends; rules about how to get along with others.

Boundary: A dividing line; space between people or things; a rule; a way somebody is supposed to act; a limit; a border; end point; a place where one thing leaves off and another begins; something that lets a person know the limits of acceptable behavior.

Physical: To do with a person's body; something one can see, touch, or feel; concrete; something that has substance; rules about whom, when, and how to touch.

Sexual: To do with sex; rules about being a man or woman; rules about people touching each other in private places; attraction between people.

Intellectual: To do with thoughts; a person's thinking; rules about a person's thoughts and how to express them.

Emotional: To do with feelings; a person's emotions; rules about who has what feelings and how to express them.

Rule: Guideline; boundary; limit; expectation; what each person agrees to do or not do.

■ CASE VIGNETTES

—*Nancy was quite clear about her personal boundaries. That meant that she knew the rules about who, when, and how to be close to others. For example, she knew she did not want her co-workers to touch her, she did not want to be touched by strangers, and she did not want people sitting too close to her at the bus stop. On the other hand, she wanted a hug from her mother, she wanted her boyfriend to kiss her, and she wanted to sit close to her friend Marge. Nancy knew that when she was feeling angry, those feelings were happening inside of herself. She knew that if someone else was mad, those feelings belonged to the other person. Nancy knew that she liked to talk about private things to her friend Marge, but she did not want Marge to tell those things to acquaintances or strangers. Nancy did not like people standing too close to her in an elevator or when she was in line at the grocery store. She did not mind sitting close to her family members when driving in a car. Nancy was clear about her rules for physical, social, and emotional closeness.*

How was Nancy clear about her personal boundaries? Can you give an example?

—*Oscar has very poor personal boundaries. Sometimes he stares at people he does not know. At other times he bumps into people when he is in line at the store. Oscar likes to talk loudly, even when someone else is talking. He does not seem to notice the normal, everyday rules for how to socialize. Oscar sits right next to somebody on the bench at the bus stop, even if there is only one person on the bench and there is plenty of room to sit away from the person. Sometimes he starts talking to strangers and tells them very private information, even though he does not have any idea who they are or how they think about things. At times Oscar is confused. He thinks that because he is feeling angry, others should know how he feels. He does not bother to tell them. Sometimes he thinks others should read his mind. For example, one day when he was at his friend Bob's house, he was very thirsty but did not ask Bob for a drink. He thought that Bob should just know how he felt. On another occasion Oscar thought that his workmate, Linda, was pretty. He walked up to her and kissed her without permission. He also touched her where he was not supposed to.*

How does Oscar have unclear personal boundaries? Can you give an example? How does he break the rules about whom, when, and how to touch others? How does he break the rules about who, when, and how to socialize with others?

■ DISCUSSION QUESTIONS

Simple/concrete questions:
    What are personal boundaries?
    What are some different types of personal boundaries?
    What are some different rules people have about physical and sexual touch?
    What are some rules which people have for socializing with others?
Personal experience/feelings questions:
    Do you set limits (personal boundaries) with other people?
    What kind of rules do you have for touching others?
    What kind of rules do you have for talking to people?
    Has anyone ever failed to respect your boundaries? Touched you without permission?
        Gotten too close when they were talking to you?
    Has anyone ever told you what you were thinking or feeling without asking you? How did
        you feel?
    Can you read someone's mind? Can you tell how people are feeling or what they are
        thinking without asking them?
Problem-solving questions:
    How can you better set personal boundaries (rules or limits) with other people?
    Why is it important to have clear personal boundaries?
    What should you do if someone touches you without permission?

■ GROUP ACTIVITIES

Facilitate a discussion about how group members set personal boundaries with others.
Participants share negative life experiences about people who do not respect their boundaries.
Group leader imitate persons with good and bad personal boundaries. Ask group members for
    feedback about each style of relating.

■ ASSESSMENT OF SKILLS LEARNED

Understands the concept of boundaries:

ALMOST NEVER	USUALLY NOT	SOMETIMES	USUALLY	ALMOST ALWAYS
1	2	3	4	5

Identifies different types of boundaries:

ALMOST NEVER	USUALLY NOT	SOMETIMES	USUALLY	ALMOST ALWAYS
1	2	3	4	5

51. *Physical and Sexual Boundaries*

This section takes a closer look at physical and sexual boundaries. Persons with developmental
disabilities are often referred to psychotherapists because of physical/sexual boundary violations. Instead of coming from sexuality problems per se, these boundary violations most often
result from a lack of ability to differentiate appropriate physical space, and to understand
social rules pertaining to physical touch. The group facilitator should review the concept of
physical/sexual boundaries, highlighting rules for closeness/distance, sharing physical space,

and how/when to touch or not touch others. This should be followed by a conversation about setting physical/sexual boundaries with others, emphasizing the need to tell others whether or not one wants to be touched, how and when to communicate about physical boundaries, getting outside help setting boundaries, and being assertive in communications about boundaries. Considering that physical/sexual/social boundaries may vary to some extent from one locale to another and from one cultural group to another, the group facilitator should be aware of, and sensitive to, the accepted social norms of the community in question. For example, southern Europeans may be more physical in their everyday expressions, often hold hands, walking with their arms around each other, and standing closer to each other during conversation. Scandinavians and Minnesotans may be more restricted in their public physical demonstrations. This topic is most appropriate for individuals with mild developmental disabilities. It may be modified for lower functioning individuals in a similar fashion as the previous topic.

■ SPECIFIC SKILLS TO BE LEARNED

Understand the concept of physical/sexual boundaries:
    Rules for how close or distant to be to others
    Rules about how to share physical space
    Rules about whether or not to touch others or let others touch you
    Rules about whom, how, and when to touch others, and to let others touch you (context of touch)
Set physical and sexual boundaries with others:
    Tell others whether or not you want them to touch you.
    Know how and when to set boundaries.
    Get help setting boundaries if necessary.
    Be assertive and repeat yourself if necessary.

■ CONCEPTS NECESSARY TO PERFORM SKILLS

Physical: To do with a person's body; something one can see, touch, or feel; concrete; something that has substance; rules about who, when and how to touch.

Sexual: To do with sex; rules about being a man or woman; rules about people touching each other in private places; attraction between people.

Boundary: A dividing line; space between people or things; rule; way somebody is supposed to act; limit; border; end point; place where one thing leaves off and another begins; something that lets a person know the limits of acceptable behavior.

Rule: Guideline; boundary; limit; expectation; what each person agrees to do or not do.

Assertive: Directly tell a person how you feel; say how you feel and why you feel that way; tell someone what is on your mind.

■ CASE VIGNETTES

—*Jessica was a very nice but quiet woman. One day she was working at her job, and a coworker, Jeff, bumped up against her. She moved away and kept working. A little while later she noticed that Jeff was smiling at her and getting close to her again. He kept asking her questions while she tried to work. She did not know what to say, but did not like him touching her. Then, just after their coffee break started, Jessica was walking to her locker and Jeff touched her where he was not supposed to. She did not like this and started crying. She just wanted Jeff to leave her alone but did not know how to tell him. Later her work supervisor saw her crying and asked what was the matter. By then Jessica was feeling awful.*

    Do you think Jessica did a good job communicating her physical boundaries to Jeff? Why or why not? What could she have done to make her boundaries more clear? Do you think Jeff had good physical boundaries? Why or why not? What should Jeff have done to be more respectful of Jessica's boundaries?

—Donna worked at a crowded table, sorting and packaging items that were sold in stores. Today she was working with a new person, Peter, who had only been at the job for a few days. She noticed Peter talked very loudly, and did not seem to listen very well. He also moved in front of others or bumped into them without excusing himself. While she was paying attention to her job, he bumped into her and then started to work right next to her, even though there was room for him to move over. Donna looked him in the eye and said, "Peter, could you please move over? I would appreciate it if you would give me enough room to do my job." Peter moved over, but a few minutes later he was back. He bumped into her again. She repeated her request for him to move over. He did not listen and kept working right next to her. She moved away, but soon he was right in her work space again. Donna told him one more time, "Peter, please move over and give me some more room to work." When he ignored her, Donna felt very angry. She quickly walked over to her supervisor's office and asked for help. She explained that Peter kept coming into her work space and bumping into her. Donna's supervisor had a talk with Peter and told him he would have to work at another table if he could not stay in his own work space.

Was Donna assertive in setting her boundaries? What did she do to set limits with Peter? Did she have to try more than once to set her boundaries? Do you think Donna was clear about her personal boundaries?

■ DISCUSSION QUESTIONS

Simple/concrete questions:

    What are some different kinds of physical touch (e.g., punching, hitting, slapping, tickling, rubbing, hugging, kissing)?

    What are some different rules for whether or not to touch somebody?

    What are some different rules for whether or not to let somebody touch you?

Personal experience/feelings questions:

    Whom do you let touch you? How? When?

    Whom do you touch? How? When?

    What are some ways that you like to be touched? What are some ways that you do not like to be touched?

    How close do you like to sit to people? Does it matter if they are friends or strangers?

    When do you look at people in the eyes (stare at people)? When is this not O.K.?

    How do you share your living space (e.g., television, telephone, bedroom, living room)?

    Whom do you let touch you in sexual ways?

Problem-solving questions:

    Who owns your body? Who has the right to touch you?

    How can you get better at setting physical/sexual boundaries?

    What should you do if someone touches you without permission?

    Where can you get help if someone tries to touch you without permission?

■ GROUP ACTIVITIES

Facilitate discussion about individual group members' good and bad experiences with physical and sexual touch.

Participants give support to others who have had physical/sexual boundary violations.

Facilitate a discussion about different types of touch and physical/sexual boundaries in different types of relationships (family, friend, acquaintance, stranger, etc.)

■ ASSESSMENT OF SKILLS LEARNED

Understands the concept of physical/sexual boundaries:

ALMOST NEVER	USUALLY NOT	SOMETIMES	USUALLY	ALMOST ALWAYS
1	2	3	4	5

Sets physical/sexual boundaries with others:

ALMOST NEVER	USUALLY NOT	SOMETIMES	USUALLY	ALMOST ALWAYS
1	2	3	4	5

52. *Social Boundaries*

This section provides a more in-depth view of social boundaries. Social boundaries are perhaps more subtle than physical/sexual ones, but are just as important and overlap them to some extent. Individuals with developmental disabilities often experience difficulty assessing appropriate boundaries in this sphere. The discussion may begin with a review of the concept of a *social* boundary. This heading subsumes sets of rules about socializing, privacy, and how close or distant to be in relationships. A detailed discussion of various social boundaries should occur. Individuals need to decide with whom to be close, and how close to be, in different types of relationships including family, significant other, friend, co-worker, schoolmate, acquaintance, and stranger. Decisions need to be made concerning with whom to talk and spend time, when to perform different activities, how physically close to be, when to make eye contact, what to talk about, how personal to get, what should be kept private from whom, where to socialize, how to let people know they are too close or personal, when to start conversing, and so forth. It must be emphasized that a different set of social boundaries applies to each category of relationship. Again, this is a very complex topic, most appropriate for those with mild developmental disabilities. Modifications in presentation can be made by simplifying the language used, focusing on concrete examples, and asking yes/no questions about a range of social boundary situations. Some examples of questions are "Is it best to talk to someone from across the room or close up?" "Should you stand next to someone when you talk to them?" "Is it O.K. to tell personal information to a stranger?" "Is it better to talk about personal problems with your work supervisor or family and friends?" "If something terrible happens to you, is it better to tell an acquaintance or a family member?" "If you are talking to people and they keep moving away from you, might you be standing too close to them?"

■ SPECIFIC SKILLS TO BE LEARNED

Understand the concept of *social* boundaries:
  Sets of rules for how and when to socialize with others (get together with, talk with others, etc.)
  Rules about privacy in social relationships
  Rules about how close or distant to be in a social relationship (family, friend, acquaintance, stranger, etc.)
Set social boundaries with others:

Decide with whom to be close:
    Family
    Significant other (e.g., boyfriend, girlfriend, husband/wife)
    Friend
    Co-worker/schoolmate
    Acquaintance
    Stranger
Decide with whom to talk or spend time.
Decide when to spend time with others (work breaks, after work, weekends, etc.).
Decide how physically close to be with others.
Decide when to make eye contact and with whom.
Decide what to talk about and with whom (decide how personal to get).
Decide what is private information.
Decide where to socialize with others.
Tell someone if he or she is too close, too personal, too nosy, or to private (if necessary, walk away, move away, say "no," etc.).
Know when to start a conversation with others.
Know how close to sit or stand when talking to someone.

■ CONCEPTS NECESSARY TO PERFORM SKILLS

Social: Related to people; to do with relationships; talk to people; take an interest in others; do things with people; get together with friends; rules about how to get along with others.

Socialize: Talk to others; get together with friends; tell people about one's life and ask about theirs; take an interest in people; do things with others; relate to people.

Boundary: A dividing line; space between people or things; a rule; a way somebody is supposed to act; a limit; a border; end point; a place where one thing leaves off and another begins; something that lets a person know the limits of acceptable behavior.

Personal: Private; confidential; intimate; things people usually keep to themselves; things usually told only to friends and family members; something a person does not want everybody to hear about; one's own special thoughts and experiences.

Private: Personal; something to be shared with only one or a few people; confidential; something told to a friend that is not to be shared with anybody else; personal and confidential talk between friends; intimate.

Rule: Guideline; boundary; limit; expectation; what each person agrees to do or not do.

Family member: Brother, sister, or parent; someone in a person's family; somebody with whom a person lives.

Friend: Somebody a person knows well; a familiar person; companion; mate; a person with whom somebody likes to do things; someone to talk to; somebody to whom a person feels close; someone a person can trust.

Co-worker: Workmate; a friend or acquaintance from work; somebody from a person's workplace.

Acquaintance: Somebody a person has seen before but does not know very well; someone with whom one has gone to school or worked but is not very familiar; a person one knows but not too well.

Stranger: Somebody a person does not know at all; a person you have never met; a person one sees for the first time; an unfamiliar person.

■ CASE VIGNETTES

—Kato had good social boundaries. When he entered a room, he frequently made a very slight bow, something he had learned in the country he came from. He had also learned the new

social boundaries of America and would smile as he greeted others. If others were talking about something, he would not interrupt them but would wait quietly until he knew what they were talking about. He might say something when the others had stopped talking. Kato was close friends with Jack and sometimes told him about personal problems; but when Kato was at the bus stop, he would keep personal matters to himself. When he was with strangers, he might engage in small talk about the weather or recent news events. When he was with strangers, he was friendly but did not share too much information. He knew it could be dangerous to say too much to people that he did not know. Another reason he said little to strangers was that he did not know what they thought or felt about things, and he did not want to offend them by saying things that would upset them. When Kato was with family and friends, he was very open and honest about his thoughts and feelings. He knew he could trust them with his personal information. At the bus stop, Kato never sat right next to somebody. He always left a little space and did not crowd others. If someone else got too close to him, Kato would politely move a little farther away. Sometimes he even stood up to wait for the bus if others were sitting too closely to him on the bench.

In what ways did Kato have good social boundaries? What did he do to get close to family and friends but keep distance with acquaintances and strangers?

—Maryann had poor social boundaries. She did not seem to know that there were different rules for relating to friends and strangers. One day she walked to the bus stop and sat right next to a stranger. She started telling him about problems with her boyfriend. Before she knew it, he invited her to go to his house for a visit. She thought that would be fun and went along with him. When they got to his house, nobody else was there. He gave her something to drink that tasted kind of funny. Maryann decided she wanted to go home, but he said he did not want her to go. He even tried to touch her where he was not supposed to. Maryann got scared and told him she was leaving. He became angry, and that made her feel even more frightened. Suddenly she thought to herself, "I'd better leave or something bad might happen." She got up and walked out the door but had a hard time finding her way back home. Finally she got home and told her counselor about what had happened.

In what ways did Maryann have poor social boundaries? Do you think that it was a good idea for her to talk about personal problems to a stranger? Why or why not? Was it a good idea for her to go home with a stranger? Why or why not? How could Maryann set better social boundaries next time?

■ DISCUSSION QUESTIONS

Simple/concrete questions:
What does it mean to socialize?
How close should you get when you talk to people?
How close should you sit to other people?
What are some rules about socializing with others?
Personal experience/feelings questions:
With whom do you like to socialize?
Do you socialize with family members? Friends? Co-workers? Strangers?
How close do you get when you talk to people?
How do you feel when you are talking to other people?
Whom do you like to spend time with?
Problem-solving questions:
What is a good way to start a conversation with others?
When is a good time to start talking to someone?
How can you set limits or boundaries on other people who try to get too close to you?

What do you do if someone wants to be your friend and you do not want to be friends with them?

How can you become a better socializer?

■ GROUP ACTIVITIES

Facilitate a discussion about different types of social boundaries for different types of relationships.

Each group member share personal experiences socializing with family, friends, co-workers, and others.

Divide into pairs and discuss various social experiences.

■ ASSESSMENT OF SKILLS LEARNED

Understands the concept of social boundaries:

ALMOST NEVER	USUALLY NOT	SOMETIMES	USUALLY	ALMOST ALWAYS
1	2	3	4	5

Sets social boundaries with others:

ALMOST NEVER	USUALLY NOT	SOMETIMES	USUALLY	ALMOST ALWAYS
1	2	3	4	5

53. *Setting Boundaries*

This topic builds on the previous three, focusing more heavily on setting one's boundaries with others. Although many individuals with developmental disabilities may recognize appropriate and inappropriate boundaries in given situations, they may lack the expressive communication skills to effectively set their boundaries with others. This topic should begin with a review of the major types of boundaries. Next, physical boundaries may be examined more closely by identifying good and bad kinds of touch, and exploring a variety of different kinds of touch between individuals. Next, members can be assisted in identifying the differences between their own thoughts or feelings and those of others, followed by another examination of the differences between various types of social relationships. The conversation should then turn to when and with whom group members would like to be close. This may lead to a discussion of ways to establish closeness, including making eye contact, moving physically closer to or touching others, beginning a conversation, talking about personal matters, and doing things together with others. Finally, a variety of ways to set personal boundaries or limits with others should be examined. These include asking someone to listen, deciding not to touch a person or let another touch oneself, backing away, saying "no," leaving a situation, deciding not to see someone again, telling a person not to touch or do something, asking somebody to stop touching, screaming at someone who will not listen, asking for help if somebody ignores boundaries, and telling someone what an individual feels, thinks and wants. This again is a higher level topic, most appropriate for those with mild developmental disabilities. For individuals with more limited intellect, similar modifications should be made as with the previous topic, focusing questions on issues around setting personal boundaries.

■ SPECIFIC SKILLS TO BE LEARNED

Identify different types of boundaries:
    Physical/sexual
    Social
    Intellectual/emotional
Identify good and bad kinds of touch:
    Punching, hitting, and kicking
    Slapping and pinching
    Hugging and kissing
    Tapping
    Poking
    Rubbing
    Tickling
    Shaking hands
    Massaging
Identify the difference between one's own thoughts/feelings and those of others.
Identify the difference between different types of social relationships:
    Family
    Friend
    Co-worker
    Acquaintance
    Stranger
Identify when and with whom one would like to be close.
Understand how to establish closeness:
    Making eye contact
    Being physically close (moving closer or touching)
    Starting a conversation
    Talking about personal matters
    Doing things together
Set boundaries (limits) with others:
    Ask someone to listen.
    Decide not to touch or let touch.
    Back away if someone is too close.
    Say "no."
    Leave a situation.
    Decide not to see somebody again.
    Tell someone not to touch you or not to do something.
    Tell somebody to stop touching.
    Scream at someone who will not listen.
    Ask for help if someone ignores boundaries.
    Tell somebody how you feel, what you think, and what you want.

■ CONCEPTS NECESSARY TO PERFORM SKILLS

Boundary: A dividing line; space between people or things; rule; way somebody is supposed to act; limit; border; end point; a place where one thing leaves off and another begins; something that lets a person know the limits of acceptable behavior.

Closeness: togetherness; how close or far away one is from another; how intimate or friendly people are with others.

Physical: To do with a person's body; something one can see, touch, or feel; concrete; something that has substance; rules about who, when and how to touch.

Sexual: To do with sex; rules about being a man or woman; rules about people touching each other in private places; attraction between people.

Social: Related to people; to do with relationships; talking to people; taking an interest in others; doing things with people; getting together with friends; rules about how to get along with others.

Intellectual: To do with thoughts; a person's thinking; rules about a person's thoughts and how to express them.

Emotional: To do with feelings; a person's emotions; rules about who has what feelings and how to express them.

■ CASE VIGNETTES

—*Miles had good personal boundaries. He knew how to set limits with others who overstepped his boundaries. When he was talking and someone was not listening closely enough, he would say, "Excuse me, I'm talking to you, will you please listen to me?" He was also clear about who he wanted to touch him and how. His mother could give him a hug, and his friend Mike could shake hands and put his arm around Miles. He let his girlfriend kiss him, but he did not want her to do this in front of other people. If somebody got too close on the bench at the bus stop, he moved further away. If others tried to touch him in a way that he did not like, Miles told them not to do it. If they did not listen, Miles would push them away or he would leave the situation. Miles knew that he could get help from his parents or counselors if someone tried to touch him in ways that he did not like. When people did things that made Miles angry, he would look them in the eyes, say how he felt, and ask them to stop doing the offensive behaviors.*

In what ways did Miles have good personal boundaries? How did he set limits on other people so that they would better respect his boundaries?

—*Laverne was not completely clear about her boundaries. She had ideas about what she liked and did not like, but she did not know how to communicate her thoughts very well to others. For example, she did not like Joe very much, but he often talked to her. She did not know how to tell him politely that she had other things to do. When he asked her if she wanted to go out for pizza on Saturday, she did not know what to say, so she told him, "I don't know, Joe." Joe kept asking her to go out. She was afraid he might be mad if she said no, so she said, "Maybe, I'm not sure." Joe was not sure either. He liked Laverne and hoped she liked him. But when he thought about her answers, he thought, "Maybe she likes me." He kept trying to see if she would spend some time with him. By the time it was Friday, Laverne was mad at Joe because he kept pestering her. Joe was mad at Laverne because she would not give him an answer about going out for pizza.*

What do you think Laverne could have done to be more clear about her boundaries with Joe? What could Joe have done to be more clear about his boundaries with Laverne? Is it O.K. to tell somebody how you feel about their behavior? Is it O.K. to tell someone that you do not want to go out for pizza with them? Is it fair to ask someone to give you a definite "yes" or "no" answer when you ask them to go out on a date?

■ DISCUSSION QUESTIONS

Simple/concrete questions:
    What is a boundary?
    What are some different kinds of touch?

What are some different types of social relationships?

What are some ways to set boundaries or limits upon others?

Personal experience/feelings questions:

How do you like to be touched? By whom?

How do you not like to be touched? By whom?

Do you like to be touched in one way by some people and in another way by others?

Whom would you like to be close to?

How do you feel when you are close to others?

How do you feel if someone does not respect your boundaries (if they do not listen when you set limits)?

Problem-solving questions:

What is a good way to get close to someone?

How can you set boundaries with other people who do not listen to you?

What should you do if someone does not respect your boundaries?

■ GROUP ACTIVITIES

Ask each person for one way that they like and do not like to be touched by others.

Facilitate a discussion about setting different types of boundaries in different types of relationships.

Lead a discussion about how to set boundaries or limits with other persons who do not listen or respect boundaries.

■ ASSESSMENT OF SKILLS LEARNED

Identifies different types of boundaries:

ALMOST NEVER	USUALLY NOT	SOMETIMES	USUALLY	ALMOST ALWAYS
1	2	3	4	5

Differentiates good and bad touch:

ALMOST NEVER	USUALLY NOT	SOMETIMES	USUALLY	ALMOST ALWAYS
1	2	3	4	5

Identifies own versus others' thoughts/feelings:

ALMOST NEVER	USUALLY NOT	SOMETIMES	USUALLY	ALMOST ALWAYS
1	2	3	4	5

Identifies different types of social relationships:

ALMOST NEVER	USUALLY NOT	SOMETIMES	USUALLY	ALMOST ALWAYS
1	2	3	4	5

Identifies when and with whom would like to be close:

ALMOST NEVER	USUALLY NOT	SOMETIMES	USUALLY	ALMOST ALWAYS
1	2	3	4	5

Understands how to establish closeness:

ALMOST NEVER	USUALLY NOT	SOMETIMES	USUALLY	ALMOST ALWAYS
1	2	3	4	5

Sets boundaries or limits with others:

ALMOST NEVER	USUALLY NOT	SOMETIMES	USUALLY	ALMOST ALWAYS
1	2	3	4	5

54. *Different Kinds of Relationships*

This topic is an extension of several previous ones, focusing on the differentiation between different types of relationships. The group facilitator should explore a wide range of relationships, including family, significant other (e.g., boyfriend, girlfriend, husband, wife, etc.), friend, workmate, boss or supervisor, acquaintance, neighbor, stranger, enemy, and so forth. The group may examine the different boundaries or levels of closeness for each type of relationship. The boundaries of each relationship can be examined according to dimensions of physical/sexual, social/intellectual/emotional, and privacy/sharing. Focus may be given to the different types of rules for different types of relationships. The point should be made that the closer the relationship, the more one expects in the way of help, caring, affection, attention, time, physical closeness, and so forth. The more distant the relationship, the less one expects. Again, this is a more complex topic than many others, most appropriate for those with mild developmental disabilities. Individuals with more limited intellectual functioning may respond to more concrete, yes/no questions, exploring which behaviors are permitted in which types of relations—for example: "John and Sheila are married. Is it O.K. for them to see each other undressing?" "Bob and JoJo are workmates. Is it a good idea for them to hug and kiss each other at work?" "Ranga and Bill live in the same house. Is it O.K. for them to tell each other how they feel about things?" "Darren noticed a stranger at the bus stop. Should he tell the stranger about his personal problems?"

■ SPECIFIC SKILLS TO BE LEARNED

Recognize different types of relationships:
  Family
  Significant other (boyfriend, girlfriend, spouse, etc.)
  Friend
  Workmate
  Boss or supervisor
  Acquaintance
  Neighbor
  Stranger
  Enemy
Recognize different boundaries for different types of relationships (different levels of closeness):
  Physical/sexual
  Social/intellectual/emotional
  Privacy/sharing
Recognize different rules for different relationships:
  The closer the relationship, the more one expects (help, caring, affection, time, attention, etc.).
  The more distant the relationship, the less one expects.

■ CONCEPTS NECESSARY TO PERFORM SKILLS

Relationship: Connection with somebody; when people know each other; to relate or do things with others; togetherness; family, friend, or acquaintance.

Boundary: A dividing line; space between people or things; rule; way somebody is supposed to act; limit; border; end point; place where one thing leaves off and another begins; something that lets a person know the limits of acceptable behavior.

Physical: To do with a person's body; something one can see, touch, or feel; concrete; something that has substance; rules about who, when and how to touch.

Sexual: To do with sex; rules about being a man or woman; rules about people touching each other in private places; attraction between people.

Social: Related to people; to do with relationships; talk to people; taking an interest in others; do things with people; get together with friends; rules about how to get along with others.

Privacy: To keep thoughts and feelings to oneself; share thoughts and feelings with only close relations; confidentiality.

Intellectual: To do with thoughts; a person's thinking; rules about a person's thoughts and how to express them.

Emotional: To do with feelings; a person's emotions; rules about who has what feelings and how to express them.

■ CASE VIGNETTES

—Roger and Peter had a close relationship. They were good friends. They had known each other for many years, and now, even though they lived across town from each other, they got together twice a month to do fun activities. Tonight they were going to a movie together. Roger had picked the movie, but Peter agreed it was a good choice. They each took the bus, and met at the shopping mall before the movie. Roger got there first. When he saw Peter, he yelled, "Over here, Pete." They shook hands and Peter patted Roger on the back. As they waited for the movie to start, they told each other about what they had done during the week. After this, Peter became more personal and told Roger about a problem he was having with his girlfriend. Soon the movie started. When it was over, they both agreed that they liked it. When they were walking out, somebody bumped into Peter and told him to look out. Because they were good friends, Roger stuck up for him and told the other man to, "Look out," himself. Soon Roger and Peter shook hands and said good-bye.

Do you think Roger and Peter were good friends? Why or why not? Do you think they had a close relationship? Why or why not? Did they touch each other at all? In what way? Was this O.K. for the type of relationship that they had?

—Isabella had a few close friends in the neighborhood. They often got together to do things and were happy when they saw each other. Isabella also had many workmates at her job. She saw her closest friends when she was away from work and did not feel too comfortable sharing personal information with her workmates. She usually ate lunch in the cafeteria where she worked. A co-worker named Genevieve often sat near her. Genevieve was very talkative and often said things that did not particularly interest Isabella. Once in a while, Genevieve would suggest that the two of them get together after work and go to a movie or out for pizza. It was not that Isabella disliked her, but she felt she did not have much in common with Genevieve. She liked different types of things. She just did not feel comfortable doing something alone with Genevieve because they did not really know each other very well. Then Isabella got an idea. She invited Genevieve to join her and her friends on Saturday. That way, Isabella felt more comfortable, and Genevieve felt happy to have somebody to do something with. Maybe they will become good friends in the future. Isabella does not know yet. In the meantime, they are becoming a bit closer and more personal than workmates, but not as close as good friends sometimes become.

What kind of relationship do Isabella and Genevieve have? Is it O.K. for Isabella to decide not to be too close to Genevieve at this point? Is it all right to get to know someone slowly before one decides to become close friends?

■ DISCUSSION QUESTIONS

Simple/concrete questions:

What are some different types of relationships?

Is it a good idea to talk about personal matters to a stranger?

Is it a good idea to let a stranger hug you?

From what kind of relationship would you expect someone to help you with personal problems? Work problems?

Personal experience/feelings questions:

Describe your relationship with family members? Workmates? Friends?

Whom would you allow to give you a back rub?

With whom would you go out for coffee?

Has anybody ever tried to be too close to you? Describe?

Have you ever tried to be too close to someone? Describe?

Problem-solving questions:

How should you deal with a person who wants to be too close?

How do you decide if you know somebody well enough to be close to them?

How can you get closer to someone if you want them for a good friend?

■ GROUP ACTIVITIES

Each participant shares a personal experience about a current or past relationship. Facilitate a discussion about different types of rules for different types of relationships.

■ ASSESSMENT OF SKILLS LEARNED

Recognizes different types of relationships:

ALMOST NEVER	USUALLY NOT	SOMETIMES	USUALLY	ALMOST ALWAYS
1	2	3	4	5

Recognizes different boundaries for different types of relationships:

ALMOST NEVER	USUALLY NOT	SOMETIMES	USUALLY	ALMOST ALWAYS
1	2	3	4	5

Recognizes different rules for different relationships:

ALMOST NEVER	USUALLY NOT	SOMETIMES	USUALLY	ALMOST ALWAYS
1	2	3	4	5

55. *Public, Private, and Secret Behaviors*

Another way to view interpersonal boundaries that involves physical, social, emotional, and intellectual categories is to think of self-presentations as either public, private, or secret. Individuals with developmental disabilities often have difficulty drawing distinctions between these three domains. The group leader should begin with a discussion about the differences between public, private, and secret phenomena. Public information and behaviors are shared with anyone, or are plain for all to see. Private information and behaviors are selectively shared in closer relationships, and it is appropriate to restrict access to these aspects of oneself. Secret information and behaviors are similarly kept to oneself or restricted to only a few other people, but should be shared with others. To illustrate this distinction, the person who has a medical problem may wish to keep this private, and rightfully so. The person who has stolen a candy bar from a store and lied about where it came from should tell someone about it and make restitution. Some examples of public phenomena are a person's name, style of dress, work behavior, attendance at public places, hair color, gender, and so forth. Examples of private phenomena include personal feelings, thoughts, matters with friends, sexual behaviors, bathroom activities, things done in the privacy of one's home, and so forth. Secret phenomena include stealing, lying, cheating, and engaging in wrongful behaviors, be they immoral, unethical, or illegal. This topic is appropriate for individuals with mild and sometimes moderate developmental disabilities. One way to modify this section for lower functioning persons is to ask yes/no questions about whether or not something belongs to one of the three categories: public, private, or secret. The use of humor is also suggested—for example: "When you use the bathroom, is what you are doing in there private or secret?" "When you change your clothes, do you do it in private or do you invite the neighborhood in to watch?" "When you have a personal problem, do you keep it private with just your family and friends, or do you announce it in public places?"

■ SPECIFIC SKILLS TO BE LEARNED

Understand the difference between public, private, and secret behaviors:
    Public (behaviors shared with anyone)
    Private (behaviors selectively shared in closer relationships)
    Secret (behaviors kept to oneself or a few others but which should be told to others)
Differentiate behaviors belonging to public, private, and secret domains:
    Public:
        Clothing
        Name
        Work behaviors
        Shopping in stores
        Visiting public places
    Private:
        Personal information
        Matters with friends
        Sexual behaviors
        Bathroom behaviors
        Bedroom behaviors
        Behaviors at home
        Things kept locked up
    Secret:
        Stealing
        Lying
        Engaging in wrongful behaviors

■ CONCEPTS NECESSARY TO PERFORM SKILLS

Public: Behaviors shared with anyone; something anybody and everybody can see.
Private: Personal; something to be shared with only one or a few people; confidential; something told to a friend that is not to be shared with anybody else; personal and confidential talk between friends; intimate.
Secret: Hidden; kept from others; something that is kept private such as stealing, lying, or wrongful behavior, which should be told to others.

■ CASE VIGNETTES

—Carlos had eaten breakfast and was walking down the sidewalk in front of his house. He lived in a crowded city neighborhood and often passed strangers on the street. Yesterday a man stopped and asked him his name. Carlos smiled and told the man his name. He felt happy because he did not always get so much attention. Then the man asked him a lot of other questions and Carlos gave him the answers. He asked, "Do you live alone?" Carlos replied, "No, I live with my mother and sister." The man questioned Carlos: "Does your mother work?" Carlos told him, "Yes, every day, she works at the restaurant." Carlos felt a little uncomfortable telling private information to a stranger. He had soon told the man that his parents were divorced, his mother returned home at five o'clock every night, his sister went to school two miles away, and many other things.

Do you think it was a good idea for Carlos to tell a stranger that much personal information? Why or why not? How should you decide if something is private? What might happen if a person tells too much personal information to a stranger?

—Annette had very good boundaries with respect to public and private behaviors. That meant that she knew what to keep private and what she could share with anyone. She knew that when she used the bathroom, she should shut the door and keep her privacy. When she took a shower or used the toilet, she did not want any company. She understood that when she wore her clothes out to the shopping mall, she was in public, and everybody could see how she was dressed. For this reason, she picked special clothes so others would know she cared about her appearance. Annette knew that her personal body was private and off limits to the public. She allowed her boyfriend to give her a hug and a kiss. She let her parents hug her, and her little sister could sit in her lap, but she did not let strangers touch her. Annette kept a diary. That was a special book in which she wrote about her personal thoughts and feelings. She kept that private except when she showed it to her friend Robin. Sometimes Annette wrote notes in her diary about different guys she liked. She did not want just any old person reading the diary.

Do you think that Annette had good personal boundaries? Was she clear about which behaviors were public and which were private?

■ DISCUSSION QUESTIONS

Simple/concrete questions:
  What are some public behaviors? Private behaviors? Secret behaviors?
  What is the difference between public and private behavior?
  What is the difference between private and secret behavior?
Personal experience/feelings questions:
  What are some of your public behaviors?
  What are some of your private behaviors?
  Do you have any secrets?
  How do you feel when you share private information with others?
Problem-solving questions:
  How can you get more privacy from others?
  What should you do if someone violates your privacy?
  How can you decide what kind of behaviors are appropriate in public?

■ GROUP ACTIVITIES

Ask each person to list one public and one private behavior. Other group members give feedback about these behaviors.

Facilitate a discussion about the difference between private and secret behaviors. Highlight the notion that one should tell secret behaviors, but private behaviors are no one else's business.

■ ASSESSMENT OF SKILLS LEARNED

Understands the difference between public, private, and secret behaviors:

ALMOST NEVER	USUALLY NOT	SOMETIMES	USUALLY	ALMOST ALWAYS
1	2	3	4	5

Lists behaviors belonging to the public, private, and secret domains:

ALMOST NEVER	USUALLY NOT	SOMETIMES	USUALLY	ALMOST ALWAYS
1	2	3	4	5

56. Borrowing and Stealing

This section takes a closer look at a special type of boundary, that between borrowing and stealing. It is included as a separate topic because individuals with developmental disabilities frequently have difficulties in this area. The group leader may begin by identifying the difference between borrowing and stealing. Borrowing has two features: taking things with permission, and taking things with the intention of giving them back. Stealing is taking things without permission and with no intention of returning them. Circumstances of appropriate borrowing can be explored. These include borrowing from the same person only occasionally, willingness to let others borrow from oneself, letting somebody know when something will be returned, and returning things on time. Next the group may discuss the types of things that people often borrow. These may include money, food, cigarettes, sports equipment, games, and other minor physical possessions. Finally, the group facilitator should help members recognize problems that can occur when borrowing or loaning things. These may include straining a friendship if something is not returned or not returned on time, resentment of the person who borrows too frequently or who does not reciprocate, losing or damaging something before it is returned, and being unable or unwilling to pay back money that one has borrowed. This topic is appropriate for individuals with mild and moderate developmental disabilities. Conceptually, it may be difficult for those with moderate developmental disabilities and those with more limited intellectual functioning. Its presentation can be modified and simplified by asking yes/no questions about a variety of items that have been either stolen or borrowed—for example: "John took a candy bar from a store without telling the clerk. Did he borrow or steal it?" "Rosemarie took Jennifer's softball glove home after Jennifer said she could use it for the weekend? Did she borrow or steal it?" "Ethel smoked one of Bill's cigarettes that he gave her when she promised to give him one tomorrow. Did she borrow or steal it?"

■ SPECIFIC SKILLS TO BE LEARNED

Identify the difference between borrowing and stealing:
    Borrow:
        Take with the intention to give back.
        Take with permission.
    Steal:
        Take with no intention to give back.
        Take without permission.

Recognize appropriate borrowing:
  Borrow from someone once in a while (not all the time).
  Be willing to let others borrow from you.
  Let the person know when you will return something.
  Return it on time.
Recognize things that people borrow:
  Money
  Food/cigarettes
  Small things (games, sports equipment, etc.)
  Physical possessions
Recognize problems that can happen when borrowing or loaning things:
  Straining friendship if one does not pay or give back
  Others resenting borrower who borrows too frequently or who does not reciprocate
  Losing something you borrow
  Borrowing money and being unable or unwilling to pay it back

■ CONCEPTS NECESSARY TO PERFORM SKILLS

Borrow: Ask permission to use something, and give it back when done; use something that belongs to someone else, but give it back; take something with permission; take with the intention of returning.

Steal: Take something without permission; borrow with no intention of giving something back; secretly take something from somebody; take something and not plan to give it back; rip something off.

Intention: What a person plans to do; if a person intends to give something back, the person plans to return it; what a person thinks he or she will do; what somebody has in mind to do.

Permission: When somebody tells you that you can do something; someone knows you are doing something and it is all right with the person; doing something by agreement; being free to do something; when another person does not mind if you do something.

Reciprocate: Pay back; one person helps now, the other helps next time; exchange; take turns doing things for each other.

■ CASE VIGNETTES

—*Darren sometimes did not think about other people. One day he forgot his lunch when he went to work. When he entered the coatroom, he noticed that there were several lunches sitting on top of the coat rack. Nobody was looking, and Darren opened a bright red lunch box, took out a sandwich, and put it in his coat pocket. He quickly closed the lunch box and put it back on the coat rack. Next, he opened another lunch box and took two cookies and an apple. Just as he was putting the lunch box back, Darren's supervisor entered the room and noticed what he was doing. The supervisor recognized that Darren was holding onto Sandy's lunch box. He had been caught red-handed, stealing from his workmates' lunch boxes.*

Was Darren stealing or borrowing food from others' lunch boxes? Did he get permission to take the food? Was he planning to give it back? How would you feel if someone stole your lunch?

—*René got to school early one day. She noticed that her friend Lucy was bouncing a ball and throwing it through a hoop in the exercise room. René smiled and said, "Throw it here, Lucy," and Lucy threw it to her. René shot at the hoop. Then they took turns catching it and throwing it through the hoop. René had great fun. She asked Lucy where she got the ball, and Lucy told her it was a gift from her brother. Lucy said she had two balls and would let René borrow that one until next week when she could buy her own. René was very thankful and promised to give it back to her next Monday. She planned to go to the store to get one on Saturday. When Monday came, René had not bought her own ball yet, but she returned Lucy's ball to her anyway. She gave it back because she did not want to break her word to a friend. She also wanted Lucy to trust and believe her next time she borrowed something.*

Did René steal or borrow Lucy's ball? Did she get permission to take it? Did she plan to give it back? Did she follow through on her word and give it back when she promised?

■ DISCUSSION QUESTIONS

Simple/concrete questions:
   What are some types of things that people borrow?
   What is the difference between borrowing and stealing?
Personal experience/feelings questions:
   How do you feel when you need to borrow things from others?
   How do you feel when other people borrow your things?
   How do you feel if someone does not pay you back the money which they borrowed?
   How do you feel if someone does not return your things which they have borrowed?
   Have you ever borrowed anything from anyone? Describe?
   Have you ever stolen anything? Describe?
Problem-solving questions:
   When might borrowing or stealing occur?
   What kinds of problems can happen if someone borrows your money? Cigarettes? Possessions? Clothing?
   What should you do if someone borrows your things and does not return them?

■ GROUP ACTIVITIES

Ask each person if he or she has ever had problems because of borrowing or loaning things.
Group members share experiences of having had things stolen.
Facilitate a discussion about strained relationships that may result from borrowing or stealing.

■ ASSESSMENT OF SKILLS LEARNED

Identifies the difference between borrowing and stealing:

ALMOST NEVER	USUALLY NOT	SOMETIMES	USUALLY	ALMOST ALWAYS
1	2	3	4	5

Recognizes appropriate borrowing:

ALMOST NEVER	USUALLY NOT	SOMETIMES	USUALLY	ALMOST ALWAYS
1	2	3	4	5

Identifies things that people borrow:

ALMOST NEVER	USUALLY NOT	SOMETIMES	USUALLY	ALMOST ALWAYS
1	2	3	4	5

Recognizes one or more problems that can happen when borrowing or loaning things:

ALMOST NEVER	USUALLY NOT	SOMETIMES	USUALLY	ALMOST ALWAYS
1	2	3	4	5

57. *Communication and Personal Boundaries*

The final topic in this section focuses on communication and personal boundaries. Communication is essential to establish and maintain boundaries with others. Individuals with developmental disabilities often have difficulties making judgments in this area. While there is a great deal of redundancy between the topics in this chapter, the notion of boundaries is so important and complex that it warrants such treatment. The discussion should examine appropriate and inappropriate times and places to communicate personal information. More information is communicated in close relationships (friends, family members, relationship partners, etc.) than with acquaintances and strangers. Communication of personal information is more likely when at home or when engaging in leisure activities, and less likely during work or school time or in public places. This topic is most appropriate for individuals with mild developmental disabilities. It may be modified for individuals with more limited intellectual resources similarly to other topics in this section.

■ SPECIFIC SKILLS TO BE LEARNED

Recognize appropriate times and places to communicate personal information with others:
> Communicate more information in close relationships (e.g., family, friend, relationship partner).
> Communicate more when at home or during leisure activities.

Recognize inappropriate times and places to communicate personal information with others:
> Communicate less information with acquaintances and strangers.
> Communicate less during work time or in public situations with strangers or acquaintances.

■ CONCEPTS NECESSARY TO PERFORM SKILLS

Communicate: To send and receive messages; to tell each other things and know what each means; to tell each other news; to listen to what somebody says, and the person also listens to what you say; to share information.

Information: Things that people talk about; ideas individuals share with each other; what people tell each other; messages; knowledge; communication about facts; advice; what people know and report.

■ CASE VIGNETTES

—*Hamilton was feeling very frustrated at his job. He was angry with one of his co-workers, Warren, who had said something nasty to him. He also felt pressure to work fast. Finally, Hamilton stomped off the job and began looking for his supervisor, who was somewhere in the plant. He could not find his supervisor, so he wandered up to the secretarial offices, where he saw a nicely dressed man sitting in the waiting area. Hamilton did not know him at all, but started talking about his job problems. He told the man about Warren, who had sworn at him, and Hamilton said that the work was going too fast. The man listened politely, so Hamilton continued to tell him about a fight he had had at home with one of his housemates. Soon one of the supervisors came into the lobby and asked Hamilton what he was doing there. He told Hamilton to return to the work floor and apologize to the man with the suit.*

Do you think it was a good idea for Hamilton to talk about his personal problems to the stranger in the waiting room? Why or why not? Who would have been a better choice for Hamilton to talk with about his problems?

—Nicholas was riding the bus home from work. He felt sad and upset because his uncle had died. He was also unhappy about how his job was going. Nicholas looked around and did not recognize any of the other bus passengers. So he decided to keep his feelings private. One lady sitting next to him asked if he had had a good day. He said it was, "Fine," and asked her the same. They engaged in some small talk about the weather and local news, but Nicholas did not tell the lady about his uncle or about his bad work day. Those things were private and he did not feel it would be appropriate to share them with a stranger.

Did Nicholas do a good job keeping personal information private? Even though he did not share personal information with her, was Nicholas polite and respectful to the lady that he met on the bus?

■ DISCUSSION QUESTIONS

Simple/concrete questions:
   What are some things about which you can talk to others?
   Is there a difference between what you would say to a friend or family member, and what you would say to a stranger?
   Do people usually talk more at work or during their free time?
Personal experience/feelings questions:
   With whom do you like to talk?
   Are you comfortable saying what you think and feel to other people? Are you more comfortable talking with friends and family members, or with strangers?
   Do people have to guess about what you feel, think and want? Are you able to tell these things to others?
Problem-solving questions:
   How do you decide to whom you should talk about personal information?
   How do you decide when to talk about very personal thoughts and feelings?
   What should you do if somebody starts telling you personal details about his or her life, and you do not know the person very well?

■ GROUP ACTIVITIES

Facilitate a discussion about whom individual group members most and least like to communicate with.
Discuss situations in which participants tried to communicate with others who either did not listen or did not care what they were saying.
Hold a discussion about the appropriate context for communicating very personal information.

■ ASSESSMENT OF SKILLS LEARNED

Recognizes appropriate times and places to communicate personal information with others:

ALMOST NEVER	USUALLY NOT	SOMETIMES	USUALLY	ALMOST ALWAYS
1	2	3	4	5

Recognizes inappropriate times and places to communicate personal information with others:

ALMOST NEVER	USUALLY NOT	SOMETIMES	USUALLY	ALMOST ALWAYS
1	2	3	4	5

8 *Developmental Issues*

THIS CHAPTER, WHICH FOCUSES on developmental issues, highlights a wide range of personal and family developmental stages that may result in problematic situations for individuals with developmental disabilities. The first three topics, individuation/separation, dependency/independency, and boundaries between self and caretakers, provide in-depth exploration of boundary issues. These topics could have been included in the previous chapter but are added here because of their importance to developmental stages. The areas of losses, death and loss, and the aging process are explored next. The issue of negative labels and ostracism is specifically addressed because of its frequent relevance to persons with developmental delay. Family illness is addressed in this chapter because it is often pivotal to individual and family change. Topics of intimacy, friendship, dating, and sexual relationships are included because of their relevance to developmental issues. These areas also could have been included easily in the previous chapter. Finally, the topic of family and residence rules is discussed because of its relationship to conflicts at particular developmental stages.

58. *Individuation/Separation*

Individuation/separation is a process that begins at birth and continues throughout an individual's life. In its early manifestation, the infant begins to realize that it has a separate body from its mother. Later, the child discovers that it has its own thoughts, feelings, and willpower. Ultimately, the healthy person comes to have an independent personal identity, a separate self from his or her caretaker. As life progresses, the individual becomes more self-reliant, independent, and separate from major caretakers.

Persons with developmental disabilities tend to experience delays in this process. They often remain significantly dependent on and attached to caretakers, in excess of what would have been expected had they been developmentally on schedule. The discussion may begin with an examination of the ways in which group members are dependent on others. Dependencies may include financial, housing, transportation, household activities, physical/medical care, shopping, leisure activities, and informational support. Next, the focus can turn to ways in which individuals have separated from caretakers and become more self-reliant. These may involve physically taking care of themselves or making independent life choices. Next, it may be examined to what extent group participants have established identities separate from others. This can be done by highlighting similarities and differences with others, and special characteristics about individuals that derive from these similarities and differences. Finally, group participants should be encouraged to share the ways in which they think and behave differently from their parents or caretakers. Conceptually, this is a very difficult topic, perhaps too difficult even for those with mild developmental delay; but when presented in a concrete fashion, it is appropriate for individuals with mild and moderate developmental disabilities. To make the discussion more accessible, it may be helpful to list many specific areas of dependency, asking individuals if they perform various activities for themselves or if others take care of them. Similarly, one may ask individuals about independent choices and similarities or differences with others, focusing on concrete aspects of these items. Some examples of questions are: "Who pays for the house that you live in?" "Where does the money come from?" "Who goes to the grocery store to get the food you eat?" "Who cooks, makes beds, washes dishes, etc., where you live?," "When you go for a walk outside your home, do you ask someone's permission to go?" "Do you do anything different than the other people you live with?" Do you have any favorite things to do that are different than others you live with?"

■ SPECIFIC SKILLS TO BE LEARNED

Recognize ways in which one is dependent on others:
    Financial (money)
    Housing (place to live)
    Transportation (rides)
    Household activities:
        Cooking
        Cleaning
    Physical/medical care
    Shopping
    Leisure activities
    Information
Recognize ways in which one has separated from caretakers and has become more self-reliant:
    Taking care of oneself
    Making independent choices
Recognize ways in which one has established an identity separate from others:
    Differences from others
    Similarities with others
    Special characteristics about oneself
Recognize ways in which one "thinks" differently from parents or caretakers.
Recognize ways in which one "behaves" differently from parents or caretakers.

■ CONCEPTS NECESSARY TO PERFORM SKILLS

Individuation: The act of becoming an individual; becoming a separate person from others; having one's own thoughts, feelings, and ways of doing things; becoming different from other people, even though one also has some similarities with them.

Separation: A boundary line; separate or less attached to someone; grown up and becoming one's own person; to have one's own thoughts, feelings, and ways of doing things.

Dependency: To depend on others for things; to let other people take care of you; when others tell a person what to think, feel, and do; not able to make choices and decisions; to trust others to take care of what you need.

Self-reliance: To do things for oneself; to take care of oneself; to make one's own decisions; to make one's own choices; not wait for others to take care of you.

Identity: Who you are; who I am; who each person is; what is special about a person; how one is like or unlike others; to be a separate person; to be an individual; to have one's own thoughts, feelings and behaviors; to know who you are and how you are the same as, or different from, others; individuality; distinctiveness.

■ CASE VIGNETTES

—*Brian was thirty-eight years old. He had lived with his mother and father all his life. He was dependent on them for many things. They told him when he had to come home at night. They paid for his food, clothes, and the bed he slept in. His mother would often tell him to dress warmer for the cold weather, and she would remind him to brush his teeth after breakfast. His father gave Brian rides to special activities. He told Brian when it was time to leave and when it was time to come home. Brian was not sure if his thoughts and feelings belonged to himself or his parents. He loved his parents very much but had a very uneasy feeling inside. He wanted to grow up, to make his own decisions, and to be a separate person with thoughts and feelings of his own. Sometimes he felt angry with his mother and father for no particular reason. He just wanted to tell them to stop making all his decisions for him; but at the same time, he was afraid to be independent and make his own choices. He was afraid that he might fail at things or that he might need help and no one would be there to help him.*

In what ways was Brian dependent on his parents? Do you think Brian had become a separate individual from his parents? What do you think scared him about being independent and making his own choices?

—*Linda lived with her parents until she was twenty-five years old. This was longer than her brothers and sisters had lived with them. Finally, Linda had decided to move away from home with the help of her parents, who loved her very much. Linda knew she would miss her mother and father and they would miss her, but she wanted to learn more about how to take care of herself. She would see them on weekends. Linda had taken an independent living class where she had learned to make beds, do dishes, cook in a microwave oven, and take care of her own apartment. She had learned how to go grocery shopping and to take the city bus. Linda would soon move into an apartment with three housemates. She would have a night staff person to help with cooking, budgeting money, and other household needs. Linda felt very good about herself because she was continuing to learn new things, growing into an adult person, and becoming more separate from her parents. Linda felt somewhat scared, but this was normal for someone moving away from home for the first time.*

In what ways was Linda becoming more independent from her parents? How was she becoming a separate adult person? Would she be receiving some extra help even while she was learning to be more independent?

■ DISCUSSION QUESTIONS

Simple/concrete questions:

What are some ways in which people depend on others for care?

What are some ways that people take care of themselves?

What are some things that make a person special?

Personal experience/feelings questions:

    For what things do you depend on others?

    How do you feel about the care you receive from others?

    Do you ever feel that you are treated too much like a child?

Problem-solving questions:

    How can a person become more independent?

    Is it a good idea to grow up and become a separate person from your parents?

    How should you decide in which ways to be similar or different from your parents?

    What kind of problems can happen if a person remains dependent on parents or caretakers for too long?

■ GROUP ACTIVITIES

Ask each person in what ways they depend on others.

Each group member share areas of their lives in which they are independent.

Participants list one or two things that make them special and separate individuals from others.

Facilitate a discussion about the negative effects of dependency, which may include anger toward caretakers and anxiety about becoming more independent.

■ ASSESSMENT OF SKILLS LEARNED

Recognizes ways in which depends on others:

ALMOST NEVER	USUALLY NOT	SOMETIMES	USUALLY	ALMOST ALWAYS
1	2	3	4	5

Recognizes ways that has separated from caretakers and become more self-reliant:

ALMOST NEVER	USUALLY NOT	SOMETIMES	USUALLY	ALMOST ALWAYS
1	2	3	4	5

Recognizes ways that has established identity separate from others:

ALMOST NEVER	USUALLY NOT	SOMETIMES	USUALLY	ALMOST ALWAYS
1	2	3	4	5

Recognizes ways that thinks and behaves differently from parents or caretakers:

ALMOST NEVER	USUALLY NOT	SOMETIMES	USUALLY	ALMOST ALWAYS
1	2	3	4	5

59. *Dependency/ Independency*

This topic explores more thoroughly the concepts of dependency and independency, which are key aspects to the individuation/separation theme and are crucial to one's developmental growth process. Individuals with developmental disabilities often remain dependent on caretakers longer than their peers at key developmental stages. For example, when their eight- to twelve-year-old peers are independently exploring their childhood universes with distant supervision, those with developmental disabilities may continue to receive continuous direct supervision. This results in more limited access to networks of friendships. When their peers begin turning outward to more complex social interactions, opposite-sex relationships, and dating, those with developmental disabilities may yet be engaging in earlier childhood tasks. As their similar-age cohorts begin forming intimate relationships, leaving home, and establishing increased separateness from parents, those with developmental disabilities may remain interested in more childlike friendships, staying at home for longer time periods, and essentially extending adolescence for a number of years beyond their emancipated peers. Because parents and caretakers of individuals with developmental disabilities do not know precisely what to expect in the area of independence, they are often surprised when their adult children begin to fight the battles of adolescence, attempting to establish their own identities, set their own boundaries, attain increased separation, and become more independent. Of course, the issue of independence is complicated by the fact that development may be uneven. The parent or caretaker can be presented with an adult body, adolescent emotions, and a child's intellect and social skills, all in the same person. The group facilitator should begin this session with a review of the different individuals on whom group members depend. These persons may include, guardians, foster providers, independent-living counselors, teachers, instructors, job supervisors, counselors, social workers, psychologists, friends, family, and other helpers. Next, members can discuss the specific ways in which they depend upon others. These may include food, clothing, shelter, money, household services, transportation, time and activity structuring, and so forth. Finally, major issues related to dependency and independency should be explored. These may include powerlessness versus competence, security versus self-esteem and confidence, stress caused by loss of dependency supports, public living versus privacy, dependency-induced depersonalization versus independency-fostered identity, fear and anxiety about independence, anger, resentment and frustration about supervision and overprotection, stubbornness and rebelliousness versus overcompliance, dealing with necessary authority, and physical and mental limitations necessitating more external care. This is a very complex topic, most appropriate for individuals with mild developmental disabilities. The topic is received best by individuals who have achieved the developmental life stage of early adolescence or later. Again, the topic must be presented as concretely as possible, and modifications can be made similar to the previous one.

■ SPECIFIC SKILLS TO BE LEARNED

Recognize upon whom one depends:
    Parents/guardians/caretakers
    Teachers/instructors
    Job supervisors
    Counselors/social workers/psychologists/psychiatrists
    Friends/family
    Other helpers
Recognize how one depends on others:
    Money
    Place to live
    Cooking
    Cleaning
    Medicine
    Shopping
    Transportation
    Structure time/activities
    Information
Recognize major issues related to dependency/independency:
    Powerlessness versus effectiveness/competence
    Safety/security versus self-esteem/confidence
    Life stress related to loss of dependency (e.g., group home staff changes, losses of parents/caretakers, loss of other supports, etc.)

Public living and lack of privacy

Depersonalization because of dependency versus special identity and individuation

Fear/anxiety about independence (e.g., fear of making decisions/choices)

Self-esteem/identity/confidence resulting from self-reliance

Anger, resentment and frustration about being supervised and overprotected

Stubbornness/rebelliousness toward caretakers and overcompliance with caretakers (two poles on the same dimension which reflect dependency)

Dealing with necessary authority figures (e.g., work supervisor)

Lack or loss of physical/mental competence, which necessitates more external care

■ CONCEPTS NECESSARY TO PERFORM SKILLS

Independent: Can do things for oneself; able to make choices for oneself; persons having their own feelings and thoughts; to make one's own choices; not wait for someone else to take care of an individual but to take care of oneself.

Dependent: Let others do things for a person; let others take care of you; when others tell someone what to do and when to do it; others make a person's decisions for him or her; trust that others will take care of one's needs.

Powerless: Helpless; cannot do anything for oneself; need to be taken care of; unable to do things for oneself; cannot take care of oneself; weak.

Competent: Know how to do a job; able to do things; can do things for oneself; able to understand things; able to make choices and decisions; not helpless and dependent; good at things.

Depersonalized: Not feel like a person; feel like an object for others to do with as they please; feel unimportant; feel that one's ideas and feelings are unimportant to others; feel that others are not treating one like a person.

Individuation: The act of becoming an individual; becoming a separate person from others; having one's own thoughts, feelings, and ways of doing things; becoming different from other people, even though one also has some similarities with them.

Self-reliance: To do things for oneself; to take care of oneself; to make one's own decisions; to make one's own choices; not wait for others to take care of you.

Self-esteem: How people feel about themselves; to feel either good or bad about oneself; to like or dislike oneself.

Confidence: Self-reliance; courage; self-assuredness; security; feeling able to take care of oneself.

■ CASE VIGNETTES

—Gail was in a wheelchair. As she rolled herself toward the door, Steve tried to grab her chair and push her through the doorway. Gail quickly said, "No, thank you, I can push the chair myself." Gail did not like others doing things for her that she could do for herself. When she got home, she was able to get in and out of the chair by herself holding onto a special metal railing. She did not want her mother to lift her. When Gail was hungry, she was able to get a snack from the refrigerator by herself. There were times when she needed somebody to help her, for example when she got onto the van to go to work. The driver had to push a special button so that her chair could be lifted into the van. She appreciated his help and thanked the driver. She also needed help to balance her checkbook, buy groceries, and cook food; but when Gail could do something for herself, she did. This gave her some power in her life. It made her feel good about herself because she was doing as much as she could for herself and was not depending on others to take care of her as though she was a helpless child.

In what ways was Gail an independent person? In what ways did she depend on others? Did she feel good when she could do things for herself?

—*Jeff was a very dependent person. He lived with his mother and aunt, and they would tell him when to get up in the morning, what to wear to work, what to eat for breakfast, and when to brush his teeth. Sometimes he wanted cereal, but his mother thought that oatmeal would be better for him. At other times, he wanted to wear a red shirt, but his aunt thought blue looked better on him. At times, Jeff would start to clear his own dishes off the table, but his mother would stop him, saying that he had a disability and did not need to do household chores. She was afraid he might break a dish. When Jeff's mother was cold, she asked him to wear a sweater. She did not bother to ask if he was feeling cold, but just made the decision for him. Sometimes Jeff would start to watch a television program, but his mother would change the channel. She thought he might be scared by the show that he was starting to watch. Jeff often felt angry and upset that his mother and aunt were making all of his decisions for him; but at the same time, he was nervous and afraid about making his own choices. He did not want his mother and aunt to be mad at him. He worried that they would not want to take care of him anymore if he disobeyed them. On the other hand, he felt powerless and helpless because they did everything for him.*

In what ways was Jeff dependent on his mother and aunt? Do you think Jeff was capable of doing some of those things for himself? Should he have made some of his own choices?

■ DISCUSSION QUESTIONS

Simple/concrete questions:

> What are some things with which people need help?
>
> What sorts of people are available to help others?

Personal experience/feelings questions:

> What are some things that you can do for yourself?
>
> What is one thing that you are able to do for yourself but for which you now receive help?
>
> What are some of the things for which you now receive help that you would like to do for yourself in the future?
>
> In what ways do you depend on other people but are not happy about your dependency?
>
> Does anything scare you about being more independent and doing things for yourself?
>
> Do you ever feel angry toward people who try to do things for you?
>
> Do you ever feel that people treat you too much like a child?

Problem-solving questions:

> How can people learn to be more independent and do things for themselves?
>
> What are some of the difficulties in becoming more self-reliant and independent?

■ GROUP ACTIVITIES

Ask each person about current areas in their lives in which they receive help. Who gives the help? How do group members feel about the help they receive?

Facilitate a discussion about any fears and anxieties related to increased independence.

■ ASSESSMENT OF SKILLS LEARNED

Recognizes on whom depends:

ALMOST NEVER	USUALLY NOT	SOMETIMES	USUALLY	ALMOST ALWAYS
1	2	3	4	5

Recognizes how depends on others:

ALMOST NEVER	USUALLY NOT	SOMETIMES	USUALLY	ALMOST ALWAYS
1	2	3	4	5

Recognizes personal issues related to dependency/independency:

ALMOST NEVER	USUALLY NOT	SOMETIMES	USUALLY	ALMOST ALWAYS
1	2	3	4	5

60. *Boundaries between Self and Caretakers*

This topic combines the areas of personal boundaries and dependency on caretakers to provide an in-depth exploration of caretaker boundaries. It is an area of particular interest to individuals with developmental disabilities, who often receive more invasive caretaking than their peers. This sometimes occurs because parents and caretakers have no guidelines about what sorts of activities persons are capable of handling at what stages of their development. Individuals may first examine boundaries between themselves and caretakers according to physical, intellectual, emotional, and behavioral dimensions. Next, rules and mutual expectations between individuals and their caretakers should be examined. Areas of interest may include listening/talking to each other, times/places for activities, involvement in activities, acceptable language, physical touch, privacy, sharing important information, use of the telephone, going into someone's bedroom, and so forth. An examination of the limits and extent of care by others, including self- and other-expectations, should be done. Finally, participants should learn to recognize good and bad care. This topic is appropriate for individuals with mild and moderate developmental disabilities. It can be modified by simplifying the language used and by asking concrete yes/no questions about rules, expectations, and care provided.

■ SPECIFIC SKILLS TO BE LEARNED

Identify boundaries between oneself and caretakers:
    Physical (body, touch, space, etc.)
    Thoughts (beliefs, ideas)
    Emotions (feelings)
    Behaviors
Identify rules and mutual expectations between oneself and caretakers:
    Listening and talking to each other
    Times and places for activities
    Involvement in activities
    Appropriate language (polite versus screaming, yelling, swearing, etc.)
    Rules for touching
    Privacy
    Sharing important information
    Use of the telephone
    Going into someone's bedroom
Identify the limits and extent of one's care by others:
    What is expected of caretaker
    What is expected of self
Recognize good and bad care.

■ CONCEPTS NECESSARY TO PERFORM SKILLS

Boundary: A dividing line; space between people or things; a rule; a way somebody is supposed to act; a limit; a border; end point; a place where one thing leaves off and another begins; something that lets a person know the limits of acceptable behavior.

Caretaker: Someone who takes care of another person; parent; guardian; foster provider; counselor; teacher; instructor; someone who helps a person do things; somebody who helps a person.

Rule: Guideline; boundary; limit; expectation; what each person agrees to do or not do.

Expectation: Rule; something somebody wants a person to do or not to do; what others expect from a person; what others think you should do.

Limits: Boundaries; borders; where some things stop and other things begin; what others do not do for you but you do for yourself.

■ CASE VIGNETTES

—*Demont lived with his parents, even though he was old enough and capable of living in his own apartment. Some of Demont's friends had moved into a townhouse with a live-in counselor who helped them with household problems. Demont's mother was worried that he would not get proper care if he moved away from home. Demont felt that his mother overprotected him and that she was too involved in his everyday life. For example, his mother always wanted to know where he was, whom he was with, and when he would be home. Sometimes she would listen when he was on the telephone to find out whom he was talking to. She woke him up every morning and reminded him when it was time to leave for work. Sometimes she called his workplace to let them know when he was sick. Demont felt that his mother invaded his privacy. She would walk into his bedroom without knocking. Sometimes she even walked into the bathroom when he was taking a shower. If he ran out of money, his mother was always there to buy the things he needed. Demont loved his mother and appreciated that she was concerned about him, but he felt that she was too interested and involved in his life. He wanted to start making his own decisions about friends and activities. He was even thinking about moving into a townhouse with his friends.*

Do you think that Demont had good boundaries between himself and his mother? Did she try to do things for him that he could do for himself? Did she respect his privacy? Why do you think it was difficult for Demont to set limits with his mother?

—*Sarah lived with her mother and father. She had been talking to them recently about the possibility of moving away from home. Both she and her parents were nervous about Sarah leaving home, but they knew it was best for her. Sarah's parents had done a very good job of taking care of her for many years. Now Sarah was older and was learning how to take care of herself. As she had grown older, her parents had given her more privacy. Eventually, she had moved into a bedroom in the basement of their house. Her parents always knocked on the door before entering her bedroom. They gave her more freedom than when she was younger. Now Sarah would let her parents know where she was going and when she would be home, but she made her own choices about where she went and with whom she did things. If her parents were worried about her, they would tell her, but they would let Sarah make her own decisions about friendships and activities. Sarah kept her own diary and did not share this with her parents. She wrote special things in her diary about her boyfriend and life activities. These were her personal and private thoughts, and her parents respected this. She counted on her mother and her father to help her balance a checkbook and get her bills paid, but she worked at a job to earn her own spending money.*

Do you think Sarah had good boundaries between she and her parents? Was she able to make some of her own choices and decisions? Did her parents respect her privacy?

■ DISCUSSION QUESTIONS

Simple/concrete questions:
> Can you list some ways which others take care of you?
> Can you list some things which you do for yourself?
> What are some different types of boundaries between you and your caretakers?

Personal experience/feelings questions:
> How do you feel about the care which you receive from others?
> Have you ever had any bad care experiences? Describe?
> Do you feel that you have enough privacy?
> Do you feel that others show enough love and affection to you?

Problem-solving questions:
> How can you let your caretakers know that you would like more independence?
> How can you develop more independence from your caretakers?
> How can you ask for more closeness from your caretakers?

■ GROUP ACTIVITIES

Ask each person to share personal experiences about good and bad care.
Discuss ways to request more or less care from others.
Break into pairs and discuss personal experiences with caretakers.

■ ASSESSMENT OF SKILLS LEARNED

Identifies boundaries between oneself and caretakers:

ALMOST NEVER	USUALLY NOT	SOMETIMES	USUALLY	ALMOST ALWAYS
1	2	3	4	5

Identifies rules and mutual expectations between oneself and caretakers:

ALMOST NEVER	USUALLY NOT	SOMETIMES	USUALLY	ALMOST ALWAYS
1	2	3	4	5

Identifies limits and extent of care by others:

ALMOST NEVER	USUALLY NOT	SOMETIMES	USUALLY	ALMOST ALWAYS
1	2	3	4	5

Recognizes good and bad care from others:

ALMOST NEVER	USUALLY NOT	SOMETIMES	USUALLY	ALMOST ALWAYS
1	2	3	4	5

61. Losses

Losses are a part of life. Individuals with developmental disabilities often experience a greater impact from losses than their peers because of more frequent school/work program changes, increased residential caretaker changes, more fragile physical/mental conditions, and fewer resources with which to deal with losses. The group facilitator should help members recognize different types of losses. Losses of valued relationships may include family, friends, relatives, schoolmates, co-workers, counselors, and other human service providers. Losses of physical/mental faculties may include general health, energy, vision/hearing, attention/concentration/memory, general reasoning ability, and major physical/mental disability. Additional losses may include money and physical possessions. Individuals should be assisted in understanding that a grief process may accompany losses. Normal feelings may include shock, anger, sadness, hurt, and other negative emotions. The discussion should turn to the inevitability of life changes and losses as one grows older. Life transformations may include aging, loss of physical capabilities, altered relationships, new schools/jobs, changing residences, meeting new people, developing new interests/activities while giving up old ones, and other lifelong learning which involves change and loss. Persons with mild and moderate developmental disabilities relate quite well to this topic and are usually willing to share experiences of their all-too-frequent losses. Lower functioning individuals can often relate to yes/no questions about specific losses, particularly of family members and caretakers.

■ SPECIFIC SKILLS TO BE LEARNED

Recognize types of losses:
  Valued relationships:
    Home, school, work, church, community
    Family, friends, relatives, counselors, staff persons, relationship partners
    Death, residence/job change
    Pets
  Physical/mental faculties:
    General health, energy
    Vision, hearing, sensory loss
    Attention/concentration/memory
    Understanding and reasoning ability
    Major physical/mental disability
  Financial (money/possessions):
    Theft
    Loss
Understand grief related to losses:
  Limited social networks of great significance
  Impact of losses:
    Shock/disbelief
    Anger
    Hurt/sadness/depression/loneliness
    Eventual acceptance and coming to terms with loss
Understand inevitability of losses:
  Life as a series of giving things up and making changes
  Inevitable life changes:
    Growing older
    Losing physical capabilities
    Changing relationships
    Changing schools/jobs
    Changing residences
    Meeting new people
    Changing interests and activities
    Lifelong learning

■ CONCEPTS NECESSARY TO PERFORM SKILLS

Loss: To lose someone or something; not have someone or something anymore; the death of a significant other; the event of a friend or family member moving away; to be cut off from a person, place or thing.

Relationship: Connection with somebody; when people know each other; to relate or do things with others; togetherness; family, friend, or acquaintance.

Physical and mental faculties: Physical and mental abilities; capabilities to see, hear, do, and understand things; capacities to pay attention, remember, and engage in activities.

Financial: Having to do with money; related to money and resources.

Grief: Sadness; loss; sorrow; distress; negative feelings at the time of a death or loss.

Life change: A new thing happening in a person's life; to do something different; stop doing something that one used to do; the experience of a loss; a person dying or moving away; to start a new school or job.

Inevitable: It will happen for sure; something that happens to everybody; an event that is bound to happen if somebody waits long enough.

■ CASE VIGNETTES

—*Carolyn was shocked and upset by the news of her mother's death. She cried and cried. It was now two months later, and Carolyn was still crying every day. She was angry because her mother had died so suddenly. She also felt guilty because she wished she had been nicer to her mother. She felt sad and lonely without her mother because they used to talk to each other every day. Carolyn did not have many friends to talk to. She had always been a loner and did not know many people. After her mother's death, Carolyn continued to live with her father, who was also very sad. He had decided to keep Carolyn home from her mother's funeral because he felt that it would upset her too much. Now she was trying to deal with her grief, mostly by herself, and she did not think that she would ever start to feel better.*

What kind of a loss did Carolyn experience? Do you think she received enough support for her loss? Do you think it would have been helpful for Carolyn to go to her mother's funeral? What could she do now that would help her deal with the loss of her mother? Do you think it would help Carolyn to meet new people and develop some friendships?

—*Brian recently moved to a new home. He continued to live with his parents after his father was transferred to a new job in another state. Brian remembered saying goodbye to all of his school friends and teachers, then saying goodbye to his neighborhood friends. He thought about how he would miss playing softball at the park and going different places with his friends. He also thought he would miss the nice house where he and his family had been living. He had had his own bedroom with special posters on the wall. Brian was not sure who lived in his new neighborhood. He was also worried about what his new school would be like.*

What kind of losses had Brian recently suffered in his life? How do you think he felt about losing his school and neighborhood friends? What do you think would make it easier for Brian to deal with his losses?

■ DISCUSSION QUESTIONS

Simple/concrete questions:
   What are some different types of losses?
   What are some typical life changes?
Personal experience/feelings questions:
   What are some losses you have suffered?
   Have any of your close friends or family members died? How did this affect you? How did you feel at the time of the loss?
   If you have lost an important person in your life, did your feelings change over time?
   Where have you lived? Worked?
   Can you describe any important changes that have happened where you live? Work?

Problem-solving questions:

How can someone prepare him or herself for the loss of a family member or friend?

What are some things a person can do to deal with a major loss?

■ GROUP ACTIVITIES

Each group member shares important life changes and losses. List both positive and negative life changes.

Facilitate a discussion about different ways to cope with losses.

■ ASSESSMENT OF SKILLS LEARNED

Recognizes possible types of losses:

ALMOST NEVER	USUALLY NOT	SOMETIMES	USUALLY	ALMOST ALWAYS
1	2	3	4	5

Understands the grief process related to losses:

ALMOST NEVER	USUALLY NOT	SOMETIMES	USUALLY	ALMOST ALWAYS
1	2	3	4	5

Recognizes the inevitability of losses:

ALMOST NEVER	USUALLY NOT	SOMETIMES	USUALLY	ALMOST ALWAYS
1	2	3	4	5

62. Death and Loss

The death of a friend or loved one is a special category of loss. It is dealt with separately to emphasize its importance as a developmental life issue. Persons with developmental disabilities experience losses by death similarly to their peers, with the exception that their understandings and coping supports are often more limited. The discussion should first recognize the inevitability of death and dying, of oneself and one's family and friends. This may be followed by a discussion of important aspects of the grief process. Elizabeth Kübler-Ross (1969) was the first person to popularize the concept of grief stages, which she characterized by the titles "denial and isolation," "anger," "bargaining," "depression," and eventual "acceptance." I recommend discussing these stages with group participants, albeit in a slightly modified format. First, feelings of shock, disbelief, and denial commonly occur at the news of a loved one's death. These feelings may be followed by anger and bargaining with God about losses. Individuals often become angry with God or with the deceased person for leaving prematurely and abandoning them. Next, the emotions of hurt, sadness, and depression may envelop the individual's consciousness. Loneliness and isolation often occur. Many individuals vacillate between the different stages of grief. Finally, at some point, individuals can begin to accept their losses and get on with their lives. Subsequent losses may rekindle unresolved grief from previous ones. The person with a mild or moderate developmental disability can easily feel the experience of a loss but may have more difficulty understanding the experience than others. It is most helpful to talk about specific losses of individual group members, questioning them concretely about different emotions and stages of grief. Lower functioning persons may be able to indicate losses of significant others by pointing to pictures and using nonverbal communications.

■ SPECIFIC SKILLS TO BE LEARNED

Recognize the inevitability of death and loss.
Recognize important aspects of the grief process:
   Shock/disbelief/denial
   Anger/bargaining
   Hurt/sadness
   Depression
   Loneliness
   Acceptance and getting on with life

■ CONCEPTS NECESSARY TO PERFORM SKILLS

Death: The end of life; the end of somebody's body; when a person no longer walks, talks and breathes; when someone is buried; when this life is left behind.
Grief: Sadness; loss; sorrow; distress; negative feelings at the time of a death or loss.

■ CASE VIGNETTES

—Rubin was very sad to hear about his mother's death. At first, he did not believe she was gone. His father had come to his house on Thursday night and told Rubin that his mother had passed away. She had been in a car accident and had died on the way to the hospital. After Rubin had time to think about it, he became very angry. He asked God if he could have his mother back. He promised to work harder and call her more often if she could just be alive again. Rubin also began to feel deeply hurt, sad, and lonely. He missed his mother and wanted to have one more chance to talk to her. Sometimes Rubin would sit on his bed crying, and at other times he seemed to forget all about his mother dying. Maybe this was because he still could not believe that she was gone. In the first couple of months after her death, Rubin was very tired and had the blues. He did not feel like working much and had trouble concentrating. Rubin had very supportive family members and friends. They called him often to see how he was feeling. They also came to visit him. Eventually, Rubin accepted the fact that his mother was gone, even though he was not happy about it. After some more time went by, Rubin's life got back to normal.

What kinds of feelings did Rubin have when he heard about his mother's death? Did his feelings change over time? Do you think it was O.K. for Rubin to have his different feelings after he lost his mother?

—Kathy lost her sister, Keri, last year. Keri had cancer and died. She was sick for a long time before she died. Kathy did not exactly know what cancer was, but she knew that it got people very sick and they sometimes died. Kathy was one year younger than Keri, and they had done everything together up until Keri went to the hospital. Even though it was over a year since Keri died, Kathy had made no new friends, and she still felt sad and lonely. She sat around the house and did not want to go outside. She felt tired and down. Kathy often cried by herself. She felt that she had no one to talk to. Kathy did not know what she would do without her sister.

What kinds of feelings did Kathy have after her sister Keri died? Why do you suppose Kathy still felt sad, lonely, and down? Was there anything else she could have done to start feeling better? Do you think she was stuck in her bad feelings about the loss of her sister Keri?

■ DISCUSSION QUESTIONS

Simple/concrete questions:
Who are some people that a person might lose?

What are some different stages of the grief process?

Personal experience/feelings questions:

Have you lost any important people in your life? Who? How old were you? How did you react?

When you think about death and dying, how do you feel? Does the thought of dying scare you?

Problem-solving questions:

How can people prepare themselves for the eventual losses of important persons?

What are some things somebody can do to cope with the loss of an important person?

■ GROUP ACTIVITIES

Facilitate a discussion about losses of important persons, the impact of the losses, and how each group member's life has been changed because of the losses.

Participants form pairs and discuss thoughts and feelings about death, dying, and the hereafter.

■ ASSESSMENT OF SKILLS LEARNED

Recognizes the inevitability of death and loss:

ALMOST NEVER	USUALLY NOT	SOMETIMES	USUALLY	ALMOST ALWAYS
1	2	3	4	5

Recognizes important aspects of the grief process:

ALMOST NEVER	USUALLY NOT	SOMETIMES	USUALLY	ALMOST ALWAYS
1	2	3	4	5

63. The Aging Process

Nobody escapes the aging process. It takes each individual on a journey through different life stages, offering various road marks along the way. Persons with developmental disabilities experience the same physical aging processes as their peers, even though their social, emotional, and intellectual development may proceed more slowly. The group facilitator should initially focus on various bodily changes associated with aging. These may include changes in mobility, weight, hair, energy level, skin, sexuality, senses, coordination, face, intellectual capabilities, and others. Next, various losses associated with aging can be examined. These may include physical prowess, intellectual ability, independence, social connections, family members, and others. It is also important to examine positive changes that accompany the aging process. These may include learning to let go of things that do not matter, wisdom, self-confidence, and others. It would be appropriate to examine the self-concept changes that often occur with the aging process. For example, how do individuals feel about themselves as they lose their physical/intellectual capabilities? Next, the focus can be on social changes associated with aging. These may include family losses, people moving away, deaths of friends, or changes of schools/jobs. Finally, the activity changes associated with aging may be explored. These can include increased sedentary activities, less vigorous physical activity/exercise, and a slower paced life-style. This area is most easily explored with aging individuals with mild developmental disabilities but can also be appropriate for younger and lower functioning persons. It will help to examine aging changes associated with the particular life stages of individual group members. It may be useful to utilize yes/no questions about specific physical, social, intellectual, and behavioral changes.

■ SPECIFIC SKILLS TO BE LEARNED

Recognize various bodily (physical) changes associated with aging:
   Mobility
   Weight changes
   Hair color
   Hair loss
   Energy level
   Skin changes
   Sexuality
   Vision/hearing/senses
   Coordination
   Facial changes
Recognize various losses connected with aging:
   Physical prowess
   Intellectual ability
   Independence
   Social life
Recognize positive aspects to growing older:
   Letting go of things that do not matter
   Wisdom
   Self-confidence
Recognize self-concept changes with the aging process.
Recognize social changes with increasing age:
   Family losses
   People moving away
   Deaths of friends
Recognize activity changes related to aging:
   Increased sedentary activity
   Less vigorous activity/exercise
   Slower moving activities

■ CONCEPTS NECESSARY TO PERFORM SKILLS

Aging: Getting older; what happens as time goes by; living to be older; growing up and growing old.

Loss: To lose someone or something; not have someone or something anymore; the death of a significant other; the event of a friend or family member moving away; to be cut off from a person, place, or thing.

■ CASE VIGNETTES

—Lucille was now almost eighty years old. She moved more slowly than when she was younger. Her hair, which used to be brown, was now silver-gray. It was also thinner than it used to be. Lucy did not have the energy she once had. She felt more tired and took a nap most afternoons. She wore glasses, and the lenses got thicker every couple of years because her eyes were getting worse. She could not hear as well as she used to, and she had a hearing aid in her right ear. She could walk by herself but sometimes used a cane to make sure that she did not fall down. Her skin was more wrinkled, but she was still the same person. Lucy had been married, but her husband had died five years earlier from a heart attack. Lucy moved in with her sister and sister's husband. She used to do her own grocery shopping, but she no longer did that. She

helped with the cooking and some of the lighter household chores. Many of Lucy's friends and family members had died. She was less able to see her other friends because she could no longer take the city bus by herself. She saw different doctors once every month or two. They told her she was doing fine but that she needed to take it easy and not work too hard.

Can you think of any changes that happened to Lucy as she got older? Do you think it was difficult for Lucy to deal with any of her life changes? What was more difficult about her life now than when she was younger?

—Bradford is now seventy-five years old. He has had a very active and full life but is slowing down quite a bit. He feels more tired, walks more slowly, and complains of more body aches and pains than when he was younger. But Bradford is a very happy man. He continues to live in his own apartment. His wife died two years ago, but he has three surviving children. One of his children lives out of state, but another son and daughter live nearby and visit him on weekends. Sometimes they bring him something to eat. They also help him with chores around the house. Bradford may be slowing down, but he is a wiser man because he has learned a lot about life in his many years. He knows how to treat people with respect and consideration. Bradford does not become as angry about small matters as he did when he was younger. He just shrugs his shoulders and ignores others who are rude. Bradford is comfortable with himself. He is not trying to impress people as he might have done when he was a young man. He is happy to receive small favors and the little things that life has to offer, like sunny days, smiles, and good food.

In what ways is Bradford different than when he was younger? In what ways has he made positive changes as he has grown older?

■ DISCUSSION QUESTIONS

Simple/concrete questions:
  When does aging begin?
  Can you stop the aging process?
  Do you get more or less physical illness when you get older?
  How does a person's body change as he or she becomes older (skin, hair, etc.)?
Personal experience/feelings questions:
  How has your body changed as you have grown older?
  How have your feelings about yourself changed as you have gotten older?
  Are you the same person now that you were five years ago?
Problem-solving questions:
  What sort of extra help might you need as you grow older?
  What changes might you need to make as you grow older?

■ GROUP ACTIVITIES

Ask each person to share one physical or bodily change resulting from growing older.
Facilitate a discussion about positive aspects of growing older.
Group members form pairs and discuss personal aging concerns with partners.

■ ASSESSMENT OF SKILLS LEARNED

Recognizes various bodily changes associated with aging:

ALMOST NEVER	USUALLY NOT	SOMETIMES	USUALLY	ALMOST ALWAYS
1	2	3	4	5

Recognizes one or more losses connected with aging:

ALMOST NEVER	USUALLY NOT	SOMETIMES	USUALLY	ALMOST ALWAYS
1	2	3	4	5

Lists at least one positive aspect of growing older:

ALMOST NEVER	USUALLY NOT	SOMETIMES	USUALLY	ALMOST ALWAYS
1	2	3	4	5

Recognizes personal self-concept changes accompanying the aging process:

ALMOST NEVER	USUALLY NOT	SOMETIMES	USUALLY	ALMOST ALWAYS
1	2	3	4	5

Recognizes social changes with ongoing age:

ALMOST NEVER	USUALLY NOT	SOMETIMES	USUALLY	ALMOST ALWAYS
1	2	3	4	5

Recognizes activity changes related to aging:

ALMOST NEVER	USUALLY NOT	SOMETIMES	USUALLY	ALMOST ALWAYS
1	2	3	4	5

64. *Negative Labels and Ostracism*

While all people are vulnerable to the possibility of receiving negative labels and ostracism, individuals with developmental disabilities are more likely than average to receive this treatment because they are often visibly different than their peers. For example, they may have unusual physical appearances because of facial or bodily deformities, or their behavior may conform less well to acceptable social standards. Their attention to neatness and personal hygiene may be more limited, and their social demeanor may be less appropriate for their specific circumstances. The topic should begin with a discussion of the concepts of negative label and ostracism. Negative labeling may be done with terms such as "retarded," "crazy," and "mentally ill." In this way, an individual is seen not as a whole person but as a stereotyped set of more narrow characteristics that fit the label. It results in others ignoring the positive qualities of the person in question. This section offers a good opportunity to discuss other types of prejudice, such as ethnic, racist, and sexist labeling. These also focus on narrow stereotypes but ignore the characters and qualities of individuals. It would also be helpful to talk about the reality of "disabilities" with group participants. This should entail an honest and open discussion with individuals about their own difficulties and limitations. It should include members' perceptions about how others treat them differently because of their disabilities. Finally, an exercise can be done to highlight the many positive characteristics of individuals unrelated to their disabilities, acknowledging their intrinsic worth as human beings, and recognizing their capabilities despite having disabilities. This topic is most appropriate for those with mild developmental disabilities, and can be utilized with some individuals with more severe limitations. The topic requires some insight on the part of group participants that they are being treated differently because of their disabilities; otherwise, it can have counterproductive effects of further calling attention to individual differences.

■ SPECIFIC SKILLS TO BE LEARNED

Recognize the concepts of negative label and ostracism:
    Labeling a whole person with a term such as "mentally retarded," "mentally ill," or "crazy"

Ignoring other positive qualities of a person
Avoiding persons with negative labels and disabilities
Other kinds of prejudice (e.g., ethnic, racial, sexist)
Recognize the reality of disability:
What is the name of your disability?
Recognizing the particular limits caused by a disability (developmental disability, mental illness, blindness, deafness, etc.)
Recognizing how others treat one differently because of a disability
Recognize positive aspects of oneself unrelated to disability:
List positive self-characteristics.
Recognize self-worth and intrinsic value as a person.
Recognize capabilities despite having a disability.

■ CONCEPTS NECESSARY TO PERFORM SKILLS

Negative label: A word people use to identify somebody or something; a name for something; a name for somebody; to call somebody "mentally retarded," "mentally ill" or "crazy."

Ostracism: To treat somebody as if they are not part of the group; refuse to include someone in fun activities; ignore somebody; banish a person; treat somebody like an outcast; treat a person as though he or she is no good.

Disability: Have a problem with part of one's body; not able to do something as well as somebody else; have special problems learning or doing things; when part of a person is damaged or not working properly; handicap.

Handicap: Disability; when somebody has a problem with his or her body or brain; to have trouble doing something as well as others; have special problems learning or doing things.

Prejudice: To make up your mind about somebody based on a negative label; decide what you think about somebody before getting to know them; to think that a person's disability is the only important thing about them; treat somebody differently because of their race, nationality, sex, or disability; have an opinion about somebody before you know them.

■ CASE VIGNETTES

—Martin was confined to a wheelchair, but he got around quite well. He lived in his own apartment with help from a residence counselor. He worked at a warehouse nearby. Martin took a special transportation service, one that picked him up with his wheelchair and gave him rides in a van. Martin would go shopping near his house by himself. He often wheeled down the sidewalk by himself. Sometimes he noticed that people would look at him and then look the other way. Sometimes they tried to walk as far away from his wheelchair as they could. Some people would talk to him, but they talked as though he was five years old even though he was grown up. It was obvious to Martin that some people had made up their minds about what kind of a person he was even though they had not gotten to know him. Martin was very friendly, though, and he soon was talking to people who used to be afraid of his wheelchair. One time he felt that a man was treating him rudely because of his wheelchair. Martin tried to be friendly, but the man did not get any nicer. Finally, Martin told him, "I may be in a wheelchair, but that doesn't mean I'm stupid." The man was surprised and walked away.

What was Martin's disability? Did Martin let other people get away with giving him negative labels? Even though Martin had a disability, do you think he still had his self-respect? Why or why not?

—Sandy was a very sensitive woman. She had been a slow learner all her life and this had been very frustrating for her. She worked hard to learn in school but always needed special help. One day she was in the hallway at her school and overheard two other students talking. One

pointed at her and said, "That's Sandy, she's mentally retarded." Then they walked away without even talking to her. Sandy felt very hurt and rejected. She felt that the other students did not want to be her friends because she was a slow learner. She knew that the word, retarded *was a bad word. It was a negative label. When she heard that word, she knew the other students were not interested in her as a person but were more interested in her slow learning. Sandy was much more than a slow learner. She was kind, friendly, helpful, and fun-loving. She was good at doing puzzles and could work on a computer. She knew how to do crafts and was a good bowler. Sandy had many friends, and her family liked her a lot. So you can see that Sandy was a very special person.*

Do you think it was fair of the other students to call Sandy "retarded"? Why or why not? Was Sandy more than a slow learner? What else was true about Sandy?

■ DISCUSSION QUESTIONS

Simple/concrete questions:
  What are some different kinds of disabilities?
  What are some positive characteristics of people which have nothing to do with disabilities?
Personal experience/feelings questions:
  What kind of disability do you have?
  How does your disability affect you?
  How do you feel when someone calls you retarded? Mentally ill?
  Have you ever felt left out by others because of your disability?
Problem-solving questions:
  What are some ways that people can overcome their disabilities?
  What are some ways that people can overcome negative labels and ostracism?

■ GROUP ACTIVITIES

Participants share information about their own disabilities. Share experiences with negative labels and ostracism.

Facilitate a discussion about individual group members' positive experiences in dealing with their disabilities.

■ ASSESSMENT OF SKILLS LEARNED

Recognizes the concepts of negative label and ostracism:

ALMOST NEVER	USUALLY NOT	SOMETIMES	USUALLY	ALMOST ALWAYS
1	2	3	4	5

Recognizes the reality of one's own limitations or disability:

ALMOST NEVER	USUALLY NOT	SOMETIMES	USUALLY	ALMOST ALWAYS
1	2	3	4	5

Recognizes positive aspects of oneself unrelated to disability:

ALMOST NEVER	USUALLY NOT	SOMETIMES	USUALLY	ALMOST ALWAYS
1	2	3	4	5

65. *Family Illness*

Acute and chronic illnesses afflict all families. The severity and duration of illnesses determine the level of impact and strain upon the family's coping resources. Individuals with developmental disabilities contribute to family stress because their disabilities require certain degrees of family adaptation and coping. Other family members illnesses call for additional coping mechanisms. The group facilitator should begin by discussing three types of family illness: physical, mental, and other disability. Next, a distinction can be made between short-term illness and chronic disability. Short-term illnesses include cold, flu, injury, and minor sickness. Longer term, chronic conditions include seizures, high blood pressure, vision/hearing loss, mental illness, developmental disability, physical disability, and so forth. The leader should stimulate a discussion about the effects of illness on the families of group members. Some of these effects may include wage earner loss, emotional stress, need for extra care from other family members, and various individual or family hardships. Most persons with mild and moderate developmental disabilities can understand and discuss the concept of family member illness. Lower functioning individuals may relate to pictures/symbols for different types of illness but will probably relate to these in a more self-centered, immediate, and concrete fashion. They will not necessarily be able to discuss impacts that illnesses have on their families.

■ SPECIFIC SKILLS TO BE LEARNED

Identify different types of family illness:
  Physical illness
  Mental illness
  Other disability
Recognize short- and long-term disability caused from illness:
  Short-term illness
      Cold
      Flu
      Injury
  Chronic conditions:
      Seizures
      High blood pressure
      Vision/hearing loss
      Mental illness
      Developmental disability
      Physical disability
  Identify effects of illness on family:
      Wage earner loss
      Emotional stress
      Need for extra care

■ CONCEPTS NECESSARY TO PERFORM SKILLS

Illness: Sickness; when a person is not feeling well; problems with one's body or brain; poor health; physical or mental distress.

Physical: To do with a person's body; something one can see, touch or feel; concrete; something that has substance; rules about whom, when, and how to touch.

Mental: To do with one's mind; thinking; what happens in somebody's head.

Disability: Have a problem with part of one's body; not be able to do something as well as somebody else; have special problems learning or doing things; when part of a person is damaged or not working properly; handicap.

■ CASE VIGNETTES

—*Edward had a disability called* cerebral palsy; *that meant that he had to use a wheelchair and had trouble speaking. Ed was a slow learner, although that is not true of all people with cerebral palsy. Ed's family made a special wheelchair ramp for him. He could push his own chair up the ramp but moved very slowly. Sometimes others would help him move faster by pushing his chair for him. When Ed talked, he had to speak very slowly and clearly so that others could understand his words. When the family went out to a restaurant, they would load Ed, wheelchair and all, into their special van, which had a wheelchair lift. Then they would wheel him in and out of the van as they left for, and came home from, the restaurant. When Ed's parents went out alone, they left somebody to watch him in case there was a fire or another emergency and he needed to be wheeled out of the house quickly. Everything was working fine in the family until Ed's Dad had an accident at work and hurt his back. Now Dad needed special help too, and Mother had to go back to work. The family did not have as much money as before, but everybody was helping so that they could do everything that needed to be done.*

Did Ed's family have any stress or problems because of illness of family members? Who had an illness and what kind? What extra help did family members need because of their illnesses?

—*Joan was a slow learner and received special help all through school. Now she was working at a job where she packaged different products. She liked her job. She lived in a semi-independent living apartment with three housemates and a live-in counselor. Joan visited her parents every week. She enjoyed her visits very much, and often talked to her workmates about family activities. Recently she was quite upset because her father was having heart problems. He saw the doctor for medicine but kept having the problems. One day he had bad chest pains and had to go into the hospital. Joan was afraid he would die. When he finally came home, he was not feeling too well and needed more rest. Joan was worried about him. His medical problems also made it more difficult for Joan's mother, who now did all the household chores and also had a part-time job to earn extra money. Joan's father received a social security check, but this was much less money than before. Now Joan could not visit home as often because her mother was busy taking care of Dad and did not feel able to come and get Joan from her apartment. Joan missed her parents but understood that their lives were more difficult since Dad's illness.*

What kind of illness was there in Joan's family? Did Joan's father's heart problem cause any changes in how the family members related to each other? What was different now that the family was dealing with her father's medical problems? How did the family change because of Dad's illness?

■ DISCUSSION QUESTIONS

Simple/concrete questions:
  What are some different types of illness?
  List some short-term illnesses? Long-term illnesses? Disabilities?
Personal experience/feelings questions:
  Have you ever been ill? Describe your illness.
  Have any of your family members ever been ill? Describe how this affected you.
  How do you feel when you are ill? How do you deal with this?
  What extra care do you need when you are ill?
  Do you have to change your family routine when someone becomes ill?
Problem-solving questions:
  What should you do if a family member becomes ill? Is this different for different illnesses?
  What are some ways that a family can cope with a chronic illness?

■ GROUP ACTIVITIES

Facilitate a discussion about individual group members' and their family members' illnesses. Discuss how each individual's family handled the illness, what treatment was received, and what individual or family stressors occurred.

Form pairs to discuss personal experiences with family illness.

■ ASSESSMENT OF SKILLS LEARNED

Identifies different types of family illness:

ALMOST NEVER	USUALLY NOT	SOMETIMES	USUALLY	ALMOST ALWAYS
1	2	3	4	5

Recognizes short- and long-term disability caused by illness:

ALMOST NEVER	USUALLY NOT	SOMETIMES	USUALLY	ALMOST ALWAYS
1	2	3	4	5

Identifies effects of illness upon own family:

ALMOST NEVER	USUALLY NOT	SOMETIMES	USUALLY	ALMOST ALWAYS
1	2	3	4	5

66. *Intimacy*

Intimacy, or emotional closeness, is a basic human need that is fulfilled differently at different stages of one's life, and in different types of relationships. Persons with developmental disabilities have the same general needs for intimacy as others but tend to have less effective skills to meet these needs. The group discussion should begin with a focus on different methods to gain attention or affection from others. These include introducing oneself, engaging in small talk, establishing common interests, listening and asking questions, sharing information about oneself, being affectionate to others, giving kindness and consideration to others, doing positive things for others, and generally extending oneself to other people. Next, the focus can turn to how to keep a relationship going once it has started. This includes showing an interest in others, doing things together, listening, and being sympathetic. The group should discuss differences between types of intimate relationships such as family, friend, dating partner, workmate, and acquaintance. It should be pointed out that different types of closeness occur in different types of relationships. For example, friends may do activities together, dating partners may engage in physical intimacies, and workmates may simply talk together on work breaks. This topic is appropriate for individuals with mild and moderate developmental disabilities. It is quite difficult for lower functioning individuals but may be modified to some extent with yes/no questions, a focus on more concrete expressions of intimacy, and the addition of nonverbal communication techniques.

■ SPECIFIC SKILLS TO BE LEARNED

Recognize different methods to gain attention or affection from others:
Introduce oneself.
Make small talk.
Establish common interests.
Listen and ask questions.
Share information about oneself.

Be affectionate to others.
Be kind to others.
Do positive things for others.
Understand how to keep a relationship going:
Show an interest in the other person.
Do things together.
Listen and be sympathetic.
Recognize the difference between different kinds of intimate relationships:
Family member
Dating partner
Friend
Workmate
Acquaintance
Stranger
Recognize different types of closeness in relationships:
Doing things together (activities)
Talking together
Physical relationship (touching and physical contact)

■ CONCEPTS NECESSARY TO PERFORM SKILLS

Intimacy: Closeness; physical touch; to talk about private things with somebody; emotional closeness; love and affection between people who feel close to each other; companionship; to relate on a personal level with somebody.

Attention: Look at somebody; talk to someone; be mindful of others; notice others; see someone; listen; watch; look, listen and notice; take notice and remember what one is doing; notice what someone is saying; keep alert; be involved in something.

Affection: Kindness; consideration; to treat somebody well; feel for someone; love; feel good about someone and show it.

Relationship: Connection with somebody; when people know each other; to relate or do things with others; togetherness; family, friend or acquaintance.

■ CASE VIGNETTES

—*René was close to many different people. But she was close to them in different ways. She loved her brother and was close to him because they had fun teasing each other. It was not mean teasing, just fun. Sometimes she tried to tickle him, but at other times she would just pretend she was going to tickle him. He made funny faces at her and they would both laugh. René was close to her boyfriend in a different way. They had a romantic relationship. Her boyfriend gave her a kiss good night, and sometimes he would hug her very closely. This was different than the way René's mother and father touched her. Sometimes they would hug her and rub her shoulders, but this was not romantic touching. She would kiss her father on the cheek before leaving the house. This showed that she cared about him. When René saw her grandmother, she would give her a big hug. She talked about many private things with her grandmother because she seemed to understand René's feelings. René was friendly with her co-workers, but she did not tell them all of her private thoughts. She had one special girlfriend, and they told each other different secrets. They promised that they would not tell anyone else. You can see that René had different kinds of intimacy in different kinds of relationships.*

What were some of the different kinds of intimacy René had with different people? What were some of the ways she got close to others?

—Ralph was a grown-up man, but he had many younger friends. That was because Ralph was a slower learner and was interested in many things that younger people liked. One problem that Ralph had was that he was confused about how to be close to others and with whom to be close. Last week he went to a family picnic. All his nieces and nephews were there. Ralph liked his ten-year-old niece, Sheila. They were playing house together, and then they threw a ball back and forth. Ralph liked her a lot. He was playing a game with her when he suddenly picked her up and kissed her right on the mouth. She was very upset and ran to tell her mother. Then her mother (who was also Ralph's sister) talked to Ralph. She said that she was very disappointed in Ralph, and that he should not kiss a ten-year-old girl on the mouth. Ralph was confused because he liked Sheila very much. He did not understand that an adult should not try to have a romantic relationship with a child. Part of Ralph's problem was that he had more fun playing with Sheila than talking to older women. Ralph's sister explained to him that romantic relationships were for adults and that it was not right to be romantic with a child.

Why was it not a good idea for Ralph to kiss Sheila on the mouth? Do you think Ralph was confused about how to be intimate or close to other people? What did Ralph need to learn so that he would not be confused about different kinds of closeness?

■ DISCUSSION QUESTIONS

Simple/concrete questions:
>   What are some different ways to get attention and affection from others?
>   What are some different kinds of relationships?

Personal experience/feelings questions:
>   How do you get attention and affection from your friends? From family members? From persons of the opposite sex?
>   Have you ever tried to get attention or affection from someone and the person did not give it to you? What happened?

Problem-solving questions:
>   What should you do if you want attention or affection from someone and the person does not want to give it?
>   What should you do if someone of the opposite sex wants to have a sexual relationship with you and you do not want this?
>   How do you know how close to get to someone or how much personal information to share with another?

■ GROUP ACTIVITIES

Each group member shares experiences with different types of relationships.
Individual participants discuss relationship problems and receive group support.
Facilitate a discussion about different levels of intimacy in different types of relationships.

■ ASSESSMENT OF SKILLS LEARNED

Recognizes different methods to gain attention or affection from others:

ALMOST NEVER	USUALLY NOT	SOMETIMES	USUALLY	ALMOST ALWAYS
1	2	3	4	5

Recognizes the difference between different kinds of intimate relationships:

ALMOST NEVER	USUALLY NOT	SOMETIMES	USUALLY	ALMOST ALWAYS
1	2	3	4	5

Recognizes different types of closeness in relationships:

ALMOST NEVER	USUALLY NOT	SOMETIMES	USUALLY	ALMOST ALWAYS
1	2	3	4	5

67. *Friendship, Dating, and Sexual Relationships*

Friendship, dating, and sexual relationships represent a natural progression in the lives of most individuals. Persons with developmental disabilities are often more protected. They have more difficulty in establishing and maintaining all of these types of relationships. They also become more easily confused about the boundaries and logistics of relationships. The group facilitator should begin with a discussion about the differences between a dating relationship and a friendship, highlighting that a dating relationship is often closer, may involve sexual attraction, and is more formal than a friendship. Next, the discussion can focus on the typical boundaries of a sexual relationship. Sexual relationships typically involve sexual attraction, sharing intimate feelings, and communications to find out if one's partner feels the same way as oneself. Sexual relationships are usually kept private, and sexual behaviors are avoided in public. Individuals have the right to say "no" to somebody who wants a sexual relationship if they do not feel the same way. There is a responsibility to listen and respect others boundaries when they say "no" to sexual relationships. The group facilitator may proceed with a discussion about special arrangements necessary for dating. These include choosing a person to date, asking them out, selecting a place to go and an activity to do, scheduling a time, arranging transportation, and obtaining necessary permissions if either person is living in a protected setting. Finally, the potential negative consequences of sexual relationships should be explored—pregnancy, sexually transmitted diseases, and the need to avoid these. This topic should be modified depending on the religious orientation, cultural background, and values of participants and their parents or guardians. In discussing sexual relationships, for those of more strict and conservative orientations, the idea of abstinence may be emphasized. For those of more liberal persuasions, the idea of pregnancy and disease prevention may be accentuated. In either case, it will be helpful to discuss the general parameters and boundaries of friendship, dating, and sexuality, as it is necessary to have concepts of these boundaries if one is to differentiate different types of relationships. This topic is most appropriate for individuals with mild developmental disabilities. It can be modified to some extent for lower functioning persons by giving more concrete examples, asking yes/no questions, and allowing for nonverbal communication.

■ SPECIFIC SKILLS TO BE LEARNED

Recognize the difference between a dating relationship and friendship:
    Dating relationship is closer.
    Dating may involve sexual attraction.
    Dating is more formal.
Recognize when a sexual relationship is appropriate or inappropriate:
    Being sexually attracted to someone
    Sharing one's feelings with somebody
    Finding out if someone else feels similarly to oneself
    Keeping sexuality private
    Avoiding sexual behaviors in public
    Saying "no" to somebody who wants a sexual relationship if one does not want this
    Paying attention when somebody says "no"
Recognize special arrangements which need to be made in order to go on a date:

Choosing a person to date and asking them out
Choosing a place to go and an activity to do
Scheduling a time
Arranging transportation
Getting necessary permissions
Recognize possible negative consequences to a sexual relationship:
Pregnancy
Sexually transmitted diseases

■ CONCEPTS NECESSARY TO PERFORM SKILLS

Friendship: Companionship; togetherness; neighborliness; comradeship; fellowship; brotherhood; closeness with others; to share thoughts, feelings and activities with others; what a person has with friends and companions.

Dating: To go out on a date; go out to dinner or to a movie with a special friend; get together with somebody at a certain time and place; what people do when they have a romantic relationship with each other; when somebody goes places with a boyfriend or girlfriend.

Sexual relationship: When people become romantic together; kissing and hugging a boyfriend or girlfriend; two people touching each other in their private places; what people do when they love each other or are more than just friends.

Pregnant: When a woman is going to have a baby; what can happen after a man and woman have sex together; what might happen if a man and woman do not use birth control methods when they have sex.

Sexually transmitted disease: A sickness that somebody may get after having sex; a disease like AIDS that can spread when people have sex together.

■ CASE VIGNETTES

—*Paul noticed Becky in the cafeteria. He thought she was pretty and also felt that she was a nice person. He was shy and did not know what to say to her, but he often sat a short distance away from her. One day she said, "Hi," and sat next to Paul. They talked about their jobs and then about more personal things. Paul found out that Becky lived in an apartment with two friends on the other side of town. She found out that he lived with his parents. In the days that followed, Paul began sitting right next to Becky at lunch. They both liked each other, and each felt the other was special. Paul wanted to go out on a date with Becky, but he did not quite know how to ask her. He was afraid she would say, "No." He was also worried about how they would make arrangements to go someplace because he did not drive a car and did not know how to take the bus by himself.*

Do you think Paul and Becky had the kind of relationship that could possibly have turned into a dating relationship? Why or why not? How could Paul have asked Becky out on a date? How could they have made arrangements to go somewhere and do something fun together? Would they have needed any special help to go out on a date?

—*Nancy had a boyfriend, Chuck. They had known each other for three years and had a very special, close relationship. Sometimes they went places together and did fun activities. They worked together in different areas of an assembly plant. One day Nancy approached Chuck and asked, "Chuck, would you like to go to a movie with me this Friday night?" Chuck said, "Yes," and said he also wanted to have dinner with her. Nancy told him that the movie was at seven-thirty and was right next to a fast food hamburger restaurant. They both agreed that they would meet at the restaurant at six o'clock so that they would have time to eat and still get in line early enough for the movie. They each knew how to take the city bus and how to get onto the right bus. They agreed that they would each pay for their own dinners and movies. Nancy invited Chuck to come over to her house for awhile when the movie was over. They held hands during the movie and later, at Nancy's house, they hugged and kissed each other. They did this because they were special friends and had a romantic relationship.*

What arrangements did Nancy and Chuck need to make to go out on their date? Do you think they did a good or bad job making their arrangements? What kind of a relationship did they have? Did they have more than just a friendship?

■ DISCUSSION QUESTIONS

Simple/concrete questions:

What is the difference between friendship and dating?

What are some arrangements that need to be made in order to go on a date?

What are some different activities that you can do on a date?

Personal experience/feelings questions:

Have you ever dated?

Have you ever had any difficulties asking someone out or making arrangements for a date?

Do you have any worry or fear about going on a date?

Problem-solving questions:

How should a person ask someone out on a date?

What should you do if someone says he or she does not want to go out with you?

What should you do if a person says he or she does not want to have a sexual relationship with you?

When might a sexual relationship happen?

How can you tell someone that you do not want to go out on a date or have sex with him or her?

■ GROUP ACTIVITIES

Facilitate a discussion about the friendship and dating experiences of different group members.

Discuss when sexual relationships may happen, and appropriate ways to talk about them with potential relationship partners.

Form pairs and discuss personal experiences with friendship and dating.

■ ASSESSMENT OF SKILLS LEARNED

Recognizes the difference between a dating relationship and friendship:

ALMOST NEVER	USUALLY NOT	SOMETIMES	USUALLY	ALMOST ALWAYS
1	2	3	4	5

Recognizes when a sexual relationship is appropriate or inappropriate:

ALMOST NEVER	USUALLY NOT	SOMETIMES	USUALLY	ALMOST ALWAYS
1	2	3	4	5

Recognizes the special arrangements necessary to go on a date:

ALMOST NEVER	USUALLY NOT	SOMETIMES	USUALLY	ALMOST ALWAYS
1	2	3	4	5

Recognizes possible negative consequences to a sexual relationship:

ALMOST NEVER	USUALLY NOT	SOMETIMES	USUALLY	ALMOST ALWAYS
1	2	3	4	5

68. *Dealing with the Loss of a Friendship*

The loss of a friendship is a normal part of life for most individuals. Friends move away, develop other interests, grow apart, and sometimes die. Individuals with developmental disabilities often experience more than their fair share of friendship losses because of frequent school, work, and residence changes. They tend to have more limited friendship networks. Consequently, each of their friends may take on more than the usual significance. This session should begin with a discussion of possible reasons for the loss of a friendship. These may include death, interpersonal conflicts, friends preferring other companionship, one or the other moving away, one person changing schools or jobs, current friends failing to show a continued interest, and occasions of conflict in which one friend violates the trust or takes advantage of another. It would be helpful to have a more in-depth discussion of reasons that one friend may become angry with another. These may include ignoring a friend, talking too much about oneself to the exclusion of one's friend, not asking questions and demonstrating an interest in a friend, selfishness, stubbornness, rudeness, and persistently trying to have things one's own way without thinking of the other's needs. Finally, possible ways to react to the loss of a friend may be examined. These may include becoming emotionally upset (hurt, angry, etc.), finding and establishing new friends, ignoring minor slights while continuing to be a good friend, picking new friends who treat one well, keeping telephone contact or writing letters to friends who have moved away, and realizing that it is all right if somebody does not want to be friends. This topic is appropriate for individuals with mild and moderate developmental disabilities. It can be modified for lower functioning individuals by using yes/no questions, pictures/symbols of friends, and nonverbal communication.

■ SPECIFIC SKILLS TO BE LEARNED

Identify possible reasons for the loss of a friendship:
    A friend dies.
    Friend is angry because of one's behavior:
        Ignoring a friend
        Talking too much about oneself and not enough about one's friend
        Not asking questions or showing an interest in a friend
        Selfishness
        Stubbornness
        Rudeness
        Having to have one's own way without thinking of a friend
    Friend chooses other friends instead of you.
    Friend moves away from one's residence, school or worksite.
    Friend shows no interest in you.
    Friend has violated trust or taken advantage of you.
Identify possible ways to react to the loss of a friend:
    Becoming emotionally upset, hurt, and angry, and blaming one's friend for problems
    Finding (making) new friends
    Ignoring slights from one's friend and continuing to try to be a good friend
    Picking new friends who treat you well
    Keeping telephone contact or writing letters to a friend who moves away
    Realizing that it is O.K. if someone does not want to be friends

■ CONCEPTS NECESSARY TO PERFORM SKILLS

Friend: Somebody a person knows well; a familiar person; companion; mate; a person with whom somebody likes to do things; someone to talk to; somebody to whom a person feels close; someone a person can trust.

Loss: To lose someone or something; not have someone or something anymore; the death of a significant other; the event of a friend or family member moving away; to be cut off from a person, place, or thing.

Interest: To show that one cares about what someone else thinks or feels; to ask about somebody; to have concern for another; to let others know they are important.

Ignore: Not pay attention; not listen; overlook; disregard; neglect; do something else when a person is trying to talk.

Rude: Mean; discourteous; offensive; doing something that bothers another person; insensitive; not paying attention to how other people feel; not caring how others feel; disregarding; vulgar; neglectful.

Selfish: Showing no interest in others; not sharing with others; thinking only of oneself; not caring about others.

Stubborn: Not willing to change; having one's mind made up; rigid; not willing to change one's behavior; always wanting to have things your way.

■ CASE VIGNETTES

—*Robert had a good friend, James. They went to a seniors program together and often sat by each other during activities. One day Robert heard the bad news that James was moving to a new home. He had medical problems and was having trouble breathing. He needed extra help for his medical problems, so he moved to a place where they had special oxygen equipment. Robert felt surprised and shocked that Jim would no longer be coming to the seniors program. He also felt sad. He knew he would miss James. After James had moved, Robert called him at his new home. He also made plans to visit him a couple of weeks later. Even though he could not see James very often, he wanted to keep in touch with him. Robert was having trouble adjusting to his senior's program without James; but he found that he had other friends there who also missed James. One day, the whole group sent James a card just to let him know they missed him.*

How do you think Robert felt when his friend James moved away? What did he do to deal with his feelings? Do you think he adjusted all right to the loss of his friend?

—*Marlene had a friend, Sally, at her day program. She and Sally often sat by each other when they worked on projects. One day Sally sat by someone else, and this upset Marlene. She wanted Sally to be her friend, and she was mad because Sally was giving her attention to somebody else. Sally did not feel very close to Marlene and enjoyed other friends as well. Marlene did not understand or accept the fact that Sally had other close friends. Sometimes Marlene would say nasty things to Sally's other friends because she was jealous. Once she even got in trouble because she hit one of Sally's friends.*

Do you think Marlene was having a difficult time dealing with the loss of Sally's friendship? Was she dealing well with the loss? Why or why not? Would there be any more adult way to handle that sort of friendship problem? Would it be okay to share friends with others?

■ DISCUSSION QUESTIONS

Simple/concrete questions:

What are some possible reasons for the loss of a friendship?

What are some different ways which a person can react to the loss of a friend?

Personal experience/feelings questions:

Have you ever lost a friend? How did you feel?

If you have lost a friend, how and why did you lose your friend?

Problem-solving questions:

What are some ways to make and keep good friendships?

What should you do if someone does not want to be your friend anymore?

■ GROUP ACTIVITIES

Facilitate a discussion about making, maintaining and/or losing friends.

Group members select partners and talk about current friendships.

■ ASSESSMENT OF SKILLS LEARNED

Identifies possible reasons for the loss of a friendship:

ALMOST NEVER	USUALLY NOT	SOMETIMES	USUALLY	ALMOST ALWAYS
1	2	3	4	5

Identifies appropriate and inappropriate ways to react to the loss of a friend:

ALMOST NEVER	USUALLY NOT	SOMETIMES	USUALLY	ALMOST ALWAYS
1	2	3	4	5

69. Family and Residence Rules: Living with Others

All people grow up in families of one sort or another, even those raised in institutions or non-traditional settings. Rules are always necessary when living space is shared by two or more individuals. Persons with developmental disabilities are more likely than usual to live in non-traditional family situations and to have extended dependencies on external caretakers. This topic focuses on the purpose of family and residence rules, beginning with a discussion of rules that help individuals get along with minimal conflict. Knowing what to do, when to do it, when not to do it, how to do it, with whom to do it, etc. helps individuals avoid unnecessary conflict. The point should be made that rules help persons share resources and responsibilities more efficiently. Resources may include television, radio, telephone, bathroom, kitchen, dining/living rooms, bedrooms, money, and so forth. Responsibilities may include food preparation, kitchen help, cleaning, garbage removal, yard work, and the like. It can be explained that some rules ensure privacy, such as those concerning knocking on or locking bedroom/bathroom doors, opening mail, private conversations, personal possessions, noise restrictions, and so forth. Rules also help families coordinate activities such as mealtimes, use of the bathroom, recreation/leisure activities, residence meetings, times to be home, sharing possessions, etc. Finally, it may be noted that rules bind people together by encouraging common experiences, providing safety/security, creating a sense of family (group) identity, and helping family members decide what is important. Establishing rules is a way of setting priorities. Rules help provide a livable framework within which individuals more easily exist than would be the case in a more anarchic situation. This topic is most appropriate for those with mild and moderate developmental disabilities, but it can be adapted for lower functioning individuals by simplifying the language, asking yes/no questions about specific family rules, and using various methods of non-verbal communication.

■ SPECIFIC SKILLS TO BE LEARNED

Identify the purpose of having family or residence rules:
  Easier for groups of people to get along together without conflict:
    What to do
    When to do it
    When not to do it
    How to do it
    With whom to do it
  More efficiently share resources and responsibilities:
    Television and radio
    Telephone
    Bathroom, kitchen, dining/living rooms
    Job tasks:
      Kitchen and food preparation
      Cleaning
      Garbage
      Yard work
      Shared bedrooms (roommates)
  Ensure privacy:
    Bedroom/bathroom doors (knock, lock, etc.)
    Mail
    Private conversation
    Respect for others' belongings
    Noise restrictions at certain times
  Coordinate activities:
    Mealtimes
    Use of bathroom
    Leisure/recreation activities (outings)
    Residence meetings
    Times to be home
    Sharing possessions
  Bind people together:
    Common experiences
    Safety/security
    A sense of family identity
    Helping people decide what is important

■ CONCEPTS NECESSARY TO PERFORM SKILLS

Rule: Guideline; boundary; limit; expectation; what each person agrees to do or not do.

Resources: Money; possessions; skills; abilities; information and knowledge.

Privacy: To keep thoughts and feelings to oneself; share thoughts and feelings with only close relations; confidentiality.

Activities: Things people do; events; happenings; how people spend time; actions; behaviors; movements.

Identity: Who you are; who I am; who each person is; what is special about a person; how one is like or unlike others; to be a separate person; to be an individual; to have one's own thoughts, feelings, and behaviors; to know who you are and how you are the same as, or different from, others; individuality; distinctiveness.

Common experience: When different people do the same thing or have the same thing happen to them; to do something together with others; when people live under the same conditions.

■ CASE VIGNETTES

—Bruce lived with five other people in a big house. Sometimes he was confused about what he was supposed to do and when he was supposed to do it. For example, when everybody else was eating supper, he sometimes wanted to watch television. When others were cleaning up the house on Saturday morning, he wanted to go for a walk instead. He was never quite sure what chore he was supposed to do, nor when to do it. This made his housemates angry. When it was time to go to bed, Bruce liked to watch television. This caused problems because Bruce turned the sound up too loud and sometimes woke the others. When asked to turn the sound lower, Bruce became upset because he was not yet ready to go to bed and felt that the others should not be tired either. Sometimes Bruce would walk into others' bedrooms without knocking, even though the rule was to knock first. At other times, he interrupted private conversations and said what he thought, even though others were not talking to him. Bruce was supposed to use the bathroom between eight and nine o'clock in the morning, and his housemates had it scheduled before and after him. Sometimes he ignored the schedule, and this made them late for their activities.

Was Bruce good at recognizing and following his residence rules? In what ways did he have trouble following the rules? How did Bruce's difficulty with rules affect his relationships with housemates? How do you think that his housemates may have felt when Bruce had trouble following the rules?

—Virginia lived in a women's dormitory with thirty other women. She had her own room but lived on the same floor as fifteen others. Virginia knew what she had to do and when she had to do it. For example, she got up at seven o'clock every morning, took a shower, and went down to breakfast in the cafeteria. Breakfast was served from seven-thirty to eight-thirty every morning. After breakfast, Virginia did her morning chores. Sometimes she cleared tables in the cafeteria, and at other times she vacuumed floors. She always did her job and then went about her day. Virginia got home at three-thirty in the afternoon. She always checked in with her residence counselor, except once in a while when she forgot. Virginia respected the privacy of her housemates. She did not go into someone's room without permission, and she did not use others' things without first asking them. Virginia knew that it was quiet time from nine-thirty until ten-thirty at night, and that lights had to be out by eleven o'clock unless someone was in the television room at the end of the hallway. She knew that everybody was supposed to be polite to each other and try to get along.

Was Virginia good at following her residence rules? In what ways did she follow the rules? How did this help all of her fellow residents when she followed the rules?

■ DISCUSSION QUESTIONS

Simple/concrete questions:

What are some reasons for family or residence rules?

How can rules help people live together more comfortably?

Personal experience/feelings questions:

Do you like the rules at your residence? Are they fair?

Are there any rules that you do not like at your residence?

Have you ever had trouble following rules? Why? What rules?

Problem-solving questions:

What is a good way to deal with rules that are difficult to follow?

What is a good way to go about changing a family or residence rule?

What should you do if your family members or housemates do not follow the rules?

■ GROUP ACTIVITIES

Facilitate a discussion about individual group members' family and residence rules. Discuss ways in which rules help people live together more easily.

Facilitate a discussion about rules that members do not like or which they have difficulty following.

■ ASSESSMENT OF SKILLS LEARNED

Identifies positive benefits of family or residence rules:

ALMOST NEVER	USUALLY NOT	SOMETIMES	USUALLY	ALMOST ALWAYS
1	2	3	4	5

Reference

Kübler-Ross, E. (1969). *On death and dying.* New York: MacMillan.

9 *Self-Advocacy*

70. *Recognizing Personal Rights*
71. *Advocating for Personal Needs and Concerns*
72. *Proactive Behavior*
73. *Differentiating between Aggressive, Passive, and Assertive Language Behavior*
74. *Appropriate Application of Assertiveness*

SELF-ADVOCACY IS AN IMPORTANT but often neglected dimension of social skills development. This chapter begins with the topic, recognizing personal rights, which facilitates awareness of the basic rights to make choices, express oneself, and receive dignified treatment from others. Next is a section focusing on self-advocacy for personal needs and concerns. It is followed by the topic of proactive behavior, which highlights the value of self-direction and personal responsibility to one's happiness. The chapter ends with topics exploring aggressive, passive, and assertive language/behavior, and appropriate application of assertiveness.

70. *Recognizing Personal Rights*

Persons with developmental delay often have no idea that they have a number of basic rights. They have frequently had histories of authoritarian treatment from caretakers and have not been taught to assert their own feelings, thoughts and desires. This skill area assists individuals in recognizing basic rights. All persons have the right to make choices and decisions to the extent to which they understand the associated implications and consequences of their actions. These include choices in areas of friendship, social relationships, leisure activities, school, and work. Each person has the right to basic self-expression of opinions, thoughts, ideas, feelings, and preferences. All individuals have the right to dignified and humane treatment. This includes protection from abuse/neglect, nonpatronizing attitudes from others, respectful interactions with peers and caretakers, and access to basic life necessities such as food, clothing, shelter, education, work, recreation, socialization, and so forth. The group facilitator should identify and describe a variety of basic rights. Individual participants may be encouraged to express and elaborate their own ideas about personal rights. This topic is appropriate for persons with mild developmental disabilities. The concepts are abstract and difficult for persons with more significant developmental delay. Some accommodation can be made for individuals with more limited cognitive and communication abilities by utilizing concrete and direct questioning of participants—for example: "Do you have the right to get something to eat when you are hungry?" "If you are angry, do you have the right to tell somebody?" "What would you rather do, play a game or work on your puzzle?"

■ SPECIFIC SKILLS TO BE LEARNED

Recognize basic rights:
    Freedom to make choices and decisions:
        Friends and social relationships
        Leisure activities

School
Work
Self-expression:
    Opinions, thoughts and ideas
    Feelings
    Preferences
Dignified and humane treatment:
    Protection from abuse and neglect
    Respectful, noncondescending attitudes and interactions
    Access to basic life necessities

■ CONCEPTS NECESSARY TO PERFORM SKILLS

Freedom: Independence; liberty to make choices and decisions; protection from unreasonable demands of others; the ability to decide things for oneself; able to have one's own way about important matters; when a person can do what he or she wishes.

Self-expression: To voice opinions, thoughts, and ideas; tell others how you feel; make choices; communicate personal preferences and wishes; share personal experiences.

Dignified: Respectful; with due regard; held in proper esteem; given proper treatment and respect; cared for without condescension; kindly but not patronizing.

■ CASE VIGNETTES

—*Tanya grew up in a very loving and caring family. She had learned early in life that she had the right to proper treatment from others. Even when she was very young, her parents had given her a choice of different activities. She could play with her blocks, write in her coloring book, or do something else that she chose. When she was old enough to go into the neighborhood, she was able to meet other children and pick her own friends. Sometimes her parents helped her to make good choices, but they always asked her how she felt and what she thought about different things. Her parents knew that it was good for her to join activities, have friends, and do schoolwork. But they were respectful of what Tanya wanted for herself, and they gave her encouragement to be successful in what she chose to do. When Tanya was sixteen years old, she wanted to have a boyfriend. Her parents were worried about her, but even so, they helped her to meet boys by taking her to activities like roller-skating and school dances. Tanya was slowly learning how to take care of herself. She was very happy that her parents treated her with respect, listened to her opinions and gave her the freedom to make choices in her life.*

    Did Tanya recognize that she had basic rights to make choices, tell her opinions, and receive respectful treatment from others? How did Tanya learn about her basic rights? Did it help to have love and concern from her family?

—*Eugene grew up in a very abusive and neglectful family. Both of his parents drank too much alcohol and yelled at each other a lot. They also yelled at Eugene and his brother. Eugene was never taught about his basic rights. In fact, he was punished if he gave his opinions or told his parents about his feelings. Sometimes, when his father was drinking, he would make fun of Eugene because he was a slow learner. At other times he called him "retarded." Eugene felt hurt and angry about this mistreatment, but if he became upset his father would spank him and send him to his room. He was told to "Be quiet" and keep out of the way. Nobody ever asked Eugene what he wanted to do. They simply told him what to do. Nobody asked him about his feelings. Nobody seemed to care much how he felt. He was never asked for his opinion about what he would like to do, what he wanted to eat, or what he thought about family matters.*

Was Eugene able to recognize his basic rights? Why or why not? Do you think Eugene was treated with dignity and respect in his family? Why or why not?

■ DISCUSSION QUESTIONS

Simple/concrete questions:

What are some basic personal rights?

What are some choices people can make about friends, hobbies, school, work, and other life activities?

Can you list one type of good (respectful) or bad (disrespectful) treatment people can give each other?

Personal experience/feelings questions:

Are you allowed to express your feelings in your family (at your residence)?

Do other people ever ask what you think about important matters?

How do you feel when you are able to make your own choices and decisions? Give an example of a choice you have made in your life.

Are you ever treated badly or disrespectfully by others? Describe.

Problem-solving questions:

How do you know if your personal rights are being respected?

How can you decide when to tell your thoughts and feelings to others?

How do you know if you are being mistreated or abused?

■ GROUP ACTIVITIES

Ask each person to share one way in which he or she makes choices in areas of friendship, leisure activities, school, or work.

Hold a discussion about various forms of mistreatment and lack of respect. Encourage individual sharing of personal experiences with patronizing or disrespectful treatment from others.

Participants practice expressing feelings, thoughts, and opinions about basic rights.

■ ASSESSMENT OF SKILLS LEARNED

Recognizes personal right to make choices about friends, activities, school and/or work:

ALMOST NEVER	USUALLY NOT	SOMETIMES	USUALLY	ALMOST ALWAYS
1	2	3	4	5

Recognizes own opinions, thoughts, and feelings about important matters:

ALMOST NEVER	USUALLY NOT	SOMETIMES	USUALLY	ALMOST ALWAYS
1	2	3	4	5

Recognizes the difference between respectful/humane and disrespectful/inhumane treatment:

ALMOST NEVER	USUALLY NOT	SOMETIMES	USUALLY	ALMOST ALWAYS
1	2	3	4	5

71. Advocating for Personal Needs and Concerns

Without the means of advocating for one's needs and wishes, an individual is at the mercy of others to meet his or her needs. Persons with developmental disabilities typically receive little training in self-advocacy. In fact, they are often reinforced much more vigorously for passive, compliant behaviors that create less work for caretakers. This topic addresses the issue of self-advocacy. Participants should be queried and informed about needs and concerns requiring advocacy. Advocacy concerns may include unreasonable restriction of choices in areas of friendship, social, leisure, school, work, and home activities. Advocacy needs may also involve unreasonable restriction of one's expression of opinions, thoughts, ideas, feelings, and preferences. Finally, advocacy needs may stem from inhumane or undignified treatment such as abuse, neglect, restricted access to basic necessities, restricted social activities, lack of appropriate opportunities for the expression of sexuality, and patronizing attitudes of others. Group members must be assisted in understanding how to advocate for personal needs and concerns. Self-advocacy may include verbalizing feelings about mistreatment, identifying desired changes in treatment, verbalizing requests for change to the perpetrators of mistreatment, repeating requests, explaining why one feels mistreated, and asking another person to help in one's advocacy. This topic involves higher level concepts most appropriate for persons with mild developmental delay. Like the previous topic, it can be modified for individuals with less cognitive ability by performing more specific and concrete questioning of individual participants.

■ SPECIFIC SKILLS TO BE LEARNED

Recognize needs and concerns requiring advocacy:
    Unreasonable restriction of choices:
        Friends and social activities
        Leisure activities
        School, work, and home activities
    Unreasonable restriction of self-expression:
        Opinions, thoughts, and ideas
        Feelings
        Preferences
    Inhumane or undignified treatment:
        Abuse/neglect
        Restricted access to life necessities:
            Food and beverages
            Rest and break times
            Clothing and shelter
        Restricted social activities
        Restricted expression of sexuality
        Condescension and patronizing attitudes of others
Understand how to advocate effectively for personal needs and concerns:
    Tell others how one feels about specific mistreatment.
    Identify specific changes in treatment one would like.
    Verbalize a request for change to the perpetrator of mistreatment.
    Repeat one's request for change.
    Explain why one feels mistreated.
    Ask another person to help in one's advocacy:
        Parent, brother, sister, or other family member
        Teacher, counselor, or job supervisor
        Social worker
        Psychologist or therapist
        Residence worker

■ CONCEPTS NECESSARY TO PEFORM SKILLS

Choice: Choose something; pick something; decide something; pick one thing or another; do one thing or another; select something; make up one's mind.

Self-expression: To voice opinions, thoughts, and ideas; tell others how you feel; make choices; communicate personal preferences and wishes; share personal experiences.

Advocate: Argue for; favor; make a case for; plead; express favorable opinions for; present reasons to support one's choices.

Unreasonable: Senseless; without good reason; without good cause; illogical; irrational; arbitrary; absurd; to advocate for something that is not in somebody's best interest.

■ CASE VIGNETTES

—George knew he had the right to make personal choices and to express his opinions. He had been working at his job for almost thirty years. He had enjoyed cleaning rooms at the hotel for many years, but now he was ready for a change. George was sixty-six years old, and he was thinking about retiring from his job. Even though he enjoyed his workmates and liked his boss, he felt that he needed something new in his life. One day he approached his job coach and stated, "Mike, I've been working here for a long time; I think I want to do something else now." Mike was surprised at first, but after listening to George he understood that George wanted a change. George explained that he was tired of cleaning rooms and that he was thinking of retiring from work just as many other people his age did. The two of them agreed that George would leave his job at the end of the month. George was not sure, but he was thinking about either working part time at a new job or joining a seniors program. Whatever George's decision would be, he was happy that Mike listened to him, took his concerns seriously, and was helping him to follow through with his own decision and choice in the matter.

Did George recognize his basic right to make choices about his job? Did he feel free to talk about his feelings and opinions related to his job? What choices did George make about his job and future? Was he able to advocate for his own needs and wishes?

—Suzanne was quite unhappy with her job. She did not particularly like working at an assembly line packaging products. She wanted to work at a hotel cleaning rooms like her friend Bertha. Suzanne did not know whom to talk to about her desire for a new job. She was afraid that if she told her job supervisor, she would get mad. One day Suzanne was at home with a residence counselor and blurted out: "Deb, I hate my job. They give me too many boxes and make me work too fast. I don't like it and I want to clean rooms at the hotel with Bertha." Suzanne's residence counselor told her: "You should feel lucky to have the job you've got. I think you're just having a bad day." Suzanne's heart sank, and she felt miserable. She did not know how to advocate effectively for her own needs, and she gave up trying to explain her wishes and feelings about her job to Deb.

Was Suzanne able to recognize her own feelings and needs related to her job? Was she able to advocate effectively for her own needs and wishes? Why or why not? Do you think Suzanne had a right to more dignified and respectful treatment from her residence counselor? How could she have continued to advocate for herself in matters related to her job?

■ DISCUSSION QUESTIONS

Simple/concrete questions:

Can you describe some possible personal choices in areas of friends, leisure activities, school, work, or home life?

Do you have the right to make personal choices and decisions? In what areas?

Personal experience/feelings questions:

Have you ever asked others to treat you differently? In what ways?

How do you feel when others do not listen to what you want?

How do you feel when others listen and try to help you get what you want?

Do others ever treat you like a little child? In what ways?

Problem-solving questions:

How can you tell somebody that you think they are mistreating you?

How can you ask others to change how they are acting toward you?

How can you let others know how you feel, and what you would like from them?

■ GROUP ACTIVITIES

Each participant list areas in which he or she currently makes personal choices. List areas in which group members would like more opportunities to make choices.

Take turns role-playing self-advocacy situations—identifying requested changes in treatment, verbalizing specific requests for change, and repeating demands for personal needs to be met.

Hold a discussion about appropriate times, places, and methods of self-advocacy.

■ ASSESSMENT OF SKILLS LEARNED

Recognizes when others unreasonably try to restrict self-expressions and choices:

ALMOST NEVER	USUALLY NOT	SOMETIMES	USUALLY	ALMOST ALWAYS
1	2	3	4	5

Identifies inhumane or undignified treatment:

ALMOST NEVER	USUALLY NOT	SOMETIMES	USUALLY	ALMOST ALWAYS
1	2	3	4	5

Advocates effectively for personal needs and concerns:

ALMOST NEVER	USUALLY NOT	SOMETIMES	USUALLY	ALMOST ALWAYS
1	2	3	4	5

72. *Proactive Behavior*

Proactive behavior is one way to avoid conflict and problems. Persons with developmental disabilities often have difficulty with proactive behaviors because these behaviors require planning, foresight, and anticipation of possible negative consequences, abilities that are often limited in this population. The group leader should begin with an explanation and examples of what it means to be a proactive person, highlighting such features as choosing one's own destiny, commitment to values, setting goals, pursuing goals with discipline, doing what is necessary to accomplish goals, looking for positives in situations, not complaining about inconveniences, taking responsibility for oneself, and not blaming other people or external circumstances for one's problems. The discussion should continue with further clarification of the proactive style of relating under various circumstances. Conceptually, this topic may be rather difficult for individuals with even mild and moderate developmental disabilities. Individuals may understand many of the specific proactive behaviors or styles of relating when they are examined separately. The topic is not appropriate for individuals with severe developmental delay.

■ SPECIFIC SKILLS TO BE LEARNED

Understand what a proactive person is:
Person who influences his or her own destiny
Person who is committed to a set of values
Person who sets goals based on values
Person who pursues goals with discipline
Person who does what he or she must in order to accomplish goals
Person who looks for the positive in any given situation
Person who does not complain about inconvenience
Person who takes responsibility for changing him- or herself or the situation in order to make things better
Person who does not blame the world or other persons for problems
Recognize proactive style of relating to the world:
Accept and commit oneself to a set of values.
Set goals for accomplishment based upon values.
Work on goals and do not give up easily (be disciplined).
Think and talk about the positive aspects of the situation.
See oneself as responsible for achieving one's goals.
If things do not work the way one wants, try doing something different to change either the situation or oneself (do not blame others).

■ CONCEPTS NECESSARY TO PERFORM SKILLS

Proactive behavior: To choose one's own goals; commit to one's own values and goals; do what a person must in order to achieve something; maintain a positive attitude while accomplishing goals; not blame others for one's problems; take responsibility for one's behavior.

Values: Beliefs; what is important to a person; ideas about what is important in life; guidelines for behavior; things which a person believes are right or true.

Goals: What people try to achieve; aims; objectives; things individuals are trying to do; what people shoot for, even if they fall short of the mark.

Personal responsibility: Decide to control one's own behavior; take control of one's life and behavior; not blame others when losing one's temper; decide to keep self-control; make a choice to do or not to do something; not blame others for one's problems; decide to do something and do it; be held accountable for your behavior; take charge of one's own life; to be dependable and reliable; to do what one says one is going to do.

■ CASE VIGNETTES

—*Brenda had a bad problem. She often picked away at the skin on her arms and hands, sometimes making herself bleed when she picked too hard. She had done this for many years, and it had become a very bad habit. One day, Brenda decided to become a proactive person. She decided to quit picking at her skin. This was very difficult, and sometimes she had to tell herself, "Stop, Brenda, quit picking at yourself. You can do it." She also asked her counselors for help. They reminded her not to pick at herself and wrapped some bandages on her skin where she needed it most. They also put soft lotion on her skin before they put the bandages on. Brenda had set her goal, to quit picking at her skin. She was now succeeding. She knew that there was no one else to blame for her problem. She was responsible for solving it and she was doing it. Brenda was no longer picking at her skin.*

Why was Brenda's behavior proactive? How was she taking responsibility for her own behavior? What might have happened if Brenda did not quit picking at her skin?

—Troy was having problems holding a job. He could do the work all right, but he often showed up late for work and was late to return to work after coffee breaks. One day he became very upset with his supervisor because she would not give him some extra time off. He became angry and frustrated, telling her that he thought she was unfair. When it came time to pick the right person for the new job in the warehouse, Troy's supervisor picked Dave even though Troy wanted the job. She told Troy that she was not sure if Troy would show up on time, and she needed a reliable person for the new job.

Was Troy a proactive person? How did he blame others for his problems? What could he have done to take charge of his life and get more respect from his job supervisor?

■ DISCUSSION QUESTIONS

Simple/concrete questions:
   What are some possible proactive behaviors?
Personal experience/feelings questions:
   Have you ever taken charge and accomplished a goal? How did you feel?
   Have you ever listened to another person whining, whimpering, and complaining because he or she got a raw deal in life? How did you feel?
   Do you think you are responsible to make your own life better? Why or why not?
Problem-solving questions:
   How can you become a more proactive person? What are some things you can do to be more proactive?
   When misfortunes and hardships happen in your life, what can you do to make it through rough times?

■ GROUP ACTIVITIES

Facilitate a discussion about the success experiences of individual group members. Keep the focus of the group on positive life experiences.
Individual group members share experiences of both success and failure, identifying what made each experience a success or failure.
Facilitate a discussion about personal responsibility as this relates to success and failure in achieving goals.

■ ASSESSMENT OF SKILLS LEARNED

Understands the concept of proactive behavior:

ALMOST NEVER	USUALLY NOT	SOMETIMES	USUALLY	ALMOST ALWAYS
1	2	3	4	5

Recognizes one or more proactive ways to relate to the world:

ALMOST NEVER	USUALLY NOT	SOMETIMES	USUALLY	ALMOST ALWAYS
1	2	3	4	5

73. *Differentiating between Aggressive, Passive, and Assertive Language/Behavior*

Assertiveness is the act of saying what one feels, thinks, wants, and needs. It requires individuals to recognize their feelings, thoughts, and wishes and to speak up about them. The group facilitator should begin with basic definitions of these concepts, which are probably somewhat familiar to participants at this point. A discussion may be conducted about basic needs and wants, exploring a variety of items including food, safety, housing, social affiliation, affection, sexuality, self-esteem, productivity, self-identity, leisure activity, and so forth. What qualifies as a basic *need* versus a *want* is open to interpretation and opinion. That is not really relevant in this context, as items from both categories provide a basis for assertive behavior. Next, the idea of basic human rights can be explored. This also establishes a rationale for assertiveness. Individuals should be told that they have the right to safety, proper care from others, personal choices, independence (if they can handle this), privacy, and respectful treatment. They have the right to say what they think, feel, and want. The idea of context should be examined, highlighting the appropriate times and places for assertive behavior, and focusing on some typical situations calling for assertive responses. Specific techniques of assertiveness may be discussed. These include repeating questions or requests and seeking outside help if necessary. Finally, the differences between passive, aggressive, and assertive behaviors should be reviewed. The topic is easily accessible to those with mild and moderate developmental disabilities, and somewhat less comprehensible to lower functioning individuals. Persons with a wide range of intellectual abilities can grasp the concepts of saying what they think and feel, but some have more difficulty understanding the appropriate context for these verbalizations. Lower functioning persons can make use of picture/symbol communication devices to express feelings and basic wants. They may also utilize gestural, sign, and other nonverbal methods in order to engage in functional communication about these matters. Mildly and moderately developmentally delayed individuals can typically understand simple appropriate contexts of assertive behaviors, such as the notion of being relatively more freely assertive in their own residence or personal space. They may also grasp the concept of assertive behaviors in situations such as waiting in lines for service or riding the bus. Lower functioning individuals, who have less understanding of situational contexts, will need to be taught more reliance on external helpers to whom they can communicate needs and wants.

■ SPECIFIC SKILLS TO BE LEARNED

Say what one feels.
Say what one thinks.
Recognize and ask for what one wants or needs:
    Food/nourishment
    Safety/protection
    Housing/transportation
    Social affiliation (being with others)
    Affection and sexual needs
    Self-esteem (feeling good about oneself)
    Productivity (accomplishing something)
    Identity (being someone)
    Leisure activities (rest, recuperation, self-development)
Recognize one's rights as a person:
    Safety
    Proper care from others
    Making personal choices
    Independence
    Privacy
    Respectful treatment
    Saying what one thinks
    Feeling what one feels
Know when and where to be assertive

Where:
    In one's own space
    At home
    On the bus
    At work/school
When:
    If one has needs/wants
    If personal rights are violated
    If personal space and property are violated
Know how to be assertive:
    Repeat questions/requests.
    Find someone else to ask/help.
Know the difference between passive, aggressive, and assertive.

■ CONCEPTS NECESSARY TO PERFORM SKILLS

Assertive: Directly tell a person how you feel; say how you feel and why you feel that way; tell someone what is on your mind.

Aggressive: Try to hurt someone; act mean to somebody; attack someone; swear or say nasty things to a person.

Passive: Indirectly tell someone how you feel; let someone guess how you feel; not say how you feel and why you feel that way; let people guess from your behavior how you feel.

Personal right: A thing that others owe to a person; something one has a right to ask for and to have; a privilege that an individual claims belongs to him- or herself; what is fair for a person to expect from others; consideration that one should receive just because he or she is a person.

Need: Something a person must have; an individual cannot live without it; something very important and necessary to someone; things that are necessary to stay alive and healthy; individuals demand that their needs be met.

Want: Something a person would very much like; a thing that somebody can live without; something very important but not necessary for survival; people want certain things to make them happy; individuals hope that their wants are satisfied.

Thought: Something somebody thinks; an idea; a thing that a person believes; activity going on in someone's head.

Behavior: Something somebody does; to act in a certain way; what somebody's body is doing

Feeling: Emotion; something somebody feels inside; nervousness, anger, surprise, happiness, sadness, excitement, loneliness, etc.; good or bad sensation happening inside of someone.

■ CASE VIGNETTES

—Suzanne walked into a nearby fast food restaurant. She was tired after a hard day of work. She had saved enough spending money during the week to buy herself a hamburger, milkshake, and French fries. As she waited in line, two other people walked right in front of her and took her place in line. She felt angry because they were so rude. They did not even look at her. Suzanne spoke up in a loud voice: "Excuse me, I was here first" They did not listen but simply ignored her. Suzanne stepped in front of them and told the clerk, "I was here first, and I want to be served first" The clerk said, "Yes, you were. I saw you, and I will wait on you first." The experience was stressful and unpleasant for Suzanne, but she knew she had a right to proper and respectful treatment. She did not want to be pushed around by strangers in a restaurant.

    Why do you think this experience was stressful for Suzanne? Was she passive or assertive?

What did she do that makes you think so?

—*Blanche was a kind and friendly person. Her friends in the neighborhood often visited her house to talk with her and play games. She often gave them treats such as soda pop or cookies. Others would often borrow things from Blanche. She was very nice and let them use her things. One day Michelle asked to borrow two dollars because she had no lunch money. Even though Blanche had very little money, she gave Michelle the two dollars. She was afraid that Michelle would not like her any more if she did not give her the money. Two days later, Michelle wanted to borrow another dollar. Blanche felt very uneasy. She could not afford to give Michelle her money, but she worried that Michelle would not like her anymore.*

Do you think that Blanche was being assertive in this situation? Why or why not? What could she have done to be more assertive? What risk would she take if she decided to be more assertive?

■ DISCUSSION QUESTIONS

Simple/concrete questions:

> Is it assertive or aggressive to yell at somebody? Hit somebody? Throw things when angry? Stomp out and slam the door behind yourself? Swear at people? Tell someone you feel angry? Ask someone not to cut in front of you in a waiting line? Ask someone to stop interrupting you?
>
> Can other people read your mind? Do they know what you are thinking or how you are feeling without asking you?

Personal experience/feelings questions:

> Have you ever wanted to say something but were afraid others would be mad at you for saying it?
>
> How do you usually feel when telling other people about your feelings?
>
> If someone takes your things without asking, is it all right to tell the person to give them back? If someone asks to borrow your money, is it all right to say "no"?
>
> Have you ever been punished for telling people what you thought or felt?

Problem-solving questions:

> What is a good way to be assertive with someone who treats you badly?
>
> What should you do if someone becomes angry with you for telling them how you feel or what you think?
>
> What is an assertive way to tell someone they are taking advantage of your friendship (e.g., borrowing money without returning it, taking your things without asking, asking you for help but not helping you when you need it)?

■ GROUP ACTIVITIES

Each participant practice various assertive statements and requests in front of the group. Facilitate a discussion about the differences between passive, aggressive, and assertive responses.

■ ASSESSMENT OF SKILLS LEARNED

Says what one feels:

ALMOST NEVER	USUALLY NOT	SOMETIMES	USUALLY	ALMOST ALWAYS
1	2	3	4	5

Says what one thinks:

ALMOST NEVER	USUALLY NOT	SOMETIMES	USUALLY	ALMOST ALWAYS
1	2	3	4	5

Recognizes and asks for what one wants/needs:

ALMOST NEVER	USUALLY NOT	SOMETIMES	USUALLY	ALMOST ALWAYS
1	2	3	4	5

Recognizes personal "rights":

ALMOST NEVER	USUALLY NOT	SOMETIMES	USUALLY	ALMOST ALWAYS
1	2	3	4	5

Recognizes when and where to be assertive:

ALMOST NEVER	USUALLY NOT	SOMETIMES	USUALLY	ALMOST ALWAYS
1	2	3	4	5

Repeats questions/requests or seeks help when it is appropriate to be assertive:

ALMOST NEVER	USUALLY NOT	SOMETIMES	USUALLY	ALMOST ALWAYS
1	2	3	4	5

Recognizes the difference between *passive, aggressive,* and *assertive* responses:

ALMOST NEVER	USUALLY NOT	SOMETIMES	USUALLY	ALMOST ALWAYS
1	2	3	4	5

74. Appropriate Application of Assertiveness

To meet one's needs and satisfy one's preferences effectively, a variety of assertive behaviors are required in specific situations. The purpose of this section is to facilitate the development of specific assertive statements and requests. The group leader should first introduce the concept of an assertive statement or request. This may be embellished with a sampling of specific assertive statements that can help members generalize the concept of *assertiveness* to different situations. Some examples are: "I'm hungry, can I please have something to eat?" "Please don't touch me that way" "I want a ride to the YMCA; will you please give me a ride?" Next, participants can be taught to repeat assertive requests, using the examples discussed. Finally, discussants may review a list of others on whom they may call to help advocate for their needs and preferences. Potential assistance may be solicited from family members, residence workers, teachers, counselors, therapists, job supervisors, or social workers. This topic is accessible to persons with mild and sometimes moderate developmental disabilities. It can be made more concrete for those with lower cognitive ability by giving individuals specific phrases to rehearse, and asking participants yes/no questions about assertive phrases.

■ SPECIFIC SKILLS TO BE LEARNED

Make an assertive statement or request:
"I'm hungry; can I have something to eat?"
"I would rather have a cheeseburger than a hamburger."
"I'm tired; can I take a break now?"
"Please don't touch me that way."
"I would like to spend some time by myself now; can we talk later?"
"It's cold outside; I need a warmer coat and some gloves."

"I would like to sign up for an arts and crafts class; can you help me?"
"I want to go to the YMCA; will you please give me a ride?"
"I would like to be friends with Jim, but I do not want to be friends with Bob."
"Excuse me! I was here first; can you please wait your turn?"
"I don't like it when you talk to me that way; can you please talk to me with respect?"
"Please don't (yell/scream/swear) at me."
"I'd rather not do that right now."
Repeat an assertive statement or request.
Ask someone to help advocate for a preference or need:
    Parent, brother, sister, or other family member
    Teacher, counselor, or job supervisor
    Social worker
Psychologist or therapist
    Residence worker

■ CONCEPTS NECESSARY TO PERFORM SKILLS

Assertive: Directly tell a person how you feel; say how you feel and why you feel that way; tell someone what is on your mind.

Request: Ask; tell somebody what you need or want; make a statement of one's preference or wish; appeal; demand.

Preference: What one desires; a wish; one's choice; the outcome that you would like; how you would like the situation to end; one's favorite choice.

■ CASE VIGNETTES

—Joe lived in a foster home. He was not very happy about living there because he did not like one of his housemates, Ed. He thought that Ed talked too loudly, made too much noise at bedtime, and was too nosy about everybody else's business. Although Joe was quite angry and resentful toward Ed, he did not talk to him directly about his anger and concerns. Joe also had a hard time asking his foster provider for help because he did not want to bother him. One day Ed asked Joe a question and Joe ignored him, simply turning and walking away. Another time Joe felt that Ed was too noisy. Joe stomped into his bedroom, slamming the door behind himself.

Was Joe able to make an assertive statement or request to Ed? Was he able to ask anyone else for help? What could Joe have done to better assert his own needs and wishes with Ed?

—Gladys lived in a residence with three housemates. They had several staff counselors who helped them live independently. Last week, one of the night counselors quit, and a new counselor named Lloyd was hired. Almost immediately, Lloyd took a special interest in Gladys. At first she was happy that Lloyd was so nice to her. But one day, when all of the other residence counselors had gone home, Lloyd put his hand on her leg and told her that she had pretty eyes. Gladys felt very uncomfortable and stood up. She said, "Lloyd, please don't touch me like that." Gladys was confused. She already had a boyfriend and did not want Lloyd for a boyfriend. She just wanted him to help with independent living tasks like cooking and budgeting. Lloyd must not have gotten the message because he touched her again the next night. Gladys again told him not to touch her that way. She also called her mother and told her what happened. She talked to the social worker and residence director, and Lloyd was taken out of Gladys's house.

Was Gladys able to make an assertive statement or request to Lloyd? When Lloyd did not listen to Gladys, to whom did she go for help?

■ DISCUSSION QUESTIONS

Simple/concrete questions:

What are some different types of assertive requests?

Personal experience/feelings questions:

How do you feel when you ask somebody for something?

Have you ever asked someone to stop doing something that bothered you? How did they respond to you?

Who can you ask if you need help telling others what you want?

Problem-solving questions:

If you are in a restaurant and somebody else tries to order your food for you, how can you speak up (assert yourself) to get what you want?

If somebody asks you to do something that you do not want to do, what should you tell them?

If you are on the telephone and the other person wants to keep talking even though you are tired, what should you say?

If you want to go to an activity but do not have a ride, what should you do?

■ GROUP ACTIVITIES

Discuss a variety of real-life situations calling for assertive responses. Practice specific assertive statements and requests.

Facilitate a discussion about individual participant's experiences in which they have had difficulties with assertiveness.

Review a variety of external sources of help when self-advocacy is not sufficient to resolve situations.

■ ASSESSMENT OF SKILLS LEARNED

Identifies a variety of life situations calling for assertive behaviors:

ALMOST NEVER	USUALLY NOT	SOMETIMES	USUALLY	ALMOST ALWAYS
1	2	3	4	5

Effectively advocates for oneself using a variety of assertive responses:

ALMOST NEVER	USUALLY NOT	SOMETIMES	USUALLY	ALMOST ALWAYS
1	2	3	4	5

Asks for help when self-advocacy is ineffective:

ALMOST NEVER	USUALLY NOT	SOMETIMES	USUALLY	ALMOST ALWAYS
1	2	3	4	5

10 *Application of Social Skills in Community Living*

Part I. Living in the Community

Part II. Keeping a Job

THE FINAL CHAPTER of this book looks outward, exploring a variety of issues related to one's vulnerability in the community. Part I, living in the community, includes seven topics. The first, planning activities, examines how to identify, locate, plan, and organize simple recreation and leisure activities. Community activities continues to build on the first topic, further identifying positive behaviors necessary in the community and how to ask for help to arrange these activities. Reality orientation focuses on necessary orientation skills to function more effectively in the community. The four topics of transportation, recognizing and avoiding dangers, money, and what to do if you lose your purse or wallet all explore practical concerns related to successful community activities. Part II, keeping a job, comprises two topics: getting along with co-workers and critical social behaviors at work. Work-related social skills deserve special attention because of the susceptibility of individuals with developmental disabilities to problems in this area.

Part I. Living in the Community

75. *Planning Activities*

It is essential to engage in planning processes if one is to participate in different activities. Individuals with developmental disabilities often have difficulty selecting activities and engaging in sustained planning to ultimately carry out these activities. At the outset of group, it would be helpful to brainstorm a list of possible activities of interest to group members. These may include going out to eat, movies, visiting friends, shopping, walking, parties, attending classes, fishing, bowling, dating, and many others. Next, attention should be devoted to understanding how one locates activities. Methods may include talking to family or friends, looking in newspapers, calling movie theaters, asking residence workers, and others. This can be followed by a discussion about how to plan and organize activities. The group leader may utilize the four "W's" to help participants remember how to plan: *"What* will I do?" *"Whom* will I do it with?" *"Where* will it happen?" *"When* will I do it?" Specific day, date, departure time, and return time should be mentioned. Costs and transportation must also be included in the discussion. Individuals with mild and moderate developmental disabilities typically are able to understand this topic. Lower functioning persons may need modifications similar to those described earlier in this section.

■ SPECIFIC SKILLS TO BE LEARNED

Recognize a variety of possible recreation/leisure activities:
  Going out to eat
  Going to movies
  Visiting friends
  Shopping
  Walking
  Going to parties
  Attending community classes
  Fishing
  Bowling
  Going on dates
Know how to find activities:
  Family/friends
  Newspapers
  Calling theaters
  Current residence workers
Know how to plan/organize activities:
  The four W's:
    What will I do?
    Whom will I do it with?
    Where will the activity take place?
    When will I do it?
      Day?
      Date?
      When will I leave?
      When will I return home?
  How much will it cost?
  How will I get there?
    Walk
    Bus
    Other transportation

■ CONCEPTS NECESSARY TO PERFORM SKILLS

Activity: To do something; movie, dance, craft, sport, church or other event; a thing to do.

Plan: What somebody is going to do; a goal; something for the future; organize; order; schedule; decide what will happen, with whom, when, and where; have an idea about what to do and how one will do something; prepare.

Recreation: Rest and recuperation; fun activity; to do something for enjoyment; leisure activity; amusement; pastime.

Leisure: Recreation; fun; enjoyment; something somebody wants to do even if the person does not have to do it; idle time; free time; spare time; restful activity; something a person likes to do.

■ CASE VIGNETTES

—John was planning his weekend. He had fifteen dollars to spend, so he decided to see a movie on Friday night, which would cost five dollars, and have dinner out on Saturday night. At the restaurant he picked, he could eat for five dollars; that meant that he had five dollars left for a treat at the Friday movie. It also meant that he had some emergency change in case he had to make a telephone call. He had looked in the newspaper and found that there was an interesting movie playing only one mile from his house on Friday night. His brother had helped him read the movie page. The movie would begin at seven o'clock, and his brother agreed to give him and his friend Joe a ride there at six-thirty. That way they would be there twenty minutes early to get tickets, buy some popcorn, and get good seats. John planned to come home after the movie and play his computer game before bed. On Saturday, he planned to get up at ten o'clock in the morning, do his chores, and then go to the park to play softball with his friends. He would come home early so that he could get ready to go out for dinner with his girlfriend, Linda. He planned to dress up in his best clothes on Saturday night. Linda and her father were going to pick him up at five-thirty that night so that they could get to the restaurant at six o'clock. They were each paying for their own dinners. It was a steak restaurant, and John had a special coupon for two steak dinners for the price of one. After dinner, he and Linda planned to walk to a nearby shopping center and look in store windows before Linda's father picked them up at eight o'clock.

Do you think John was a good activity planner? What kind of arrangements did he make for his weekend? Did he plan whom he was going to see? When he would see them? Where they would go? How much it would cost?

—Mela finished working at four o'clock on Friday. She had just gotten her paycheck but did not know what she would do for the weekend. She had made no plans. When she got got home, she called her friend Doris to ask if she wanted to come over for pizza, but Doris had already made plans to go to a movie with her boyfriend. Then Mela called her sister, Jessica, to see if she wanted to come over for a visit. But Jessica had already left for dinner with a friend. Finally Mela decided to make a frozen pizza in the oven and watch television by herself. When she thought about it, she realized that she should have done some planning earlier in the week. Now everybody else was busy, and she was all alone. As she ate her pizza, she thought she might like to go to the circus tomorrow, but when she called the ticket office, all of the tickets were sold out until next week. Mela realized that she would need to plan ahead if she wanted to do fun things with her friends.

How could Mela have planned better for her weekend? Should people wait until the last minute before they plan their weekend activities? Why or why not?

■ DISCUSSION QUESTIONS

Simple/concrete questions:

Can you list some possible recreation/leisure activities?

What are the four W's?

What are some things that a person needs to do to plan activities?

Personal experience/feelings questions:

What activities do you like to do? Why?

Do you ever have trouble planning activities? Describe?

Problem-solving questions:

How can you find different activities or things to do?

■ GROUP ACTIVITIES

Facilitate a discussion about a variety of activities that members may plan and organize.
Facilitate a discussion about the importance of planning activities instead of waiting for things
to happen.

■ ASSESSMENT OF SKILLS LEARNED

Recognizes a variety of possible recreation/leisure activities:

ALMOST NEVER	USUALLY NOT	SOMETIMES	USUALLY	ALMOST ALWAYS
1	2	3	4	5

Knows how to find community activities:

ALMOST NEVER	USUALLY NOT	SOMETIMES	USUALLY	ALMOST ALWAYS
1	2	3	4	5

Plans/organizes activities:

ALMOST NEVER	USUALLY NOT	SOMETIMES	USUALLY	ALMOST ALWAYS
1	2	3	4	5

76. *Community Activities*

Participating in community activities requires a certain degree of social competence. Individuals
with developmental disabilities may lack some of the skills necessary to independently become
involved in community activities. Their skills deficits may also result in related misfortunes,
such as getting lost or suffering from mistreatment. The group leader should first define the term
community activity, emphasizing that it is any event that happens away from home. Group members may be encouraged to list a variety of different types of community activities, which might
include church, school, work, shopping, movies, going out to eat, and so forth. A discussion can
take place about positive behaviors necessary when venturing into the community. These may
include politeness, consideration for others, and dressing appropriately for activities. Finally, the
group may focus on how to ask for help in order to participate in community activities. This topic
is most appropriate for individuals with mild and moderate developmental disabilities. It can be
modified for lower functioning individuals utilizing pictures/symbols, yes/no questions about
places/activities, and allowing for nonverbal communication.

■ SPECIFIC SKILLS TO BE LEARNED

Define a community activity.
List possible community activities of interest:
    Church
    School
    Work
    Shopping
    Movies
    Out to eat
Recognize positive behaviors necessary in the community:

Politeness and consideration
Dressing appropriately for activities
Learn to ask for help in order to participate in community activities:
Find out what, where, and when.
Tell residence counselor or helper.
Work out rides, money, schedule.

■ CONCEPTS NECESSARY TO PERFORM SKILLS

Community: A place away from home; church, school, work, store, movie theater, or other place away from home; where people get together to do things; a gathering place.
Activity: To do something; movie, dance, craft, sport, church, or other event; a thing to do.
Polite: Courteous; caring; kind; considerate of others; letting others know that you care about how they feel; showing respect for others.

■ CASE VIGNETTES

—*Sam was independent in his community activities. He knew how to take buses, get rides, or walk places he wanted to go. He took the city bus to and from work. He walked to a nearby grocery store to buy snacks. He got a ride from his residence counselor to go to the bank. Sam had a girlfriend, Betty, and he liked to go to movies with her. He took the bus to her house, and they walked together to a nearby movie theater. Sam usually called the movie theater to find out when the movie started; then he gave himself plenty of time to get to Betty's house and walk to the movie. He also asked the movie theater worker how much the movie would cost, so that he would have enough money to pay for it. Sometimes he paid for Betty, and sometimes she paid for him. Sam was polite to others in the community, but he was not overly friendly with strangers.*

Was Sam independent in the community? Why or why not? What did he do to plan for a community event such as a movie?

—*Natalie was not completely independent, but she liked to participate in community events. Usually she asked others for help to go places and do things. She lived with her parents, and they often gave her rides. Tonight she wanted to go roller skating with her friends at seven o'clock. She told her mother that she needed five dollars to go to the roller rink, and that she needed a ride there. Her mother told Natalie that she had twenty-three dollars in her moneybox, which was more than enough to go roller skating. Her mother said that she would drive Natalie and her friend Julie to the roller rink, but Natalie needed to get a ride home. Natalie called Julie, and Julie said that her father would drive them home. They both had a good time roller skating and came home at ten o'clock that night, the exact time she told her mother she would be there.*

Even though Natalie was not completely independent in her community activities, did she know how to get help to participate in those activities? What arrangements did she make to go roller skating?

■ DISCUSSION QUESTIONS

Simple/concrete questions:
What are some possible community activities?
Personal experience/feelings questions:

What community activities do you like to attend?

Would you like to join any new community activities? Which ones?

Do you have any restrictions upon your community activities? Do you need any special help in order to go into the community?

Problem-solving questions:

What should you do if you want to join a community activity but do not have a ride?

How can you find out about new community activities?

■ GROUP ACTIVITIES

Group members share particular community activities in which they are involved. Describe how arrangements are made.

Facilitate a discussion about the importance of participating in community activities.

■ ASSESSMENT OF SKILLS LEARNED

Understands what is a community activitity:

ALMOST NEVER	USUALLY NOT	SOMETIMES	USUALLY	ALMOST ALWAYS
1	2	3	4	5

Recognizes positive behaviors necessary in the community:

ALMOST NEVER	USUALLY NOT	SOMETIMES	USUALLY	ALMOST ALWAYS
1	2	3	4	5

Knows how to ask for help to participate in community activities:

ALMOST NEVER	USUALLY NOT	SOMETIMES	USUALLY	ALMOST ALWAYS
1	2	3	4	5

77. *Reality Orientation*

Each person needs to be properly oriented in terms of time of day, place of activity, date, persons with whom he or she is interacting, and general surroundings. This places one's present life in context and allows one to reference it to past as well as future activities and relationships. For lack of a better term, this will be called one's *reality orientation*. It tends to be a problematic area for individuals with developmental disabilities because of general and specific cognitive limitations that impair their orientations. The discussion should explore each individual's orientation, beginning with news about what is happening around the person. Categories of interest in this area may include family, friends, relatives, home life, work, school, city/state/national/world news, and so forth. Next, an examination may be made of each person's awareness of past, present, and future calendar events, attempting to put these into a coherent perspective. This can be followed by participants orienting themselves in time and space, utilizing categories of who the person is now with, day of the week, time of day, month, year, place, birth date, and so forth. Next, a conversation may transpire about group members' conversations/activities in various time perspectives, including today, yesterday, last week, last month, last year, many years ago, and so forth. Finally participants can discuss how each appears to the others in the present situation, noting style of dress, grooming/hygiene, physical demeanor, tone of voice, and impressions made on others. Various elements of this topic can and should be interjected into other group sessions as a way of orienting individuals to important life events/activities, sharing personal information, and maintaining more personal connections with each other. Conceptually, this group is most appropriate for individuals with mild developmental disabilities. It can be modified by asking yes/no questions about individuals' orientations in different dimensions, using pictures, maps or calendars, and nonverbal communication.

■ SPECIFIC SKILLS TO BE LEARNED

Recognize what is happening around oneself:
    Family, friends, relatives
    Home
    Work/school
    City
    State
    Country
    World
Recognize calendar events and occurrences:
    Past
    Present
    Future
Orient oneself in time and space:
    With whom
    Day of week
    Time of day
    Month, day of month, year
    Place
    Birthdate
Recall one's conversations and activities with others:
    Today
    Yesterday
    Last week
    Last month
    Last year
    Many years ago
Understand how one appears to others:
    Style of dress
    Grooming/hygiene
    Physical demeanor
    Tone of voice
    Impressions made on others

■ CONCEPTS NECESSARY TO PERFORM SKILLS

Reality: What is real; what is happening around a person; to see things as other people see them; to be in touch with what is real or true; to know who you are, where you are, time of day, whom you are with.

Calendar events: Things on the calendar; the order in which activities occur; events that happen on different days.

Time: The past, present, and future; what happens as people live their lives; all the different moments of a person's life.

Past: What has already happened; five minutes ago, an hour ago, yesterday, last week, last month, last year, and a long time ago.

Present: What is happening right now; this moment; what we are doing, seeing, hearing, and talking about now; here and now.

Future: What will happen later; five minutes from now, an hour from now, tomorrow, next week, next month, next year, and a long time from now; what is yet to come; what will happen.

Physical appearance: What a person looks like; how one appears to others; a person's body, style of dress, and the way he or she acts.

■ CASE VIGNETTES

—Ann was very disoriented. She was confused about the time, where she was, what day it was, and what she was doing. When she started talking, she often forgot what she was trying to say. She had a hard time recognizing other people, even after she had met them several times. She could not remember much of her childhood and had trouble remembering what activities she had done in the recent past. She could not remember what she ate for breakfast and could not remember what she was planning to do on a certain day. Ann listened to the radio and watched the television news, but she still could not remember much about what was happening in her city, state, and country. Ann often wore dirty clothing and did not take a shower every day, but she had no idea that she looked unkempt and smelled bad to others. Ann was drifting through life and had no goals. She simply got up in the morning and did the things her counselors and instructors told her to do. Ann was very disoriented and had poor contact with reality.

In what ways did Ann have a poor orientation? How was she out of touch with reality? What could she have done to develop a better reality orientation?

—Dale had a good reality orientation. He knew who he was and where he was going. He was aware of family, friends, and relatives; he called them on the telephone and saw them regularly. When he saw them, he asked about what they had talked about on previous occasions, because he could remember what they had told him in the past and he wanted them to know that he was interested in their lives. Dale knew that he had graduated from high school three years ago, then had gone to a vocational school, and now worked as a custodian cleaning buildings. His future goal was to work in a restaurant as a cook's helper. Dale knew what was happening in his town because he listened to local television and radio news. He also knew what was happening in the country and the world because he listened to the national news as well. Dale arrived places on time because he looked at his watch and remembered where he had to be.He showed up on time for his different activities because he kept a weekly calendar. He knew that bowling was on Thursday night at seven o'clock and that he went to movies on Saturday night.

In what ways did Dale have a good reality orientation? Did Dale recognize familiar people? Did he remember when and where to be different places? Did Dale remember his own history? Did he have goals for the future?

■ DISCUSSION QUESTIONS

Simple/concrete questions:
   What are some things happening in your home? Workplace?
   What are some events happening in your city? State? Country?
   What are some things happening in other parts of the world?
   What are some important historical events of the past?
Personal experience/feelings questions:
   What are some important things happening in your life right now?

What important things did you do yesterday? Last week? Last month? Last year? Many years ago?

What important things would you like to have happen in your future?

How do you feel about the events happening in your life right now?

Problem-solving questions:

What problems can happen if you forget what happened in your past?

What problems can happen if you cannot remember the time? Day of the week? Month? Day of the month? Year?

■ GROUP ACTIVITIES

Facilitate a discussion about important life events of group members, past, present, and anticipated future.

Facilitate a discussion of why reality orientation is important.

■ ASSESSMENT OF SKILLS LEARNED

Recognizes what is happening around oneself (e.g., family, friends, work/school, community, world):

ALMOST NEVER	USUALLY NOT	SOMETIMES	USUALLY	ALMOST ALWAYS
1	2	3	4	5

Recognizes calendar events and occurrences:

ALMOST NEVER	USUALLY NOT	SOMETIMES	USUALLY	ALMOST ALWAYS
1	2	3	4	5

Orients self in time and space:

ALMOST NEVER	USUALLY NOT	SOMETIMES	USUALLY	ALMOST ALWAYS
1	2	3	4	5

Recalls conversations with others:

ALMOST NEVER	USUALLY NOT	SOMETIMES	USUALLY	ALMOST ALWAYS
1	2	3	4	5

Understands how one appears to others:

ALMOST NEVER	USUALLY NOT	SOMETIMES	USUALLY	ALMOST ALWAYS
1	2	3	4	5

78. *Transportation*

Individuals with developmental disabilities are often more vulnerable than their peers in the community. Because of their limited adaptive behaviors, they are often reliant on others to arrange and provide transportation to and from different places. This topic should begin with a discussion of different types of transportation, which include automobile, city bus, taxi, special modified van, walking, wheelchair, bicycle, motorcycle, airplane, train, and boat. Once the idea of transportation has been sufficiently communicated, the group should examine different types of difficulties or problems that may occur with common types of transportation. Some difficulties include making arrangements, reading bus schedules, following bus schedules, physical barriers to wheelchairs, getting help for wheelchair transfers, waiting for rides, rudeness or mistreatment from strangers, accidents, having enough money for rides, and inappropriate behavior of drivers. This topic is appropriate for individuals with mild and moderate developmental disabilities. It can be modified for lower functioning individuals by simplifying the language, asking yes/no questions about transportation, using pictures/symbols to represent different types of transportation, and utilizing other nonverbal communications.

■ SPECIFIC SKILLS TO BE LEARNED

Identify different types of transportation:
  Automobile
  City bus
  Taxi
  Special transportation
  Walking/jogging
  Wheelchair
  Bicycle
  Motorcycle
  Airplane
  Train
  Boat
Identify difficulties or problems that may occur with different types of transportation:
  Arranging transportation
  Following bus schedules
  Reading bus schedules
  Physical barriers to wheelchairs (e.g., stairs)
  Getting help for wheelchair transfers
  Waiting for rides
  Mistreatment from strangers
  Accidents
  Having correct change for the bus
  Payment for transportation
  Inappropriate behavior of drivers

■ CONCEPTS NECESSARY TO PERFORM SKILLS

Transportation: Ways to go places; methods of travel; how to get somewhere; to ride a bicycle, car, bus, train, plane, boat, etc.

Time schedule: Calendar of events; the day, hour, and minute somebody plans to do something; a list of things somebody will do at certain times.

Physical barrier: Something in the way; when a wheelchair cannot get up the steps; when something is blocking somebody; when someone is traveling somewhere and something gets in the way.

Waiting: When a ride has not yet arrived; to sit and wait until a ride comes; not do something now but do it later.

■ CASE VIGNETTES

—Kevin lived by himself with the support of his independent living counselor. He knew how to take the city bus different places. Today he was going to a doctor appointment that he had arranged last month. He had scheduled the appointment for ten o'clock in the morning. He scheduled it at this time because that would give him enough time for breakfast and the bus ride to the doctor's office. He had arranged to take the number 12 bus at eight-thirty in the morning. Then he would transfer to the number 4 bus downtown at nine-fifteen, and that one

would get him to the doctor's office by nine forty-five in the morning. This gave him fifteen minutes extra in case the bus was late. Kevin caught the number 12 bus on time, but the number 4 bus was ten minutes late. Because of his good planning, he still got to the doctor's office five minutes early. He had his checkup and then returned home on the bus. While he was waiting at the bus stop, a man came along and asked Kevin for some money. Kevin said, "No," because he had saved money from his job and did not understand why he should give it away to a stranger. The man asked him again, but Kevin just ignored him. When the bus came, Kevin got on and gave the driver the exact bus change. He was always prepared with extra money in his coin purse in case he needed bus change or to make a telephone call.

Was Kevin good at arranging and taking his own transportation? How did he prepare the possibility that he would be late? Did he make any plans in case of an emergency?

—Theresa was able to take the city bus by herself, but sometimes she had problems. Yesterday she got onto the wrong bus because she forgot to look closely at the bus number. She went for two miles before she realized her mistake. By then it was too late to get off, so she rode the bus until it got downtown. Then she switched to another bus and came home. She missed out on her bowling league that day. Last week she was planning to take the number 10 bus to a doctor appointment scheduled for one o'clock in the afternoon. She forgot to leave for the bus stop early enough and missed the noon bus. By the time the next bus came, it was twelve-forty five in the afternoon, and she got to the doctor's office a half hour late. The nurse was upset because she was late, and Theresa had to reschedule her doctor appointment.

What kind of trouble did Theresa have when she was taking the bus? Do you think she needed to pay closer attention to the time and to the different bus numbers? Should Theresa have planned ahead better so that she would not have trouble catching the bus on time?

■ DISCUSSION QUESTIONS

Simple/concrete questions:
> What are some different types of transportation?
> What are some different kinds of problems that may happen when you arrange transportation?

Personal experience/feelings questions:
> What kind of transportation do you use most often?
> How do you feel about your method of transportation?
> Do you ever feel frustrated or angry while waiting for transportation?
> Do you ever feel nervous or afraid about your transportation?
> Have you ever had any problems while you were being transported?

Problem-solving questions:
> What should you do if your bus or transportation is late?
> What sorts of dangers should you look out for when you are taking transportation?

■ GROUP ACTIVITIES

Group members share their methods of transportation and feelings about that transportation. Facilitate a discussion about dealing with transportation problems.

■ ASSESSMENT OF SKILLS LEARNED

Identifies different types of transportation:

ALMOST NEVER	USUALLY NOT	SOMETIMES	USUALLY	ALMOST ALWAYS
1	2	3	4	5

Identifies one or more problems which may occur with different types of transportation:

ALMOST NEVER	USUALLY NOT	SOMETIMES	USUALLY	ALMOST ALWAYS
1	2	3	4	5

79. Recognizing and Avoiding Dangers

To maintain personal safety, an individual must know how to recognize and avoid dangers. Persons with developmental disabilities experience more difficulties than their peers in this area. The group leader should begin with a discussion of possible dangers in one's everyday life. These include getting lost; threats or intimidation from strangers; physical, sexual, or emotional abuse by family, caretakers, or others; losing one's money, wallet, or purse; having things stolen; fire; physical injury; bad business deals or self-defeating agreements with others; bad occurrences when out alone after dark; venturing alone into unfamiliar places; reckless behavior; and so forth. Next, group participants should learn to recognize a variety of persons who may take advantage of them. The list may include family members, caretakers, relatives, friends, co-workers, schoolmates, acquaintances, and strangers. Finally, attention can be turned to identifying ways to avoid dangers. These may involve planning ahead, going places with a friend, not talking too much to strangers, carrying extra coins for the telephone or city bus, carrying a personal identification card, having a fire extinguisher at home, knowing how to call for emergency help, looking around oneself and thinking about how to keep safe, looking both ways before crossing streets, and avoiding reckless/careless behaviors. This topic is appropriate for individuals with mild and moderate developmental disabilities. It can be modified for lower functioning persons by simplifying the language, utilizing yes/no questions about dangers and danger-avoidant behaviors, making use of pictures/symbols, and allowing for nonverbal communications.

■ SPECIFIC SKILLS TO BE LEARNED

Recognize possible dangers in everyday living:
  Getting lost
  Threats/intimidation by strangers
  Abuse by family/caretakers (physical/sexual/emotional)
  Losing money/wallet/purse
  Having things stolen
  Fire
  Cutting oneself or physical injury
  Business deals gone bad
  Going out alone after dark (e.g., rape, attack)
  Going into unfamiliar places alone
  Reckless behavior (e.g., fast driving, carelessness)
Recognize a variety of persons who may take advantage of one:
  Family/caretakers
  Relatives/friends
  Co-workers/schoolmates
  Acquaintances/strangers
Identify ways to avoid danger:
  Plan ahead.
  Go places with a friend.
  Do not talk too much to strangers.

Carry extra change for the telephone or city bus.

Carry identification (name, telephone number, address).

Have a fire extinguisher.

Know how to call 911.

Look around oneself and think about how to avoid danger.

Look both ways before crossing streets.

Avoid careless/reckless behaviors.

■ CONCEPTS NECESSARY TO PERFORM SKILLS

Danger: When something bad might happen; a situation in which something might go wrong; when something is risky; a hazard; something scary that might hurt someone; an unsafe situation.

Threat/intimidation: When people act as if they might hurt others; when someone acts as though he or she will harm somebody else; to bully or push around; to scare somebody; to give a warning that you might hurt somebody.

Abuse: Harm; hurt; damage; mistreat; injure; scold; curse.

Plan: What somebody is going to do; a goal; something for the future; organize; order; schedule; decide what will happen with whom, when, and where; have an idea about what and how one will do something; prepare.

Identification: Something that lets somebody know who you are; a driver's license or social security card; a picture of somebody.

911: Emergency telephone number; a way to call the police, fire department, or emergency helpers; a number to call if somebody is hurt or in trouble.

■ CASE VIGNETTES

—Bradley was a very impulsive young man. That meant he often acted before he thought about things. For example, one day, when he was playing catch with his friend Luke, their baseball rolled into the street. Before he looked, Bradley ran out into the street and almost got hit by a car. Another time, Brad and his friends were walking near a road construction site. There was a flashing yellow light and two benches to keep cars away from a big hole in the road. Bradley walked past the benches and the light, and fell into the hole. He was lucky that his friends were nearby to help him climb out; otherwise, he might have been stuck there for a long time. Bradley did not think ahead when he went places. One day he took the city bus to see his friend Bill, and forgot to bring enough money for a bus ride home. The driver was not going to let him back onto the bus but changed his mind because Bradley started crying. He made Brad promise to pay him the next day. On another occasion, a stranger asked Brad if he could borrow ten dollars, all the money Bradley had for the week. The stranger told Brad that he would pay him back the next day. After Bradley gave him the money, he never saw the stranger again.

Did Bradley think ahead to avoid dangers? What is one way that Brad acted before he thought? Would Brad's life have been easier if he planned ahead to avoid dangers?

■ DISCUSSION QUESTIONS

Simple/concrete questions:

What are some different types of dangers?

Who are some different types of people who might take advantage of you?

Personal experience/feelings questions:

Have you ever been in danger? How?

Have you ever felt that someone took advantage of you? Who?

Problem-solving questions:
How can a person avoid dangerous situations

■ GROUP ACTIVITIES

Each group member lists one possible danger.
Participants share personal experiences in which they felt someone took advantage of them.
Facilitate a discussion of how to avoid possible dangerous situations.

■ ASSESSMENT OF SKILLS LEARNED

Recognizes several possible dangers in everyday living:

ALMOST NEVER	USUALLY NOT	SOMETIMES	USUALLY	ALMOST ALWAYS
1	2	3	4	5

Recognizes a variety of persons who may take advantage of oneself:

ALMOST NEVER	USUALLY NOT	SOMETIMES	USUALLY	ALMOST ALWAYS
1	2	3	4	5

Identifies ways to avoid danger:

ALMOST NEVER	USUALLY NOT	SOMETIMES	USUALLY	ALMOST ALWAYS
1	2	3	4	5

80. *Money*

Money is a necessary element in one's life in order to meet basic needs. Individuals with developmental disabilities are extremely vulnerable in this regard. They often rely on others to either provide money and commodities or to manage their money so that they are able to plan their expenditures and purchase life's necessities. A good starting point for this topic is to explore what money belongs to which individual group participants. What money do they or their caretakers control for their benefits? Next, the group may discuss and recognize things for which money is required. These may include housing, food, clothing, recreation, and others. Various sources of money can be discussed, as these are relevant to group members. Monetary sources may include government (e.g., social security, medical payments, housing subsidies), employment earnings, parent and family member contributions, residence funds, and so forth. Individuals who help participants with their money should be identified. These persons may include family members, residence workers, social workers, conservators, and guardians. Finally, participants should discuss ways to ensure that they are treated fairly with their money. These may involve asking a trusted friend or relative to review one's money situation, learning to recognize and estimate correct change, asking for more change if necessary, carrying only small amounts of money at one time, getting help with correct monetary amounts before going to a store, buying things where one is known by clerks, and having two different people help with one's budgeting so that one of them can be a check on the other. This topic is most appropriate for individuals with mild developmental disabilities. It can be modified to some extent for lower functioning persons similarly to previous topics.

■ SPECIFIC SKILLS TO BE LEARNED

Recognize what money belongs to oneself.
Recognize things for which money is needed:

Housing
Food
Clothing
Spending money
Understand different sources of money:
Government (social security, medical payments, housing payments, etc.)
Work earnings
Parents or family members
Residence funds
Other
Identify who helps an individual with his or her money:
Family member
Residence worker
Social worker
Conservator/guardian
Other
Recognize ways to make sure that one is being treated fairly with money:
Ask a trusted relative or friend to help review your money situation.
Learn to recognize and estimate correct change.
Ask for more change if necessary.
Carry only small amounts of money.
Get help with correct monetary amounts before going to the store.
Buy things where you know the clerks and they know you.
Have two different people help with budgeting so that one can be a check on the other.

■ CONCEPTS NECESSARY TO PERFORM SKILLS

Money: What somebody uses to buy something; what one pays for things; finances; budget; coins and dollars; cash, dough, or moola; what things cost.
Government: City, state, and county workers; a place where some people get help with money; where social security, medical assistance, and housing monies come from.
Work earnings: Money earned by working; paycheck; salary; wages; money given to somebody for his or her work.

■ CASE VIGNETTES

—Jeanette was very frugal. That meant that she knew how to save her money and spend it only on the things she really needed. Jeanette received a certain amount of money each month from the government social security department, extra money for food stamps, and a small housing subsidy. After paying her rent, she had a small amount of money left over each month to pay for her telephone, electricity, clothing, and other things. Jeanette went shopping every week at the supermarket, where she used coupons, food stamps, and other money to buy as many groceries as she could. Her sister helped her shop so that she would get the lowest prices on things. Jeanette liked movies, but she saw them on Saturday afternoons when the prices were lower. She walked or rode her bicycle to nearby places so that she would not spend all of her money on bus rides. Jeanette did not smoke or drink alcohol, so she saved money that she would have spent on those things. She was able to put a small amount of money every month into a savings account. That way, she had a little extra money for special occasions or emergencies. For example, one time she bought her sister a birthday present. Another time she bought a new pair of shoes when the heel broke on her old pair. Jeanette liked to put something in the collection

plate at church on Sunday. Because she was a good planner, Jeanette made her money last until the end of each month.

What did Jeanette do to manage her own money successfully? How did she make her money last until the end of each month?

—*Ramoan lived in a townhouse with three housemates. Every month his social worker sent money to pay for his food, rent, and clothing. Ramoan's residence counselor gave him and his housemates each a small amount of money every week to spend on treats and leisure activities. It was their special needs money. This worked very well because Ramoan's counselor also helped him plan how to spend the money to make it last. One day Ramoan came home to find that a new residence counselor had taken the job, and his old one had moved to a new job. The new counselor was nice at first but soon started giving Ramoan and his housemates less spending money. Some weeks, he told them that there was no spending money left in their accounts. Ramoan told his brother that he was no longer getting any spending money at his residence. His brother called the social worker, and the social worker called the director of the residence program. It turned out that Ramoan's new counselor was stealing their money and keeping it for himself. The new counselor was fired from the job.*

What did Ramoan do that helped catch the person who was stealing his money? Is it a good idea to tell someone if you think somebody is unfairly taking your money? Whom should you tell and why?

■ DISCUSSION QUESTIONS

Simple/concrete questions:
   What are some things for which people need money?
   Who are some people who might be able to help you with money problems?
Personal experience/feelings questions:
   What are some problems that you have had in the past with your money?
   Do you trust the people who help you with your money?
   How do you feel about your money situation? Do you have enough money?
Problem-solving questions:
   How do you know if you are being treated fairly with your money?
   How can you get help for your money matters?

■ GROUP ACTIVITIES

Group members share their sources of money and problems related to money matters. Facilitate a discussion about things that money will and will not buy.

■ ASSESSMENT OF SKILLS LEARNED

Recognizes own money:

ALMOST NEVER	USUALLY NOT	SOMETIMES	USUALLY	ALMOST ALWAYS
1	2	3	4	5

Understands different sources of money:

ALMOST NEVER	USUALLY NOT	SOMETIMES	USUALLY	ALMOST ALWAYS
1	2	3	4	5

Identifies persons who help with money:

ALMOST NEVER	USUALLY NOT	SOMETIMES	USUALLY	ALMOST ALWAYS
1	2	3	4	5

Recognizes one or more methods to ensure fair treatment with money:

ALMOST NEVER	USUALLY NOT	SOMETIMES	USUALLY	ALMOST ALWAYS
1	2	3	4	5

81. *What to Do If You Lose Your Purse or Wallet*

Losing one's purse or wallet is an inconvenience, to say the least, and may cause hardship because of lost money, identification, medical cards, and other valued personal items. Individuals with developmental disabilities are much more prone to such losses than their peers because of increased difficulty attending to details, and less ability to notice subtle perceptual differences. This topic may begin with a discussion of the importance of the contents of one's wallet or pocketbook, including identification, money, bus card, valuable papers, and personal effects. This can lead to a discussion of what to do if one's purse or wallet is lost. Problem-solving activities may include trying to remember when and where an item was lost, going to look for it, telling others about the loss, asking for help finding it, telling residence caretakers or work/school personnel, contacting the police, reporting it to the lost and found, or getting new identification and replacement cards. The topic is most appropriate for persons with mild developmental disabilities. It can be modified for lower functioning individuals by simplifying the language, using pictures/symbols to represent personal effects, asking yes/no questions about the purse/wallet and its loss, and utilizing nonverbal communication.

■ SPECIFIC SKILLS TO BE LEARNED

Recognize the importance of one's wallet or pocketbook contents:
   Identification
   Money, bus cards, and valuable papers
   Personal effects (e.g., pictures)
Understand what to do if purse or wallet is lost:
   Try to remember when/where it was last seen.
   Go look for it.
   Tell other people and ask for help finding it.
   Tell a residence counselor, work supervisor, or school instructor.
   If unable to find wallet/purse, get new identification and replacement cards.
   Contact the police.
   Contact lost-and-found office.

■ CONCEPTS NECESSARY TO PERFORM SKILLS

Wallet: Moneyholder; place for identification, money, and other small cards or pictures; bill-fold; purse; pocketbook.
Purse: Handbag; pocketbook; moneybag; place for identification, money, and personal effects.
Pocketbook: Purse; wallet; billfold; handbag.
Lose: Be unable to find something; a person had something but now it is gone; misplace; something slips through somebody's fingers; something is missing.
Identification: Something that lets somebody know who you are; a drivers license or social security card; a picture of somebody.

■ CASE VIGNETTES

—Lonnie went to the baseball game on Friday night. He took a ten dollar bill out of his wallet to pay for his ticket, and was given five dollars back. He then walked into the open-air bleachers at the high school stadium. He sat in the tenth row, just in from the isle. While he was there, he spent another three dollars on a hot dog and lemonade. Now, home again, it was twelve o'clock noon on Saturday, and he could not find his wallet. He did not remember seeing it since the night before at the baseball game. First, he looked all around his bedroom, then in his pants pocket from the previous day; but he could not find it. He told his housemates, who helped look for it but could not find it either. Lonnie also told his residence counselor, who suggested going back to the baseball field benches where he had last seen it and looking underneath. Two of Lonnie's housemates offered to go with him. He remembered that he had sat in row 10, just in from the isle. They all looked around on the ground beneath where he had been sitting. Sure enough, they found it, right near to where Lonnie had been sitting the night before.

Did Lonnie understand what to do when he could not find his wallet? Was he smart about how he went about finding it? What kind of help did he get from others?

—Sandy was at home on Tuesday evening. She noticed that her purse was gone. She could not remember when she had last seen it but thought she had had it on Monday when she was at work. Sandy cried because she had her spending money, identification card, family pictures, and important papers in her purse. She did not know where to begin looking for it and did not know whom to ask for help. Sandy decided to go watch television and worry about her purse later. She never did find it.

What do you think Sandy could have done to have had a better chance of getting back her purse? Was there anybody to whom she could have gone for help? Would it have been possible for her to think of the last places she might have seen her purse, so that she could have had someplace to start looking for it? Do you think that it was a good idea for her to sit and watch television, or should she have tried to get help right away to find her purse? Why or why not?

■ DISCUSSION QUESTIONS

Simple/concrete questions:
   What type of things are kept in a wallet or pocketbook?
Personal experience/feelings questions:
   Have you ever lost your wallet or pocketbook? How did you feel when you lost it?
Problem-solving questions:
   Why is a wallet or pocketbook important?
   What are some things you should do if you lose your wallet or pocketbook?

■ GROUP ACTIVITIES

Group members share the types of things that they keep in their wallets or pocketbooks.
Facilitate a discussion of the importance of a wallet or pocketbook, and what can be done if it
   is lost.

■ ASSESSMENT OF SKILLS LEARNED

Recognizes the importance of one's wallet or pocketbook contents:

ALMOST NEVER	USUALLY NOT	SOMETIMES	USUALLY	ALMOST ALWAYS
1	2	3	4	5

Understands what to do if one loses one's wallet or pocketbook:

ALMOST NEVER	USUALLY NOT	SOMETIMES	USUALLY	ALMOST ALWAYS
1	2	3	4	5

Part II. Keeping a Job

82. Getting Along with Co-Workers

Conflicts in the work setting are common for individuals with developmental disabilities. This section takes a more in-depth look at how to relate positively with co-workers. The discussion should begin with a description of the Golden Rule: "Treat others how you want to be treated." Then a discussion may ensue about a number of positive ways to treat others. These include being generous, forgiving of faults, tolerant of imperfections, accepting, kindly, friendly, respectful, considerate, not too picky, uncritical, attentive, like an adult, and so forth. Though simple for individuals with mild developmental disabilities, the topic is more abstract and difficult for individuals with moderate and severe disabilities. It may help to give many concrete examples of positive treatment that reflects the Golden Rule. For example, the leader may say, "I share with you, and you share with me," then practice giving something to, and taking something from, a group member. Another modification is to say, "John smiles at Joan, and Joan smiles at John," while showing pictures of two smiling individuals. In this way, the notion of reciprocity may be explained. Lower functioning persons may learn best from a combination of verbal statements and nonverbal demonstrations, in addition to the pictorial schematics and nonverbal communication strategies described in previous topics.

■ SPECIFIC SKILLS TO BE LEARNED

Identify the Golden Rule: "Treat others how you want to be treated."
Identify positive ways in which to treat others:
   Generously
   Forgiving of faults or weaknesses
   Tolerant of imperfections
   Accepting
   Kindly
   Friendly
   Respectfully
   Considerately
   Not too picky
   Not critically
   Attentively
   Like an adult

■ CONCEPTS NECESSARY TO PERFORM SKILLS

Generous: Sharing one's things with others; ignoring others' faults and shortcomings; giving things to people in need; sharing one's time with others; doing things for others; kind; not blaming or criticizing; being helpful, considerate, and giving.

Tolerant: Not critical; friendly and forgiving; not expecting too much from someone; lenient; not yelling at someone when the person makes a mistake; not blaming someone for small matters.

Forgiving: Tolerant; not critical; not expecting too much from someone; letting others make small mistakes without punishing them; lenient.

Accepting: Letting others know they are O.K. the way they are; not trying to change someone; forgiving; believing what someone says; approving of someone.

Respect: Esteem; consideration; showing others that you care about them; letting people know that you care about how they think and feel; listen and pay attention to someone; treat others well.

Considerate: Kind; respectful; thinking about others; treating others as one would like to be treated.

■ CASE VIGNETTES

—*Earl had a hard time getting along with others because he was very demanding. Earl would not share his treats with others but always wanted somebody else to buy him a can of pop or give him one of their snacks. When he was in line at the vending machines, he was intolerant. That meant that he would yell at others to "Hurry up" or get out of his way. When he was at the machines, he would slowly make up his mind what to buy even if others were waiting. When Earl was working, he did not tolerate anyone coming into his work space. But he frequently invaded the work space of others and took things that were in front of co-workers. He also told them that they were working too slowly. Once, when it was time to get on the bus, Earl nearly knocked down Jean, who walked with a metal walker. He wanted to be the first person on the bus and did not much care if he bumped into others.*

Do you think Earl was considerate of others? Did he follow the Golden Rule? Why or why not? Do you think others liked being around Earl? Why or why not?

—*Renalda is a friendly woman. Even though she walks with a cane and cannot see very well, she always says "Hello" when she hears people go by. She asks them, "How are you today?" and continues to talk if they stop. When someone talks about a bad experience, Renalda is the first one to tell the person that she is sorry to hear about it. She always offers to help if she can. She is respectful and waits her turn in lines. She offers to share her treats with others. Yesterday, she had five cookies and gave two to Jeff, who had none. Renalda thinks about what others may want or need, not just about herself.*

Why do you think everybody likes Renalda? What does she do to show consideration for others? Does she follow the Golden Rule?

■ DISCUSSION QUESTIONS

Simple/concrete questions:
   What are some things that make a person easy to get along with?
   What are some things that make someone difficult to get along with?
Personal experience/feelings questions:
   How do you like to be treated by others?
   Have you ever had someone treat you badly? How did you handle it?
   How do you usually get along with others?
Problem-solving questions:
   How can you become better at getting along with others?
   How can you get along with somebody who is rude and inconsiderate?

■ GROUP ACTIVITIES

Facilitate a discussion about positive and negative experiences in relationships with others.
Each person select a partner and discuss different ways to get along well with others.
Lead a discussion about why some people act rude, inconsiderate, and insensitive.

■ ASSESSMENT OF SKILLS LEARNED

Identifies the "Golden Rule":

ALMOST NEVER	USUALLY NOT	SOMETIMES	USUALLY	ALMOST ALWAYS
1	2	3	4	5

Identifies several positive ways to treat others:

ALMOST NEVER	USUALLY NOT	SOMETIMES	USUALLY	ALMOST ALWAYS
1	2	3	4	5

83. *Critical Social Behaviors at Work*

There is a host of skills related to getting and keeping a job. Individuals with developmental disabilities are particularly vulnerable to losing jobs because of social skills deficits. This session focuses on a variety of behaviors that are necessary in order to keep a job. These may include showing up for work in the morning, being punctual, getting back to work on time after breaks, learning to do the job well, listening, paying attention to the supervisor, accepting supervision, doing what the supervisor requests, asking for help when needed, showing respect for others, being polite/friendly, keeping a positive attitude, avoiding excessive socializing at the job, visiting with friends at breaktime but not during work time, keeping on task, ignoring distractions, working without distracting others, staying awake/attentive, leaving personal problems at home, talking to the supervisor about problems that affect work, keeping one's hands to oneself, avoiding making negative remarks to co-workers, and so forth. This topic is appropriate for those with mild and moderate developmental disabilities. It can be modified for lower functioning individuals utilizing pictures/symbols, yes/no questioning, and nonverbal communication.

■ SPECIFIC SKILLS TO BE LEARNED

Recognize various behaviors necessary to keep a job:
  Be punctual, show up for work, do not be late from work breaks.
  Learn how to do the job, and do it well.
  Pay attention to one's supervisor, listen.
  Accept supervision, do what the supervisor asks.
  If one needs help, ask for it.
  Respect others, get along, be polite and friendly, have a positive attitude.
  Do not socialize on the job, see friends at breaktime.
  Stay on task, ignore distractions, do not talk and distract others, do not sleep at the job.
  Try not to take personal problems to work, take care of personal problems outside of work.
  Talk to one's supervisor if having a problem that affects work.
  Keep one's hands to oneself, not on one's co-workers.
  Avoid making negative remarks to co-workers.

■ CONCEPTS NECESSARY TO PERFORM SKILLS

Punctual: On time; doing something when one is supposed to do it; being where you say you will be when you say you will be there.

Supervision: To watch somebody's work and help the person do it right; to oversee; to help; to direct somebody's work.

On task: Staying with one thing until it is done; keeping at what one is supposed to be doing; keeping doing what you are doing; not stopping something until you finish it; not becoming distracted.

Respect: Esteem; consideration; showing others that you care about them; letting people know that you care about how they think and feel; listening and paying attention to someone; treating others well.

Personal problem: Private problem; a problem one shares only with friends and family members; something a person does not want everybody to hear about.

■ CASE VIGNETTES

—Jane was a good worker. She left her house early enough so that she would be on time for work every day. In fact, she usually got there early to talk with her friends in the morning. She spent her coffee breaks with friends but got back to work when it was time. She looked at the clock in the break room so that she would remember to go back on time. Jane paid attention to her work supervisor and stayed at her job. When others talked about matters unrelated to work, she kept working and did not get distracted. Jane sometimes asked her supervisor how to do things. She also remembered what she was supposed to do and did it. She was friendly and did not say rude things to others. She left her personal problems at home so that she could concentrate on her job. She was a fast worker and earned more money than others because she finished a great deal of work.

Why was Jane a good worker? Was she good at keeping a job? What did she do that helped her keep her job?

—Dick was a nice man but a poor worker. He often came to work late and returned to his job late from breaks. He did not pay attention when the boss explained different jobs, and Dick often needed the boss to tell him more than once how to do things. Dick talked a great deal to other workers when he was supposed to be working. He often forgot to stay at his job and wandered around the work floor. His mind tended to wander, and he would think about his weekend while he was supposed to be thinking about his job. Sometimes Dick said rude things to co-workers. He teased them and told nasty jokes that they did not think were very funny. Sometimes he tried to touch women at work, even when they told him to keep his hands to himself.

Why was Dick a poor worker? Why do you think his boss was thinking about firing him? Do you think his fellow workers liked to be around him? Why or why not? What could Dick have done to be a better worker?

■ DISCUSSION QUESTIONS

Simple/concrete questions:
   What are some important things you need to do to keep a job?
Personal experience/feelings questions:
   Do you have a job? If so, do you like your job?
   Have you ever had trouble at work? What kind of trouble?

Problem-solving questions:
How should you react when your job supervisor asks you to do something?
What should you do when a co-worker yells at you while you are working?
What should you do when a co-worker is noisy and distracts you from your work?
What should you do if your ride is late to your workplace?

■ GROUP ACTIVITIES

Individuals share positive and negative job experiences.
Facilitate a discussion about the importance of positive work behaviors in order to keep a job.

■ ASSESSMENT OF SKILLS LEARNED

Recognizes various behaviors necessary to keep a job:

ALMOST NEVER	USUALLY NOT	SOMETIMES	USUALLY	ALMOST ALWAYS
1	2	3	4	5

Appendix I

Abandonment: When important people leave and never come back; when someone forgets about another person; when others lose interest and no longer have anything to do with somebody; when people turn their backs on others.

Abuse: Harm; hurt; damage; mistreat; injure; scold; curse.

Accept: Take; receive; like yourself for who you are; know that one is a good person even if needing to change some things; feel good as you are.

Accepting: Letting others know they are okay the way they are; not trying to change someone; forgiving; believing what someone says; approving of someone.

Accuse: Say that somebody did something; blame somebody for something; slur; condemn; complain about someone's behavior.

Acknowledge: Listen; let individuals know that you hear them; repeat back what one hears; show that a person understands what someone has said.

Acquaintance: Somebody a person has been before but does not know very well; someone with whom one has gone to school or worked but is not very familiar; a person one knows, but not too well.

Active and passive listening: Sometimes people sit back and do not look like they are listening (passive) and other times they sit up, look at you, and ask about what you are saying (active).

Activities: Things people do; events; happenings; how people spend time; actions; behaviors; movements.

Activity: To do something; movie, dance, craft, sport, church or other event; a thing to do.

Adaptable: Able to make changes; able to change behavior in new and different situations; flexible; willing to try new things.

Adult behavior: To act in an adult fashion; behave as a grown-up; control one's behavior; not tantrum and lose control; think before acting.

Advocate: Argue for; favor; make a case for; please; express favorable opinions for; present reasons to support one's choices.

Affection: Kindness; consideration; treating somebody well; feeling for someone; love; feeling good about someone and showing it.

Aggressive: Trying to hurt someone; acting mean to somebody; attacking someone; swearing or saying nasty things to a person.

Aging: Getting older; what happens as time boes by; living to be older; growing up and growing old.

Ally: On somebody's side; friend; companion; someone who supports another; willing to fight for someone; helper.

Alternative: One possible choice; something a person can pick or choose; one of the different choices some-

one can make; one way to do things; one way to solve a problem; one of several things that will make a problem go away; solution; answer.

Angry: Mad; upset; rageful; irritated; annoyed; resentful.

Angry behavior: Performing angry behaviors such as yelling, screaming, hitting, kicking, and breaking things; doing something mean or nasty when feeling emotionally upset.

Angry feeling: To feel angry, mad, upset, rageful, irritated, annoyed, or resentful; an unpleasant emotional experience that one feels inside him- or herself.

Anxiety: Worry; nervousness; to feel threatened; concern; to feel that something bad might happen; afraid something will go wrong; trembling and shaking.

Argument: Disagreement; conflict; a problem between two people; dispute; spat; squabble; to yell or swear at somebody.

Ask: Question somebody; make a request of someone; one can "tell" somebody to do something or can "ask" the person if he or she wants to do it; a person "asks" questions and "tells" statements.

Assertive: Directly tell a person how you feel; say how you feel and why you feel that way; tell someone what is on your mind.

Attack/blame others: Tell someone, "You're wrong"; say, "You're stupid"; tell people they never do anything right; say, "It's your fault"; tell a person, "I don't like you"; say mean things to someone.

Attention: Look at somebody; talk to someone; be mindful of others; notice others; see someone; listen; watch; look, listen and notice; take notice and remember what one is doing; notice what someone is saying; keep alert; be involved in something.

Autobiography: One's personal story; an individual's life story.

Bad behaviors: Bad behaviors happen on the outside; yelling, swearing, hitting, and other misbehaviors; what people do when they get out of control.

Bad feelings: Bad feelings happen on the inside of a person; someone can have bad feelings of anger, hurt, and upset but not do any bad behaviors; to feel emotionally upset.

Behavior: Something somebody does; to act in a certain way; what somebody's body is doing.

Belongingness: Feeling that one belongs somewhere; feeling that one fits into a group; feeling like a part of the gang; feeling that one has a place with others.

Blocks to communication: Things that get in the way when people are talking; fear of telling one's real thoughts or feelings; anything that makes it hard to listen and share things with others.

Borrow: Ask permission to use something and then give

it back when done; use something that belongs to someone else but give it back; take something with permission; take with the intention of returning.

Boundary: A dividing line; space between people or things; rule; way somebody is supposed to act; limit; border; end point; place where one thing leaves off and another begins; something that lets a person know the limits of acceptable behavior.

Calendar events: Things on the calendar; the order in that activities occur; events which happen on different days.

Caretaker: Someone who takes care of another person; parent; guardian; foster provider; counselor; teacher; instructor; someone who helps a person do things; somebody who helps a person.

Category of information: A topic somebody wants to know about; something that interests someone; a type of news about someone or something.

Child behavior: To act like a child; lose control; have a temper tantrum; act like a youngster.

Choice: Choose something; pick something; decide something; pick one thing or another; do one thing or another; select something; make up one's mind.

Cleanliness: To keep neat and clean; throw away old food; wash dishes; bathe or shower one's body with soap and water; wash clothes; keep one's room picked up.

Closeness: Togetherness; how close or far away one is from another; how intimate or friendly people are with others.

Closing: Ending a conversation; saying, "See you later," "Good-bye," "Have a nice day," or "Nice talking to you"; a friendly way to stop talking to someone so that you can each do something else.

Co-worker: Workmate; a friend or acquaintance from work; somebody from a person's workplace.

Coalition: When two family members team up together against someone else in the family; two or more family members who disagree with others in the family.

Cohesion: Togetherness; when people find it easy to talk to each other; individuals enjoying being together; when persons are feeling emotionally close to each other.

Collect background information: Ask somebody about him or herself; get to know someone; find out what people like to eat, watch on television, do in their spare time, and so on; find out about somebody's present life and history.

Commitment: Decide to do something and do it; make a choice and stay with it; keep doing something that one chooses to do; not give up; not change one's mind; stay with what you decide.

Common experience: When different people do the same thing or have the same thing happen to them; to do something together with others; when people live under the same conditions.

Communicate: To send and receive messages; to tell each other things and know what each means; to tell each other news; to listen to what somebody says, and the person listens to what you say; to share information.

Communication: To send and receive messages; to tell each other things and know what each means; to tell each other news; to listen to what somebody says, and the person listens to what you say; to share information.

Community: A place away from home; church, school, work, store, movie theater, or other place away from home; where people get together to do things; a gathering place.

Competent: Knowing how to do a job; able to do things; able to do things for oneself; able to understand things; able to make choices and decisions; not helpless and dependent; good at things.

Compliment: Say something nice to someone; tell others what you like about them; tell someone what you like about his or her behavior; tell somebody what you like about his or her personality; praise someone; congratulate a person; tell others that you like them.

Compromise: Do both what you want to do and what a friend wants to do; give a little and take a little; settle for part of what you want so that others can have some of what they want; one person can choose this time and the other may pick next time.

Confidence: Self-reliance; courage; self-assuredness; security; feeling able to take care of oneself.

Confident: Brave; sure of oneself; secure; feeling able to deal with things; not worried about what will happen; knowing that one can do something with no problem.

Confidentiality: Privacy; to keep private information between friends; not tell secrets to others; not talk about group matters outside of group sessions.

Conflict: Problem; disagreement; argument; when a person sees something differently than someone else and becomes upset about it.

Considerate: Kind; respectful; to think about others; to treat others as one would like to be treated.

Constructive: Good; positive; helpful; give information to help somebody change his or her behavior.

Coping skills: Ways to get what a person wants; ways to deal with not having what someone wants; behaviors a person can use to handle anger, frustration, and emotional upset; abilities and behaviors that help a person avoid problems.

Courtesy: Saying "Please," and "Thank-you"; waiting one's turn; letting others know you care about how they feel; helping others in small ways such as holding doors for them or letting them go first; kindness and consideration.

Criticism: Giving someone feedback about his or her behavior; telling others what you think about their behavior; helping someone make changes by telling the person what you think about what he or she is doing; saying what you think is good or bad about a person's behavior; judging someone's behavior; telling a person how you feel about his or her behavior.

Danger: When something bad might happen; a situation in which something might go wrong; when something is risky; a hazard; something scary that might hurt someone; an unsafe situation.

Dating: To go out on a date; go out to dinner or to a movie with a special friend; get together with somebody at a certain time and place; what people do when they have a romantic relationship with each other; when somebody goes places with a boyfriend or girlfriend.

Death: The end of life; the end of somebody's body; when a person no longer walks, talks and breathes; when someone is buried; when this life is left behind.

Decision: Deciding something; making a choice; picking one thing or another; doing one thing or another; doing this or that; picking this or that; making up one's mind.

Defense against feelings: Block out your feelings; forget how you feel; try not to think about how you feel; act the opposite of how you feel; yell at one person when mad at somebody else; break things when angry with somebody; pretend to feel good when feeling bad; act tough or angry when feeling scared.

Dependency: To depend on others for things; to let other people take care of you; when others tell a person what to think, feel, and do; unable to make choices and decisions; trusting others to take care of what you need.

Dependent: Letting others do things for a person; letting others take care of you; when others tell someone what to do and when to do it; others make a person's decisions for him or her; trust that others will take care of one's needs.

Depersonalized: Not feeling like a person; feeling like an object for others to do with as they please; feel unimportant; feeling that one's ideas and feelings are unimportant to others; feeling that others are not treating one like a person.

Depressed: Down; upset; having a lowered mood; unhappy; tired and gloomy; having the blues; slowed down; feel badly.

Destructive: Bad; negative; hurtful; not helpful; wasteful; putting someone down; shaming or blaming a person; trampling on someone's feelings.

Difference: What is not alike between people; what is not the same about things; something that sets two people apart; something that is special about a person or thing.

Direct expression of feelings: Telling others how you feel with words.

Directions: Telling somebody which way to go; telling someone how to get somewhere; tell a person what to do; give instructions; letting a person know how to do something.

Disability: Having a problem with part of one's body; not able to do something as well as somebody else; having special problems learning or doing things; when part of a person is damaged or not working properly; handicap.

Disagreement: When two people fight; when two individuals have different ideas about what to do; when people each have different answers to a problem; when someone argues or yells at somebody else.

Disease: Sickness; when germs get into food and on a person's body because one is not clean; what can happen if a person eats old and unrefrigerated food; what might occur if a person eats food that has not been cooked long enough.

Displacement: Yell at one person when mad at somebody else; feel upset with one person and take it out on someone else.

Distraction: Something that interrupts a person; an event that makes somebody lose concentration; something that gets somebody's attention while the person is trying to do something else.

Dyad/triad: Two family members or three family members; how any two or three family members get along together; family teams; who is on whose side in family disagreements; who gets along with whom in a family.

Emotion: Feeling; something somebody feels inside; nervousness, anger, surprise, happiness, sadness, excitement, loneliness, or other feeling; good or bad sensation happening inside of someone.

Emotional: To do with feelings; a person's emotions; rules about who has what feelings and how to express them.

Energy: Enthusiasm; what makes a person feel excited; vigor; life; vitality; high spirits; get-up-and-go; pep, vim and vigor.

Esteem: How individuals feel about themselves; how much people like themselves.

Expectation: Rule; something somebody wants a person to do or not to do; what others expect from a person; what others think you should do.

Eye contact: Look someone in the eyes; look at somebody instead of looking away.

Fable: Lie; untruth; falsehood; a made up story; fiction.

Falsehood: Lie; not tell the truth; fable; made up story; say something that is not true.

Familial: A family relationship; to do with family; something about one's family; oneself, parents, brothers and sisters, grandparents, and one's entire family.

Family boundaries: Family rules; space between family members; how close family members feel; how close family members are to each other; how much privacy family members have; how much sharing family members do with each other.

Family loss: Someone dying or leaving the family; a family member going away to school; theft of family property; illness or disability of a family member; a family member getting separated or divorced.

Family member: Brother, sister or parent; someone in a person's family; somebody with whom a person lives.

Family tree: Everybody in a family; all of a person's relatives; parents, children, aunts, uncles, cousins, grandparents, and all of someone's relatives.

Fear: Worry about a real danger; nervous because something dangerous is happening; to feel startled by something scary and dangerous; terror; fright; panic.

Feedback: Tell others how one thinks or feels about what was said; share how one thinks or feels about others' behaviors; tell a person how one sees his or her appearance; tell somebody how his or her appearance and behavior affect others.

Feeling: Emotion; something somebody feels inside; nervousness, anger, surprise, happiness, sadness, excitement, loneliness, or other emotion; good or bad sensation happening inside of someone.

Fiction: Falsehood; fable; untruth; made up story; lie.

Financial: Having to do with money; related to money and resources.

Flexible: Able to change behavior in new situations; able to make changes to deal with new problems; able to do things differently than before when a person or family has a new problem; ability of individuals or family members to trade jobs.

Follow-up: Ask something new after asking the first question; keep talking about the same topic but ask or tell new things about it.

Forgiving: Tolerant; not critical; not expecting too much from someone; letting others make small mistakes without punishing them; lenient.

Friend: Somebody a person knows well; a familiar person; companion; mate; a person with whom somebody likes to do things; someone to talk to; somebody to whom a person feels close; someone a person can trust.

Friendship: Companionship; togetherness; neighborliness; comradeship; fellowship; brotherhood; closeness with others; to share thoughts, feelings and activities with others; what a person has with friends and companions.

Frustration: Irritation; inconvenience; something is in somebody's way; something is keeping a person from getting what he or she wants; something or someone is in the way of what somebody wants to do; when people have to wait for things they want.

Frustration tolerance: Ability to deal with frustrating situations; patience to wait for things; ability to control one's behavior while upset; can manage tough problems without getting too upset; able to solve problems without losing control.

Future: What will happen later; five minutes from now; an hour from now, tomorrow, next week, next month, next year, and a long time from now; what is yet to come; what will happen.

Generation: A group of people about the same age; you and your friends are one generation, and your parents are another generation; a whole group of people who were born at about the same time.

Generous: Sharing one's things with others; ignoring others' faults and shortcomings; giving things to people in need; share one's time with others; doing things for others; kind; not blaming or criticizing; to be helpful, considerate and giving.

Germ: A very small living thing that can make food spoil; a creature that goes away if you wash your hands, clean your body, and keep your food in the refrigerator; a thing that can give a person a cold, sore throat, or other sickness.

Goals: What people try to achieve; aims; objectives; things individuals are trying to do; what people shoot for, even if they fall short of the mark.

Golden Rule: Treat others how you want to be treated.

Good faith: Give your word and try to keep it; mean what you say; not lie; try not to deceive someone.

Gossip: Say things about someone which may or may not be true; say something behind somebody's back without telling the person; spread rumors; whisper about somebody.

Government: City, state, and county workers; a place where some people get help with money; where social security, medical assistance and housing monies come from.

Greet: Say, "Hi," "Hello," "How are you?" "Nice to see you," "What's happening?" "Nice day," "Good day," etc.; say something to let somebody know that you have noticed the person; say something when first encountering somebody else.

Grief: Sadness; loss; sorrow; distress; negative feelings at the time of a death or loss.

Grief stages: Emotional changes that occur after a loss; different feelings such as denial, disbelief, shock, anger, guilt, anxiety, depression, sadness, hurt, etc., which take place after a loss; different moods a person may experience after losing somebody or something.

Group belongingness: People feeling that they are accepted in their group; a person feeling that he or she has a place in a group; feeling that one is like others in a group; feeling cared about by fellow group members.

Group cohesion: Togetherness; when people find it easy to talk to each other; individuals enjoying being together; when persons are feeling emotionally close to each other.

Group format: The kinds of things a group talks about; the order of group activities.

Group process: The way things are worked on in group; the manner in which topics are talked about in group; how things are done in group.

Group rule: A thing upon which group members agree; order so that everybody can get along together in group; what each person expects or wants from others in a group.

Guilt: Feel badly because one does something wrong; a bad feeling that lets a person know that a behavior should be changed; a bad feeling resulting from a bad behavior.

Handicap: Disability; when somebody has a problem with his or her body or brain; to have trouble doing something as well as others; have special problems learning or doing things.

Hear: Open your ears and listen to what somebody says; know what a person is saying because you are listening.

Help: Do something for somebody; share the work; work with somebody so that the person can get the job done faster; do things for others that they cannot do for themselves; assist someone.

Hierarchy: A group or family pecking order; who is the boss over whom; who makes group or family decisions and who follows them; who gets to decide what happens in a group or family.

History: Somebody's life story; a story; all the things that happen to a person in his or her life; all of the things that someone experiences during his or her life.

Honest: Truthful; tell the truth; say what really happened; say what is true.

Hygiene: Neatness and cleanliness; to keep germs away by washing with soap and water; to wash away body odor and use deodorant.

Identification: Something that lets somebody know who you are; a driver's license or social security card; a picture of somebody.

Identity: Who you are; who I am; who each person is; what is special about a person; how one is like or unlike others; to be a separate person; to be an individual; to have one's own thoughts, feelings, and behaviors; to know who you are and how you are the same as, or different from, others; individuality; distinctiveness.2

Ignore: Not pay attention; not listen; overlook; disregard; neglect; do something else when a person is trying to talk.

Illness: Sickness; when a person is not feeling well; problems with one's body or brain; poor health; physical or mental distress.

Impulsive: Act before thinking; not control your behavior; do or say things right away instead of thinking about them.

Independent: Can do things for oneself; able to make choices for oneself; persons having their own feelings and thoughts; to make one's own choices; not wait for someone else to take care of an individual but to take care of oneself.

Individual name: What people call themselves; "My name is _____"; a special word for *you* or *me;* a word that tells whom one is talking to, whom one is talking about, or whom is speaking to an individual.

Individuation: The act of becoming an individual; becoming a separate person from others; having one's own thoughts, feelings, and ways of doing things; becoming different from other people, even though one also has some similarities with them.

Inevitable: It will happen for sure; something that happens to everybody; an event that is bound to happen if somebody waits long enough.

Information: Things that people talk about; ideas individuals share with each other; what people tell each other; messages; knowledge; communication about facts; advice; what people know and report.

Initiate: Start; begin; introduce; begin to talk to somebody; ask to do something with somebody.

Inside self: One's thoughts and feelings; the private world of an individual; one's personal experience of the world.

Instruction: Direction; tell someone what to do; an order; a command.

Intellectual: To do with thoughts; a person's thinking; rules about a person's thoughts and how to express them.

Intention: What a person plans to do; if a person intends to give something back, the person plans to return it; what a person thinks he or she will do; what somebody has in mind to do.

Interest: To show that one cares about what someone else thinks or feels; to ask about somebody: to have concern for another; to let others know they are important.

Interfere: get in the way; butt in; meddle; hinder; try to help when others do not want help #46

Interrupt: Start to talk before someone else is finished speaking; come into or leave a room when someone is talking; butt in when someone is talking; start talking before somebody else is finished; make noise when someone is talking.

Intimacy: Closeness; physical touch; to talk about private things with somebody; emotional closeness; love and affection between people who feel close to each other; companionship; to relate on a personal level with somebody.

Intimate: Feel close to someone; loving closeness; two people feeling care and affection for each other; emotional closeness between people; to share very personal thoughts and feelings with someone.

Introduce: Present somebody to others; share a new friend with existing friends; help acquaint a person with others; let people know who is one's new friend.

Kind: Considerate; helpful; to show someone that you care about how he or she feels; avoid doing things to hurt or upset others; to be mindful of the needs of others.

Leisure: Recreation; fun; enjoyment; something somebody wants to do even if the person does not have to do it; idle time; free time; spare time; restful activity; something a person likes to do.

Lie: Say something that is false; tell an untruth; make up a story that is not true; deceive.

Life change: A new thing happening in a person's life; to do something different; stop doing something that one used to do; the experience of a loss; a person dying or moving away; to start a new school or job.

Life timeline: The order of experiences that have happened in someone's life; the order of important events in the life of a person.

Limits: Boundaries; borders; where some things stop and other things begin; what others do not do for you but you do for yourself.

Listen: Pay attention to what someone says; hear and understand what somebody says; open your ears and close your mouth; let others know that you know what they are saying.

Lose: Unable to find something; a person had something but now it is gone; misplace; something slips through somebody's fingers; something is missing.

Loss: To lose someone or something; not have someone or something anymore; the death of a significant other; the event of a friend or family member moving away; to be cut off from a person, place, or thing.

Love: Kindness; attention; affection; admiration; care for someone; nurturance.

Mental: To do with one's mind; thinking; what happens in somebody's head.

Mistreat: Treat badly; act with disrespect; treat poorly; abuse; do bad things to someone; say bad things to a person.

Money: What somebody uses to buy something; what one pays for things; finances; budget; coins and dollars; cash, dough or moola; what things cost.

Mythology: T•things family members believe; things that people believe that may or may not be true; ways that families see things and think people should act.

Name: What others call someone; a word for somebody so that people know whom one is talking about; what a person calls him or herself.

Need: Something a person must have; an individual cannot live without it; something very important and necessary to someone; things that are necessary to stay alive and healthy; individuals demand that their needs be met.

Negative: Bad; having undesirable qualities; disagreeable; unpleasant; not helpful; not worthwhile.

Negative frustration reaction: Loss of control when frustrated; tantrum; acting like a spoiled child; anger, emotional upset, and out-of-control behavior.

Negative label: A word people use to identify somebody or something; a name for something; a name for somebody; to call somebody "mentally retarded," "mentally ill," or "crazy."

Negative statement: Say something bad; tell a bad thing about yourself; say something that is not nice about yourself or someone else; tell a bad thing about a person.

Nervous: Worried; agitated; uptight; edgy; unsettled; tense; fearful; jittery; jumpy.

911: Emergency telephone number; a way to call the police, fire department or emergency heepers; a number to call if somebody is hurt or in trouble.

Nonverbal and verbal communication: Sometimes our bodies and sometimes our mouths tell things to others; a frowning or smiling face may tell you that someone is sad or happy but things can also be said with words; say things either with your body or with words.

Nonverbal behavior: What a person's face and body are doing while the person talks; smile, shake hands, nod one's head, wave good-bye, etc.

Nurturance: Love; affection; attention; care; kindness; comfort.

Occupational: Related to work; things related to jobs, hobbies, schoolwork, and productive activities; things done to improve oneself.

On-task: Stay with one thing until it is done; keep at what one is supposed to be doing; keep doing what you are doing; do not stop something until you finish it; do not become distracted.

Option: An alternative; a choice someone can make; one way to decide something; one possible pick.

Ostracism: To treat somebody like they are not part of the group; refuse to include someone in fun activities; ignore somebody; banish a person; treat somebody as an outcast; treat a person as though he or she is no good.

Other-respect: Have respect of others; to be important to others; to be valued by people; others think that one is worthwhile.

Outside self: How one's voice, face, body, and speech look and sound to others; behaviors and body movements; one's appearance.

Passive: indirectly tell someone how you feel; let some-one guess about how you feel; not say how you feel and why you feel that way; let people guess from your behavior how you feel.

Passive-aggressive: Do mean or hostile things to someone but refuse to say why; give somebody the silent treat-ment or refuse to talk to the person but not say why; do small things to bother someone but not say why; walk out of a room and slam the door behind yourself.

Past: What has already happened; five minutes ago, an hour ago, yesterday, last week, last month, last year, and a long time ago.

Pay attention: Listen; remember what somebody says; do what you are told; hear what someone says; keep one's mind on something; not talk while listening to somebody.

Permission: When somebody tells you that you can do something; someone knows you are doing something and it is all right with the person; do something by agreement; free to do something; another person does not mind if you do something.

Personal: Private; confidential; intimate; things people usually keep to themselves; things usually told only to friends and family members; something a person does not want everybody to hear about; one's own special thoughts and experiences.

Personal experience: A thing that happens to someone; something a person thinks or feels; what happens in a person's life; how a person sees him- or herself and other people.

Personal growth: To make changes for the better; im-prove oneself; mature; grow up; learn new things; develop a better understanding of life, people and oneself.

Personal history: What happens to a person over time; a person's past, present, and future life; how somebody lives and changes over time; someone's life story.

Personal problem: Private problem; a problem one shares only with friends and family members; some-thing a person does not want everybody to hear about.

Personal responsibility: Decide to control one's own be-havior; take control of one's life and behavior; not blame others when losing one's temper; decide to keep self-control; make a choice to do or not to do some-thing; not blame others for one's problems; decide to do something and do it; be held accountable for your behavior; take charge of one's own life; to be depend-able and reliable; to do what one says he or she is going to do.

Personal right: A thing that others owe to a person; some-thing one has a right to ask for and to have; a privi-lege which an individual claims belongs to him- or herself; what is fair for a person to expect from oth-ers; consideration which one should receive just be-cause he or she is a person.

Personal sharing or self-revelation: Tell things about yourself; let others know personal information about oneself; tell your real feelings; tell people what you think; tell others about your life.

Personal strength: Something somebody does well; something good about a person; a skill; to know how to do something; a thing someone likes about him or herself; something others like about a person.

Personal weakness or limitation: Something a person wants to do better; a thing about oneself that is not yet as good as one would like; something an individual wishes he or she could do better, but even when tying hard it continues to be difficult; what a person does not like about him or herself; a characteristic that somebody does not like about a person.

Physical: To do with a person's body; something one can see, touch or feel; concrete; something that has sub-stance; rules about whom, when, and how to touch.

Physical appearance: What a person looks like; how one appears to others; a person's body, style of dress, and the way he or she acts.

Physical barrier: Something in the way; when a wheel-chair cannot get up the steps; when something is block-ing somebody; when someone is traveling somewhere and something gets in the way.

Physical and mental faculties: Physical and mental abili-ties; capabilities to see, hear, do, and understand things; capacities to pay attention, remember, and engage in activities.

Plan: What somebody is going to do; a goal; something for the future; organize; order; schedule; decide what will happen with whom, when, and where; have an idea about what and how one will do something; prepare.

Please: people say "Please" to get something; "Please" means you are asking for something.

Pocketbook: Purse; wallet; billfold; handbag.

Polite: Courteous; caring; kind; considerate of others; to let others know that you care about how they feel; to show respect for others.

Positive: Good; has desirable qualities; agreeable; pleas-ant; helpful; worthwhile.

Positive statement: Say something good; tell a good thing about yourself; say something nice; tell a good thing about a person.

Potential: Something that a person might do; something one may achieve; a person has not yet done some-thing but may do it; a thing that has not yet been done but could be if one worked at it; a dream that may or may not come true.

Power structure: Who controls the power in a group or family; who can make what decisions; who does what jobs; who has the authority to decide things in a group or family.

Powerless: Helpless; cannot do anything for oneself; need to be taken care of; unable to do things for oneself; cannot take care of oneself; weak.

Preference: What one desires; a wish; one's choice; the outcome that you would like; how you would like the situation to end; one's favorite choice.

Pregnant: When a woman is going to have a baby; what can happen after a man and woman have sex together; what might happen if a man and woman do not use birth control methods when they have sex.

Prejudice: To make up your mind about somebody based on a negative label; decide what you think about somebody before getting to know them; to think that a person's disability is the only important thing about them; treat somebody differently because of their race, nationality, sex, or disability; have an opinion about somebody before you know them.

Present: What is happening right now; this moment; what we are doing, seeing, hearing, and talking about now; here and now.

Privacy: To keep thoughts and feelings to oneself; share thoughts and feelings only with close relatives; confidentiality.

Private: Personal; something to be shared with only one or a few people; confidential; something told to a friend that is not to be shared with anybody else; personal and confidential talk between friends; intimate.

Proactive behavior: To choose one's own goals; commit to one's own values and goals; do what a person must in order to achieve something; maintain a positive attitude while accomplishing goals; not blame others for one's problems; take responsibility for one's behavior.

Problem: Conflict; puzzle; disagreement with somebody; when a person needs help; an argument with somebody; when someone or something gets in one's way.

Public: Behaviors shared with anyone; something anybody and everybody can see.

Punctual: On time; do something when one is supposed to do it; be where you say you will be when you say you will be there.

Purse: Handbag; pocketbook; moneybag; place for identification, money and personal effects.

Question: Ask somebody something; ask about something; inquire.

Reality: What is real; what is happening around a person; to see things as other people see them; to be in touch with what is real or true; to know whom you are, where you are, time of day, who you are with, etc.

Reassure: Tell somebody that everything is okay; let someone know you will help; tell someone that things will turn out all right; promise help or support.

Reciprocate: Pay back; one person helps now, the other helps next time; exchange; take turns doing things for each other.

Recreation: Rest and recuperation; fun activity; to do something for enjoyment; leisure activity; amusement; pastime.

Rejection: To be put aside by others; when someone is ignored; when family members or friends no longer want to see a person or talk to them; when a group of persons do not include another in their activities.

Relationship: Connection with somebody; when people know each other; to relate or do things with others; togetherness; family, friend or acquaintance.

Relaxed: Calm; peaceful; at ease; restful.

Request: Ask; tell somebody what you need or want; make a statement of one's preference or wish; appeal; demand.

Resources: Money; possessions; skills; abilities; information and knowledge.

Respect: Esteem; consideration; show others that you care about them; let people know that you care about how they think and feel; listen and pay attention to someone; treat others well.

Rigid: Not willing to change; unable to change; to do the same thing even if it is not working anymore; not flexible or adaptable.

Role: What job somebody performs; a person's position in a family or group.

Rude: Mean; discourteous; offensive; do something that bothers another person; insensitive; not pay attention to how other people feel; not care how others feel; disregarding; vulgar; neglectful.

Rule: Guideline; boundary; limit; expectation; what each person agrees to do or not do.

Rumor: Something that may or may not be true; hearsay; gossip; report something without knowing all the facts.

Sad: Unhappy; gloomy; down in the dumps; blue; heavy-hearted; sorrowful.

Safe: Secure; not worry that bad things will happen; feel comfortable with others; not afraid to tell others how one feels and thinks.

Sarcasm: Say something mean and funny; embarrass someone with a snappy remark; humiliate a person; make fun of somebody with an angry joke.

Secret: hidden; kept from others; something that is kept private such as stealing, lying, or wrongful behavior, which should be told to others.

Secure: Trust others with one's feelings; confident; safe; feel comfortable with oneself and accepted by others.

Security: Feeling safe to tell others about yourself; feeling accepted as you are; feeling comfortable with others; trusting others with one's feelings.

Self-acceptance: To like yourself for who you are; to know that one is a good person even if needing to change some things; to feel good as you are.

Self-actualization: To reach one's potential; what happens when somebody works hard to achieve something; continue to get better at things; become more mature; do the best one can with his or her abilities; make things happen; act and make choices.

Self-affirmation: Say something nice about oneself; think a positive thought about oneself; say something that is good about yourself; talk about a happy thought or feeling.

Self-esteem: How people feel about themselves; to feel either good or bad about oneself; to like or dislike oneself.

Self-expression: To voice opinions, thoughts, and ideas; tell others how you feel; make choices; communicate personal preferences and wishes; share personal experiences.

Self-monitor: Pay attention to what one is doing; notice what you are doing and how you are doing it; notice how fast or slow one is doing something.

Self-reliance: To do things for oneself; to take care of oneself; to make one's own decisions; to make one's own choices; not wait for others to take care of you.

Self-respect: Respect oneself; feel that one is important; value oneself; feel worthwhile; see yourself as a good person.

Self-statement: Telling something about yourself; sharing personal information tell one's thoughts or feelings.

Self-talk: What a person says about him or herself; say good or bad things about oneself; talk about yourself.

Self-worth: What individuals think they are worth; how important a person feels; how good or bad someone feels about him or herself; what people think they deserve from others and from their lives.

Selfish: Showing no interest in others; not sharing with others; thinking only of oneself; not caring about others.

Separation: A boundary line; separate or less attached to someone; grown up and becoming one's own person; to have one's own thoughts, feelings, and ways of doing things.

Sexual: To do with sex; rules about being a man or woman; rules about people touching each other in private places; attraction between people.

Sexual relationship: When people become romantic together; kissing and hugging a boyfriend or girlfriend; two people touching each other in their private places; what people do when they love each other or are more than just friends.

Sexually transmitted disease: A sickness that somebody may get after having sex; a disease like AIDS that can spread when people have sex together.

Shame: Feel like a "no good" person; feel as though one is "totally bad"; feel inadequate; feel "not good enough"; feel like a disgrace.

Share: Take turns using things; give some of your treat to somebody else; take turns doing something.

Show interest: Listen to others; pay attention; care how others feel and let them know it.

Similarity: How people or things are the same; how people or things are alike.

Small talk: Discuss things that are not too personal; talk about things like news, weather, and sports; converse about small matters before talking about more important topics; a way to make contact with others without taking the risk of telling them information that is too personal.

Social: Related to people; to do with relationships; talk to people; take an interest in others; do things with people; get together with friends; rules about how to get along with others.

Social skill: Able to socialize well with others; get along with others; know how to talk to others; able to listen and talk to others; to be sociable; good at doing things with others.

Social support: Someone available who understands a person; friend, family, or relative; somebody to talk to or do things with; the act of listening, believing, caring about, helping, and otherwise considerately treating another person.

Socialize: Talk to others; get together with friends; tell people about one's life and ask about theirs; take an interest in people; do things with others; relate to people.

Solution: The answer to a problem; when a person gets rid of a problem; when a person's problem goes away.

Spiritual: Related to beliefs and values; what one thinks is important in life; a belief in something greater than oneself; something having to do with the meaning of life; what is important to a person.

Statement: Something that someone says; tell something; say something about yourself or someone else.

Steal: Take something without permission; borrow with no intention of giving something back; secretly take something from somebody; take something and not plan to give it back; rip something off.

Stranger: Somebody a person does not know at all; a person you have never met; a person one sees for the first time; an unfamiliar person.

Stubborn: Not willing to change; to have one's mind made up; rigid; not willing to change one's behavior; always want to have things your way.

Supervision: To watch somebody's work and help the person do it right; to oversee; to help; to direct somebody's work.

Support: Listen; care about; believe what someone says; tell others they are O.K.; tell a person one is on his or her side; be helpful; treat others kindly; be considerate; tell others one is with them and cares about how they feel.

Tease: Make fun of; ridicule; laugh at; poke fun of; embarrass; harass; mock; tantalize.

Tell: Say something to someone; give information; explain something; say what one feels, thinks, or wants; make a statement.

Temper: Mood; disposition; anger; emotional outburst; tantrum.

Thank-you: Tell others that you appreciate their compliments; let someone know that you like what he or she said to you; be gracious; accept a compliment.

Thought: Something somebody thinks; an idea; a thing that a person believes; activity going on in someone's head.

Threat/intimidation: When people act as though they might hurt others; when someone acts as though he or she will harm somebody else; to bully or push around; to scare somebody; to give a warning that you might hurt somebody.

Threaten: Say one will hurt another; try to hurt someone; do something to scare somebody; intimidate.

Time: The past, present, and future; what happens as people live their lives; all of the different moments of a person's life.

Time schedule: Calendar of events; the day, hour and minute somebody plans to do something; a list of things somebody will do at certain times.

Tolerant: Not critical; friendly and forgiving; not expecting too much from soneone; lenient; not yelling at someone when the person makes a mistake; not blaming someone for small matters.

Topic: The main thing people are talking about; a particular thing that someone thinks is important; the subject about which people ask questions or tell things; the main point of a discussion.

Train of thought: Keep one's mind on one thing; follow along during the conversation; stay with one topic; not let distractions interrupt a person; not get off task because of noises and movements of others.

Transportation: Ways to go places; methods of travel; how to get somewhere; to ride a bicycle, car, bus, train, plane, or boat, etc.

Trust: Feel safe with others; feel you can tell personal things without being attacked by others; feel that others will treat you with respect; know that it is O.K. to tell someone how you feel or what you think; not worry that somebody will try to blame or hurt you; feel good, comfortable, or relaxed with someone.

Trustworthy: Deserve the trust of others; be truthful; not lie; be honest; be direct; do what you say you will do; tell the truth; keep one's word; not steal, lie, or cheat.

Truthful: Tell the truth; be honest; tell the real facts; say what is true; tell what really happened.

Understand: Know what someone is saying; know what somebody means when they tell you something; know what a person is telling you.

Unreasonable: Senseless; without good reason; without good cause; illogical; irrational; arbitrary; absurd; to advocate for something that is not in somebody's best interest.

Value: What is important to a person; a belief; guideline for behavior; what somebody thinks is right or true.

Values: Beliefs; what is important to a person; ideas about what is important in life; guidelines for behavior; things that a person believes are right or true.

Valuing self: To feel that one is important; to have positive self-worth; to think that one deserves something good from life; to feel that one deserves good treatment from others.

Verbal behavior: The words people say to each other when they talk; use words to explain things; talk to others and tell them things.

Violate a confidence: Tell private things to somebody without permission; when one friend tells another to keep something private but the person tells it to somebody else anyway; break a trust.

Wait: When a person cannot have what he or she wants right now but can get it later; to let somebody else go first; to take your turn after someone else.

Waiting: When a ride has not yet arrived; to sit and wait until a ride comes; not do something now but do it later.

Wallet: Moneyholder; place for identification, money and other small cards or pictures; billfold; purse; pocketbook.

Want: Something a person would very much like; a thing that somebody can live without; something very important but not necessary for survival; people want certain things to make them happy; individuals hope that their wants are satisfied.

Work earnings: Money earned by working; paycheck; salary; wages; money given to somebody for his or her work.

Worry: Nervousness; fretting; uneasiness; fearfulness.

Appendix II

1. Beginning Social Skills

1. Introduction to Group

Understands concepts of confidentiality and privacy:

ALMOST NEVER	USUALLY NOT	SOMETIMES	USUALLY	ALMOST ALWAYS
1	2	3	4	5

Understands the concept of social skill:

ALMOST NEVER	USUALLY NOT	SOMETIMES	USUALLY	ALMOST ALWAYS
1	2	3	4	5

Gives opinion about group rules:

ALMOST NEVER	USUALLY NOT	SOMETIMES	USUALLY	ALMOST ALWAYS
1	2	3	4	5

Understands and follows group process and format:

ALMOST NEVER	USUALLY NOT	SOMETIMES	USUALLY	ALMOST ALWAYS
1	2	3	4	5

Shares former group experiences:

ALMOST NEVER	USUALLY NOT	SOMETIMES	USUALLY	ALMOST ALWAYS
1	2	3	4	5

2. Listening Skills

Makes eye contact:

ALMOST NEVER	USUALLY NOT	SOMETIMES	USUALLY	ALMOST ALWAYS
1	2	3	4	5

Orients toward speaker and has good listening posture:

ALMOST NEVER	USUALLY NOT	SOMETIMES	USUALLY	ALMOST ALWAYS
1	2	3	4	5

Gives reaction to indicate listening:

ALMOST NEVER	USUALLY NOT	SOMETIMES	USUALLY	ALMOST ALWAYS
1	2	3	4	5

Repeats back what someone says:

ALMOST NEVER	USUALLY NOT	SOMETIMES	USUALLY	ALMOST ALWAYS
1	2	3	4	5

Asks others to repeat themselves:

ALMOST NEVER	USUALLY NOT	SOMETIMES	USUALLY	ALMOST ALWAYS
1	2	3	4	5

Asks others to explain themselves:

ALMOST NEVER	USUALLY NOT	SOMETIMES	USUALLY	ALMOST ALWAYS
1	2	3	4	5

3. Introducing Oneself

Recognizes appropriate times and places for introduction:

ALMOST NEVER	USUALLY NOT	SOMETIMES	USUALLY	ALMOST ALWAYS
1	2	3	4	5

Gives a greeting:

ALMOST NEVER	USUALLY NOT	SOMETIMES	USUALLY	ALMOST ALWAYS
1	2	3	4	5

Tells name to others:

ALMOST NEVER	USUALLY NOT	SOMETIMES	USUALLY	ALMOST ALWAYS
1	2	3	4	5

Asks others their names:

ALMOST NEVER	USUALLY NOT	SOMETIMES	USUALLY	ALMOST ALWAYS
1	2	3	4	5

Shakes hands:

ALMOST NEVER	USUALLY NOT	SOMETIMES	USUALLY	ALMOST ALWAYS
1	2	3	4	5

Looks someone in eyes when introducing self:

ALMOST NEVER	USUALLY NOT	SOMETIMES	USUALLY	ALMOST ALWAYS
1	2	3	4	5

Smiles when introducing self:

ALMOST NEVER	USUALLY NOT	SOMETIMES	USUALLY	ALMOST ALWAYS
1	2	3	4	5

4. Beginning a Conversation

Chooses someone to talk to:

ALMOST NEVER	USUALLY NOT	SOMETIMES	USUALLY	ALMOST ALWAYS
1	2	3	4	5

Greets others:

ALMOST NEVER	USUALLY NOT	SOMETIMES	USUALLY	ALMOST ALWAYS
1	2	3	4	5

Engages in small talk:

ALMOST NEVER	USUALLY NOT	SOMETIMES	USUALLY	ALMOST ALWAYS
1	2	3	4	5

Chooses a topic of discussion:

ALMOST NEVER	USUALLY NOT	SOMETIMES	USUALLY	ALMOST ALWAYS
1	2	3	4	5

Closes a conversation:

ALMOST NEVER	USUALLY NOT	SOMETIMES	USUALLY	ALMOST ALWAYS
1	2	3	4	5

5. Asking a Question

Chooses a person to whom to ask a question:

ALMOST NEVER	USUALLY NOT	SOMETIMES	USUALLY	ALMOST ALWAYS
1	2	3	4	5

Selects a topic about which to ask a question:

ALMOST NEVER	USUALLY NOT	SOMETIMES	USUALLY	ALMOST ALWAYS
1	2	3	4	5

Gives a greeting and asks permission to ask a question:

ALMOST NEVER	USUALLY NOT	SOMETIMES	USUALLY	ALMOST ALWAYS
1	2	3	4	5

Smiles when greeting someone:

ALMOST NEVER	USUALLY NOT	SOMETIMES	USUALLY	ALMOST ALWAYS
1	2	3	4	5

Makes eye contact:

ALMOST NEVER	USUALLY NOT	SOMETIMES	USUALLY	ALMOST ALWAYS
1	2	3	4	5

Asks a question:

ALMOST NEVER	USUALLY NOT	SOMETIMES	USUALLY	ALMOST ALWAYS
1	2	3	4	5

Thanks a person for listening or answering a question:

ALMOST NEVER	USUALLY NOT	SOMETIMES	USUALLY	ALMOST ALWAYS
1	2	3	4	5

6. Maintaining a Conversation

Asks a question:

ALMOST NEVER	USUALLY NOT	SOMETIMES	USUALLY	ALMOST ALWAYS
1	2	3	4	5

Shares personal information without being asked:

ALMOST NEVER	USUALLY NOT	SOMETIMES	USUALLY	ALMOST ALWAYS
1	2	3	4	5

Asks a follow-up question about the topic of discussion:

ALMOST NEVER	USUALLY NOT	SOMETIMES	USUALLY	ALMOST ALWAYS
1	2	3	4	5

Asks a follow-up question to move a topic in a new direction (changes the topic):

ALMOST NEVER	USUALLY NOT	SOMETIMES	USUALLY	ALMOST ALWAYS
1	2	3	4	5

Shares personal information in response to a question:

ALMOST NEVER	USUALLY NOT	SOMETIMES	USUALLY	ALMOST ALWAYS
1	2	3	4	5

Recognizes the difference between a question and a statement (asking versus telling):

ALMOST NEVER	USUALLY NOT	SOMETIMES	USUALLY	ALMOST ALWAYS
1	2	3	4	5

Asks repeated follow-up questions:

ALMOST NEVER	USUALLY NOT	SOMETIMES	USUALLY	ALMOST ALWAYS
1	2	3	4	5

Intermixes questions and self-statements:

ALMOST NEVER	USUALLY NOT	SOMETIMES	USUALLY	ALMOST ALWAYS
1	2	3	4	5

7/8. Giving a Compliment/Saying Thank-You

Chooses someone to compliment:

ALMOST NEVER	USUALLY NOT	SOMETIMES	USUALLY	ALMOST ALWAYS
1	2	3	4	5

Makes eye contact when complimenting a person:

ALMOST NEVER	USUALLY NOT	SOMETIMES	USUALLY	ALMOST ALWAYS
1	2	3	4	5

Lists several possible areas to compliment:

ALMOST NEVER	USUALLY NOT	SOMETIMES	USUALLY	ALMOST ALWAYS
1	2	3	4	5

Smiles and is friendly when complimenting:

ALMOST NEVER	USUALLY NOT	SOMETIMES	USUALLY	ALMOST ALWAYS
1	2	3	4	5

Uses the person's name when complimenting:

ALMOST NEVER	USUALLY NOT	SOMETIMES	USUALLY	ALMOST ALWAYS
1	2	3	4	5

Listens to a compliment:

ALMOST NEVER	USUALLY NOT	SOMETIMES	USUALLY	ALMOST ALWAYS
1	2	3	4	5

Recognizes a compliment:

ALMOST NEVER	USUALLY NOT	SOMETIMES	USUALLY	ALMOST ALWAYS
1	2	3	4	5

Says "Thank you" after a compliment:

ALMOST NEVER	USUALLY NOT	SOMETIMES	USUALLY	ALMOST ALWAYS
1	2	3	4	5

Lets the person know why they are being thanked:

ALMOST NEVER	USUALLY NOT	SOMETIMES	USUALLY	ALMOST ALWAYS
1	2	3	4	5

9. Introducing Others

Asks someone for personal background information:

ALMOST NEVER	USUALLY NOT	SOMETIMES	USUALLY	ALMOST ALWAYS
1	2	3	4	5

Asks questions and listens to what other people say:

ALMOST NEVER	USUALLY NOT	SOMETIMES	USUALLY	ALMOST ALWAYS
1	2	3	4	5

Remembers what other people say:

ALMOST NEVER	USUALLY NOT	SOMETIMES	USUALLY	ALMOST ALWAYS
1	2	3	4	5

Names a person while introducing him or her:

ALMOST NEVER	USUALLY NOT	SOMETIMES	USUALLY	ALMOST ALWAYS
1	2	3	4	5

Tells background information when introducing a person:

ALMOST NEVER	USUALLY NOT	SOMETIMES	USUALLY	ALMOST ALWAYS
1	2	3	4	5

Identifies and describes categories of interest to introduce someone:

ALMOST NEVER	USUALLY NOT	SOMETIMES	USUALLY	ALMOST ALWAYS
1	2	3	4	5

2. Feelings

10. Types of Feelings

Identifies what is a feeling:

ALMOST NEVER	USUALLY NOT	SOMETIMES	USUALLY	ALMOST ALWAYS
1	2	3	4	5

Lists different types of feelings:

ALMOST NEVER	USUALLY NOT	SOMETIMES	USUALLY	ALMOST ALWAYS
1	2	3	4	5

Identifies the difference between a feeling and behavior:

ALMOST NEVER	USUALLY NOT	SOMETIMES	USUALLY	ALMOST ALWAYS
1	2	3	4	5

Identifies the difference between a feeling and a thought:

ALMOST NEVER	USUALLY NOT	SOMETIMES	USUALLY	ALMOST ALWAYS
1	2	3	4	5

Identifies two groups of feelings: good and bad:

ALMOST NEVER	USUALLY NOT	SOMETIMES	USUALLY	ALMOST ALWAYS
1	2	3	4	5

Understands the difference between emotional and physical feelings:

ALMOST NEVER	USUALLY NOT	SOMETIMES	USUALLY	ALMOST ALWAYS
1	2	3	4	5

11. Recognizing and Accepting Feelings

Recognizes that feelings happen inside oneself:

ALMOST NEVER	USUALLY NOT	SOMETIMES	USUALLY	ALMOST ALWAYS
1	2	3	4	5

Recognizes that feelings show on the outside of oneself:

ALMOST NEVER	USUALLY NOT	SOMETIMES	USUALLY	ALMOST ALWAYS
1	2	3	4	5

Relates feelings to body postures and sensations:

ALMOST NEVER	USUALLY NOT	SOMETIMES	USUALLY	ALMOST ALWAYS
1	2	3	4	5

Recognizes feelings when receiving feedback about them from others:

ALMOST NEVER	USUALLY NOT	SOMETIMES	USUALLY	ALMOST ALWAYS
1	2	3	4	5

Accepts unpleasant feelings while controlling behavior:

ALMOST NEVER	USUALLY NOT	SOMETIMES	USUALLY	ALMOST ALWAYS
1	2	3	4	5

12. Appropriately Expressing Feelings

Tells others how feels:

ALMOST NEVER	USUALLY NOT	SOMETIMES	USUALLY	ALMOST ALWAYS
1	2	3	4	5

Tells feelings directly:

ALMOST NEVER	USUALLY NOT	SOMETIMES	USUALLY	ALMOST ALWAYS
1	2	3	4	5

Understands the concept of *indirect* expression of feelings:

ALMOST NEVER	USUALLY NOT	SOMETIMES	USUALLY	ALMOST ALWAYS
1	2	3	4	5

Recognizes one or more *defenses* against feelings:

ALMOST NEVER	USUALLY NOT	SOMETIMES	USUALLY	ALMOST ALWAYS
1	2	3	4	5

Expresses feelings in appropriate fashion:

ALMOST NEVER	USUALLY NOT	SOMETIMES	USUALLY	ALMOST ALWAYS
1	2	3	4	5

Recognizes situations in which it is better to keep feelings to oneself:

ALMOST NEVER	USUALLY NOT	SOMETIMES	USUALLY	ALMOST ALWAYS
1	2	3	4	5

13. Dealing with Fear and Anxiety

Recognizes when feeling fearful/anxious:

ALMOST NEVER	USUALLY NOT	SOMETIMES	USUALLY	ALMOST ALWAYS
1	2	3	4	5

Is able to engage in anxiety- or fear-reducing task(s) when feeling anxious/fearful:

ALMOST NEVER	USUALLY NOT	SOMETIMES	USUALLY	ALMOST ALWAYS
1	2	3	4	5

Recognizes useless worry and fretting:

ALMOST NEVER	USUALLY NOT	SOMETIMES	USUALLY	ALMOST ALWAYS
1	2	3	4	5

Lists things that are anxiety-provoking:

ALMOST NEVER	USUALLY NOT	SOMETIMES	USUALLY	ALMOST ALWAYS
1	2	3	4	5

14. Dealing with Sadness and Depression

Recognizes when feeling sad or depressed:

ALMOST NEVER	USUALLY NOT	SOMETIMES	USUALLY	ALMOST ALWAYS
1	2	3	4	5

Recognizes causes of sadness/depression:

ALMOST NEVER	USUALLY NOT	SOMETIMES	USUALLY	ALMOST ALWAYS
1	2	3	4	5

Engages in one or more activities to reduce sadness/depression:

ALMOST NEVER	USUALLY NOT	SOMETIMES	USUALLY	ALMOST ALWAYS
1	2	3	4	5

Accepts sadness and depression as normal responses to loss:

ALMOST NEVER	USUALLY NOT	SOMETIMES	USUALLY	ALMOST ALWAYS
1	2	3	4	5

15. Dealing with Anger and Frustration

Recognizes the difference between angry feelings and angry behaviors:

ALMOST NEVER	USUALLY NOT	SOMETIMES	USUALLY	ALMOST ALWAYS
1	2	3	4	5

Identifies causes of frustration and anger:

ALMOST NEVER	USUALLY NOT	SOMETIMES	USUALLY	ALMOST ALWAYS
1	2	3	4	5

Uses one or more coping skills to deal with anger/frustration:

ALMOST NEVER	USUALLY NOT	SOMETIMES	USUALLY	ALMOST ALWAYS
1	2	3	4	5

Recognizes displaced anger:

ALMOST NEVER	USUALLY NOT	SOMETIMES	USUALLY	ALMOST ALWAYS
1	2	3	4	5

Understands the difference between controlling behavior and controlling feelings:

ALMOST NEVER	USUALLY NOT	SOMETIMES	USUALLY	ALMOST ALWAYS
1	2	3	4	5

Verbalizes angry/frustrated feelings without violating the rights of others:

ALMOST NEVER	USUALLY NOT	SOMETIMES	USUALLY	ALMOST ALWAYS
1	2	3	4	5

16. Dealing with Grief and Loss

Recognizes one or more types of loss that can result in grief:

ALMOST NEVER	USUALLY NOT	SOMETIMES	USUALLY	ALMOST ALWAYS
1	2	3	4	5

Recognizes stages of grief:

ALMOST NEVER	USUALLY NOT	SOMETIMES	USUALLY	ALMOST ALWAYS
1	2	3	4	5

Lists one or more helpful activities to deal with grief/loss:

ALMOST NEVER	USUALLY NOT	SOMETIMES	USUALLY	ALMOST ALWAYS
1	2	3	4	5

Understands one positive aspect to grief/loss:

ALMOST NEVER	USUALLY NOT	SOMETIMES	USUALLY	ALMOST ALWAYS
1	2	3	4	5

3. Personal Hygiene, Self-Care, and Manners

17. Personal Hygiene

Identifies two or more areas of personal cleanliness/hygiene:

ALMOST NEVER	USUALLY NOT	SOMETIMES	USUALLY	ALMOST ALWAYS
1	2	3	4	5

Identifies one or more areas of personal space that require cleanliness:

ALMOST NEVER	USUALLY NOT	SOMETIMES	USUALLY	ALMOST ALWAYS
1	2	3	4	5

Lists one or more food hygiene skills:

ALMOST NEVER	USUALLY NOT	SOMETIMES	USUALLY	ALMOST ALWAYS
1	2	3	4	5

Understands why personal hygiene/cleanliness is important:

ALMOST NEVER	USUALLY NOT	SOMETIMES	USUALLY	ALMOST ALWAYS
1	2	3	4	5

18. Courtesy, Public Manners, and Socially Offensive Behaviors

Says, "Please," "Thank you," and "Excuse me," at appropriate times:

ALMOST NEVER	USUALLY NOT	SOMETIMES	USUALLY	ALMOST ALWAYS
1	2	3	4	5

Listens without interrupting:

ALMOST NEVER	USUALLY NOT	SOMETIMES	USUALLY	ALMOST ALWAYS
1	2	3	4	5

Speaks politely, without sarcasm, abruptness, and rudeness:

ALMOST NEVER	USUALLY NOT	SOMETIMES	USUALLY	ALMOST ALWAYS
1	2	3	4	5

Smiles, compliments, and shows an interest in others:

ALMOST NEVER	USUALLY NOT	SOMETIMES	USUALLY	ALMOST ALWAYS
1	2	3	4	5

Speaks in a normal tone of voice:

ALMOST NEVER	USUALLY NOT	SOMETIMES	USUALLY	ALMOST ALWAYS
1	2	3	4	5

Waits for others, holds doors, takes turns and shares things with others:

ALMOST NEVER	USUALLY NOT	SOMETIMES	USUALLY	ALMOST ALWAYS
1	2	3	4	5

Helps others at appropriate times:

ALMOST NEVER	USUALLY NOT	SOMETIMES	USUALLY	ALMOST ALWAYS
1	2	3	4	5

Follows simple directions:

ALMOST NEVER	USUALLY NOT	SOMETIMES	USUALLY	ALMOST ALWAYS
1	2	3	4	5

19. Self-Control

Controls behavior when angry or upset:

ALMOST NEVER	USUALLY NOT	SOMETIMES	USUALLY	ALMOST ALWAYS
1	2	3	4	5

Thinks ahead to avoid losing control when upset:

ALMOST NEVER	USUALLY NOT	SOMETIMES	USUALLY	ALMOST ALWAYS
1	2	3	4	5

20. Dealing with Frustration

Waits patiently for people and things:

ALMOST NEVER	USUALLY NOT	SOMETIMES	USUALLY	ALMOST ALWAYS
1	2	3	4	5

Handles disappointment, letdown, and anger without negative behaviors:

ALMOST NEVER	USUALLY NOT	SOMETIMES	USUALLY	ALMOST ALWAYS
1	2	3	4	5

Reacts calmly when having to wait for things:

ALMOST NEVER	USUALLY NOT	SOMETIMES	USUALLY	ALMOST ALWAYS
1	2	3	4	5

Thinks calmly about possible solutions to problems without a display of anger, irritability, and negative emotions:

ALMOST NEVER	USUALLY NOT	SOMETIMES	USUALLY	ALMOST ALWAYS
1	2	3	4	5

Tells oneself an appropriate positive message if unable to have something immediately:

ALMOST NEVER	USUALLY NOT	SOMETIMES	USUALLY	ALMOST ALWAYS
1	2	3	4	5

Recognizes one active and one passive coping skill:

ALMOST NEVER	USUALLY NOT	SOMETIMES	USUALLY	ALMOST ALWAYS
1	2	3	4	5

21. Respect for Others

Recites the Golden Rule:

ALMOST NEVER	USUALLY NOT	SOMETIMES	USUALLY	ALMOST ALWAYS
1	2	3	4	5

Recognizes polite behaviors:

ALMOST NEVER	USUALLY NOT	SOMETIMES	USUALLY	ALMOST ALWAYS
1	2	3	4	5

Recognizes generous behaviors:

ALMOST NEVER	USUALLY NOT	SOMETIMES	USUALLY	ALMOST ALWAYS
1	2	3	4	5

Understands how to ask questions to get to know someone better:

ALMOST NEVER	USUALLY NOT	SOMETIMES	USUALLY	ALMOST ALWAYS
1	2	3	4	5

Avoids rude behaviors:

ALMOST NEVER	USUALLY NOT	SOMETIMES	USUALLY	ALMOST ALWAYS
1	2	3	4	5

4. Self-Esteem

22. Introduction and Cohesion Building

Recognizes/understands group topics and format:

ALMOST NEVER	USUALLY NOT	SOMETIMES	USUALLY	ALMOST ALWAYS
1	2	3	4	5

Understands group rules:

ALMOST NEVER	USUALLY NOT	SOMETIMES	USUALLY	ALMOST ALWAYS
1	2	3	4	5

Shares personal information; bonds with others:

ALMOST NEVER	USUALLY NOT	SOMETIMES	USUALLY	ALMOST ALWAYS
1	2	3	4	5

23. Basic Needs and Personal Growth Opportunities

Identifies basic needs:

ALMOST NEVER	USUALLY NOT	SOMETIMES	USUALLY	ALMOST ALWAYS
1	2	3	4	5

Identifies personal growth opportunities:

ALMOST NEVER	USUALLY NOT	SOMETIMES	USUALLY	ALMOST ALWAYS
1	2	3	4	5

Distinguishes between a *need* and a *want:*

ALMOST NEVER	USUALLY NOT	SOMETIMES	USUALLY	ALMOST ALWAYS
1	2	3	4	5

24. Self-Worth and Self-Acceptance

Lists several personal strengths:

ALMOST NEVER	USUALLY NOT	SOMETIMES	USUALLY	ALMOST ALWAYS
1	2	3	4	5

Identifies several personal weaknesses or things to change:

ALMOST NEVER	USUALLY NOT	SOMETIMES	USUALLY	ALMOST ALWAYS
1	2	3	4	5

Differentiates between personal *limits* and *inadequacies:*

ALMOST NEVER	USUALLY NOT	SOMETIMES	USUALLY	ALMOST ALWAYS
1	2	3	4	5

Identifies an area of potential self-fulfillment:

ALMOST NEVER	USUALLY NOT	SOMETIMES	USUALLY	ALMOST ALWAYS
1	2	3	4	5

Accepts oneself even if wanting to make changes:

ALMOST NEVER	USUALLY NOT	SOMETIMES	USUALLY	ALMOST ALWAYS
1	2	3	4	5

Understands the importance of self-improvement:

ALMOST NEVER	USUALLY NOT	SOMETIMES	USUALLY	ALMOST ALWAYS
1	2	3	4	5

25. Self-Esteem
    Verbalizes several positive self-statements:

ALMOST NEVER	USUALLY NOT	SOMETIMES	USUALLY	ALMOST ALWAYS
1	2	3	4	5

Recognizes positive and negative feelings related to self-esteem:

ALMOST NEVER	USUALLY NOT	SOMETIMES	USUALLY	ALMOST ALWAYS
1	2	3	4	5

26. Self-Identity
    Identifies similarities between self and others:

ALMOST NEVER	USUALLY NOT	SOMETIMES	USUALLY	ALMOST ALWAYS
1	2	3	4	5

Identifies differences between self and others:

ALMOST NEVER	USUALLY NOT	SOMETIMES	USUALLY	ALMOST ALWAYS
1	2	3	4	5

27. Personal History
    Recognizes the importance of a personal history:

ALMOST NEVER	USUALLY NOT	SOMETIMES	USUALLY	ALMOST ALWAYS
1	2	3	4	5

Shares personal history with others:

ALMOST NEVER	USUALLY NOT	SOMETIMES	USUALLY	ALMOST ALWAYS
1	2	3	4	5

Lists several important areas of personal history:

ALMOST NEVER	USUALLY NOT	SOMETIMES	USUALLY	ALMOST ALWAYS
1	2	3	4	5

28. Family Constellation
    Describes personal family tree:

ALMOST NEVER	USUALLY NOT	SOMETIMES	USUALLY	ALMOST ALWAYS
1	2	3	4	5

Differentiates between family of origin and current family situation if different:

ALMOST NEVER	USUALLY NOT	SOMETIMES	USUALLY	ALMOST ALWAYS
1	2	3	4	5

Understands concept of family boundaries:

ALMOST NEVER	USUALLY NOT	SOMETIMES	USUALLY	ALMOST ALWAYS
1	2	3	4	5

Recognizes family communication patterns:

ALMOST NEVER	USUALLY NOT	SOMETIMES	USUALLY	ALMOST ALWAYS
1	2	3	4	5

Identifies family values, roles, rules, and mythology:

ALMOST NEVER	USUALLY NOT	SOMETIMES	USUALLY	ALMOST ALWAYS
1	2	3	4	5

Recognizes family secrets:

ALMOST NEVER	USUALLY NOT	SOMETIMES	USUALLY	ALMOST ALWAYS
1	2	3	4	5

Identifies stresses and strains acting on family:

ALMOST NEVER	USUALLY NOT	SOMETIMES	USUALLY	ALMOST ALWAYS
1	2	3	4	5

Describes family member roles:

ALMOST NEVER	USUALLY NOT	SOMETIMES	USUALLY	ALMOST ALWAYS
1	2	3	4	5

Identifies family emotional tone:

ALMOST NEVER	USUALLY NOT	SOMETIMES	USUALLY	ALMOST ALWAYS
1	2	3	4	5

Describes family relationships with outsiders:

ALMOST NEVER	USUALLY NOT	SOMETIMES	USUALLY	ALMOST ALWAYS
1	2	3	4	5

Identifies major family member losses:

ALMOST NEVER	USUALLY NOT	SOMETIMES	USUALLY	ALMOST ALWAYS
1	2	3	4	5

29. Socialization

Identifies one or more social experiences:

ALMOST NEVER	USUALLY NOT	SOMETIMES	USUALLY	ALMOST ALWAYS
1	2	3	4	5

Recognizes why socialization is important:

ALMOST NEVER	USUALLY NOT	SOMETIMES	USUALLY	ALMOST ALWAYS
1	2	3	4	5

30. Nurturance

Understands the concept of nurturance:

ALMOST NEVER	USUALLY NOT	SOMETIMES	USUALLY	ALMOST ALWAYS
1	2	3	4	5

Identifies personal sources of nurturance:

ALMOST NEVER	USUALLY NOT	SOMETIMES	USUALLY	ALMOST ALWAYS
1	2	3	4	5

Lists one or more ways to influence others to provide nurturance:

ALMOST NEVER	USUALLY NOT	SOMETIMES	USUALLY	ALMOST ALWAYS
1	2	3	4	5

31. Guilt and Shame

Understands emotions of guilt and shame:

ALMOST NEVER	USUALLY NOT	SOMETIMES	USUALLY	ALMOST ALWAYS
1	2	3	4	5

Recognizes events that lead to the development of shame:

ALMOST NEVER	USUALLY NOT	SOMETIMES	USUALLY	ALMOST ALWAYS
1	2	3	4	5

Recognizes feelings that accompany guilt and shame:

ALMOST NEVER	USUALLY NOT	SOMETIMES	USUALLY	ALMOST ALWAYS
1	2	3	4	5

Lists one or more ways to deal with guilt and shame:

ALMOST NEVER	USUALLY NOT	SOMETIMES	USUALLY	ALMOST ALWAYS
1	2	3	4	5

32. Positive Self-Affirmations

Understands the concept of a positive self-affirmation:

ALMOST NEVER	USUALLY NOT	SOMETIMES	USUALLY	ALMOST ALWAYS
1	2	3	4	5

States several positive self-affirmations:

ALMOST NEVER	USUALLY NOT	SOMETIMES	USUALLY	ALMOST ALWAYS
1	2	3	4	5

Demonstrates the ability to direct mind away from negative thoughts:

ALMOST NEVER	USUALLY NOT	SOMETIMES	USUALLY	ALMOST ALWAYS
1	2	3	4	5

33. Wellness

Identifies several areas of wellness:

ALMOST NEVER	USUALLY NOT	SOMETIMES	USUALLY	ALMOST ALWAYS
1	2	3	4	5

States several ways to increase wellness:

ALMOST NEVER	USUALLY NOT	SOMETIMES	USUALLY	ALMOST ALWAYS
1	2	3	4	5

34. Physical and Mental Energy

Identifies physical and mental sources of energy:

ALMOST NEVER	USUALLY NOT	SOMETIMES	USUALLY	ALMOST ALWAYS
1	2	3	4	5

Identifies several reasons for physical/mental tiredness:

ALMOST NEVER	USUALLY NOT	SOMETIMES	USUALLY	ALMOST ALWAYS
1	2	3	4	5

States several methods to combat tiredness:

ALMOST NEVER	USUALLY NOT	SOMETIMES	USUALLY	ALMOST ALWAYS
1	2	3	4	5

5. Problem Solving and Conflict Management

35. Problem Solving

Lists different types of problems:

ALMOST NEVER	USUALLY NOT	SOMETIMES	USUALLY	ALMOST ALWAYS
1	2	3	4	5

Identifies what is a conflict:

ALMOST NEVER	USUALLY NOT	SOMETIMES	USUALLY	ALMOST ALWAYS
1	2	3	4	5

States personal feelings about a problem:

ALMOST NEVER	USUALLY NOT	SOMETIMES	USUALLY	ALMOST ALWAYS
1	2	3	4	5

States more than one possible alternative to solve a problem:

ALMOST NEVER	USUALLY NOT	SOMETIMES	USUALLY	ALMOST ALWAYS
1	2	3	4	5

Picks one of several possible solutions to a problem:

ALMOST NEVER	USUALLY NOT	SOMETIMES	USUALLY	ALMOST ALWAYS
1	2	3	4	5

36. Making Decisions

Understands what is a decision:

ALMOST NEVER	USUALLY NOT	SOMETIMES	USUALLY	ALMOST ALWAYS
1	2	3	4	5

Recognizes that making a choice involves picking between alternatives:

ALMOST NEVER	USUALLY NOT	SOMETIMES	USUALLY	ALMOST ALWAYS
1	2	3	4	5

Lists possible alternative choices in a decision-making process:

ALMOST NEVER	USUALLY NOT	SOMETIMES	USUALLY	ALMOST ALWAYS
1	2	3	4	5

Rules out less good alternatives in a decision-making process:

ALMOST NEVER	USUALLY NOT	SOMETIMES	USUALLY	ALMOST ALWAYS
1	2	3	4	5

Identifies different types of decisions:

ALMOST NEVER	USUALLY NOT	SOMETIMES	USUALLY	ALMOST ALWAYS
1	2	3	4	5

Recognizes one or more stressors associated with decisions:

ALMOST NEVER	USUALLY NOT	SOMETIMES	USUALLY	ALMOST ALWAYS
1	2	3	4	5

Follows through on decisions/choices:

ALMOST NEVER	USUALLY NOT	SOMETIMES	USUALLY	ALMOST ALWAYS
1	2	3	4	5

37. Asking for Help

Recognizes various sources of help:

ALMOST NEVER	USUALLY NOT	SOMETIMES	USUALLY	ALMOST ALWAYS
1	2	3	4	5

Recognizes several situations that may necessitate help:

ALMOST NEVER	USUALLY NOT	SOMETIMES	USUALLY	ALMOST ALWAYS
1	2	3	4	5

Understands how and when to ask for help:

ALMOST NEVER	USUALLY NOT	SOMETIMES	USUALLY	ALMOST ALWAYS
1	2	3	4	5

38. Getting Help for Personal Problems

Identifies one or more personal problems:

ALMOST NEVER	USUALLY NOT	SOMETIMES	USUALLY	ALMOST ALWAYS
1	2	3	4	5

Recognizes one or more persons who might help with a personal problem:

ALMOST NEVER	USUALLY NOT	SOMETIMES	USUALLY	ALMOST ALWAYS
1	2	3	4	5

Identifies one or more ways to work through personal problems:

ALMOST NEVER	USUALLY NOT	SOMETIMES	USUALLY	ALMOST ALWAYS
1	2	3	4	5

39. Following Directions

Listens to a person giving instructions:

ALMOST NEVER	USUALLY NOT	SOMETIMES	USUALLY	ALMOST ALWAYS
1	2	3	4	5

Makes eye contact:

ALMOST NEVER	USUALLY NOT	SOMETIMES	USUALLY	ALMOST ALWAYS
1	2	3	4	5

Pays attention to what others say:

ALMOST NEVER	USUALLY NOT	SOMETIMES	USUALLY	ALMOST ALWAYS
1	2	3	4	5

Complies with simple requests:

ALMOST NEVER	USUALLY NOT	SOMETIMES	USUALLY	ALMOST ALWAYS
1	2	3	4	5

Recognizes when it is necessary to follow directions:

ALMOST NEVER	USUALLY NOT	SOMETIMES	USUALLY	ALMOST ALWAYS
1	2	3	4	5

40. Keeping on Task

Focuses attention on a task:

ALMOST NEVER	USUALLY NOT	SOMETIMES	USUALLY	ALMOST ALWAYS
1	2	3	4	5

Stays on the topic of conversation:

ALMOST NEVER	USUALLY NOT	SOMETIMES	USUALLY	ALMOST ALWAYS
1	2	3	4	5

Ignores distractions during activities:

ALMOST NEVER	USUALLY NOT	SOMETIMES	USUALLY	ALMOST ALWAYS
1	2	3	4	5

Performs a task without interruptions:

ALMOST NEVER	USUALLY NOT	SOMETIMES	USUALLY	ALMOST ALWAYS
1	2	3	4	5

Self-monitors activities for specified time periods:

ALMOST NEVER	USUALLY NOT	SOMETIMES	USUALLY	ALMOST ALWAYS
1	2	3	4	5

41. Giving and Receiving Constructive Criticism

Understands the difference between constructive and destructive criticism:

ALMOST NEVER	USUALLY NOT	SOMETIMES	USUALLY	ALMOST ALWAYS
1	2	3	4	5

Effectively uses constructive criticism:

ALMOST NEVER	USUALLY NOT	SOMETIMES	USUALLY	ALMOST ALWAYS
1	2	3	4	5

Responds appropriately to constructive criticism:

ALMOST NEVER	USUALLY NOT	SOMETIMES	USUALLY	ALMOST ALWAYS
1	2	3	4	5

Responds appropriately to destructive criticism:

ALMOST NEVER	USUALLY NOT	SOMETIMES	USUALLY	ALMOST ALWAYS
1	2	3	4	5

42. Conflicts with Housemates, Family, and Friends

Understands what is a conflict:

ALMOST NEVER	USUALLY NOT	SOMETIMES	USUALLY	ALMOST ALWAYS
1	2	3	4	5

Recognizes one or more problems which may result in conflict:

ALMOST NEVER	USUALLY NOT	SOMETIMES	USUALLY	ALMOST ALWAYS
1	2	3	4	5

Identifies one or more positive ways to deal with conflict:

ALMOST NEVER	USUALLY NOT	SOMETIMES	USUALLY	ALMOST ALWAYS
1	2	3	4	5

Avoids negative reactions to conflict:

ALMOST NEVER	USUALLY NOT	SOMETIMES	USUALLY	ALMOST ALWAYS
1	2	3	4	5

43. Dealing with Negative Gossip, Teasing, and False Accusations

Recognizes negative gossip, teasing, and false accusations:

ALMOST NEVER	USUALLY NOT	SOMETIMES	USUALLY	ALMOST ALWAYS
1	2	3	4	5

Lists one or more ways in which gossip can hurt others:

ALMOST NEVER	USUALLY NOT	SOMETIMES	USUALLY	ALMOST ALWAYS
1	2	3	4	5

Lists one or more ways in which false accusations can hurt others:

ALMOST NEVER	USUALLY NOT	SOMETIMES	USUALLY	ALMOST ALWAYS
1	2	3	4	5

Lists one or more ways in which teasing can hurt others:

ALMOST NEVER	USUALLY NOT	SOMETIMES	USUALLY	ALMOST ALWAYS
1	2	3	4	5

Identifies one or more positive ways to respond to gossip, false accusations, and teasing:

ALMOST NEVER	USUALLY NOT	SOMETIMES	USUALLY	ALMOST ALWAYS
1	2	3	4	5

44. Staying Out of Others' Problems

Recognizes the difference between one's own and others' problems:

ALMOST NEVER	USUALLY NOT	SOMETIMES	USUALLY	ALMOST ALWAYS
1	2	3	4	5

Understands one or more ways to avoid getting involved in others' problems:

ALMOST NEVER	USUALLY NOT	SOMETIMES	USUALLY	ALMOST ALWAYS
1	2	3	4	5

45. Dealing with Mistreatment from Others

Recognizes various types of mistreatment:

ALMOST NEVER	USUALLY NOT	SOMETIMES	USUALLY	ALMOST ALWAYS
1	2	3	4	5

Recognizes one or more ways to deal with mistreatment:

ALMOST NEVER	USUALLY NOT	SOMETIMES	USUALLY	ALMOST ALWAYS
1	2	3	4	5

6. Friendship and Social Support

46. Making a Friend

Recognizes how to initiate a friendship:

ALMOST NEVER	USUALLY NOT	SOMETIMES	USUALLY	ALMOST ALWAYS
1	2	3	4	5

Lists several ways to be a friend to others:

ALMOST NEVER	USUALLY NOT	SOMETIMES	USUALLY	ALMOST ALWAYS
1	2	3	4	5

Recognizes where friendship fits into the range of relationships:

ALMOST NEVER	USUALLY NOT	SOMETIMES	USUALLY	ALMOST ALWAYS
1	2	3	4	5

47. Keeping a Friend

Recognizes the difference between a friend and other types of relationships:

ALMOST NEVER	USUALLY NOT	SOMETIMES	USUALLY	ALMOST ALWAYS
1	2	3	4	5

Identifies several ways to keep a friendship going:

ALMOST NEVER	USUALLY NOT	SOMETIMES	USUALLY	ALMOST ALWAYS
1	2	3	4	5

48. Giving and Receiving Support

Recognizes several types of support:

ALMOST NEVER	USUALLY NOT	SOMETIMES	USUALLY	ALMOST ALWAYS
1	2	3	4	5

Recognizes one or more ways to give support:

ALMOST NEVER	USUALLY NOT	SOMETIMES	USUALLY	ALMOST ALWAYS
1	2	3	4	5

Requests one or more types of support:

ALMOST NEVER	USUALLY NOT	SOMETIMES	USUALLY	ALMOST ALWAYS
1	2	3	4	5

49. Trusting Others

Recognizes the level of trustworthiness of others:

ALMOST NEVER	USUALLY NOT	SOMETIMES	USUALLY	ALMOST ALWAYS
1	2	3	4	5

Recognizes the difference between intentional and unintentional unreliability of others:

ALMOST NEVER	USUALLY NOT	SOMETIMES	USUALLY	ALMOST ALWAYS
1	2	3	4	5

7. Personal Boundaries and Sexuality

50. Personal Boundaries

Understands the concept of boundaries:

ALMOST NEVER	USUALLY NOT	SOMETIMES	USUALLY	ALMOST ALWAYS
1	2	3	4	5

Identifies different types of boundaries:

ALMOST NEVER	USUALLY NOT	SOMETIMES	USUALLY	ALMOST ALWAYS
1	2	3	4	5

51. Physical and Sexual Boundaries

Understands the concept of physical/sexual boundaries:

ALMOST NEVER	USUALLY NOT	SOMETIMES	USUALLY	ALMOST ALWAYS
1	2	3	4	5

Sets physical/sexual boundaries with others:

ALMOST NEVER	USUALLY NOT	SOMETIMES	USUALLY	ALMOST ALWAYS
1	2	3	4	5

52. Social Boundaries

Understands the concept of social boundaries:

ALMOST NEVER	USUALLY NOT	SOMETIMES	USUALLY	ALMOST ALWAYS
1	2	3	4	5

Sets social boundaries with others:

ALMOST NEVER	USUALLY NOT	SOMETIMES	USUALLY	ALMOST ALWAYS
1	2	3	4	5

53. Setting Boundaries

Identifies different types of boundaries:

ALMOST NEVER	USUALLY NOT	SOMETIMES	USUALLY	ALMOST ALWAYS
1	2	3	4	5

Differentiates good and bad touch:

ALMOST NEVER	USUALLY NOT	SOMETIMES	USUALLY	ALMOST ALWAYS
1	2	3	4	5

Identifies own versus others' thoughts/feelings:

ALMOST NEVER	USUALLY NOT	SOMETIMES	USUALLY	ALMOST ALWAYS
1	2	3	4	5

Identifies different types of social relationships:

ALMOST NEVER	USUALLY NOT	SOMETIMES	USUALLY	ALMOST ALWAYS
1	2	3	4	5

Identifies when and with whom one would like to be close:

ALMOST NEVER	USUALLY NOT	SOMETIMES	USUALLY	ALMOST ALWAYS
1	2	3	4	5

Understands how to establish closeness:

ALMOST NEVER	USUALLY NOT	SOMETIMES	USUALLY	ALMOST ALWAYS
1	2	3	4	5

Sets boundaries or limits with others:

ALMOST NEVER	USUALLY NOT	SOMETIMES	USUALLY	ALMOST ALWAYS
1	2	3	4	5

54. Different Kinds of Relationships

Recognizes different types of relationships:

ALMOST NEVER	USUALLY NOT	SOMETIMES	USUALLY	ALMOST ALWAYS
1	2	3	4	5

Recognizes different boundaries for different types of relationships:

ALMOST NEVER	USUALLY NOT	SOMETIMES	USUALLY	ALMOST ALWAYS
1	2	3	4	5

Recognizes different rules for different relationships:

ALMOST NEVER	USUALLY NOT	SOMETIMES	USUALLY	ALMOST ALWAYS
1	2	3	4	5

55. Public, Private, and Secret Behaviors

Understands the difference between public, private, and secret behaviors:

ALMOST NEVER	USUALLY NOT	SOMETIMES	USUALLY	ALMOST ALWAYS
1	2	3	4	5

Lists behaviors belonging to public, private, and secret domains:

ALMOST NEVER	USUALLY NOT	SOMETIMES	USUALLY	ALMOST ALWAYS
1	2	3	4	5

56. Borrowing and Stealing

Identifies the difference between borrowing and stealing:

ALMOST NEVER	USUALLY NOT	SOMETIMES	USUALLY	ALMOST ALWAYS
1	2	3	4	5

Recognizes appropriate borrowing:

ALMOST NEVER	USUALLY NOT	SOMETIMES	USUALLY	ALMOST ALWAYS
1	2	3	4	5

Identifies things that people borrow:

ALMOST NEVER	USUALLY NOT	SOMETIMES	USUALLY	ALMOST ALWAYS
1	2	3	4	5

Recognizes one or more problems that can happen when borrowing or loaning things:

ALMOST NEVER	USUALLY NOT	SOMETIMES	USUALLY	ALMOST ALWAYS
1	2	3	4	5

57. Communication and Personal Boundaries

Recognizes appropriate times and places to communicate personal information with others:

ALMOST NEVER	USUALLY NOT	SOMETIMES	USUALLY	ALMOST ALWAYS
1	2	3	4	5

Recognizes inappropriate times and places to communicate personal information with others:

ALMOST NEVER	USUALLY NOT	SOMETIMES	USUALLY	ALMOST ALWAYS
1	2	3	4	5

8. Developmental Issues

58. Individuation/Separation

Recognizes ways in which depends on others:

ALMOST NEVER	USUALLY NOT	SOMETIMES	USUALLY	ALMOST ALWAYS
1	2	3	4	5

Recognizes ways that has separated from caretakers and become more self-reliant:

ALMOST NEVER	USUALLY NOT	SOMETIMES	USUALLY	ALMOST ALWAYS
1	2	3	4	5

Recognizes ways that has established identity separate from others:

ALMOST NEVER	USUALLY NOT	SOMETIMES	USUALLY	ALMOST ALWAYS
1	2	3	4	5

Recognize ways that one thinks and behaves differently from parents or caretakers:

ALMOST NEVER	USUALLY NOT	SOMETIMES	USUALLY	ALMOST ALWAYS
1	2	3	4	5

59. Dependency/Independency

Recognizes on whom one depends:

ALMOST NEVER	USUALLY NOT	SOMETIMES	USUALLY	ALMOST ALWAYS
1	2	3	4	5

Recognizes how one depends on others:

ALMOST NEVER	USUALLY NOT	SOMETIMES	USUALLY	ALMOST ALWAYS
1	2	3	4	5

Recognizes personal issues related to dependency/independency:

ALMOST NEVER	USUALLY NOT	SOMETIMES	USUALLY	ALMOST ALWAYS
1	2	3	4	5

60. Boundaries between Self and Caretakers

Identifies boundaries between self and caretakers:

ALMOST NEVER	USUALLY NOT	SOMETIMES	USUALLY	ALMOST ALWAYS
1	2	3	4	5

Identifies rules and mutual expectations between self and caretakers:

ALMOST NEVER	USUALLY NOT	SOMETIMES	USUALLY	ALMOST ALWAYS
1	2	3	4	5

Identifies limits and extent of care by others:

ALMOST NEVER	USUALLY NOT	SOMETIMES	USUALLY	ALMOST ALWAYS
1	2	3	4	5

Recognizes good and bad care from others:

ALMOST NEVER	USUALLY NOT	SOMETIMES	USUALLY	ALMOST ALWAYS
1	2	3	4	5

61. Losses

Recognizes possible types of losses:

ALMOST NEVER	USUALLY NOT	SOMETIMES	USUALLY	ALMOST ALWAYS
1	2	3	4	5

Understands the grief process related to losses:

ALMOST NEVER	USUALLY NOT	SOMETIMES	USUALLY	ALMOST ALWAYS
1	2	3	4	5

Recognizes the inevitability of losses:

ALMOST NEVER	USUALLY NOT	SOMETIMES	USUALLY	ALMOST ALWAYS
1	2	3	4	5

62. Death and Loss

Recognizes the inevitability of death and loss:

ALMOST NEVER	USUALLY NOT	SOMETIMES	USUALLY	ALMOST ALWAYS
1	2	3	4	5

Recognizes important aspects of the grief process:

ALMOST NEVER	USUALLY NOT	SOMETIMES	USUALLY	ALMOST ALWAYS
1	2	3	4	5

63. The Aging Process

Recognizes various bodily changes associated with aging:

ALMOST NEVER	USUALLY NOT	SOMETIMES	USUALLY	ALMOST ALWAYS
1	2	3	4	5

Recognizes one or more losses connected with aging:

ALMOST NEVER	USUALLY NOT	SOMETIMES	USUALLY	ALMOST ALWAYS
1	2	3	4	5

Lists at least one positive aspect of growing older:

ALMOST NEVER	USUALLY NOT	SOMETIMES	USUALLY	ALMOST ALWAYS
1	2	3	4	5

Recognizes personal self-coancept changes accompanying the aging process:

ALMOST NEVER	USUALLY NOT	SOMETIMES	USUALLY	ALMOST ALWAYS
1	2	3	4	5

Recognizes social changes with ongoing age:

ALMOST NEVER	USUALLY NOT	SOMETIMES	USUALLY	ALMOST ALWAYS
1	2	3	4	5

Recognizes activity changes related to aging:

ALMOST NEVER	USUALLY NOT	SOMETIMES	USUALLY	ALMOST ALWAYS
1	2	3	4	5

64. Negative Labels and Ostracism

Recognizes the concepts of negative label and ostracism:

ALMOST NEVER	USUALLY NOT	SOMETIMES	USUALLY	ALMOST ALWAYS
1	2	3	4	5

Recognizes the reality of own limitations or disability:

ALMOST NEVER	USUALLY NOT	SOMETIMES	USUALLY	ALMOST ALWAYS
1	2	3	4	5

Recognizes positive aspects of self unrelated to disability:

ALMOST NEVER	USUALLY NOT	SOMETIMES	USUALLY	ALMOST ALWAYS
1	2	3	4	5

65. Family Illness

Identifies different types of family illness:

ALMOST NEVER	USUALLY NOT	SOMETIMES	USUALLY	ALMOST ALWAYS
1	2	3	4	5

Recognizes short- and long-term disability caused by illness:

ALMOST NEVER	USUALLY NOT	SOMETIMES	USUALLY	ALMOST ALWAYS
1	2	3	4	5

Identifies effects of illness on one's own family:

ALMOST NEVER	USUALLY NOT	SOMETIMES	USUALLY	ALMOST ALWAYS
1	2	3	4	5

66. Intimacy

Recognizes different methods to gain attention or affection from others:

ALMOST NEVER	USUALLY NOT	SOMETIMES	USUALLY	ALMOST ALWAYS
1	2	3	4	5

Recognizes the difference between different kinds of intimate relationships:

ALMOST NEVER	USUALLY NOT	SOMETIMES	USUALLY	ALMOST ALWAYS
1	2	3	4	5

Recognizes different types of closeness in relationships:

ALMOST NEVER	USUALLY NOT	SOMETIMES	USUALLY	ALMOST ALWAYS
1	2	3	4	5

67. Friendship, Dating, and Sexual Relationships

Recognizes the difference between a dating relationship and friendship:

ALMOST NEVER	USUALLY NOT	SOMETIMES	USUALLY	ALMOST ALWAYS
1	2	3	4	5

Recognizes when a sexual relationship is appropriate or inappropriate:

ALMOST NEVER	USUALLY NOT	SOMETIMES	USUALLY	ALMOST ALWAYS
1	2	3	4	5

Recognizes the special arrangements necessary to go on a date:

ALMOST NEVER	USUALLY NOT	SOMETIMES	USUALLY	ALMOST ALWAYS
1	2	3	4	5

Recognizes possible negative consequences to a sexual relationship:

ALMOST NEVER	USUALLY NOT	SOMETIMES	USUALLY	ALMOST ALWAYS
1	2	3	4	5

68. Dealing with the Loss of a Friendship

Identifies possible reasons for the loss of a friendship:

ALMOST NEVER	USUALLY NOT	SOMETIMES	USUALLY	ALMOST ALWAYS
1	2	3	4	5

Identifies appropriate and inappropriate ways to react to the loss of a friend:

ALMOST NEVER	USUALLY NOT	SOMETIMES	USUALLY	ALMOST ALWAYS
1	2	3	4	5

69. Family and Residence Rules: Living with Others

Identifies positive benefits of family or residence rules:

ALMOST NEVER	USUALLY NOT	SOMETIMES	USUALLY	ALMOST ALWAYS
1	2	3	4	5

9. Self-Advocacy

70. Recognizing Personal Rights

Recognizes personal right to make choices about friends, activities, school, and/or work:

ALMOST NEVER	USUALLY NOT	SOMETIMES	USUALLY	ALMOST ALWAYS
1	2	3	4	5

Recognizes own opinions, thoughts, and feelings about important matters:

ALMOST NEVER	USUALLY NOT	SOMETIMES	USUALLY	ALMOST ALWAYS
1	2	3	4	5

Recognizes the difference between respectful/humane and disrespectful/inhumane treatment:

ALMOST NEVER	USUALLY NOT	SOMETIMES	USUALLY	ALMOST ALWAYS
1	2	3	4	5

71. Advocating for Personal Needs and Concerns

Recognizes when others unreasonably try to restrict self-expressions and choices:

ALMOST NEVER	USUALLY NOT	SOMETIMES	USUALLY	ALMOST ALWAYS
1	2	3	4	5

Identifies inhumane or undignified treatment:

ALMOST NEVER	USUALLY NOT	SOMETIMES	USUALLY	ALMOST ALWAYS
1	2	3	4	5

Effectively advocates for personal needs and concerns:

ALMOST NEVER	USUALLY NOT	SOMETIMES	USUALLY	ALMOST ALWAYS
1	2	3	4	5

72. Proactive Behavior
Understands the concept of proactive behavior:

ALMOST NEVER	USUALLY NOT	SOMETIMES	USUALLY	ALMOST ALWAYS
1	2	3	4	5

Recognizes one or more proactive ways to relate to the world:

ALMOST NEVER	USUALLY NOT	SOMETIMES	USUALLY	ALMOST ALWAYS
1	2	3	4	5

73. Differentiating between Aggressive, Passive, and Assertive Language/Behavior
Says what one feels:

ALMOST NEVER	USUALLY NOT	SOMETIMES	USUALLY	ALMOST ALWAYS
1	2	3	4	5

Says what one thinks:

ALMOST NEVER	USUALLY NOT	SOMETIMES	USUALLY	ALMOST ALWAYS
1	2	3	4	5

Recognizes and asks for what one wants/needs:

ALMOST NEVER	USUALLY NOT	SOMETIMES	USUALLY	ALMOST ALWAYS
1	2	3	4	5

Recognizes personal rights:

ALMOST NEVER	USUALLY NOT	SOMETIMES	USUALLY	ALMOST ALWAYS
1	2	3	4	5

Recognizes when and where to be assertive:

ALMOST NEVER	USUALLY NOT	SOMETIMES	USUALLY	ALMOST ALWAYS
1	2	3	4	5

Repeats questions/requests or seeks help when it is appropriate to be assertive:

ALMOST NEVER	USUALLY NOT	SOMETIMES	USUALLY	ALMOST ALWAYS
1	2	3	4	5

Recognizes the difference between *passive, aggressive,* and *assertive* responses:

ALMOST NEVER	USUALLY NOT	SOMETIMES	USUALLY	ALMOST ALWAYS
1	2	3	4	5

74. Appropriate Application of Assertiveness
Identifies a variety of life situations calling for assertive behaviors:

ALMOST NEVER	USUALLY NOT	SOMETIMES	USUALLY	ALMOST ALWAYS
1	2	3	4	5

Effectively advocates for self using a variety of assertive responses:

ALMOST NEVER	USUALLY NOT	SOMETIMES	USUALLY	ALMOST ALWAYS
1	2	3	4	5

Asks for help when self-advocacy is ineffective:

ALMOST NEVER	USUALLY NOT	SOMETIMES	USUALLY	ALMOST ALWAYS
1	2	3	4	5

10. Applications of Social Skills in Community Living

Part I. Living in the Community

75. Planning Activities

Recognizes a variety of possible recreational/leisure activities:

ALMOST NEVER	USUALLY NOT	SOMETIMES	USUALLY	ALMOST ALWAYS
1	2	3	4	5

Knows how to find community activities:

ALMOST NEVER	USUALLY NOT	SOMETIMES	USUALLY	ALMOST ALWAYS
1	2	3	4	5

Plans/organizes activities:

ALMOST NEVER	USUALLY NOT	SOMETIMES	USUALLY	ALMOST ALWAYS
1	2	3	4	5

76. Community Activities

Understands what is a community activity:

ALMOST NEVER	USUALLY NOT	SOMETIMES	USUALLY	ALMOST ALWAYS
1	2	3	4	5

Recognizes positive behaviors necessary in the community:

ALMOST NEVER	USUALLY NOT	SOMETIMES	USUALLY	ALMOST ALWAYS
1	2	3	4	5

Knows how to ask for help to participate in community activities:

ALMOST NEVER	USUALLY NOT	SOMETIMES	USUALLY	ALMOST ALWAYS
1	2	3	4	5

77. Reality Orientation

Recognizes what is happening around oneself (e.g., family, friends, work/school, community, world):

ALMOST NEVER	USUALLY NOT	SOMETIMES	USUALLY	ALMOST ALWAYS
1	2	3	4	5

Recognizes calendar events and occurrences:

ALMOST NEVER	USUALLY NOT	SOMETIMES	USUALLY	ALMOST ALWAYS
1	2	3	4	5

Orients oneself in time and space:

ALMOST NEVER	USUALLY NOT	SOMETIMES	USUALLY	ALMOST ALWAYS
1	2	3	4	5

Recalls conversations with others:

ALMOST NEVER	USUALLY NOT	SOMETIMES	USUALLY	ALMOST ALWAYS
1	2	3	4	5

Understands how one appears to others:

ALMOST NEVER	USUALLY NOT	SOMETIMES	USUALLY	ALMOST ALWAYS
1	2	3	4	5

78. Transportation

Identifies different types of transportation:

ALMOST NEVER	USUALLY NOT	SOMETIMES	USUALLY	ALMOST ALWAYS
1	2	3	4	5

Identifies one or more problems that may occur with different types of transportation:

ALMOST NEVER	USUALLY NOT	SOMETIMES	USUALLY	ALMOST ALWAYS
1	2	3	4	5

79. Recognizing and Avoiding Dangers

Recognizes several possible dangers in everyday living:

ALMOST NEVER	USUALLY NOT	SOMETIMES	USUALLY	ALMOST ALWAYS
1	2	3	4	5

Recognizes a variety of persons who may take advantage of oneself:

ALMOST NEVER	USUALLY NOT	SOMETIMES	USUALLY	ALMOST ALWAYS
1	2	3	4	5

Identifies ways to avoid danger:

ALMOST NEVER	USUALLY NOT	SOMETIMES	USUALLY	ALMOST ALWAYS
1	2	3	4	5

80. Money

Recognizes own money:

ALMOST NEVER	USUALLY NOT	SOMETIMES	USUALLY	ALMOST ALWAYS
1	2	3	4	5

Understands different sources of money:

ALMOST NEVER	USUALLY NOT	SOMETIMES	USUALLY	ALMOST ALWAYS
1	2	3	4	5

Identifies persons who help with money:

ALMOST NEVER	USUALLY NOT	SOMETIMES	USUALLY	ALMOST ALWAYS
1	2	3	4	5

Recognizes one or more methods to ensure fair treatment with money:

ALMOST NEVER	USUALLY NOT	SOMETIMES	USUALLY	ALMOST ALWAYS
1	2	3	4	5

81. What to Do If You Lose Your Purse or Wallet

Recognizes the importance of wallet or pocketbook contents:

ALMOST NEVER	USUALLY NOT	SOMETIMES	USUALLY	ALMOST ALWAYS
1	2	3	4	5

Understands what to do if one loses one's wallet or pocketbook:

ALMOST NEVER	USUALLY NOT	SOMETIMES	USUALLY	ALMOST ALWAYS
1	2	3	4	5

Part II. Keeping a Job

82. Getting Along with Co-Workers
    Identifies the Golden Rule:

ALMOST NEVER	USUALLY NOT	SOMETIMES	USUALLY	ALMOST ALWAYS
1	2	3	4	5

Identifies several positive ways to treat others:

ALMOST NEVER	USUALLY NOT	SOMETIMES	USUALLY	ALMOST ALWAYS
1	2	3	4	5

83. Critical Social Behaviors at Work
    Recognizes various behaviors necessary to keep a job:

ALMOST NEVER	USUALLY NOT	SOMETIMES	USUALLY	ALMOST ALWAYS
1	2	3	4	5

Bibliography

Akridge, R. L., Farley, R. C., & Rice, B. D. (1987). An empirical evaluation of the effects of peer counseling training on a sample of vocational rehabilitation facility clients. *Journal of Applied Rehabilitation Counseling, 18*(3), 20–24.

American Psychiatric Association. (1994). *Diagnostic and statistical manual of mental disorders* (4th ed.). Washington, DC: Author.

Anderson, D. J., Lakin, K. C., Hill, B. K., & Chen, T. H. (1992). Social integration of older persons with mental retardation in residential facilities. *American Journal on Mental Retardation, 96*(5), 488–501.

Andron, L., & Sturm, M. L. (1973). Is "I do" in the repertoire of the mentally retarded? *Mental Retardation, 11*, 31–34.

Baran, F. N. (1972). Group therapy improves mental retardates' behavior. *Hospital and Community Psychiatry, 23*, 7–11.

Bates, P. (1980). The effectiveness of interpersonal skills training on the social skill acquisition of moderately and mildly retarded adults. *Journal of Applied Behavior Analysis, 13*, 237–248.

Benson, B. (1992). *Teaching anger management to persons with mental retardation*. Chicago, IL: International Diagnostics Systems.

Berliner, A. K. (1986). Overcoming obstacles to counseling with the mentally retarded. *British Journal of Mental Subnormality, 32*(62, Part 1), 42–48.

Bradway, K. P. (1937). Social competence of exceptional children: I. Measurements of social competence. *Journal of Exceptional Children, 4*, 38–42, 64–69.

Castles, E. E., & Glass, C. R. (1986). Empirical generation of measures of social competence for mentally retarded adults. *Behavioral Assessment, 8*(4), 319–330.

Cavaiuolo, D., & Nasca, M. (1991). The relevance of social survival skills in job retention of workers with mental retardation. *Vocational Evaluation and Work Adjustment Bulletin, 24*(1), 27–31.

Chadsey-Rusch, J. (1992). Toward defining and measuring social skills in employment settings. *American Journal on Mental Retardation, 96*(4), 405–418.

Chadsey-Rusch, J., DeStefano, L., O'Reilly, M., Gonzalez, P., & Collet-Klingberg, L. (1992). Assessing the loneliness of workers with mental retardation. *Mental Retardation, 30*(2), 85–92.

Charlesworth, W. R. (1987). Resources and resource acquisition during ontogeny. In MacDonald, K. B. (Ed.), *Sociobiological perspectives on human development* (pp. 42–117). New York: Springer-Verlag.

Clegg, J. A., & Standen, P. J. (1991). Friendship among adults who have developmental disabilities. *American Journal on Mental Retardation, 95*(6), 663–671.

Collet-Klingberg, L., & Chadsey-Rusch, J. (1991). Using a cognitive-process approach to teach social skills. *Education and Training in Mental Retardation, 36*(3), 258–270.

Cotzin, M. (1948). Group psychotherapy with mentally defective problem boys. *American Journal of Mental Deficiency, 53*, 268–283.

Darwin, C. (1962). *The origin of species*. New York: Collier-Macmillan.

Doll, E. A. (1945). Influence of environment and etiology on social competence. *American Journal of Mental Deficiency, 50*(1), 89–94.

Fletcher, R. (1984, June). Group therapy with mentally retarded persons with emotional disorders. *Psychiatric Aspects of Mental Retardation Reviews, 3*(6), 21–24

Foxx, R. M., & Faw, G. D. (1992). An eight-year follow-up of three social skills training studies. *Mental Retardation, 30*(2), 63–66.

Foxx, R. M., McMorrow, M. J., Storey, K., & Rogers, B. M. (1984). Teaching social/sexual skills to mentally retarded adults. *American Journal of Mental Deficiency, 89*(1), 9–15.

Fritz, M. F. (1990). A comparison of social interactions using a friendship awareness activity. *Education and Training in Mental Retardation, 25*(4), 352–359.

Gorlow, L., Butler, A., Einig, K. G., & Smith, J. A. (1963). An appraisal of self-attitudes and behavior following group psychotherapy with retarded young adults. *American Journal of Mental Deficiency, 67*, 893–898.

Greenspan, S., & Granfield, J. M. (1992). Reconsidering the construct of mental retardation: Implications of a model of social competence. *American Journal on Mental Retardation, 96*(4), 442–453.

Gresham, F. M., & Elliott, S. N. (1993). Social skills intervention guide: Systematic approaches to social skills training. *Special Services in the Schools, 8*(1), 137–158.

Guralnick, M. J. (1990). Social competence and early intervention. *Journal of Early Intervention, 14*(1), 3–14.

Haring, T. G., & Breen, C. G. (1992). A peer-mediated social network intervention to enhance the social integration of persons with moderate and severe disabilities. *Journal of Applied Behavior Analysis, 25*(2), 319–333.

Haseltine, B., & Miltenberger, R. G. (1990). Teaching self-protection skills to persons with mental retardation. *American Journal on Mental Retardation, 95*(2), 188–197.

Hayden, M. F., Lakin, K. C., Hill, B. K., Bruininks, R. H., & Copher, J. I. (1992). Social and leisure integration of people with mental retardation in foster homes and small group homes. *Education and Training in Mental Retardation, 27*(3), 187–199.

Healey, K. N., & Masterpasqua, F. (1992). Interpersonal cognitive problem-solving among children with mental retardation. *American Journal on Mental Retardation, 96*(4), 367–372.

Helsel, W. J., & Matson, J. L. (1988). The relationship of depression to social skills and intellectual functioning in mentally retarded adults. *Journal of Mental Deficiency Research, 32*(5), 411–418.

Herbert, J. T., & Ishikawa, T. (1991). Employment-related interpersonal competence among workers with mental retardation. *Vocational Evaluation and Work Adjustment Bulletin, 24*(3), 87–94.

Hobson, R. P. (1993). The emotional origins of social understanding. *Philosophical Psychology, 6*(3), 227–249.

Jackson, D. A., Jackson, N. F., Bennett, M. L., Bynum, D. M., & Faryna, E. (1991). *Learning to get along: Social effectiveness training for people with developmental disabilities.* Champaign, IL: Research Press.

Jageman, L. W., & Myers, J. E. (1987). A conceptual model for counseling adult mentally retarded persons. *Journal of Applied Rehabilitation Counseling, 18*(1), 17–21.

Kaldeck, R. (1958). Group psychotherapy with mentally defective adolescents and adults. *International Journal of Group Psychotherapy, 8,* 185–192.

Kamps, D. M., Dugan, E. P., Leonard, B. R., & Daoust, P. M. (1994). Enhanced small group instruction using choral responding and student interaction for children with autism and developmental disabilities. *American Journal on Mental Retardation, 99*(1), 60–73.

Kamps, D. M., Leonard, B. R., Vernon, S., Dugan, E. P., & Delquadri, J. C. (1992). Teaching social skills to students with autism to increase peer interactions in an integrated first-grade classroom. *Journal of Applied Behavior Analysis, 25,* 281–288.

Kopp, C. B., Baker, B. L., & Brown, K. W. (1992). Social skills and their correlates: Preschoolers with developmental delays. *American Journal on Mental Retardation, 96*(4), 357–366.

Krantz, P. J., & McClannihan, L. E. (1993). Teaching children with autism to initiate to peers: Effects of a script-fading procedure. *Journal of Applied Behavior Analysis, 26,* 121–132.

Krauss, M. W., Seltzer, M. M., & Goodman, S. J. (1992). Social support networks of adults with mental retardation who live at home. *American Journal on Mental Retardation, 96*(4), 432–441.

Kübler-Ross, E. (1969). *On death and dying.* New York: Macmillan.

Lancioni, G. E. (1982). Normal children as tutors to teach social responses to withdrawn mentally retarded schoolmates: Training, maintenance, and generalization. *Journal of Applied Behavior Analysis, 15*(1), 17–40.

Laterza, P. (1979). An eclectic approach to group work with the mentally retarded. *Social Work with Groups, 2*(3), 235–245.

Lee, D. Y. (1977). Evaluation of a group counseling program designed to enhance social adjustment of mentally retarded adults. *Journal of Counseling Psychology, 24*(4), 318–323.

Lignugaris-Kraft, B., Salzberg, C. L., Rule, S., & Stowitschek, J. J. (1988). Social-vocational skills of workers with and without mental retardation in two community employment sites. *Mental Retardation, 26*(5), 297–305.

Lindsay, W. R., & Baty, F. J. (1989). Group relaxation training with adults who are mentally handicapped. *Behavioral Psychotherapy, 17*(1), 43–51.

Long, N. (1988). Training social skills to severely mentally retarded multiply handicapped adolescents. *Research in Developmental Disabilities, 9*(2), 195–208.

Lovett, D. L., & Harris, M. B. (1987). Identification of important community living skills for adults with mental retardation. *Rehabilitation Counseling Bulletin, 31*(1), 34–41.

Maslow, A. H. (1970). *Motivation and Personality,* 2nd ed. New York: Harper & Row.

Mathias, J. L., & Nettelbeck, T. (1992). Reliability of seven measures of social intelligence in a sample of adolescents with mental retardation. *Research in Developmental Disabilities, 13*(2), 131–143.

Mathias, J., & Nettelbeck, T. (1992). Validity of Greenspan's models of adaptive and social intelligence. *Research in Developmental Disabilities, 13*(2), 113–129.

Matson, J. L., & Barrett, R. P. (1993). *Psychopathology in the mentally retarded.* Boston: Allyn and Bacon.

Matson, J. L., & Senatore, V. (1981). A comparison of traditional psychotherapy and social skills training for improving interpersonal functioning of mentally retarded adults. *Behavior Therapy, 12,* 369–382.

May, E., House, W. C., & Kovacs, K. V. (1982). Group relaxation therapy to improve coping with stress. *Psychotherapy: Theory, Research and Practice, 19*(1), 102–109.

Meyer, L. H., Cole, D. A., McQuarter, R., & Reichle, J. (1990). Validation of the assessment of social competence (ASC) for children and young adults with developmental disabilities. *Journal of the Association for Persons with Severe Handicaps, 15*(2), 57–68.

Miezio, S. (1967). Group therapy with mentally retarded adolescents in institutional settings. *International Journal of Group Psychotherapy, 17,* 321–327.

Minskoff, E. H. (1980). Teaching approach for developing nonverbal communication skills in students with social perception deficits: Part I. The basic approach and body language clues. *Journal of Learning Disabilities, 13,* 118–124.

Minskoff, E. H. (1980). Teaching approach for developing nonverbal communication skills in students with social perception deficits: Part II. Proxemic, vocalic, and artifactual cues. *Journal of Learning Disabilities, 13*(4), 203–208.

Misra, A. (1992). Generation of social skills through self-monitoring by adults with mild mental retardation. *Exceptional Children, 58*(6), 495–507.

Morgan, R. L., & Salzberg, C. L. (1992). Effects of video-assisted training on employment-related social skills of adults with severe mental retardation. *Journal of Applied Behavior Analysis, 25,* 365–383.

National Information Center for Handicapped Children and Youth. (1987). *Social skills* (No. 6), pp. 1–7. Washington, DC: U. S. Government Printing Office.

Newton, J. S., & Horner, R. H. (1993). Using a social guide to improve social relationships of people with severe disabilities. *Journal of the Association for Persons with Severe Handicaps, 18*(1), 36–45.

O'Dononue, W., & Krasner, L. (Eds.). (1995). *Handbook of psychological skills training: Clinical techniques and applications.* Boston: Allyn and Bacon.

Oswald, D. P., & Ollendick, T. H. (1989). Role taking and social competence in autism and mental retardation. *Journal of Autism and Developmental Disorders, 19*(1), 119–127.

Ouellette, L., Horner, R. H., & Newton, J. S. (1994). Changing activity patterns to improve social networks: A descriptive analysis. *Behavioral Interventions, 9*(1), 55–66.

Park, H. S., & Gaylord-Ross, R. (1989). A problem-solving approach to social skills training in employment settings with mentally retarded youth. *Journal of Applied Behavior Analysis, 22*(4), 373–380.

Perry, M., & Cerreto, M. C. (1977). Structured learning training of social skills for the retarded. *Mental Retardation, 15,* 31–34.

Pfadt, A. (1991). Group psychotherapy with mentally retarded adults: Issues related to design, implementation, and evaluation. *Research in Developmental Disabilities, 12,* 261–285.

Pray, B. S., Hall, C. W., & Markley, R. P. (1992). Social skills training: An analysis of social behaviors selected for individualized education programs. *Remedial and Special Education, 13*(5), 43–49.

Quinn, J. M., Sherman, J. A., Sheldon, J. B., Quinn, L. M., & Harchik, A. E. (1992). Social validation of component behaviors of following instructions, accepting criticism, and negotiating. *Journal of Applied Behavior Analysis, 25*(2), 401–413.

Richards, L. D., & Lee, K. A. (1972). Group processes in social habilitation of the retarded. *Social Casework, 53*(1), 30–37.

Robinson, H. B., & N. M. (1965). *The mentally retarded child: A psychological approach.* New York: McGraw-Hill.

Sherman, J. A., Sheldon, J. B., Harchik, A. E., Edwards, K., & Quinn, J. M. (1992). Social evaluation of behaviors comprising three social skills and a comparison of the performance of people with and without mental retardation. *American Journal on Mental Retardation, 96*(4), 419–431.

Sievert, A. L., Cuvo, A. J., & Davis, P. K. (1988). Training self-advocacy skills to adults with mild handicaps. *Journal of Applied Behavior Analysis, 21,* 299–309.

Silverman, R., Zigmond, N., & Sansone, J. (1981). Teaching coping skills to adolescents with learning problems. *Focus on Exceptional Children, 13*(6), 1–20.

Siperstein, G. N. (1992). Social competence: An important construct in mental retardation. *American Journal on Mental Retardation, 96*(4), iii–vi.

Siperstein, G. N., & Bak, J. J. (1989). Social relationships of adolescents with moderate mental retardation. *Mental Retardation, 27*(1), 5–10.

Smith, H. M., Gottsegen, M., & Gottsegen, G. (1955). A group technique for mental retardates. *International Journal of Group Psychotherapy, 5,* 84–90.

Soodak, L. C. (1990). Social behavior and knowledge of social "scripts" among mentally retarded adults. *American Journal on Mental Retardation, 94*(5), 515–521.

Sternlight, M. (1964). Establishing an initial relationship in group psychotherapy with delinquent retarded male adolescents. *American Journal of Mental Deficiency, 69,* 39–41.

Stowitschek, J. J., McConaughy, E. K., Peatross, D., Salzberg, C. L., & Lignugaris-Kraft, B. (1988). Effects of group incidental training on the use of social amenities by adults with mental retardation in work settings. *Education and Training in Mental Retardation, 23*(3), 202–212.

Sundel, S. S. (1994). Videotaped training of job-related social skills using peer modeling: An evaluation of social validity. *Research on Social Work Practice, 4*(1), 40–52.

Szivos, S. E., & Griffiths, E. (1990). Group processes involved in coming to terms with a mentally retarded identity. *Mental Retardation, 28*(6), 333–341.

Valenti-Hein, D. C., Yarnold, P. R., & Mueser, K. T. (1994). Evaluation of the dating skills program for improving heterosexual interactions in people with mental retardation. *Behavior Modification, 18*(1), 32–46.

Von Bertalanffy, L. (1968). *General system theory.* New York: George Braziller.

Waite, L. M. (1993). Drama therapy in small groups with the developmentally disabled. *Social Work with Groups, 16*(4), 95–108.

Wheeler, J. J., Bates, P., Marshall, K. J., & Miller, S. R. (1988). Teaching appropriate social behaviors to a young man with moderate mental retardation in a supported competitive employment setting. *Education and Training in Mental Retardation, 23*(2), 105–116.

Wilcox, G. T., & Guthrie, G. M. (1957). Changes in adjustment of institutionalized female defectives following group psychotherapy. *Journal of Clinical Psychology, 13,* 9–13.

Williamson, W. W., & Byrd, E. K. (1986). Some suggested counseling techniques in moving toward placement for persons with mental retardation. *Journal of Applied Rehabilitation Counseling, 17*(4), 48–50.

Wittmann, J. P., Strohmer, D. C., & Prout, H. T. (1989). Problems presented by persons of mentally retarded and borderline intellectual functioning in counseling: An exploratory investigation. *Journal of Applied Rehabilitation Counseling, 20*(2), 8–13.

Yanok, J., & Beifus, J. A. (1993). Communicating about loss and mourning: Death education for individuals with mental retardation. *Mental Retardation, 31*(3), 144–147.

Zigler, E. (1961). Social deprivation and rigidity in the performance of feeble-minded children. *Journal of Abnormal and Social Psychology, 62*(2), 413–421.

Zisfein, L., & Rosen, M. (1974). Effects of a personal adjustment training group counseling program. *Mental Retardation, 12,* 50–53.

Index